Business Process Change
A Guide for Business Managers and BPM and Six Sigma Professionals
Second Edition

Every organization wants to improve the way it does business—to improve its ability to respond rapidly and dynamically to market forces and to competition, and to produce goods and services more efficiently, while increasing profits. Leading companies are increasingly using business process management techniques to define and align their processes, vertically and horizontally. At the same time they are implementing process governance and performance measurement systems to assure cost-effective and consistent outcomes. Managers face many challenges when they try to implement these techniques. *Business Process Change, 2nd Edition* provides a comprehensive and balanced discussion of business process change today. It describes the concepts, methodologies, and tools managers need to improve or redesign processes and to implement business process management systems in their organizations.

Features

This is a complete revision and update to the popular 1st Edition of *Business Process Change*. It includes new material on all aspects of process change including Business Process Management Systems (BPMS), Business Rules, Business Process Architectures, Enterprise Architectures, Business Frameworks, Performance Metrics, Process Redesign, and Six Sigma and Lean methodologies.

- Includes the most comprehensive, up-to-date look at state of the art business process improvement methodologies.
- Shows you how all the different process elements fit together.
- Presents a methodology based on current best practices that can be tailored for specific needs, and that maintains a focus on the human aspects of process redesign.
- Provides all new detailed case studies showing how all these methodologies are successfully being implemented by leading companies.

About the Author

Paul Harmon is Executive Editor and Senior Analyst at Business Process Trends (www.bptrends.com), the most trusted source of information and analysis on trends, directions, and best practices in business process management. He is the co-author and editor of the *BPTrends Product Reports*, the most widely read reports available on BPM software products. In addition, he is the Chief Methodologist and a Principal Consultant at BPTrends Associates, a professional services company providing consulting, executive education, and training services to organizations interested in understanding and implementing business process change programs.

Paul is an acknowledged BPM thought leader and a respected author and consultant who has helped numerous companies apply business process technologies and methodologies to solve their business problems. He has developed and presented, seminars, keynotes and executive briefings on BPM to conferences and major organizations throughout the world.

It's a relief for process professionals to be able to move beyond theoretical BPM with case studies and find techniques and methodologies which provide great results in applied BPM. Paul Harmon's writing has been an invaluable guide for me for several years, and his methodologies in combination with the open-standard framework based on SCOR®, benchmarking, and methodologies we have been using at Supply-Chain Council provide a complete end-to-end approach for organizations to take themselves not just to the next level, but to place themselves permanently on the top-level of performance. This is a must read for process professionals, whether you're coming at it from "the business" or "the IT" side, a "Wade-Mecum" for the Third-Wave Generation of process experts.

—*Joe Francis, CTO, Supply-Chain Council.*

I enjoyed the writing style because it took some complex concepts and ideas and boiled them down into very simple, easy to understand concepts. Considering that there is lots of differing opinions on BPM by press, analysts and vendors, it makes it very difficult for the end customer to get a true understanding of the concepts. The two chapters that I read make it very easy to grasp the concepts. It makes very easy reading for the busy executive or the practitioner who wants to get an understanding of the BPM market.

—*Trevor Naidoo, Director, ARIS Solution Engineering, IDS Scheer North America.*

Harmon takes a clear-eyed look at the "movements," the standards, the strategies and the tactics and distills it into a clear picture of how to manage an agile business in the 21st century. As change accelerates and margins fall, this book becomes a must-read for survivors-to-be.

—*Dr. Richard Mark Soley, CEO, The Object Management Group (OMG).*

Business Process Change

A Guide for Business Managers
and BPM and Six Sigma Professionals

Second Edition

Business Process Change

A Guide for Business Managers and BPM and Six Sigma Professionals

Second Edition

Paul Harmon
Executive Editor, *www.BPTrends.com*
Chief Methodologist, Business Process Trends Associates

Foreword by Tom Davenport

ELSEVIER

AMSTERDAM • BOSTON • HEIDELBERG • LONDON
NEW YORK • OXFORD • PARIS • SAN DIEGO
SAN FRANCISCO • SINGAPORE • SYDNEY • TOKYO

Morgan Kaufmann Publishers is an imprint of Elsevier

MORGAN KAUFMANN PUBLISHERS

Publishing Director	Denise Penrose
Acquisitions Editor	Diane D. Cerra
Publishing Services Manager	George Morrison
Project Manager	Kathryn Liston
Editorial Assistant	Mary James
Marketing Manager	Misty Bergeron
Cover Design	Eric DeCicco
Production Services	www.BorregoPublishing.com
Interior printer	Edwards Brothers Malloy
Cover printer	Phoenix Color Corporation

Morgan Kaufmann Publishers is an imprint of Elsevier.
30 Corporate Drive, Suite 400, Burlington, MA 01803, USA

 This book is printed on acid-free paper.

Library of Congress Cataloging-in-Publication Data

(Application Submitted.)

ISBN: 978-0-12-374152-3

For information on all Morgan Kaufmann publications,
visit our Web site at *www.mkp.com* or *www.books.elsevier.com*

Printed in the United States of America.
Transferred to Digital Printing, 2013

To Celia Wolf and Roger Burlton,
my business partners and my friends

Foreword

Tom Davenport
President's Distinguished Professor of Information Technology and Management
Director, Process Management Research Center
Babson College
Wellesley, Massachusetts

Paul Harmon has a knack for writing clearly about topics that other people tend to obfuscate. Whether the topic is expert systems, e-business, or process management, he cuts through needless complexity and uses clear terminology to get the relevant points across. In this book, of course, he has focused on process management and associated technologies. There are unfortunately many possibilities for obfuscation in this topic area. Other people might confuse the technologies with the actual business change involved in process management, but not Harmon. He is always careful, for example, to note that "BPM" means business process management, and "BPMS" means systems that help accomplish BPM. If only that other writers and speakers on these topics were so careful.

In this regard and in many other ways, *Business Process Management* is a model of clarity. All books on business process management should be this clear. In fact, all books about how to manage anything should be this clear. Process management should be treated—as it is in these pages—as one of the basic principles of contemporary management, rather than anything exotic or esoteric.

Why is an extremely clear approach to process management particularly important? One reason is that process management has been somewhat faddish in the past. As a management topic it has been a bit immature, coming in and out of fashion over time. For some reason managers and firms have often latched onto the more fashionable, short-term elements of the approach instead of the more timeless ones. There have been multiple flavors or different religions of the movement, including Total Quality Management (TQM), Reengineering, Six Sigma, Lean, and so forth.

Each decade seems to see the rise of a new flavor, although as Harmon describes, many of the underlying principles are similar. Perhaps the excitement of a "new" approach (or at least a new combination of previous ideas with a new name) is necessary to get people excited, but there is a downside to this approach. The problem is that devotees of a new process religion become bored as rapidly as they were converted. Basic business process management may not be new or sexy, but it is clearly necessary. Perhaps it should be adopted whether it is sexy or not, and then perhaps it will persist over the long term without cycles or fads. This book goes a long way toward advancing that perspective on processes.

It's also apparent that process management, as it has changed over time, is a synthetic discipline. Each new process management approach has built on previous foundations, and added one or more new elements. This book, I am happy to note, also takes a synthetic, broad approach to process management. Ideally, an organization would be able to draw upon all of the elements or tools available to meet the process management needs of any individual project. Harmon provides a methodology for process management that contains most if not all of the attributes an organization could need with regard to improving processes.

The book also takes—at least to my mind—the appropriate perspective on information technology in the process context. Most approaches to process management either devote too much attention to information technology or too little. Some devotees of reengineering and BPM technologies act as if IT is literally all that matters in improving processes. They usually achieve no business change as a result. Advocates of Six Sigma and Lean usually ignore technology altogether. However, IT is a powerful tool, and to ignore it is to leave a lot of potential change on the table. Harmon's approach is like Goldilocks' porridge: just right. It treats IT not as the primary objective of BPM, but as an enabler. Yet the book has plenty of detail and useful knowledge on how IT can help in managing and improving processes. Harmon has carefully updated the book since the 2002 edition to address the latest technologies in the realm of process management.

Finally, process management advocates—like enthusiasts for other management trends—often pretend that process management is the only business idea that matters. Get that right, the argument goes, and everything else about a business is either irrelevant or will automatically fall into place. Harmon is under no such illusions. He knows that processes must coexist with strategies, value disciplines, enterprise systems, and other aspects of organizational life. The book provides useful guidance on how process management relates to, and can support, other modern management ideas. As with other aspects of the book, it's a sober and realistic approach.

You've picked up the right book for just about any goal you have in process management. If you're an enterprise process architect or manager, Harmon tells you what you need to think about and do at the enterprise level. If you are an owner or improver of a particular business process, there's an entire section devoted to managing particular processes. If you're charged with using IT to support processes, you are similarly in luck. The book should be on the desk, in the briefcase, or on the bedside table of anyone who believes business processes are an important way to understand businesses and make them better.

Contents

Preface to the Second Edition

BUSINESS PROCESS CHANGE was originally written in 2002, and published at the beginning of 2003. Since then, the interest in business process and the number of business process projects have increased dramatically. In 2002, there were no Business Process Management (BPM) conferences in the U.S. In 2006, there were eleven major BPM conferences and dozens of other meetings on more specialized aspects of process change. In 2002, most corporate process work was focused on specific business process improvement projects. Today, leading organizations are focused on enterprise business process architectures and on developing corporate performance management and measurement systems that will allow senior executives to plan, monitor and manage enterprise-wide transformation efforts. Many of these enterprise efforts are being facilitated by newly available business process frameworks, like eTOM and SCOR, that make it possible to create enterprise models and performance measurement systems in weeks rather than months.

During this same period, new tools and methodologies have become common among those undertaking business process change projects. Six Sigma programs in most major corporations have expanded and now include Lean technologies. Several Six Sigma groups have extended their practices to include Human Performance techniques or aligned their practices with frameworks like SCOR. New process modeling notations have begun to replace earlier notations. There has also been significant work done to integrate business process modeling techniques with business rules technologies.

In a similar way, new software tools have made it possible to automate the day-to-day management of processes. BPMS products were unavailable in 2002 and are now widely available and becoming very popular. During the same time period a number of technical standards have been created to support these new software tools.

This book focuses on the entire range of options that business managers face when they try to redesign, improve or automate their company's business processes. I have tried to emphasize the relationships between the various approaches. I am convinced, as a result of years of work with leading companies, that the companies that succeed, over the long term, are those that figure out how to integrate and coordinate all their different business process change options. Any one approach may seem like a fad. In any given year, one or another of the approaches will get more attention in the popular business press. But, over the long term all are necessary. Six Sigma with its emphasis on quality and its powerful grassroots organizing abilities, IT with its automation techniques, and those who are focused on strategy, business process architectures, and process management training and evaluation all understand important aspects of process. Smart managers will insist that the practitioners from each of these areas coordinate their efforts to assure that their organizations achieve outstanding results.

In 2003, just as Business Process Change was published, Celia Wolf and I founded Business Process Trends (*www.bptrends.com*), a web portal that publishes a wide variety of articles on business process practices. As the Executive Editor of BPTrends, I have been well positioned to observe the evolution of the business process market and realized, as 2006 was drawing to a close, that a new edition of Business Process Change was necessary if the book was to continue to serve as a comprehensive guide for managers and practitioners who need up-to-date information on current business process practices.

To reflect the major shift that has occurred in business process practice in the last four years, I have reorganized the book and divided it into three major sections, one focused on Enterprise Level Concerns, one on Business Process Project Concerns, and a third on Implementation Technology Concerns. I have added significant new material to each section. I discuss the new emphasis on business process architectures and the use of business process frameworks in the Enterprise section. I include new process redesign and improvement techniques—like Lean—in the Process section, and I describe Business Process Management System products and several new standards in the Implementation section. Throughout the text I have updated discussions to reflect the evolving practices. Overall, perhaps half of the text has changed in whole or in part.

Business Process Change sold well during the past four years and many readers told me that they liked the way the book provided a comprehensive overview of all of the options that were available to managers and practitioners. I have tried to maintain that approach, updating earlier material and adding new material to assure that this second edition will continue to provide readers with the broadest overview of the techniques and practices that are being used to effect business process change in today's leading organizations.

Today, our Business Process Trends Web site (*www.bptrends.com*) provides an excellent extension to this book. Each month we publish current information on new techniques and case studies that illustrate trends in business process practices. In the earlier edition of *Business Process Change*, we included an extensive Glossary and a Bibliography, which quickly became out of date as new terms and books became popular. In this edition we have omitted both and have placed them, instead, on the BPTrends Web site so they can be frequently updated.

I want to thank the many, many readers of *Business Process Change* and the members of the Business Process Trends Web site who have talked with me and sent me email. Business process change is complex and expanding and I have been able to cover it as well as I have only because of the many different people who have taken the time to teach me about all of the different kinds of process work that is being undertaken in organizations throughout the world. I can hardly name them all, but I can at least name a few who have provided special insights.

The first book originated in conversations I held with Geary A. Rummler. I worked for Geary in the late sixties and learned the basics of process analysis from him. I've continued to learn from him and read everything he writes.

In 2003, Celia Wolf and I founded Business Process Trends. Two years ago Celia and I joined with Roger Burlton, Artie Mahal and Sandra Foster to found Business Process Trends Associates, an education, training, and consulting services group. As I have worked with Roger, Artie, and Sandy to create the BPTrends Associates curriculum, I have benefited from their extensive and practical experience in affecting business process change.

A number of people stand out for their role in teaching me about specific technologies. I have never met Michael Porter, but his books and writings have taught me almost everything I know about strategy, value chains, and the development of competitive advantage. Joseph Francis, currently the CTO of the Supply Chain Council first convinced me of the importance of business frameworks and proceeded to demonstrate their power at Hewlett-Packard. George Brown of Intel has also been very helpful in regard to both the SCOR framework and the VRM framework. I owe Pam Garretson and Eric Anderson a great deal for teaching me how Boeing GMS organized its entire division using a process-centric approach. They really demonstrated what a dedicated management team can do to create a process-centric company. I owe a debt to Roxanne O'Brasky, Executive Director of ISSSP, Don Redinius and Ron Recker of AIT Group and David Silverstein of the Breakthrough Management Group (BMG) for teaching me more about Six Sigma. I owe a similar debt to Howard Smith of CSC, Derek Miers, and Rashid Kahn for teaching me about the nature and potential of BPMS products. I owe thanks to Stephen White for his many conversations on notation and BPMN and to David Frankel, Sridhar Iyengar, and Richard Mark Soley for their ongoing insights into the evolution of the software market and the OMG's standards setting process. I also owe a debt of gratitude to Curt Hall for his continuing conversations on business rules and artificial intelligence in all its manifestations. And I want to thank Thomas Davenport for his insight and support over the last few years and for writing the Foreword.

This just scratches the surface; however, and I also owe thanks to lots of others for their special insights into business process practices and technologies. With apologies to anyone I've accidentally omitted, this list includes: Wil van der Aalst, Roger Addison, John Alden, Paul Allen, Michael Anthony, Gopala Krishna Behara, Oscar Barros, Conrad Bock, Peter Bolstorff, David Burke, Allison Burkett, Frits Bussemaker, Richard Butler, Mike Costa, David Chappell, Brett Champlin, Fred Cummins, Bill Curtis, Joseph DeFee, George Diehl, Jean-Jacques Dubray, Chuck Faris, Paul Fjelstra, Peter Fingar, Layna Fischer, David Fisher, Mike Forster, Kiran Garimella, Ismael Ghalimi, Mike Gilger, Praveen Gupta, Keith Harrison-Broninski, Hideshige Hasegawa, David Heidt, Stan Hendryx, Jenny Huang, Casper Hunsche, Brian James, John Jeston, Gladys Lam, Antoine Lonjon, Mike Marin, Mark McGregor, Mike Melenovsky, Amit Mitra, Michael zur Muehlen, Johan Nelis, Mark Nelson, James Odell, Ken Orr, Nathaniel Palmer, Ron Peliegrino, Jan Popkin, Carlos Pratis, John Pyke, Alan Ramias, Pete Rivett, Mike Rosen, Michael Rosemann, Ron Ross, Rick Rummler, Jim Sinar, Andrew Spanyi, Steve Stanton, David Straus, Keith Swanson, Doug Timmel, Donald Tosti, Alan Trefler, Cedric Tyler, Guy Wallace, Michael Webb, Cherie Wilkins, Bruce Williams, and James Womack.

Each of these individuals helped make this book better than it would have been otherwise. Needless to say, in the end, I took everything that everyone offered and fitted it into my own perspective and expressed it in my own words. Those who helped can take credit for the many good things they suggested, but can hardly be blamed for the mistakes I'm sure I've introduced.

I also want to thank my editor, Diane Cerra, who has worked with me on a variety of books over the years. She makes a difficult task as easy as it can be.

Finally, I want to thank Celia Wolf one more time. She critiqued the entire manuscript and kept asking insightful questions about the market, the strategies and services of the various vendors, and company practices, until I finally understood them and could explain them to her satisfaction. We have worked together over the past five years to create the Business Process Trends Web site and Business Process Trends Associates. She has consistently proven to be both a wise partner and a wonderful friend. I couldn't have done it without her support and encouragement.

—Paul Harmon, San Francisco

Introduction

WE LIVE IN A WORLD that changes faster all the time. What worked only yesterday may not work today or tomorrow. Smart managers know that organizations that succeed do so because they adjust to keep up with the changes that are taking place. This book is about business process change. It describes how smart managers analyze, redesign, and improve the business processes they manage.

Every year dozens of books are written by management consultants to propose a great new management idea. Some of these new ideas have merit, but most are simply fads that are popular for a year or two and then gradually fade. This book is not such a book. In the first place, this book describes a variety of process change techniques that have been proven over the course of two decades. It describes how companies can achieve efficiencies by integrating and improving their business processes and by aligning those business processes with corporate strategies and goals. Companies that routinely practice business process improvement, using the techniques described in this book, are able to consistently improve on the results obtained from existing processes. Companies that undertake more extensive business process redesign efforts frequently achieve improvements in excess of 50%. This isn't miraculous; it simply reflects the fact that most existing processes are less efficient than they could be and that new technologies make it possible to design much more efficient processes.

This book wasn't written to hype the idea of process change. If you need convincing or motivation, you should read one of the popular books that have been written to do just that. This book is designed to help you actually make process change happen, systematically and consistently.

Levels of Concerns

Companies undertake process change initiatives for a variety of different reasons. Organizations new to process work usually start by deciding to improve a specific business process. More experienced companies usually have some kind of corporate business process architecture and a BPM group assigned to consider all possible process change initiatives, to prioritize interventions, to coordinate efforts, and to document results. Organizations that have more sophistication usually support a number of ongoing activities that are managed at the enterprise level. These initiatives include the maintenance of a corporate business process architecture, the ongoing measurement and analysis of process performance, and some kind of corporate process management. These activities are not, typically, projects, but ongoing managerial processes performed to support executive decision-making efforts and to define specific process change opportunities.

At the same time, these organizations normally undertake a variety of specific projects to create, redesign or improve specific business processes. These projects are usually managed by divisional or departmental managers. We refer to these projects as *process level concerns.*

Allied to the projects at the process level, but at a further remove, are more specific projects undertaken to acquire and install new software applications or to create new training courses that will actually implement changes defined at the process level. Thus, for example, an *enterprise level* BPM group might decide that a company supply chain is operating inefficiently. The BPM group initiates a *supply chain process redesign* effort. The supply process redesign project team undertakes a study of the supply chain, considers options, and concludes that a number of different changes should be made. Once the process level project team's recommendations are approved by senior management, IT launches an *implementation level* project to acquire new ERP software to support some of the changes in the supply chain. At the same time, Training creates new job descriptions and launches a separate implementation level project to develop a new training course to provide new employees with the skills they will need to implement the new supply chain process.

One of the major insights we've drawn from studying a wide variety of business process efforts during the past three years is that it is very useful to distinguish between the various levels of concern. Projects or activities at different levels require different participants, different methodologies, and different types of support. We illustrate these three different levels of concern with the business process pyramid shown in Figure I.1.

Figure I.1 The BPTrends Business Process Pyramid.

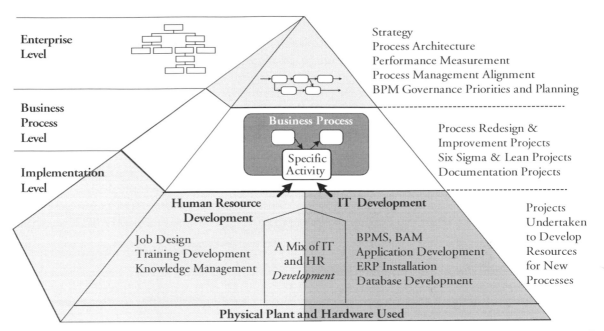

Throughout this book we will rely on the distinction between different levels of concern to help organize our discussion. We will describe the major process initiatives being undertaken at each of the three levels and present appropriate methodologies for work at each of these levels. Some of the material will be the same as it was in the first edition of *Business Process Change*, but there are also new insights and concepts and techniques that have evolved and become popular during the past three years. This is especially true at the enterprise level, where business process architectures are now the focus of efforts at leading companies, and at the IT implementation level, where new business process management software (BPMS) products have become popular. Each of these developments, and others besides, are rippling through all aspects of business process work and effecting subtle changes in emphasis and practice.

In early 2006 the *Business Process Trends* Web site undertook a survey of its readers to determine what companies were doing to support business process change. The questionnaire remained online for a little over one month, and during that time 348 people completed the questionnaire. The respondents came from large and small companies from throughout the world and from a wide variety of different industries. Given the size of the response and the distribution of the respondents, we believe this represents the best current data on worldwide business process activity.

One question asked if the respondent's organizations were active in any aspect of business process change. Figure I.2 shows how the survey participants responded. In

2001, when we conducted the survey reported in the first edition of this book, 17% of our respondents indicated that they weren't involved in any aspect of process improvement or redesign. In early 2006, only 6% suggested that they had no interest.

Figure I.2 Responses to the question: What commitment has your company made?

We also asked respondents to indicate what the term "BPM" meant to them.

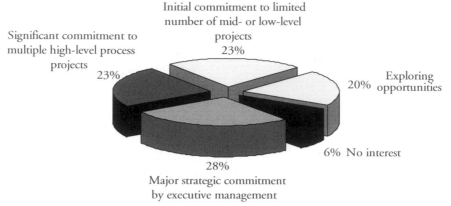

Figure I.3 shows how the respondents answered. This response is consistent with lots of other data about why companies undertake business process projects. In bad times, companies seek to make their processes more efficient to save money. In expansive times, companies seek to redesign processes to make them more competitive, to offer new services, or to get into new lines of business. Or they acquire companies and have to integrate the processes used at the two different organizations. In addition, especially during expansive periods, companies look to see if they can gain a competitive advantage by incorporating a new technology. During the past several years, much of the technology-driven work has been a result of developments in Internet technologies and companies have redesigned processes to let customers or employees access information and make purchases via the Web, or to take advantage of the communication efficiencies offered by email or Internet-based phone services.

The fourth major reason for undertaking business process change is perhaps the most interesting, and ultimately the most revolutionary. A growing number of leading companies have begun to believe that a corporate-wide focus on process provides a superior way of managing the company. These companies tend to be in industries that are undergoing rapid, extensive changes. Their senior executives have concluded that they need the insights and the agility provided by a process-oriented approach to management in order to respond quickly and effectively. These are the organizations that are making

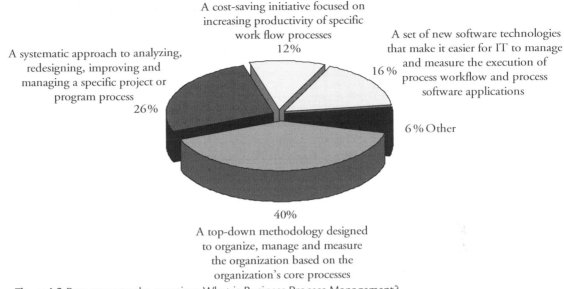

Figure I.3 Responses to the question: What is Business Process Management?

major commitments to develop enterprise-level business process tools and management systems to assure that they have aligned all their business resources and functions to their value chains and can manage those processes in something close to real time.

To summarize this more graphically, consider Figure I.4. In this case, we use the process pyramid to suggest changes that have occurred between the emphasis on process that was typical of leading organizations in the nineties and the emphasis we see at leading organizations today.

In the nineties, most organizations were focused on business process redesign or reengineering projects. Leading companies focused on processes that cut across departmental or functional lines, but most companies concentrated on redesigning processes within specific departments or functional units. At the same time, Six Sigma was popular in manufacturing organizations for process improvement efforts. Toward the end of the nineties, standard or off-the-shelf software applications (ERP, CRM) became a popular way to standardize processes and reporting systems. During this same period, workflow systems became popular as tools to automate document-processing systems. In the past six years, all of these process change strategies have continued to be popular. Today, however, leading companies are putting more emphasis on developing enterprise-wide business process architectures and corporate performance management systems. They seek to standardize specific processes throughout their divi-

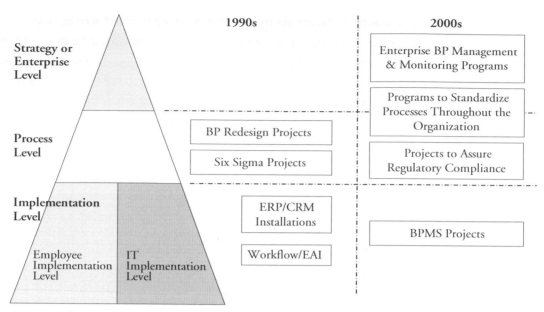

Figure I.4 Changes in focus at leading companies.

sions and subsidiary organizations to assure that the same ERP or CRM modules can be used throughout the corporation and they seek to understand their corporate value chains to assure regulatory compliance. At the same time, there is a major emphasis on installing new software automation technologies—usually termed *Business Process Management Systems* (BPMS)—to automate the day-to-day control of processes and to provide real-time performance data for senior management.

This book is written for today's manager and focuses on the business process change problems today's managers face. This book was written to educate managers in the best practices available for today's challenges and to provide practical tips for anyone undertaking the development of a business process architecture, undertaking a business process change project, or considering the development of a BPMS application.

Business Process Change and Management

Every company wants to improve the way it does business, to produce things more efficiently, and to make greater profits. Nonprofit organizations are also concerned with efficiency, productivity, and with achieving the goals they set for themselves. Every manager understands that achieving these goals is a part of his or her job.

Consider the management of the automobile industry. The first internal-combustion automobiles were produced by Karl Benz and Gottlieb Daimler in Germany in 1885. In the decades that followed, some 50 entrepreneurs in Europe and North America set up companies to build cars. In each case, the companies built cars by hand, incorporating improvements with each model. Henry Ford was one among many who tried his hand at building cars in this manner.

In 1903, however, Henry Ford started his third company, the Ford Motor Company, and tried a new approach to automobile manufacturing. First, he designed a car that would be of high quality, not too expensive, and easy to manufacture. Next he organized a moving production line. In essence, workmen began assembling a new automobile at one end of the factory building and completed the assembly as it reached the far end of the plant. Workers at each point along the production line had one specific task to do. One group moved the chassis into place, another welded on the side panels, and still another group lowered the engine into place when each car reached their station. In other words, Henry Ford conceptualized the development of an automobile as a single process and designed and sequenced each activity in the process to assure that the entire process ran smoothly and efficiently. Clearly, Henry Ford had thought deeply about the way cars were assembled in his earlier plants and had a very clear idea of how he could improve the process.

By organizing the process as he did, Henry Ford was able to significantly reduce the price of building automobiles. As a result, he was able to sell cars for such a modest price that he made it possible for every middle-class American to own a car. At the same time, as a direct result of the increased productivity of the assembly process, Ford was able to pay his workers more than any other auto assembly workers. Within a few years, Ford's new approach had revolutionized the auto industry, and it soon led to changes in almost every other manufacturing process as well.

Ford's success is a great example of the power of innovation and process improvement to revolutionize the economics of an industry. Other examples could be drawn from the dawn of the Industrial Revolution or from the early years of computers, when mainframes revolutionized the census process in the United States and began to change the way companies managed their accounting and payroll processes.

The bottom line, however, is that the analysis of business processes and their improvement in order to increase the efficiency and productivity of companies is a perennial management responsibility. Managers, of course, have other responsibilities, but one of the most important requires that they constantly examine the processes by which their companies produce products and services and upgrade them to assure that they remain as efficient and effective as possible.

Some business process gurus have advocated crash programs that involve major changes in processes. In a sense they are advocating that today's managers do what Henry Ford did when he created the moving production line. In some cases this kind of radical redesign is necessary. Today's managers can often use computers to automate processes and achieve major gains in productivity. Similarly, in responding to challenges created by the Internet, some managers have been forced to create new business processes or to make major changes in existing processes. eBay and Amazon.com come to mind. In most cases, however, gradual improvements are more effective.

There are other times, however, when a crash program is too far reaching and a gradual improvement effort wouldn't be enough. These are cases that we refer to as business process redesign projects. They implement a significant change without redesigning the entire process. Many projects that automate a portion of an existing process fall in this category. In some cases, redesign takes place in a series of steps in order to minimize disruption. A series of modules, for example, could be installed over the course of several months, one after another, with enough time between each change to assure that the employees can adjust as the changes are made.

The Evolution of an Organization's Understanding of Process

Managers have been thinking about business process change for several decades now. Some organizations are more sophisticated in their understanding of business processes than others. Software organizations, for example, have spent quite a bit of time thinking about the software development process. In the 1990s, the Department of Defense funded a major effort to determine how the software development process could be improved. This task was entrusted to the Software Engineering Institute (SEI), which is located at Carnegie Mellon University. The SEI/DOD effort resulted in a model of the stages that software organizations go through in their understanding and management of processes.

The SEI model is known as the Capability Maturity Model (CMM). It was initially described in a book, *The Capability Maturing Model: Guidelines for Improving the Software Process*, published in 1995. In essence, the CMM team defined five stages that organizations go through as they move from an immature to a mature understanding of business processes. These stages were defined using examples from software organizations, but they apply equally to any large organization.

Although the CMM model is more commonly applied to large organizations, the model can also serve as an excellent reference model for small- and medium-size firms. Remember the key point of such reference models is to help you understand where you are today and to assist in developing a road map to help you get where you want to go. No one is suggesting that all companies should attempt to follow the model in the same exact way.

The key assumption that the CMM team makes is that immature organizations don't perform consistently. Mature organizations, on the other hand, produce quality products or services effectively and consistently. In the CMM book, they describe it this way:

> In a mature organization, managers monitor the quality of the software products and the processes that produce them. There is an objective, quantitative basis for judging product quality and analyzing problems with the product and process. Schedules and budgets are based on historical performance and are realistic; the expected results for cost, schedule, functionality, and quality of the product are usually achieved. In general, the mature organization follows a disciplined process consistently because all of the participants understand the value of doing so, and the necessary infrastructure exists to support the process.

Watts Humphrey, one of the leading gurus behind the CMM effort, describes it this way:

> An immature software process resembles a Little League baseball team. When the ball is hit, some players run toward the ball, while others stand around and watch, perhaps not even thinking about the game. In contrast, a mature organization is like a professional baseball team. When the ball is hit, every player reacts in a disciplined manner. Depending on the situation, the pitcher may cover home plate, infielders may set up for a double play, and outfielders prepare to back up their teammates.

CMM identified five levels or steps that describe how organizations typically evolve from immature organizations to mature organizations. The steps are illustrated in Figure I.5.

The CMM model defines the evolution of a company's maturity as follows:

▶ *Level 1: Initial.* The process is characterized by an ad hoc set of activities. The process isn't defined and success depends on individual effort and heroics.
▶ *Level 2: Repeatable.* At this level, basic project management processes are established to track costs, to schedule, and to define functionality. The discipline is

available to repeat earlier successes on similar projects.

▶ *Level 3: Defined.* The process is documented for both management and engineering activities and standards are defined. All projects use an approved, tailored version of the organization's standard approach to developing and maintaining software.

▶ *Level 4: Managed.* Detailed measures of the software process and product quality are collected. Both the software process and products are quantitatively understood and controlled.

▶ *Level 5: Optimizing.* Continuous process improvement is enabled by quantitative feedback from the process and from piloting innovative ideas and technologies.

Figure I.5 The five levels of SEI's Capability Maturity Model (CMM).

The CMM approach is very much in the spirit of the Total Quality Management (TQM) movement that was popular in engineering and manufacturing during the late eighties. (The latest version of CMM is termed CMMI. We'll consider CMMI and some alternative process maturity models later in the book.)

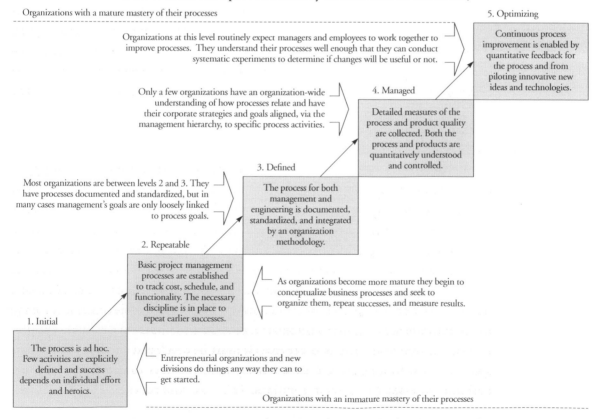

Every organization can be assigned a maturity level. Most software organizations studied by SEI were in either level 2 or 3. In effect, they had processes, but in most cases they weren't as well defined as they could be. Their management systems were not well aligned with their processes, and they weren't in a position to routinely improve their processes. Put a different way, most organizations today are focused on redesigning specific, departmental-level processes and only beginning to move to a more comprehensive process architecture. Leading companies today, however, are focused on moving from level 4 to level 5. They have created comprehensive business process architectures that describe how all the processes fit together (level 3) and have then moved on to create management systems that measure process performance and assign specific managers with responsibilities for assuring that processes perform as necessary (level 4). The best organizations have integrated management systems that automatically trigger process improvement efforts whenever there is a failure to achieve targeted process goals (level 5). This progress reflects the concerns we illustrated in Figure I.4.

In this book we won't make any assumptions about where your organization is today. We will, however, put lots of emphasis on how companies document processes, how they develop process architectures that describe how processes relate to each other, and how they align management systems to assure that corporate goals are aligned with managerial goals; and we will stress the importance of routine, continuous process improvement. In effect, this is a book that should help managers conceptualize where their organization should go and provide the tools they need to help with the transition.

The Variety of Options

If there were one way of handling all business process problems, we would be happy to elaborate it. Unfortunately, there are many different types of business process change problems. They vary by the organization's level of concern, by industry, and by the nature of the environmental change that needs to be accommodated. Some changes are undertaken to provide executives with the tools they need to manage a process-centric organization. Other changes only require modest improvements in existing processes. Still others require the complete redesign of an existing process or the creation of a new process. Some focus on changes in how people perform, while others involve the use of software applications to automate a process. In some cases a software application can be purchased, and in other cases it must be developed and tailored for your specific needs. In a nutshell, there are many different ways to improve or redesign business processes. Managers face options. This book will provide you with an overview of all the options and describe the best practices available to help you choose the approach that is best for your situation.

The Variety of Solutions

One of the problems with the business process field is that various authors and vendors use the same terms in different ways. In this book we will use certain terms in very precise ways to avoid confusion.

Process improvement refers to relatively minor, specific changes that one makes in an existing business process. Every manager responsible for a process should always be considering process improvements. In addition, on occasion, special process improvement efforts are required to get everyone focused on improving a specific process. Six Sigma is a good example of a popular approach to process improvement.

Process design or redesign refers to a major effort that is undertaken to significantly improve an existing process or to create a new business process. Process redesign considers every aspect of a process and often results in changes in the sequence in which the process is done, in employee jobs, and in the introduction of automation. Business Process Reengineering, the BPTrends Process Redesign methodology, and the Supply Chain Council's SCOR methodology are all good examples of popular approaches to process redesign.

Process automation refers to the use of computers and software applications to assist employees or to replace employees in the performance of a business process. The use of BPMS tools, workflow systems, or XML business process languages are ways to automate the management of processes or activities. The use of off-the-shelf ERP and CRM applications are also examples of automation. Similarly, software development methodologies like Rational Software's Unified Process or the Object Management Group's Model Driven Architecture are other examples of popular approaches to process automation.

Many authors use the term *business process management* (BPM) to refer to process automation efforts. It is used to refer to the fact that, once processes are automated, the day-to-day execution of the process can be managed by means of software tools. Business executives, however, often use the term *business process management* in a more generic sense to refer to efforts on the part of business executives to organize and improve the human management of business processes. On the corporate level, *business process management* is also used to refer to the development and maintenance of a business process architecture. We will use the term BPM in its most generic sense, to refer to how business managers organize and control processes. When we want to use it in the more specialized sense, to refer to automated systems, we will use the term "Business Process Management Software" or BPMS.

How This Book Is Organized

This book provides a pragmatic introduction to business process change. It's designed to provide managers with an overview of process concepts and best practices and to explain the options managers face as they seek to improve, redesign, or automate their business processes.

We will start with an overview of the kind of systematic business process improvement methodologies companies have used during the past decade. In effect, Chapter 1 will provide a brief history of business process change, just to assure we understand the basic options and are all using the same vocabulary.

The remainder of the book is divided into three major parts. Chapters 2 through 7 consider enterprise level concerns. Chapters 8 through 14 focus on process level concerns. Then, in Chapters 15, 16 and 17, we discuss implementation level concerns. Chapter 18 pulls together all of these concerns and provides some final advice. Now let's consider this plan in a little more detail.

Part I: Enterprise Level Concerns

In Chapter 2 we consider how companies develop strategies and define goals. This introduction to the strategic process will necessarily be rather general, but it will establish important themes, including ideas such as strategic positioning, value chains, and the importance of well-integrated processes for companies that want to achieve a competitive advantage.

In Chapter 3 we'll discuss enterprise level process concerns in a more practical way. We'll introduce the BPTrends Enterprise Methodology, and then consider what a company needs to do to develop a good basic understanding of the processes that make up an organization.

In Chapter 4 we'll consider the nature of a business process architecture. In essence, it is the business process architecture that defines how the various business processes work together to create value. It is also the key to linking the organization's strategic goals to process goals and then to specific managerial goals. The business process architecture also provides a basis for prioritizing process change initiatives. And it provides the means by which business managers and IT managers can work together to establish a corporate software infrastructure and prioritize software development efforts. We'll also discuss business process frameworks in this chapter and consider how they can help an organization in the rapid development of a business process architecture.

In Chapter 5, on process management, we'll consider the role that managers play in organizing and maintaining an organization's business processes. We will also look at some frameworks that define best practices for process management.

Chapter 6 will focus on measuring process performance. We'll consider the development of a process performance measurement system in more detail. We'll discuss the Balanced Scorecard system that many companies use and see how it can be modified to support a more sophisticated process monitoring system.

In Chapter 7 we will examine the functions that a executive-level business process management group—or Process Center of Excellence—can provide. A BPM group can assist in all aspects of process change and it can, in particular, serve as the center for prioritizing, planning, and coordinating a company's business process redesign or improvement projects.

Part II: Process Level Concerns

In Chapter 8, we will provide a general introduction to the overall analysis of process problems. We will provide a basic approach to conceptualizing process problems and analyzing the nature of the gap between what is now and what kind of process you would like to create. Then we will use that knowledge to scope specific redesign or improvement projects.

In Chapter 9, we will pause to define the basic concepts and modeling techniques used to create process diagrams. There are lots of ways of diagramming processes, and we have chosen the simplest we know about that is specifically designed for business mangers. As automation has increasingly become a major part of any process redesign effort, there has been a tendency to discuss processes in the more technical terms that software analysts sometimes employ. We believe this is a serious mistake, since it makes it harder for average business managers to understand the processes that they are ultimately responsible for managing. We rely on a very simple way of modeling organizations and processes that assures that business managers can stay in control of the effort.

In Chapters 10 we drill down a bit further and consider what is involved in analyzing specific activities and defining the tasks or procedures that employees must follow and maintaining employee performance. We will also consider how we might define the rules that employees use to make decisions as they perform specific activities.

Chapter 11 considers what is involved in day-to-day management of a business process. Unlike Chapter 6, which considered enterprise-wide process management issues, this chapter focuses on the specific activities that supervisors must master to be effective process managers.

Chapter 12 shifts and focuses on a specific, popular process improvement methodology, Six Sigma. Six Sigma is derived from operations research and provides a systematic way to measure and refine the output of specific processes. We do not go into the statistical techniques used in the Six Sigma process, but focus instead on the overall process and on how Six Sigma practitioners relate goals and measures to satisfying customers. We will also consider the Lean methodology that is increasingly being combined with Six Sigma.

In Chapter 13 we discuss a methodology for systematically redesigning a business process. The BPTrends Process Redesign methodology we consider is one we use and teach to those new to business process redesign. It combines and integrates all of the techniques we have discussed in Part II. Our stress in this chapter is not only on process analysis and redesign, but on the other things one must do to assure the success of a project, including the organization and management of the project, the gathering of information and facilitation of discussions, and the communication and change management skills necessary to assure that others will join you in making the changed process a success.

Chapter 14 presents a major case study of a hypothetical manufacturing company that redesigns its order-fulfillment process using the approach, concepts, and techniques we have discussed in these chapters.

Part III. Implementation Level Concerns

Chapter 15 is the first of three chapters that focus on business process software tools and automation. In Chapter 15 we begin with an overview of the types of software tools available to those who seek to redesign or automate business processes. We then proceed to consider the use of business process modeling tools and how they facilitate process analysis and redesign.

In Chapter 16 we shift and consider Business Process Management Suites, software tools that allow companies to manage the real-time execution of business processes on a day-to-day basis. These exciting new tools combine the best features of an earlier generation of workflow and EAI tools and offer a powerful way to help companies achieve new levels of integration and automation. And they rely on new Internet protocols and techniques like those embodied in the Service Oriented Architecture (SOA), which we will briefly consider.

In Chapter 17 we focus on ERP (enterprise resource planning) applications, systems of software modules that companies can use to support or automate established business processes like inventory and accounting operations. We also consider some of the newer packaged applications used for CRM (customer-relationship management) automation. In addition, we focus on the modeling languages commonly used for the design of ERP and CRM systems. We will conclude by considering how ERP and BPMS applications are likely to evolve in the near future.

Finally, in Chapter 18 we will try to pull together all the main points we make in this book. The chapter recapitulates the major options we have discussed and makes some suggestions about when each of the techniques is likely to be most effective. This book doesn't advocate a single methodology or a single set of practices to deal with business process change. Instead, we believe that business managers need to understand their options and then use the practices best suited to specific problems they face.

We have included appendices on BPMN and on various BPM standards to provide a succinct summary of some of the standards efforts underway.

Our goal was not to write a long book but, instead, to create a book that a wide variety of managers could turn to when they needed information and insight on one or another aspect of their business process change. We hope this will serve as a guide and a tool for the business managers who will lead their companies through the changes that will challenge organizations in the decade ahead.

Notes and References

All references to anything published by Business Process Trends (BPTrends) can be accessed on the BPTrends Web site: *www.bptrends.com.* All information on the BPTrends Web site is available without charge.

Specifically, BPTrends has published a series of surveys. To access the complete survey cited in this chapter, go to *www.BPTrends.com* and click on the tab marked BPTrends Surveys.

McCraw, Thomas K. (Ed.), *Creating Modern Capitalism: How Entrepreneurs, Companies, and Countries Triumphed in Three Industrial Revolutions*, Harvard University Press, 1997. There are several books that describe the Industrial Revolution and the birth of modern corporations. This is my favorite, and it's where I got my basic information on Henry Ford and the Ford Motor Company.

Paulk, Mark C., Charles V. Weber, Bill Curtis, and Mary Beth Chrissis (principal contributors and editors), *The Capability Maturity Model: Guidelines for Improving the Software Process*, Addison-Wesley, 1995. This book provides a good introduction to the concepts underlying CMM. To access information about CMM, check *www.esi.cmu.edu/cmm*.

Chrissis, Mary Beth, Mike Konrad, and Sandy Shrum. *CMMI: Second Edition: Guidelines for Process Integration and Product Improvement*. Addison-Wesley, 2007. This book provides a summary of where CMMI is today.

1

Business Process Change

THIS CHAPTER PROVIDES a brief history of corporate business process change initiatives. Individuals working in one tradition, whether BPR, Six Sigma, or ERP, often imagine that their perspective is the only one, or the correct one. We want to provide managers with several different perspectives on business process change in order to give everyone an idea of the range of techniques and methodologies available today. In the process we will define some of the key terms that will occur throughout the remainder of the book.

People have always worked at improving processes. Some archaeologists find it useful to organize their understanding of early human cultural development by classifying the techniques and processes that potters used to create their wares. In essence, potters gradually refined the pot-making process, creating better products, while probably also learning how to make them faster and cheaper.

The Industrial Revolution that began in the late 18th century led to factories and managers who focused considerable energy on the organization of manufacturing processes. Any history of industrial development will recount numerous stories of entrepreneurs who changed processes and revolutionized an industry. In the introduction we mentioned how Henry Ford created a new manufacturing process and revolutionized the way automobiles were assembled. He did that in 1903.

In 1911, soon after Henry Ford launched the Ford Motor Company, another American, Frederick Winslow Taylor, published a seminal book: *Principles of Scientific Management.* Taylor sought to capture some of the key ideas that good managers used to improve processes. He argued for simplification, for time studies, for systematic experimentation to identify the best way of performing a task, and for control systems that measured and rewarded output. Taylor's book became an international bestseller, and many would regard him as the father of operations research, a branch of engineering that seeks to create efficient and consistent processes. From 1911 on, managers have sought ways to be more systematic in their approaches to process change.

New technologies have often led to new business processes. The introduction of the train and the automobile, and of radio, telephones, and television, have each led to new and improved business processes. Since the end of World War II, computers and software systems have provided a major source of new efficiencies.

Two recent developments in management theory deserve special attention. One was the popularization of systems thinking, and the other was the formalization of the idea of a value chain.

Organizations as Systems

Many different trends led to the growing focus on systems that began in the 1960s. Some derived from operations research and studies of control systems. Some resulted from the emphasis on systems current in the computer community. Today's emphasis on systems also arose out of contemporary work in biology and the social sciences. At the same time, however, many management theorists have contributed to the systems perspective. One thinks of earlier writers like Ludwig von Bertalanffy, Stafford Beer, and Jay W. Forrester and more recent management theorists like John D. Sterman and Peter M. Senge.

In essence, the systems perspective emphasizes that everything is connected to everything else and that it's often worthwhile to model businesses and processes in terms of flows and feedback loops. A simple systems diagram is shown in Figure 1.1.

The idea of treating a business as a system is so simple, especially today when it is so commonplace, that it is hard for some to understand how important the idea really is. Systems thinking stresses linkages and relationships and flows. It emphasizes that any given employee or unit or activity is part of a larger entity and that ultimately those entities, working together, are justified by the results they produce.

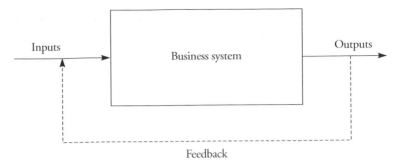

Figure 1.1 A business entity as a system.

To make all this a bit more concrete, consider how it is applied to business processes in the work of Michael E. Porter.

Systems and Value Chains

The groundwork for the current emphasis on comprehensive business processes was laid by Michael Porter in his 1985 book, *Competitive Advantage: Creating and Sustaining Superior Performance.* Porter is probably best known for his earlier book, *Competitive Strategy,* published in 1980, but it's in *Competitive Advantage* that he lays out his concept of a *value chain*—a comprehensive collection of all of the activities that are performed to design, produce, market, deliver, and support a product line. Figure 1.2 shows the diagram that Porter has used on several occasions to illustrate a generic value chain.

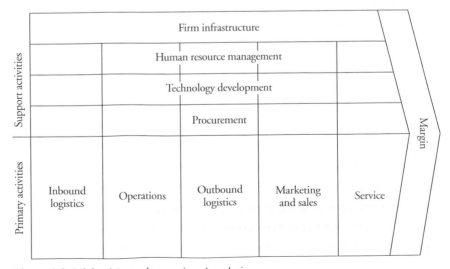

Figure 1.2 Michael Porter's generic value chain.

Although Porter doesn't show it on this diagram, you should assume that some primary activity is initiated on the lower left of the diagram when a customer orders a product, and ends on the right side when the product is delivered to the customer. Of course it may be a bit more complex, with marketing stimulating the customer to order and service following up the delivery of the order with various services, but those details are avoided in this diagram. Figure 1.2 simply focuses on what happens between the order and the final delivery—on the value chain or large-scale business process that produces the product. What's important to Porter's concept is that every function involved in the production of the product, and all of the support services, from information technology to accounting, should be included in a single value chain. It's only by including all of the activities involved in producing the product that a company is in position to determine exactly what the product is costing and what margin the firm achieves when it sells the product.

As a result of Porter's work, a new approach to accounting, *Activity-Based Costing* (ABC), has become popular and is used to determine the actual value of producing specific products.

When Porter's concept of a value chain is applied to business processes, a different type of diagram is produced. Figure 1.3 illustrates a value chain or business process that cuts across five departmental or functional boundaries, represented by the underlying organizational chart. The boxes shown within the process arrow are subprocesses. The subprocesses are initiated by an input from a customer, and the process ultimately produces an output that is consumed by a customer. As far as I know, this type of diagram was first used by another management systems theorist, Geary Rummler, in 1984.

Geary Rummler was the second major business process guru of the 1980s. With a background in business management and behavioral psychology, Rummler worked for years on employee training and motivation issues. Eventually, Rummler and his colleagues established a specialized discipline that is usually termed *Human Performance Technology* (HPT). Rummler's specific focus was on how to structure processes and activities to guarantee that employees—be they managers, salespeople, or production line workers—would function effectively. In the 1960s and 1970s he relied on behavioral psychology and systems theory to explain his approach, but during the course of the 1980s he focused increasingly on business process models.

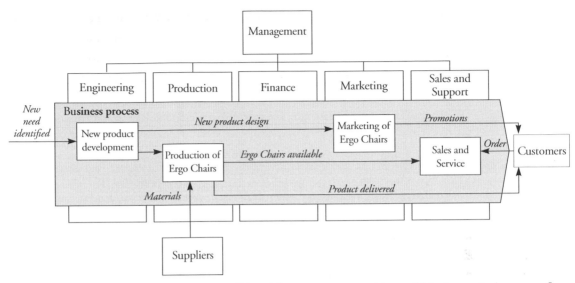

Figure 1.3 A business process cuts across traditional departments to combine activities into a single process flow. (After Rummler, 1984.)

At the end of the eighties Rummler and a colleague, Alan Brache, wrote a book, *Improving Performance: How to Manage the White Space on the Organization Chart*, that described the approach they had developed while consulting on process improvement during the course of the eighties. Rummler focused on organizations as systems and worked from the top down to develop a comprehensive picture of how organizations were defined by processes and how people defined what processes could accomplish. He provided a detailed methodology for how to analyze an organization, how to analyze processes, how to redesign and then improve processes, how to design jobs, and how to manage processes once they were in place. The emphasis on "the white space on the organization chart" stressed the fact that many process problems occurred when one department tried to hand off things to the next. The only way to overcome those interdepartmental problems, Rummler argued, was to conceptualize and manage processes as wholes.

Later, in the nineties, Hammer and Davenport would exhort companies to change and offered lots of examples about how changes had led to improved company performance. Similarly, IDS Scheer would offer a software engineering methodology for process change. Rummler and Brache offered a systematic, comprehensive approach designed for business managers. The book that Rummler and Brache wrote did not launch the BPR movement in the nineties. The popular books written by Hammer and Davenport launched the Reengineering movement. Once managers became interested in Reengineering, however, and began to look around for practical advice about how to actually accomplish process change, they frequently arrived at *Improving Performance*. Thus, the Rummler-Brache methodology became the most widely used, systematic business process methodology in the mid-1990s.

One of the most important contributions made by Rummler and Brache was a framework that showed, in a single diagram, how everything related to everything else. They define three levels of performance: (1) an organizational level, (2) a process level, and (3) a job or performer level. This is very similar to our levels of concern, except that we refer to level 3 as the implementation level to emphasize that an activity can be performed by an employee doing a job or by a computer executing a software application. Otherwise, our use of levels of concern in this book mirrors the levels described in Rummler-Brache in 1990.

Rummler and Brache also introduced a matrix that they obtained by crossing their three levels with three different perspectives. The perspectives are goals and measures, design and implementation issues, and management. Figure 1.4 illustrates the matrix. Software architects today would probably refer to it as a framework. The important thing is that it identifies nine different concerns that anyone trying to change processes in an organization must consider. Approaches that focus only on processes or on performance level measures or on process management are limited perspectives.

	Goals and measures	Design and implementation	Management
Organizational level	Organizational goals and measures of organizational success	Organizational design and implementation	Organizational management
Process level	Process goals and measures of process success	Process design and implementation	Process management
Activity or performance level	Activity goals and measures of activity success	Activity design and implementation	Activity management

Figure 1.4 A performance framework (modified after a figure in Rummler and Brache's *Improving Performance*).

Notice how similar the ideas expressed in the Rummler-Brache framework are to the ideas expressed in the SEI Capability Maturity Model we considered in the introduction. Both seek to describe an organization that is mature and capable of taking advantage of systematic processes. Both stress that we must be concerned not only with the design of processes themselves, but also with measures of success and with the management of processes. In effect, the CMM diagram described how organizations evolve toward process maturity, and the Rummler-Brache framework describes all of the things that a mature organization must master.

Mature organizations must align both vertically and horizontally. Activity goals must be related to process goals, which must, in turn, be derived from the strategic goals of the organization. Similarly, a process must be an integrated whole, with goals and measures, a good design that is well implemented, and a management system that uses the goals and measures to assure that the process runs smoothly and, if need be, is improved.

The Rummler-Brache methodology has helped everyone involved in business process change to understand the scope of the problem, and it provides the foundation on which all of today's comprehensive process redesign methodologies are based.

Prior to the work of systems and management theorists like Porter and Rummler, most companies had focused on dividing processes into specific activities that were assigned to specific departments. Each department developed its own standards and procedures to manage the activities delegated to it. Along the way, in many cases, departments became focused on doing their own activities in their own way, without much regard for the overall process. This is often referred to as *silo thinking*, an image that suggests that each department on the organization chart is its own isolated silo.

In the early years of business computing, a sharp distinction was made between corporate computing and departmental computing. A few systems like payroll and accounting were developed and maintained at the corporate level. Other systems were created by individual departments to serve their specific needs. Typically, one departmental system wouldn't talk to another, and the data stored in the databases of sales couldn't be exchanged with data in the databases owned by accounting or by manufacturing. In essence, in an effort to make each department as professional and efficient as possible, the concept of the overall process was lost.

The emphasis on value chains and systems in the 1980s and the emphasis on business process reengineering in the early 1990s was a revolt against excessive departmentalism and a call for a more holistic view of how activities needed to work together to achieve organizational goals.

The Six Sigma Movement

The third main development in the 1980s evolved from the interaction of the Rummler-Brache approach and the quality control movement. In the early 1980s, Rummler had done quite a bit of consulting at Motorola and had helped Motorola University set up several courses in process analysis and redesign. In the mid-1980s, a group of quality control experts wedded Rummler's emphasis on process with quality and measurement concepts derived from quality control gurus W. Edwards Deming and Joseph M. Juran to create a movement that is now universally referred to as Six Sigma. Six Sigma is more than a set of techniques, however. As Six Sigma spread, first from Motorola to GE, and then to a number of other manufacturing companies, it developed into a comprehensive training program that sought to create process awareness on the part of all employees in an organization. Organizations that embrace Six Sigma not only learn to use a variety of Six Sigma tools, but also embrace a whole culture dedicated to training employees to support process change throughout the organization.

Prior to Six Sigma, quality control professionals had explored a number of different process improvement techniques. ISO 9000 is a good example of another quality control initiative. This international standard describes activities organizations should undertake to be certified ISO 9000 compliant. Unfortunately, ISO 9000 efforts usually focus on simply documenting and managing procedures. Recently, a newer version of this standard, ISO9000:2000, has become established. Rather than focusing so much on documentation, the new standard is driving many companies to think in terms of processes. In many cases this has prompted management to actually start to analyze processes and use them to start to drive change programs. In both cases, however, the emphasis is on documentation, while what organizations really need are ways to improve quality.

At the same time that companies were exploring ISO 9000, they were also exploring other quality initiatives like statistical process control (SPC), total quality management (TQM), and just-in-time manufacturing (JIT). Each of these quality-control initiatives contributed to the efficiency and quality of organizational processes. All this jelled at Motorola with Six Sigma, which has evolved into the most popular corporate process movement today. Unfortunately, Six Sigma's origins in quality control and its heavy emphasis on statistical techniques and process improvement has often put it at odds with other, less statistical approaches to process redesign, like the Rummler-Brache methodology, and with process automation. That, however, is beginning to change and today Six Sigma groups in leading corporations are reaching out to explore the whole range of business process change techniques. This book is not written from a traditional Six Sigma perspective, but we believe that Six Sigma practitioners will find the ideas described here useful and we are equally convinced that readers from other traditions will find it increasingly important and useful to collaborate with Six Sigma practitioners.

Business Process Change in the 1990s

Much of the current corporate interest in business process change can be dated from the business process eeengineering (BPR) movement that began in 1990 with the publication of two papers: Michael Hammer's "Reengineering Work: Don't Automate, Obliterate" (*Harvard Business Review*, July/August 1990) and Thomas Davenport and James Short's "The New Industrial Engineering: Information Technology and Business Process Redesign" (*Sloan Management Review*, Summer 1990). Later, in 1993, Davenport wrote a book, *Process Innovation: Reengineering Work through Information Technology*, and Michael Hammer joined with James Champy to write *Reengineering the Corporation: A Manifesto for Business Revolution*.

BPR theorists like Champy, Davenport, and Hammer insisted that companies must think in terms of comprehensive processes, similar to Porter's value chains and Rummler's Organization Level. If a company focused only on new product development, for example, the company might improve the new product development subprocess, but it might not improve the overall process. Worse, one might improve new product development at the expense of the overall value chain. If, for example, new process development instituted a system of checks to assure higher-quality documents, it might produce superior reports, but take longer to produce them, delaying marketing and manufacturing's ability to respond to sudden changes in the marketplace. Or the new reports might be organized in such a way that they made better sense to the new process development engineers, but became much harder for marketing or manufacturing readers to understand.

Stressing the comprehensive nature of business processes, BPR theorists urged companies to define all of their major processes and then focus on the processes that offered the most return on improvement efforts. Companies that followed this approach usually conceptualized a single business process for an entire product line, and ended up with only 5–10 value chains for an entire company, or division, if the company was very large. The good news is that if companies followed this advice, they were focusing on everything involved in a process and were more likely to identify ways to significantly improve the overall process. The bad news is that when one conceptualizes processes in this way, one is forced to tackle very large redesign efforts that typically involve hundreds or thousands of workers and dozens of major IT applications.

Business process reengineering was more than an emphasis on redesigning large-scale business processes. The driving idea behind the business process reengineering movement was best expressed by Thomas Davenport, who argued that information technology had made major strides in the 1980s, and was now capable of creating major improvements in business processes. Davenport's more reasoned analysis, however, didn't get nearly the attention that Michael Hammer attracted with his more colorful rhetoric.

Hammer argued that previous generations of managers had settled for using information technologies to simply improve departmental functions. In most cases, the departmental functions hadn't been redesigned but simply automated. Hammer referred to this as "paving over cow paths." In many cases, he went on to say, departmental efficiencies were maximized at the expense of the overall process. Thus, for example, a financial department might use a computer to assure more accurate and up-to-date accounting records by requiring manufacturing to turn in reports on the status of the production process. In fact, however, many of the reports came at inconvenient times and actually slowed down the manufacturing process. In a similar way, sales might initiate a sales campaign that resulted in sales that manufacturing couldn't produce in the time allowed. Or manufacturing might initiate changes in the product that made it easier and more inexpensive to manufacture, but which made it harder for salespeople to sell. What was needed, Hammer argued, was a completely new look at business processes. In most cases, Hammer argued that the existing processes should be "obliterated" and replaced by totally new processes, designed from the ground up to take advantage of the latest information system technologies.. Hammer promised huge improvements if companies were able to stand the pain of such comprehensive business process reengineering.

In addition to his call for total process reengineering, Hammer joined Davenport in arguing that processes should be integrated in ways they hadn't been in the past. Hammer argued that the economist Adam Smith had begun the movement toward increasingly specialized work. Readers will probably all recall that Adam Smith compared data on pin manufacture in France in the late 18th century. He showed that one man, working alone, could create a given number of straight pins in a day. But a team, each doing only one part of the task, could produce many times the number of pins per day that the individual members of the team could produce, each working alone. In other words, the division of labor paid off with handsome increases in productivity. In essence, Ford had only been applying Smith's principle to automobile production when he set up his continuous production line in Michigan in the early 20th century. Hammer, however, argued that Smith's principle had led to departments and functions that each tried to maximize its own efficiency at the expense of the whole. In essence, Hammer claimed that large companies had become more inefficient by becoming larger and more specialized. The solution, according to Hammer, Davenport, and Champy was twofold: First, processes needed to be conceptualized as complete, comprehensive entities that stretched from the initial order to the delivery of the product. Second, Information Technology (IT)[1] needed to be used to integrate these comprehensive processes.

As a broad generalization, the process initiatives, like Six Sigma and Rummler-Brache, that began in the 1980s put most of their emphasis on improving how people performed while BPR, in the 1990s, put most of the emphasis on using IT more effectively and on automating processes wherever possible.

The Role of Information Technology in BPR

Both Hammer and Davenport had been involved in major process improvement projects in the late 1980s and observed how IT applications could cut across departmental lines to eliminate inefficiencies and yield huge gains in coordination. They described some of these projects and urged managers at other companies to be equally bold in pursuing similar gains in productivity.

In spite of their insistence on the use of IT, however, Hammer and his colleagues feared the influence of IT professionals. Hammer argued that IT professionals were usually too constrained by their existing systems to recognize major new opportunities.

---

[1] Different organizations use different terms to refer to their information technology (IT) or information systems (IS) or data processing (DP) groups. We'll use these terms and abbreviations interchangeably. In all cases, they refer to the organizational group responsible for analyzing needs, acquiring computer hardware, acquiring or creating computer software, and maintaining the same, or to the systems created and maintained, or to both.

He suggested that IT professionals usually emphasized what couldn't be done rather than focusing on breakthroughs that could be achieved. To remedy this, Hammer and Champy argued that the initial business process redesign teams should exclude IT professionals. In essence, they argue that the initial Business Process Reengineering team should consist of business managers and workers who would have to implement the redesigned process. Only after the redesign team had decided how to change the entire process, Hammer argued, should IT people be called in to advise the team on the systems aspects of the proposed changes.

In hindsight, one can see that the BPR theorists of the early 1990s underestimated the difficulties of integrating corporate systems with the IT technologies available at that time. The BPR gurus had watched some large companies achieve significant results, but they failed to appreciate that the sophisticated teams of software developers available to leading companies were not widely available. Moreover, they failed to appreciate the problems involved in scaling up some of the solutions they recommended. And they certainly compounded the problem by recommending that business managers redesign processes without the close cooperation of their IT professionals. It's true that some IT people resisted major changes, but in many cases they did so because they realized, better than most business managers, just how much such changes would cost. Worse, they realized that many of the proposed changes could not be successfully implemented at their companies with the technologies and manpower they had available.

Some of the BPR projects undertaken in the mid-1990s succeeded and produced impressive gains in productivity. Many others failed and produced disillusionment with BPR. Most company managers intuitively scaled down their BPR efforts and didn't attempt anything as large or comprehensive as the types of projects recommended in the early BPR books.

Misuses of BPR

During this same period, many companies pursued other goals under the name of BPR. Downsizing was popular in the early to mid-1990s. Some of it was justified. Many companies had layers of managers whose primary function was to organize information from line activities and then funnel it to senior managers. The introduction of new software systems and tools that made it possible to query databases for information also meant that senior managers could obtain information without the need for so many middle-level managers. On the other hand, much of the downsizing was simply a natural reduction of staff in response to a slowdown in the business cycle. The latter was appropriate, but it led many employees to assume that any BPR effort would result in major reductions in staff.

Because of some widely discussed failures, and also as a result of employee distrust, the term "business process reengineering" became unpopular during the late 1990s and has gradually fallen into disuse. As an alternative, most companies began to refer to their current business process projects as "business process improvement" or "business process redesign."

Other Process Change Work in the 1990s

Many of the approaches to business process redesign that emerged in the mid-1990s were driven by software technologies. Some companies used software applications, called *workflow systems*, to automate applications. In essence, early workflow systems controlled the flow of documents from one employee to another. The original document is scanned into a computer. Then, an electronic copy of the document is sent to the desk of any employees who need to see or approve the document. To design workflow systems, one creates a flow plan, like the diagram shown in Figure 1.3, that specifies how the document moves from one employee to the next. The workflow system developers or managers can control the order that electronic documents show up on employees' computers by modifying the diagram. Workflow systems became a very popular way to automate document-based processes. Unfortunately, in the early 1990s, most workflow systems were limited to automating departmental processes and couldn't scale up to the enterprise-wide processes.

During this same period, vendors of off-the-shelf software applications began to organize their application modules so that they could be represented as a business process. In effect, one could diagram a business process by simply deciding how to link a number of application modules. Vendors like SAP, People Soft, Oracle, and J. D. Edwards all offered systems of this kind, which were usually called enterprise resource planning (ERP) systems. In effect, a business analyst was shown an ideal way that several modules could be linked together. A specific company could elect to eliminate some modules and change some of the rules controlling the actions of some of the modules but, overall, one was limited to choosing and ordering already-existing software application modules. Many of the modules included customer-interface screens and therefore controlled employee behaviors relative to particular modules. In essence, an ERP system is controlled by another kind of "workflow" system.[2] Instead of moving documents from one employee workstation to another, the ERP systems offered by SAP and others allowed managers to design processes that moved information and control from one software module to another. ERP systems allowed companies to replace older software applications with new applications, and to organize the new applications into an organized business process. This worked best for processes that were well understood and common between companies. Thus, accounting, inventory, and human resource processes were all popular targets for ERP systems.

SAP, for example, offers the following modules in their financials suite: Change Vendor or Customer Master Data, Clear Open Items, Deduction Management, Payment with Advice, Clearing of Open Items at Vendor, Reporting for External Business Partners, and SEM: Benchmark Data Collection. They also offer "blueprints," which are, in essence, alternative flow diagrams showing how the financial modules might be assembled to accomplish different business processes.

Davenport supported and promoted the use of ERP packaged applications as a way to improve business processes. At the same time, August-Wilhelm Scheer, a software systems theorist, advocated the use of ERP applications for systems development, and wrote several books promoting this approach and the use of a modeling methodology that he named ARIS.

Most large companies explored the use of document workflow systems and the use of ERP systems to automate at least some business processes. The use of document workflow and ERP systems represented a very different approach to process redesign than that advocated by the BPR gurus of the early 1990s. Gurus like Hammer had advocated a total reconceptualization of complete value chains. Everything was to be reconsidered and redesigned to provide the company with the best possible new business process. The workflow and ERP approaches, on the other hand, focused on automating existing processes and replacing existing, departmentally focused legacy systems with new software modules that were designed to work together. These systems were narrowly focused and relied heavily on IT people to put them in place. They provided small-scale improvements rather than radical redesigns.

We have already considered two popular software approaches to automating business processes: workflow and the use of systems of packaged applications. Moving beyond these specific techniques, any software development effort could be a response to a business process challenge. Any company that seeks to improve a process will

---

[2] Systems that coordinate the flow of work from one software application to another are usually called *Enterprise Application Integration* (EAI) systems.

at least want to consider if the process can be automated. Some processes can't be automated with existing technology. Some activities require people to make decisions or to provide a human interface with customers. Over the course of the past few decades, however, a major trend has been to increase the number of tasks performed by computers. As a strong generalization, automated processes reduce labor costs and improve corporate performance.

Software engineering usually refers to efforts to make the development of software more systematic, efficient, and consistent. Increasingly, software engineers have focused on improving their own processes and on developing tools that will enable them to assist business managers to automate business processes. We mentioned the work of the Software Engineering Institute at Carnegie Mellon University on CMM, a model that describes how organizations mature in their use and management of processes.

At the same time, software engineers have developed modeling languages for modeling software applications and tools that can generate code from software models. Some software theorists have advocated developing models and tools that would allow business analysts to be more heavily involved in designing the software, but to date this approach has been limited by the very technical and precise nature of software specifications. As an alternative, a good deal of effort has been focused on refining the concept of *software requirements*—the specification that a business process team would hand to a software development team to indicate exactly what a software application would need to do to support a new process.

The more complex and important the business process change, the more likely a company will need to create tailored software to capture unique company competencies. Whenever this occurs, then languages and tools that communicate between business process teams and IT teams become very important.

The Internet and Y2K

During the same period that the enthusiasm for BPR was declining, and at the same time that companies began to explore workflow and ERP approaches, new software technologies began to emerge that really could deliver on the promise that the early BPR gurus had oversold. Among the best known are the Internet, email, and the Web, which provide powerful ways to integrate employees, suppliers, and customers.

In the early 1990s, when Hammer and Davenport wrote their books, the most popular technique for large-scale corporate systems integration was EDI (electronic data interchange). Many large companies used EDI to link with their suppliers. In general, however, EDI was difficult to install and expensive to maintain. As a practical matter, EDI could only be used to link a company to its major suppliers. Smaller suppliers couldn't afford to install EDI and didn't have the programmers required to maintain an EDI system. The Internet changed that.

The Internet doesn't require proprietary lines, but runs instead on ordinary telephone lines. At the same time, the Internet depends on popular, open protocols that were developed by the government and were widely accepted by everyone. A small company could link to the Internet and to a distributor or supplier in exactly the same way that millions of individuals could surf the Web, by simply acquiring a PC and a modem and using browser software. Just as the Internet provided a practical solution for some of the communications problems faced by companies, email and the Web created a new way for customers to communicate with companies. In the late 1990s, customers rapidly acquired the habit of going to company Web sites to find out what products and services were available. Moreover, as fast as companies installed Web sites that would support it, customers began to buy products online. In effect, the overnight popularity of the Internet, email, and the Web in the late 1990s made it imperative that companies reconsider how they had their business processes organized in order to take advantage of the major cost savings that the use of the Internet, Web, and email could provide.

Of course the story is more complex. A number of "dot.com" companies sprang up, promising to totally change the way companies did business by using the Internet, Web, and email. Some have carved new niches for themselves, but most disappeared when the stock market finally realized that their business models were unsound. That process encouraged large, established companies to consider how they could use Internet technologies, but it also distracted them and encouraged some to attempt rash ventures to compete with the dot.coms that achieved extraordinary stock valuations in the late 1990s.

At the same time, other technology gurus began to warn of the approach of the end of the millennium. Too many software systems had been created in the last half of the 20th century with two-digit dates (e.g., instead of representing the year 1965 with four digits, it was represented as "65"). This had been done on the assumption that the systems created in that manner would be retired well before the end of the millennium. Most hadn't, and that posed a significant problem, since it was possible that a system given the date "01" would read it as "1901" rather than "2001" and make costly, and in some cases life-threatening, mistakes. Thus, in spite of the opportunity for process improvement created by Internet techniques, many companies diverted IT resources to checking their existing software applications to assure that they didn't contain what became popularly known as the Y2K bug.

The overall result is that change that might have happened in the late 1990s was delayed, but it is now at the top of most companies' agenda in the first decade of the new millennium.

A Quick Summary

Figure 1.5 provides a summary overview of some of the historic business process technologies we have described in this chapter. Most are still actively evolving. As you can see in the figure, business process management is made up of a diverse collection of ideas and traditions. We have grouped them, very loosely, into three general traditions, the Operations Research/Quality Control tradition that is primarily focused on improving operational processes, the Management and Business Process Redesign tradition that is focused on aligning or changing major business processes to significantly improve organizational performance, and the IT tradition, which is primarily focused on process automation. Most large companies have groups working in each of these traditions, and, increasingly the different traditions are borrowing from each other. And, of course, none of the groups has confined itself to a single tradition. Thus, Lean Six Sigma is focused on process improvement, but it also supports process management and process redesign initiatives. Similarly, IT is focused on automation, but IT process groups are often heavily involved in process redesign projects and are strongly committed to architecture initiatives that incorporate process architectures.

The author of this book comes from the Management and Process Redesign tradition—he began his process work as an employee of a consulting company managed by Geary Rummler—and this book describes that tradition in more detail than any other. However, the author has worked with enough different companies to know that no solution fits every situation. Thus, he is firmly committed to a best-practices approach that seeks to combine the best from all the process change traditions and provides information on the other traditions whenever possible to encourage the evolving synthesis of the different process traditions. Senior managers do not make the fine distinctions that we illustrate in Figure 1.5. Executives are interested in results and, increasingly, effective solutions require practitioners from the different traditions to work together. Indeed, one could easily argue that the term "business process management"

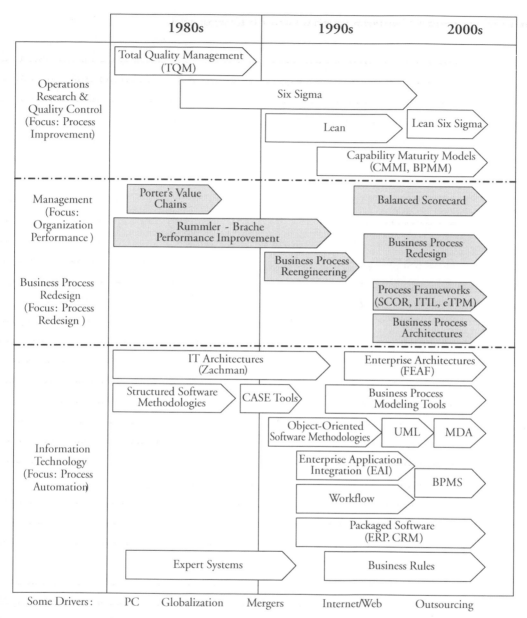

Figure 1.5 Some key ideas and groups that are part of the business process management movement.

was coined to suggest the emergence of a more synthetic, comprehensive approach to process change that combines the best of process management, redesign, process improvement and process automation.

Business Process Change in the New Millennium

For awhile, the new millennium didn't seem all that exciting. Computer systems didn't shut down as the year 2000 began. The collapse of the dot.com market and a recession seemed to provide a brief respite from the hectic business environment of the nineties. By 2002, however, the sense of relentless change had resurfaced.

The corporate interest in business process change, which seemed to die down a bit toward the end of the century, resurfaced with a vengeance. Many people working in IT realized that they could integrate a number of diverse technologies that had been developed in the late 1990s to create a powerful new approach to facilitate the day-to-day management of business processes. The book that best reflected this new approach was called *Business Process Management: The Third Wave* by Howard Smith and Peter Fingar. They proposed that companies combine workflow systems, software applications integration systems, and Internet technologies to create a new type of software application. In essence the new software—a Business Process Management System (BPMS)—would coordinate the day-to-day activities of both employees and software applications. The BPMS applications would use process models to define their functionality, and make it possible for business managers to change their processes by changing the models or rules that directed the BPMS applications. All of these ideas had been tried before, with earlier technologies, but in 2003 it all seemed to come together, and dozens of vendors rushed to create BPMS products. As the enthusiasm spread, the vision was expanded and other technologists began to suggest how BPMS applications could drive management dashboards that would let managers control processes in something close to real time.

In 2002 there were no BPM conferences in the U.S. In 2006 there were 11 major BPM meetings in the U.S., and there will be as many in 2007. In 2003 Gartner suggested that BPMS vendors earned around $500 million dollars. Gartner now projects that the market for BPMS will exceed $1 billion by 2009.

If everyone were only excited about BPMS, then we might suggest that the market was simply a software market, but that's hardly the case. All the various aspects of business process have advanced during the same period. Suddenly large companies are making major investments in the creation of business process architectures. To create these architectures, they seek to define and align their processes while simultaneously defining metrics to measure process success. Similarly, there is a broad movement toward reorganizing managers to support process goals. Balanced Scorecard has played a major role in this. There has been a renewed interest in using maturity models to evaluate corporate progress. A number of industry groups have defined business process frameworks, like the Supply Chain Council's SCOR and the TeleManagement Forum's eTOM, and management has adopted these frameworks to speed the development of enterprise level architectures and measurement systems.

Process redesign and improvement have also enjoyed a renaissance and Six Sigma has expanded from manufacturing to every possible industry while simultaneously incorporating Lean. A dozen new process redesign methodologies and notations have been published in the past three years and over 100 books on the various aspects of process change have been published. It's hard to find a business publication that isn't talking about the importance of process change. Clearly this interest in business process change isn't driven by just BPMS or by any other specific technology. Instead, it is being driven by the deeper needs of today's business managers.

What Drives Business Process Change?

So far, we have spoken of various approaches to business process change. To wrap up this discussion, perhaps we should step back and ask what drives the business interest in business processes in the first place. The perennial answers are very straightforward. In economically bad times, when money is tight, companies seek to make their processes more efficient. In economically good times, when money is more available, companies seek to expand, to ramp up production and to enter new markets. They improve processes to offer better products and services in hopes of attracting new customers or taking customers away from competitors.

Since the 1980s, however, the interest in process has become more intense. The new interest in process is driven by change. Starting in the 1980s, large U.S. companies became more engaged in world trade. At the same time, foreign companies began to show up in the U.S. and compete with established market leaders. Thus, in the 1970s, most Americans who wanted to buy a car chose among cars sold by General Motors, Ford and Chrysler. By the mid-1980s, Americans were just as likely to consider a VW, a BMW, a Nissan, or a Honda. Suddenly, the automobile market had moved from a continental market to a world market. This development has driven constant changes in the auto market and it's not about to let up in the next few years.

Increased competition also led to mergers and acquisitions, as companies attempted to acquire the skills and technologies they needed to control their markets or enter new ones. Every merger between rivals in the same industry created a company with two different sets of processes and someone had to figure out which processes the combined company would use going forward.

During this same period, IT technology was remaking the world. The first personal computers appeared at the beginning of the 1980s. The availability of relatively cheap desktop computers made it possible to do things in entirely different and much more productive ways. In the mid-1990s the Internet burst on the scene and business was revolutionized again. Suddenly people bought PCs for home use so they could communicate via email and shop on-line. Companies reorganized their processes to support web portals. That, in turn, suddenly increased competitive pressures as customers in one city could as easily buy items from a company in another city or country as from the store in their neighborhood. Amazon.com revolutionized the way books are bought and sold.

The Internet and the Web and the broader trend toward globalization also made it easier for companies to coordinate their efforts with other companies. Increased competition and the search for greater productivity led companies to begin exploring all kinds of outsourcing. If another company could provide all the services your company's Human Resources or IT departments used to provide, and was only an email away, it was worth considering. Suddenly companies that had historically been manufacturers were outsourcing the manufacture of their products to China and were focusing instead on sticking close to their customers, so they could specialize in designing and selling new products that would be manufactured by overseas companies and delivered by companies who specialized in the worldwide delivery of packages.

In part, new technologies like the Internet and the Web are driving these changes. They make worldwide communication easier and less expensive than in the past. At the same time, however, the changes taking place are driving companies to jump on any new technology that seems to promise them an edge over their competition. Wireless laptops, cell phones and personal digital assistants are being used by business people to work more efficiently. At the same time, the widespread purchase of iPods by teenagers is revolutionizing the music industry and driving a host of far-reaching changes and realignments.

We won't go on. Lots of authors and many popular business magazines write about these changes each month. Suffice it to say that change and competition have become relentless. Large companies are reorganizing to do business on a worldwide scale, and, predictably, some will do it better than others and expand, while those that are less successful will disappear. Meantime, smaller companies are using the Internet and the Web to explore the thousands of niche service markets that have been created.

Change and relentless competition calls for constant innovation and for constant increases in productivity, and those both call for an intense focus on how work gets done. To focus on how the work gets done is to focus on business processes. Every manager knows that if his or her company is to succeed it will have to figure out how to do things better, faster, and cheaper than they are being done today, and that's what the focus on process is all about.

Notes and References

We provided a wide-ranging history of the evolution of business process techniques and concerns. We have included a few key books that provide a good overview to the concepts and techniques we described.

McCraw, Thomas K. (Ed.), *Creating Modern Capitalism: How Entrepreneurs, Companies, and Countries Triumphed in Three Industrial Revolutions*, Harvard University Press, 1997. A good overview of the Industrial Revolution, the rise of various early companies, the work of various entrepreneurs, and the work of management theorists like F. W. Taylor.

Taylor, Frederick W., *The Principles of Scientific Management*, Harper's, 1911. For a modern review of the efficiency movement and Taylor, check Daniel Nelson's *Frederick W. Taylor and the Rise of Scientific Management*, University of Wisconsin Press, 1980.

Bertalanffy, Ludwig von, *General Systems Theory: Foundations, Development, Applications*, George Braziller, 1968. An early book that describes how engineering principles developed to control systems ranging from thermostats to computers provided a better way to describe a wide variety of phenomena.

Beer, Stafford, *Brain of the Firm*, Harmondsworth, 1967. Early, popular book on how managers should use a systems approach.

Forrester, Jay, *Principles of Systems*, Pegasus Communications, 1971. Forrester was an influential professor at MIT who wrote a number of books showing how systems theory could be applied to industrial and social systems. Several business simulation tools are based on Forrester's ideas, which are usually referred to as *systems dynamics*, since they focus on monitoring and using changing rates of feedback to predict future activity.

Sterman, John D., *Business Dynamics: Systems Thinking and Modeling for a Complex World*, Irwin McGraw-Hill, 2000. Sterman is one of Forrester's students at MIT, and this is a popular textbook for those interested in the technical details of systems dynamics, as applied to business problems.

Senge, Peter M., *The Fifth Discipline: The Art and Practice of the Learning Organization*, Currency Doubleday, 1994. Senge is also at the Sloan School of Management at MIT, and a student of Forrester. Senge has created a more popular approach to systems dynamics that puts the emphasis on people and the use of models and feedback to facilitate organizational development. In the Introduction we described mature process organizations as organizations that totally involved people in constantly improving the process. Senge would describe such an organization as a learning organization.

Porter, Michael E., *Competitive Advantage: Creating and Sustaining Superior Performance*, The Free Press, 1985. This book focuses on the idea of competitive advantage and discusses how companies obtain and maintain it. One of the key techniques Porter stresses is an emphasis on value chains and creating integrated business processes that are difficult for competitors to duplicate.

Hammer, Michael, "Reengineering Work: Don't Automate, Obliterate," *Harvard Business Review*. July–August 1990. This article, and the one below by Davenport and Short, kicked off the BPR fad. The books that these authors are best known for didn't come until a couple of years later.

Rummler, Geary, and Alan Brache, *Performance Improvement: Managing the White Space on the Organization Chart*, Jossey-Bass, 1990. Still the best introduction to business process redesign for senior managers. Managers read Hammer and Davenport in the early 1990s, and then turned to Rummler and Brache to learn how to actually do business process redesign. So many ideas that we now associate with business process change originated with Geary Rummler. Davenport, Thomas H., and James Short, "The New Industrial Engineering: Information Technology and Business Process Redesign," *Sloan Management Review*, Summer 1990.

Hammer, Michael, and James Champy, *Reengineering the Corporation: A Manifesto for Business Revolution*, HarperBusiness, 1993. This was a runaway bestseller that got everyone in business talking about reengineering in the mid-1990s. It argued for a radical approach to redesign. Some companies used the ideas successfully; most found it too disruptive.

Davenport, Thomas H., *Process Innovation: Reengineering Work through Information Technology*, Harvard Business School Press, 1993. This book doesn't have the breathless marketing pizzazz that Hammer's book has, but it's more thoughtful. Overall, however, both books advocate radical change to take advantage of the latest IT technologies.

Smith, Adam, *The Wealth of Nations*, (any of several editions). Classic economics text that advocates, among other things, the use of work specialization to increase productivity.

Fischer, Layna (Ed.), *The Workflow Paradigm: The Impact of Information Technology on Business Process Reengineering* (2nd ed.), Future Strategies, 1995. A good overview of the early use of workflow systems to support BPR efforts.

Davenport, Thomas H., *Mission Critical: Realizing the Promise of Enterprise Systems,* Harvard Business School Press, 2000. This is the book in which Davenport laid out the case for using ERP systems to improve company processes.

Ramias, Alan. *The Mists of Six Sigma*, www.bptrends.com, Oct. 2005. Excellent history of the early development of Six Sigma at Motorola.

Scheer, August-Wilhelm, *Business Process Engineering: Reference Models for Industrial Enterprises* (2nd ed.), Springer, 1994. Scheer has written several books, all very technical, that describe how to use IT systems and modeling techniques to support business processes.

Harry, Mikel J., and Richard Schroeder, *Six Sigma: The Breakthrough Management Strategy Revolutionizing the World's Top Corporations*, Doubleday and Company, 1999. An introduction to Six Sigma by the Motorola engineer who is usually credited with originating the Six Sigma approach.

Harrington, H. James, Erik K.C. Esseling and Harm Van Nimwegen, *Business Process Improvement Workbook,* McGraw-Hill, 1997. A very practical introduction to process improvement, very much in the Six Sigma tradition, but without the statistics and with a dash of software diagrams.

Boar, Bernard H., *Practical Steps for Aligning Information Technology with Business Strategies: How to Achieve a Competitive Advantage*, Wiley, 1994. Lots of books have been written on business-IT alignment. This one is a little out of date, but still very good. Ignore the methodology, which gets too technical, but focus on the overviews of IT and how they support business change.

CIO, "Reengineering Redux," *CIO Magazine*, March 1, 2000, pp. 143–156. A roundtable discussion between Michael Hammer and four other business executives on the state of reengineering today. They agree on the continuing importance of process change. For more on Michael Hammer's current work, check his Web site: *www.hammerandco.com*.

Smith, Howard and Peter Fingar, *Business Process Management, The Third Wave*, Meghan-Kiffer Press, 2003. Although this book is a bit over the top in some of its claims, like Hammer and Champy's *Reengineering the Corporation*, it got people excited about the idea of Business Process Management Software systems and helped kick off the current interest in BPM.

ENTERPRISE-LEVEL CONCERNS

UNTIL RECENTLY, MOST BUSINESS PROCESS efforts focused on redesigning or improving specific business processes. In the past few years, however, leading organizations have realized that they cannot achieve the results they want by modifying specific processes in isolation from one another. The only way to achieve a significant competitive advantage is to assure that all the processes that make up a common value chain are integrated and support each other. This insight, in turn, has led organizations to begin to focus on enterprise-level concerns.

In essence, an enterprise focus shifts from trying to improve processes to conceptualizing the entire organization as a system of interacting processes and working to maximize the effectiveness of the whole system. Once executives shift from worrying about specific processes to worrying about all the processes in the organization, they naturally want an enterprise model that shows how all the organization's processes fit together, a set of enterprise process measures that show how processes support enterprise strategies and goals, and how all the process and subprocess are aligned to achieve those goals. They also want a system that defines responsibilities for managing the processes in the organization. This entire set of models and measures, and the resources alignment to support them, is referred to as a *business process architecture.*

In the 1990s, when companies focused on improving specific processes, most process change was project oriented. One started with a broken process and worked till it was fixed. As companies shift to enterprise-level process work, they are finding that they need to develop tools and organizational structures to support a sustained effort. A business process architecture isn't a product that can be developed in one push. A business process architecture is usually developed in stages over a period of time. It's usually easiest to begin with a description of an organization's processes and then progress to defining measures and managerial responsibilities. The sophistication of the architecture tends to evolve as managers learn to use it as a tool for strategizing and decision making. Moreover, to be useful, an architecture needs to be maintained and that requires an organization to constantly monitor processes and changes and incorporating them into the architecture. Thus, as companies begin to focus on enterprise-level process concerns, they find that they need to adopt an entirely new attitude and a new level of commitment to generate the desired results.

Restated in slightly different terms, any organization that shifts from focusing on specific processes to enterprise-level concerns is making a major shift in its process maturity. It is undertaking a shift from CMM Level 2 to CMM Levels 3 and 4. Today it is common to refer to organizations whose executives decide to commit to organizing around processes as *process-centric organizations*.

In this section we are going to focus on some of the key enterprise-level concepts and practices that organizations need to understand and implement to become process-centric organizations.

In Chapter 2 we will discuss organization goals and strategies and how they can be tied to processes and to competitive advantage.

In Chapter 3 we will present an overview of the BPTrends Enterprise Methodology, one approach to defining and implementing the tools and practices needed to manage processes at the enterprise level. We will also consider what's involved in understanding an enterprise and defining its major value chains and key business processes.

In Chapter 4 we will consider the idea of a business process architecture. A process architecture defines the major processes in a value chain, establishes their relationships, defines their performance measures, determines who manages each process, and describes how the processes are aligned to other organizational resources, including, for example, goals and policies, business rules, IT resources, training programs and knowledge-management systems.

We can't consider all aspects of a business process architecture in a single chapter, so we focus on modeling processes and resource alignment in Chapter 4 and then consider process management in Chapter 5 and process measurement in Chapter 6.

In Chapter 7 we conclude our discussion of enterprise-level concerns by considering how a BPM group—or BPM Center of Excellence—can be used to maintain the business process architecture, provide executives with timely reports, and support the on-going process activities of an organization. We will also look at a case study in Chapter 7 to see how one organization has managed to implement all of the enterprise-level tools we have discussed in Part I.

2

Strategy, Value Chains and Competive Advantage

T HE CONCEPT OF A BUSINESS STRATEGY has been around for decades, and the models and process used to develop a company strategy are taught at every business school. A business strategy defines how a company will compete, what its goals will be, and what policies it will support to achieve those goals. Put a different way, a company's strategy describes how it will create value for its customers, its shareholders, and its other stakeholders. Developing and updating a company's business strategy is one of the key responsibilities of a company's executive officers.

We are going to start our discussion of enterprise-level process concerns with a look at how business people talk about business strategy. This will establish a number of the terms we will need for our subsequent discussion of processes. To develop a business strategy, senior executives need to consider the strengths and weaknesses of their own company and its competitors. They also need to consider trends, threats, and opportunities within the industry in which they compete, as well as in the broader social, political, technological, and economic environments in which the company operates.

There are different schools of business strategy. Some advocate a formal process that approaches strategic analysis very systematically, while others support less formal processes. A few argue that the world is changing so fast that companies must depend on the instincts of their senior executives and evolve new positions on the fly in order to move rapidly.

The formal approach to business strategy analysis and development is often associated with the Harvard Business School. In this brief summary we'll begin by describing a formal approach that is derived from Harvard professor Michael E. Porter's book, *Competitive Strategy*. Published in 1980 and now in its 60th printing, *Competitive Strategy* has been the bestselling strategy textbook throughout the past two decades. Porter's approach is well known, and it will allow us to examine some models that are well established among those familiar with strategic management literature.

Defining a Strategy

Porter defines business strategy as "a broad formula for how a business is going to compete, what its goals should be, and what policies will be needed to carry out these goals." Figure 2.1 provides an overview of the three-phase process that Porter recommends for strategy formation.

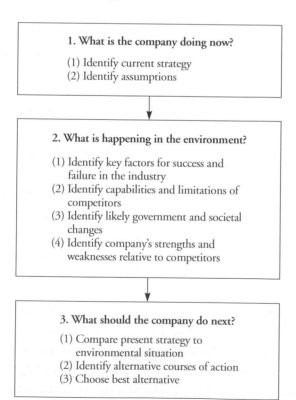

Figure 2.1 Porter's process for defining a company strategy (after Porter, *Competitive Strategy*).

▶ *Phase 1: Determine the current position of the company.* The formal strategy process begins with a definition of where the company is now—what its current strategy is—and the assumptions that the company managers commonly make about the company's current position, strengths and weaknesses, competitors, and industry trends. Most large companies have a formal strategy and have already gone through this exercise several times. Indeed, most large companies have a strategy committee that constantly monitors the company's strategy.

▶ *Phase 2: Determine what's happening in the environment.* In the second phase of Porter's strategy process (the middle box in Figure 2.1), the team developing the strategy considers what is happening in the environment. In effect, the team ignores the assumptions the company makes at the moment and gathers intelligence that will allow them to formulate a current statement of environmental constraints and opportunities facing all the companies in their industry. The team examines trends in the industry the company is in and reviews the capabilities and limitations of competitors. It also reviews likely changes in society and government policy that might affect the business. When the team has finished its current review, it reconsiders the company's strengths and weaknesses, relative to the current environmental conditions.

▶ *Phase 3: Determine a new strategy for the company.* During the third phase, the strategy team compares the company's existing strategy with the latest analysis of what's happening in the environment. The team generates a number of scenarios or alternate courses of action that the company could pursue. In effect, the company imagines a number of situations the company could find itself in a few months or years hence and works backward to imagine what policies, technologies, and organizational changes would be required, during the intermediate period, to reach each situation. Finally, the company's strategy committee, working with the company's executive committee, selects one alternative and begins to make the changes necessary to implement the company's new strategy.

Porter offers lots of qualifications about the need for constant review and the necessity for change and flexibility but, overall, Porter's model was designed for the relatively calmer business environment that existed 20 years ago. Given the constant pressures to change and innovate that we've all experienced during the last three decades, it may be hard to think of the 1980s as a calm period, but everything really is relative. When you contrast the way companies approached strategy development just 10 years ago with the kinds of changes occurring today, as companies scramble to adjust to the world of the Internet, the 1980s were relatively sedate. Perhaps the best way to illustrate this is to look at Porter's general model of competition.

Porter's Model of Competition

Porter emphasizes that "the essence of formulating competitive strategy is relating a company to its environment." One of the best-known diagrams in Porter's *Competitive Strategy* is the one we have illustrated in Figure 2.2. Porter's diagram, which pulls together lots of information about how managers conceptualize the competition when they formulate strategy, is popularly referred to as the "five forces model."

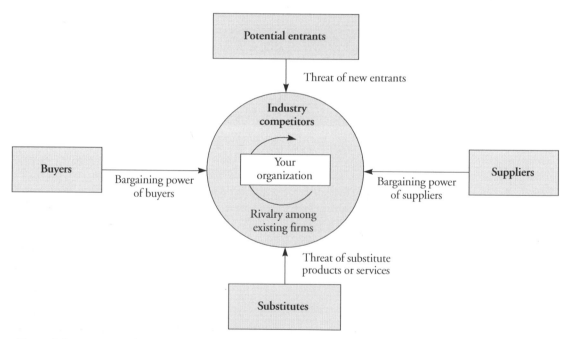

Figure 2.2 Porter's model of the five forces driving industry competition (after Porter, *Competitive Strategy*).

Porter identifies five changes in the competitive environment that can force a company to adjust its business strategy. The heart of the business competition, of course, is the set of rival companies that comprise an industry. The company and its competitors are represented by the circle at the center of Figure 2.2.

▶ *Industry competitors.* As rival companies make moves, the company must respond. Similarly, the company may opt to make changes itself, in order to place its rivals at a disadvantage. Porter spends several chapters analyzing the ways companies compete within an industry, and we'll return to that in a moment.

Beyond the rivalry between the companies that make up the industry, there are changes in the environment that can potentially affect all the companies in an industry. Porter classifies these changes into four groups: (1) buyers, (2) suppliers, (3) potential new companies that might enter the field, and (4) the threat that new products or services will become desirable substitutes for the company's existing products and services.

▶ *Buyers.* Buyers or customers will tend to want to acquire the company's products or services as inexpensively as possible. Some factors give the seller an advantage: If the product is scarce, if the company is the only source of the product, or the only local source of the product, or if the company is already selling the product more cheaply than its competitors, then the seller will tend to have better control of its prices. The inverse of factors like these give the customer more bargaining power and tend to force the company to reduce its prices. If there are lots of suppliers competing with each other, or if it's easy for customers to shop around, prices will tend to fall.

▶ *Suppliers.* In a similar way, suppliers would always like to sell their products or services for a higher price. If the suppliers are the only source of a needed product, if they can deliver it more quickly than their rivals, or if there is lots of demand for a relatively scarce product, then suppliers will tend to have more bargaining power and will increase their prices. Conversely, if the supplier's product is widely available, or available more cheaply from someone else, the company (buyer) will tend to have the upper hand and will try to force the supplier's price down.

▶ *Substitutes.* Companies in every industry also need to watch to see that no products or services become available that might function as substitutes for the products or services the company sells. At a minimum, a substitute product can drive down the company's prices. In the worst case, a new product can render the company's current products obsolete. The manufacturers of buggy whips were driven into bankruptcy when internal combustion automobiles replaced horse-drawn carriages in the early years of the 20th century. Similarly, the availability of plastic products has forced the manufacturers of metal, glass, paper, and wood products to reposition their products in various ways.

▶ *Potential entrants.* Finally, there is the threat that new companies will enter an industry and thereby increase the competition. More companies pursuing the same customers and trying to purchase the same raw materials tend to give both the suppliers and the customers more bargaining power, driving up the cost of goods and lowering each company's profit margins.

Historically, there are a number of factors that tend to function as barriers to the entry of new firms. If success in a given industry requires a large capital investment, then potential entrants will have to have a lot of money before they can consider trying to enter the industry. The capital investment could take different forms. In some cases, a new entrant might need to build large factories and buy expensive machinery. The cost of setting up a new computer chip plant, for example, runs to billions of dollars, and only a very large company could consider entering the chip manufacturing field. In other cases, the existing companies in an industry may spend huge amounts on advertising and have well-known brand names. Any new company would be forced to spend at least as much on advertising to even get its product noticed. Similarly, access to established distribution channels, proprietary knowledge possessed by existing firms, or government policies can all serve as barriers to new companies that might otherwise consider entering an established industry.

Until recently, the barriers to entry in most mature industries were so great that the leading firms in each industry had a secure hold on their positions and new entries were very rare. In the past three decades the growing move toward globalization has resulted in growing competition among firms that were formerly isolated by geography. Thus, prior to the 1960s, the three large auto companies in the United States completely controlled the U.S. auto market. Starting in the 1970s, and growing throughout the next two decades, foreign auto companies began to compete for U.S. buyers and U.S. auto companies began to compete for foreign auto buyers. By the mid-1980s, a U.S. consumer could choose between cars sold by over a dozen firms. The late 1990s witnessed a sharp contraction in the auto market, as the largest automakers began to acquire their rivals and reduced the number of independent auto companies in the market. A key to understanding this whole process, however, is to understand that these auto companies were more or less equivalent in size and had always been potential rivals, except that they were functioning in geographically isolated markets. As companies became more international, geography stopped functioning as a barrier to entry, and these companies found themselves competing with each other. They all had similar strategies, and the most successful had gradually reduced the competition by acquiring their less successful rivals. In other words, globalization created challenges, but it didn't radically change the basic business strategies that were applied by the various firms engaged in international competition.

In effect, when a strategy team studies the environment, it surveys all of these factors. They check to see what competitors are doing, if potential new companies seem likely to enter the field, or if substitute products are likely to be offered. And they check on factors that might change the future bargaining power that buyers or sellers are likely to exert.

Industries, Products, and Value Propositions

Obviously Porter's model assumes that the companies in the circle in the middle of Figure 2.2 have a good idea of the scope of the industry they are in and the products and services that define the industry. Companies are sometimes surprised when they find that the nature of the industry has changed and that companies that were not formerly their competitors are suddenly taking away their customers. When this happens, it usually occurs because the managers at a company were thinking too narrowly or too concretely about what it is that their company was selling.

To avoid this trap, sophisticated managers need to think more abstractly about what products and services their industry provides. A "value proposition" refers to the value that a product or service provides to customers. Managers should always strive to be sure that they know what business (or industry) their company is really in. That's done by being sure they know what value their company is providing to its customers.

Thus, for example, a bookseller might think he or she is in the business of providing customers with books. In fact, however, the bookseller is probably in the business of providing customers with information or entertainment. Once this is recognized, then it becomes obvious that a bookseller's rivals are not only other book stores, but magazine stores, TV, and the Web. In other words, a company's rivals aren't simply the other companies that manufacture similar products, but all those who provide the same general value to customers. Clearly Rupert Murdoch realizes this. He has gradually evolved from being a newspaper publisher to managing a news and entertainment conglomerate that makes movies, owns TV channels and TV satellites, and sells books. His various companies are constantly expanding their interconnections to offer new types of value to their customers. Thus, Murdoch's TV companies and newspapers promote the books he publishes. Later, the books are made into movies that are shown on his TV channels and once again promoted by his newspapers.

If customers ever decide they like reading texts on computer screens in some automated book device, like an iPod, then companies that think of themselves as booksellers are in serious trouble. In this situation it will be obvious that the real value being provided is information and that the information could be downloaded from a computer just as well as printed in a book format. Many magazines are already producing online versions that allow customers to read articles on the Web or download articles in electronic form. Record and CD vendors are currently struggling with a version of this problem as copies of songs are exchanged over the Internet. In effect, one needs to understand that it's the song that has the value, and not the record or CD on which it's placed. The Web and a computer become a substitute for a CD if they can function as effective media for transmitting and playing the song to the customer.

Good strategists must always work to be sure they really understand what customer needs they are satisfying. Strategists must know what value they provide customers before they can truly understand what business they are really in and who their potential rivals are. A good strategy is focused on providing value to customers, not narrowly defined in terms of a specific product or service.

In some cases, of course, the same product may provide different value to different customers. The same car, for example, might simply be a way of getting around for one group of customers, but a status item for another set of customers.

In spite of the need to focus on providing value to customers, historically, in designing their strategies, most companies begin with an analysis of their core competencies. In other words, they begin by focusing on the products or services they currently produce. They move from products to ways of specializing them and then to sales channels until they finally reach their various targeted groups of customers. Most e-business strategists suggest that companies approach their analysis in reverse. The new importance of the customer, and the new ways that products can be configured for the Web, suggest that companies should begin by considering what Web customers like and what they will buy over the Web, and then progress to what product the company might offer that would satisfy the new Web customers. This approach, of course, results in an increasingly dynamic business environment.

Strategies for Competing

Earlier, we mentioned that Potter places a lot of emphasis on the ways existing companies can compete within an existing industry. In his 1980 book on *Competitive Strategy*, Potter described competition in most traditional industries as following one of three generic strategies: (1) cost leadership, (2) differentiation, or (3) niche specialization.

▶ *Cost leadership.* The cost leader is the company that can offer the product at the cheapest price. In most industries, price can be driven down by economies of scale, by the control of suppliers and channels, and by experience that allows a company to do things more efficiently. In most industries, large companies dominate the manufacture of products in huge volume and sell them more cheaply than their smaller rivals.

▶ *Differentiation.* If a company can't sell its products for the cheapest price, an alternative is to offer better or more desirable products. Customers are often willing to pay a premium for a better product, and this allows companies specializing in producing a better product to compete with those selling a cheaper but less desirable product. Companies usually make better products by using more expensive materials, relying on superior craftsmanship, creating a unique design, or tailoring the design of the product in various ways.

▶ *Niche specialization.* Niche specialists focus on specific buyers, specific segments of the market, or buyers in particular geographical markets and often only offer a subset of the products typically sold in the industry. In effect, they represent an extreme version of differentiation, and they can charge a premium for their products, since the products have special features beneficial to the consumers in the niche.

Figure 2.3 provides an overview of one way strategists think of positioning and specialization. As a broad generalization, if the product is a commodity, it will sell near its manufacturing cost, with little profit for the seller.

The classic example of a company that achieved cost leadership in an industry was Ford Motor Company. The founder, Henry Ford, created a mass market for automobiles by driving the price of a car down to the point where the average person could afford one. To do this, Ford limited the product to one model in one color and set up a production line to produce large numbers of cars very efficiently. In the early years of the 20th century, Ford completely dominated auto production in the United States.

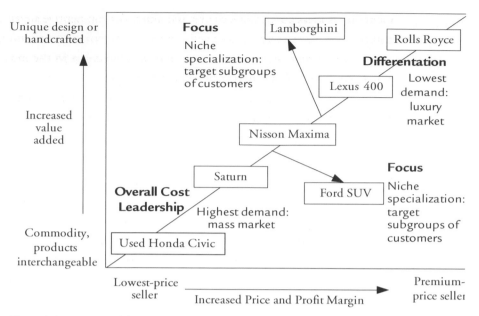

Figure 2.3 Some considerations in positioning a company or product.

As the U.S. economy grew after World War I, however, General Motors was able to pull ahead of Ford, not by producing cars as cheaply, but by producing cars that were nearly as cheap and that offered a variety of features that differentiated them. Thus, GM offered several different models in a variety of colors with a variety of optional extras. In spite of selling slightly more expensive cars, GM gradually gained market share from Ford because consumers were willing to pay more to get cars in preferred colors and styles.

Examples of niche specialists in the automobile industry are companies that manufacture only taxi cabs or limousines.

Porter's Theory of Competitive Advantage

Michael Porter's first book was *Competitive Strategy: Techniques for Analyzing Industries and Competitors*. This is the book in which he analyzed the various sources of environmental threats and opportunities and described how companies could position themselves in the marketplace. Porter's second book, *Competitive Advantage: Creating and Sustaining Superior Performance*, was published in 1985. *Competitive Advantage* extended Porter's basic ideas on strategy in several important ways. For our purposes, we will focus on his ideas about value chains, the sources of competitive advantage, and the role that business processes play in establishing and maintaining competitive advantage.

We've already encountered the idea of a value chain in the introduction. Figure 1.2 illustrates Porter's generic value chain diagram.

Porter introduced the idea of the value chain to emphasize that companies ought to think of processes as complete entities that begin with new product development and customer orders and end with satisfied customers. To ignore processes or to think of processes as things that occur within departmental silos is simply a formula for creating a suboptimized company. Porter suggested that company managers should conceptualize large-scale processes, which he termed *value chains*, as entities that include every activity involved in adding value to a product or service sold by the company.

We've used the terms *value proposition* and *value chain* several times now, so we should probably offer a definition. The term *value*, as it is used in any of these phrases, refers to value that a customer perceives and is willing to pay for. The idea of the value chain is that each activity in the chain or sequence adds some value to the final product. It's assumed that if you asked the customer about each of the steps, the customer would agree that the step added something to the value of the product. A value proposition describes, in general terms, a product or service that the customer is willing to pay for.

It's a little more complex, of course, because everyone agrees that there are some activities or steps that don't add value, directly, but facilitate adding value. These are often called *value-enabling* activities. Thus, acquiring the parts that will later be used to assemble a product is a value-enabling activity. The key reason to focus on value, however, is ultimately to identify activities that are *non-value-adding* activities. These are activities that have been incorporated into a process, for one reason or another, that no longer add any value to the final product. Non-value-adding activities should be eliminated. We'll discuss all this in later chapters when we focus on analyzing processes.

Figure 1.2 emphasizes that lots of individual subprocesses must be combined to create a complete value chain. In effect, every process, subprocess, or activity that contributes to the cost of producing a given line of products must be combined. Once all the costs are combined and subtracted from the gross income from the sale of the products, one derives the profit margin associated with the product line. Porter discriminates between primary processes or activities, and includes inbound logistics, operations, outbound logistics, marketing and sales, and service. He also includes support processes or activities, including procurement, technology development, human resource management, and firm infrastructure, which includes finance and senior management activities. Porter's use of the term *value chain* is similar to Hammer's use of *core process*. Many companies use the term *process* to refer to much more specific sets of activities. For example, one might refer to the Marketing and Sales Process, the Order Fulfillment Process, or even the Customer Relationship Management Process. In this book, when we want to speak of comprehensive, large-scale processes, we'll use the term *value chain*. In general, when we use the term *process*, we will be referring to some more specific set of activities.

Although it doesn't stand out in Figure 1.2, if we represented each of the functions shown in the figure as boxes and connected them with arrows, we could see how a series of functions results in a product or service delivered to a customer. If we had such a representation, we could also ask which functions added value to the process as it passed through that box. The term *value chain* was originally chosen to suggest that the chain was made up of a series of activities that added value to products the company sold. Some activities would take raw materials and turn them into an assembled mechanism that sold for considerably more than the raw materials cost. That additional value would indicate the value added by the manufacturing process. Later, when we consider activity costing in more detail, we will see how we can analyze value chains to determine which processes add value and which don't. One goal of many process redesign efforts is to eliminate or minimize the number of non-value-adding activities in a given process.

Having defined a value chain, Porter went on to define *competitive advantage* and show how value chains were the key to maintaining competitive advantage. Porter offered these two key definitions:

A *strategy* depends on defining a company position that the company can use to maintain a competitive advantage. A *position* simply describes the goals of the company and how it explains those goals to its customers.

A *competitive advantage* occurs when your company can make more profits selling its product or service than its competitors can. Rational managers seek to establish a long-term competitive advantage. This provides the best possible return, over an extended period, for the effort involved in creating a process and bringing a product or service to market. A company with a competitive advantage is not necessarily the largest company in its industry, but it makes its customers happy by selling a desirable product, and it makes its shareholders happy by producing excellent profits.

Thus, a company anywhere in Figure 2.3 could enjoy a competitive advantage.

Porter cites the example of a small bank that tailors its services to the very wealthy and offers extraordinary service. It will fly its representatives, for example, to a client's yacht anywhere in the world for a consultation. Compared with larger banks, this bank doesn't have huge assets, but it achieves the highest profit margins in the banking industry and is likely to continue to do so for many years. Its ability to satisfy its niche customers gives it a competitive advantage.

Two fundamental variables determine a company's profitability or the margin it can obtain from a given value chain. The first is the industry structure. That imposes broad constraints on what a company can offer and charge. The second is a competitive advantage that results from a strategy and a well-implemented value chain that lets a company outperform the average competitor in an industry over a sustained period of time.

A competitive advantage can be based on charging a premium because your product is more valuable, or it can result from selling your product or service for less than your competitors because your value chain is more efficient. The first approach relies on developing a good *strategic position*. The second advantage results from *operational effectiveness*.

As we use the terms, a *strategy*, the *positioning* of a company, and *a strategic position* are synonyms. They all refer to how a company plans to function and present itself in a market.

In the 1990s, many companies abandoned strategic positioning and focused almost entirely on operational effectiveness. Many companies speak of focusing on *best practices*. The assumption seems to be that a company can be successful if all of its practices are as good as, or better than, its competitors. The movement toward best practices has led to outsourcing and the use of comparison studies to determine the best practices for any given business process. Ultimately, Porter argues operational effectiveness can't be sustained. In effect, it puts all the companies within each particular industry on a treadmill. Companies end up practicing what Porter terms "hypercompetition," running faster and faster to improve their operations. Companies that have pursued this path have not only exhausted themselves, but they have watched their profit margins gradually shrink. When companies locked in hypercompetition have exhausted all other remedies, they usually end up buying up their competitors to obtain some relief. That temporarily reduces the pressure to constantly improve operational efficiency, but it usually doesn't help improve the profit margins.

The alternative is to define a strategy or position that your company can occupy where it can produce a superior product for a given set of customers. The product may be superior for a wide number of reasons. It may satisfy the very specific needs of customers ignored by other companies, it may provide features that other companies don't provide, or it may be sold at a price other companies don't choose to match. It may provide customers in a specific geographical area with products that are tailored to that area.

Porter argues that, ultimately, competitive advantage is sustained by the processes and activities of the company. Companies engaged in hypercompetition seek to perform each activity better than their competitors. Companies competing on the basis of strategic positioning achieve their advantage by performing different activities or organizing their activities in a different manner.

Put a different way, hypercompetitive companies position themselves in the same manner as their rivals and seek to offer the same products or services for less money. To achieve that goal, they observe their rivals and seek to assure that each of their process- es and activities is as efficient as, or more efficient than, those of their rivals. Each time a rival introduces a new and more efficient activity, the company studies it and then proceeds to modify its equivalent activity to match or better the rival's innovation. In the course of this competition, since everyone introduces the same innovations, no one gains any sustainable advantage. At the same time margins keep getting reduced. This critique is especially telling when one considers the use of ERP applications, and we will consider this in detail later.

Companies relying on strategic positioning focus on defining a unique strategy. They may decide to focus only on wealthy customers and provide lots of service, or on customers that buy over the Internet. They may decide to offer the most robust product, or the least expensive product, with no frills. Once the company decides on its competitive position, it translates that position into a set of goals and then lets those goals dictate the organization of its processes.

Porter remarks that a good position can often be defined by what the company decides not to do. It is only by focusing on a specific set of customers or products and services that one can establish a strong position. Once one decides to focus, manage- ment must constantly work to avoid the temptation to broaden that focus in an effort to acquire a few more customers.

If a company maintains a clear focus, however, then the company is in a position to tailor business processes and to refine how activities interact. Porter refers to the way in which processes and activities work together and reinforce one another as *fit*. He goes on to argue that a focus on fit makes it very hard for competitors to quickly match any efficiencies your company achieves. As fit is increased and processes are more and more tightly integrated, duplicating the efficiency of an activity demands that the competitor rearrange its whole process to duplicate not only the activity, but the whole process, and the relation of that process to related processes, and so on. Good fit is often a result of working to assure that the handoffs between departments or functions are as efficient as possible.

In Porter's studies, companies that create and sustain competitive advantage do it because they have the discipline to choose a strategic position and then remain focused on it. More important, they gradually refine their business processes and the fit of their activities so that their efficiencies are very hard for competitors to duplicate. It is process integration or fit that provides the basis for long-term competitive advantage and that provides better margins without the need for knee-jerk efforts to copy the best practices of rivals.

Porter's Strategic Themes

After writing *Competitive Advantage* in 1985, Porter shifted his focus to international competition. Then, in 1996 he returned to strategy concerns and wrote an article for the *Harvard Business Review* entitled "What is Strategy?" which is still worth close study today. In addition to laying out his basic arguments against a simple-minded operational efficiency and in favor of strategic positioning and the importance of integrated processes, Porter threw in the idea that strategists ought to create maps of activity systems to "show how a company's strategic position is contained in a set of tailored activities designed to deliver it."

Porter suggested that strategists create network diagrams that show how a limited set of high-level strategic themes, and the activities associated with those themes, fit together to support a strategic position.

Porter provided several examples and we've chosen one to illustrate this idea. In the early 1990s, the executives at Southwest Airlines decided on a strategy that emphasized their being the dependable, low-cost airline. Figure 2.4 illustrates the Activity-System map Porter provided for Southwest Airlines. The themes are in the rectangles and a set of activities are shown in circles. To charge low prices, Southwest limited service. They only operated from secondary airports and didn't assign seats or check baggage through to subsequent flights. They didn't serve meals and attendants cleaned the planes between flights. By limiting service they were able to avoid activities that

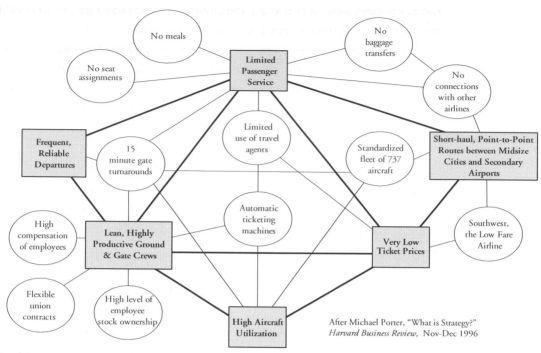

Figure 2.4 A Strategic Activity-System Map for Southwest airlines.

took time at check-in and were able to achieve faster turn around and more frequent departures. Thus, Southwest averaged more flights, with the same aircraft, between set locations, than their rivals. By standardizing on a single aircraft they were also able to minimize maintenance costs and reduce training costs for maintenance crews.

Porter argued that too many companies talked strategy, but didn't follow through on the implications of their strategy. They didn't make the hard choices required to actually implement a specific strategy and, hence, they didn't create the highly integrated business processes that were very hard for rivals to duplicate. When companies do make the hard choices, as Southwest did, they find that the themes reinforce one another and the activities fit together to optimize the strategic position.

We've read lots of discussions of how business processes ought to support corporate strategies, and we certainly agree. Those who manage processes have an obligation to work to assure that their process outcomes achieve corporate goals. Companies should work hard to align their process measures with corporate performance measures and to eliminate subprocesses that are counter to corporate goals. Different theorists have proposed different ways of aligning process activities and outcomes to goals.

Most, however, assume that when executives announce goals that process people will simply create processes that will implement those goals.

Porter suggests something subtler. He suggests that smart senior executives think in terms of processes. In effect, one strategic goal of the organization should be to create value chains and processes that are unique and that fit together to give the organization a clear competitive advantage that is difficult for rivals to duplicate. He doesn't suggest that senior executives should get into the design or redesign of specific business processes, but he does suggest that they think of the themes that will be required to implement their strategies, which are ultimately defined by products and customers, and think about the hard choices that will need to be made to assure that the themes and key processes will fit together and be mutually reinforcing.

This isn't an approach that many companies have taken. However, a process manager can use this concept to, in effect, "reverse engineer" a company's strategy. What are your value chains? What products do your value chains deliver to what customers? What is your positioning? What value propositions does your organization present to your customers when you advertise your products? Now, develop an ideal Activity-System Map to define your company's strategic positioning. Then compare it with your actual themes and activities. Do your major themes reinforce each other, or do they conflict? Think of a set of well-known activities that characterize one of your major processes. Do they support the themes that support your company's strategic positioning?

This exercise has led more than one process manager to an "Ah Ha! Moment" and provided insight into why certain activities always seem to be in conflict with each other.

As Porter argues, creating a strategy is hard work. It requires thought and then it requires the discipline to follow through with the implications of a given strategic position. If it is done correctly, however, it creates business processes that are unique and well integrated and that lead to successes that are difficult for rivals to duplicate.

The alternative is for everyone to try to use the same best practices, keep copying each other's innovations, and keep lowering profit margins till everyone faces bankruptcy. Given the alternative, senior management really ought to think about how strategy and process can work together to generate competitive advantage.

Treacy and Wiersema's Positioning Strategies

Two other strategy theorists, Michael Treacy and Fred Wiersema, generated a lot of discussion in the mid-1990s with their book, *The Discipline of Market Leaders*, which extended Porter's ideas on generic strategies by focusing on customers and company cultures. Treacy and Wiersema suggest that there are three generic types of customers: 1) those whose primary value is high-performance products or services, 2) those whose primary value is personalized service, and 3) those who most value the lowest-priced product. It's easy to see how these might be mapped to Porter's generic strategies, but they capture subtle differences. Like Porter, Treacy and Wiersema argue in favor of strategic differentiation and assert that "no company can succeed today by trying to be all things to all people. It must instead find the unique value that it alone can deliver to a chosen market." The authors argue that companies can study their customers to determine what value proposition is most important to them. If they find that their customers are a mix of the three types, the company needs to have the discipline to decide which group they most want to serve and focus their efforts accordingly. According to Treacy and Wiersema, the three value positions that companies must choose between are:

▶ *Product Leadership.* These companies focus on innovation and performance leadership. They strive to turn new technologies into breakthrough products and focus on product lifecycle management.
▶ *Customer Intimacy.* These companies focus on specialized, personal service. They strive to become partners with their customers. They focus on customer relationship management.
▶ *Operational Excellence.* These companies focus on having efficient operations in order to deliver the lowest-priced product or service to their customers. They focus on their supply chain and distribution systems in order to reduce the costs of their products or services.

Just as one can conceive of three types of customers, one can also imagine three types of company cultures. A company culture dominated by technologists is likely to focus on innovation and on product leadership. A company culture dominated by marketing or sales people is more likely to focus on customer intimacy. A company culture dominated by financial people or by engineers is likely to focus on cutting costs and operational excellence.

Using this approach, we can represent a market as a triangle, with the three value positions as three poles. Then we can draw circles to suggest the emphasis at any given organization. It is common to begin a discussion with executives and hear that they believe that their organization emphasizes all three of these positions equally. Invariably, however, as the discussion continues and you consider what performance measures the executives favor and review why decisions were taken, one of these positions emerges as the firm's dominant orientation. In Figure 2.5, we show the basic triangle and then overlay a circle to suggest how we would represent a company that was primarily focused on customer-intimacy and secondarily focused on product leadership.

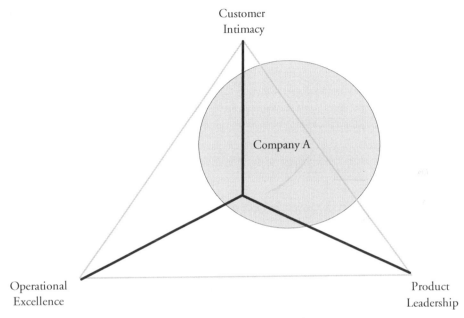

Figure 2.5 Treacy and Wiersema's three positioning strategies.

Obviously, an MBA student learns a lot more about strategy. For our purposes, however, this brief overview should be sufficient. In essence, business managers are taught to evaluate a number of factors and arrive at a strategy that will be compatible with the company's strengths and weaknesses and that will result in a reasonable profit. Historically, companies have developed a strategy and, once they succeeded, continued to rely on that strategy, with only minor refinements, for several years.[1]

The Balanced Scorecard Approach to Strategy

Robert S. Kaplan and David P. Norton are consultants who are closely related to the Harvard approach to strategy. Their influence began when they wrote an article titled "The Balanced Scorecard—Measures That Drive Performance," which appeared in the Jan/Feb 1992 issue of the *Harvard Business Review* (HBR). Since then, Kaplan and Norton have produced several other articles, a series of books, and a consulting company, all committed to elaborating the themes laid down in the initial "Balanced Scorecard" article.

Kaplan and Norton published *Strategy Maps*, their third book, in 2004. In the introduction they explained that their journey began in 1990 when they undertook a research project to explore ways that organizations measured performance. At the time, they believed that knowledge-based assets—primarily employees and IT—were becoming increasingly important for companies' competitive success, but that, in spite of that, most companies were still focused on measuring short-term financial performance. They also believed that "financial reporting systems provided no foundation for measuring and managing the value created by enhancing the capabilities of an organization's intangible assets." They argued that organizations tended to get what they measured. The result of this research effort was the Balanced Scorecard approach.

In essence, the Balanced Scorecard approach insists that management track four different types of measures: *financial* measures, *customer* measures, *internal business* (process) measures, and *innovation and learning* measures. Using the Balanced Scorecard approach, an organization identifies corporate objectives within each of the four categories, and then aligns the management hierarchy by assigning each manager his or her own scorecard with more specific objectives in each of the four categories. Properly used, the system focuses every manager on a balanced set of performance measures.

As soon as they published their now classic *Harvard Business Review* article on the Balanced Scorecard methodology, they found that: "while executives appreciated a more comprehensive new performance measurement system, they wanted to use their new system in a more powerful application than we had originally envisioned. The executives wanted to apply the system to solve the more important problem they faced—how to implement new strategies."

In a series of articles and books, Kaplan and Norton have gradually refined a methodology that seeks to align a balanced set of measures to an organization's strategy. They use a top-down method that emphasizes starting with the executive team and defining the organization's strategic goals, and then passing those goals downward, using the balanced scorecard. They argue that success results from a Strategy-Focused Organization, which, in turn, results from Strategy Maps and Balanced Scorecards.

Figure 2.7 provides an overview of a Strategy Map. Kaplan and Norton claim that this generic map reflects a generalization of their work with a large number of companies for whom they have developed specific Strategy Maps. Notice that the four sets of Balanced Scorecard measures are now arranged in a hierarchical fashion, with financial measures at the top, driven by customer measures, which are in turn the result of internal (process) measures, which in turn are supported by innovation and learning measures.

Their approach to strategy is explained in their Sept–Oct 2000 *HBR* article, "Having Trouble with Your Strategy? Then Map It." The main thing the new book adds is hundreds of pages of examples, drawn from a wide variety of different organizations. For those that need examples, this book is valuable, but for those who want theory, the HBR article is a lot faster read.

Given our focus on process, we looked rather carefully at the *themes*, which are, in essence, described as the internal perspective on the Strategy Map. Kaplan and Norton identify four themes, which they go on to describe as "value-creating processes." Scanning across on the Strategy Map in Figure 2.6, the themes are *operations manage-*

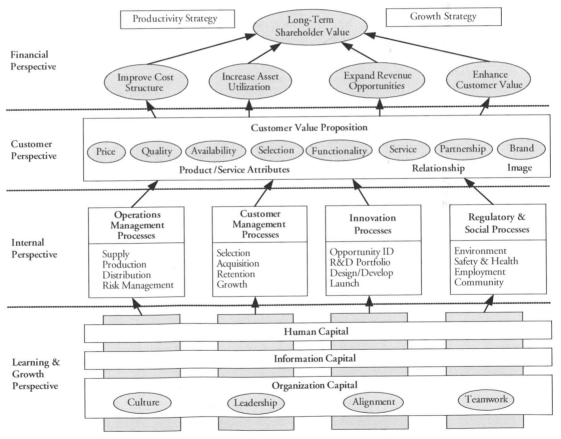

Figure 2.6 The Balanced Scorecard approach to strategy. (After Kaplan and Norton.)

ment processes (supply chain management), *customer management processes* (customer relationship management), *innovation processes* (the design and development of new products and services), and *regulatory and social processes*. The latter is obviously a support process and doesn't go with the other three, but would be better placed in their bottom area where they treat other support processes like HR and IT. Obviously, identifying these large-scale business processes is very much in the spirit of the times. Software vendors have organized around SCM and CRM, and the Supply Chain Council is seeking to extend the SCOR model by adding a Design Chain model and a Customer Chain model.

The problem with any of these efforts is that, if they aren't careful, they get lost in business processes, and lose the value chain that these business processes enable. Going further, what is missing in *Strategy Maps* is any sense of a value chain. One Strategy Map actually places an arrow behind the four themes or sets of processes in the internal perspective, to suggest they somehow fit together to generate a product or service, but the idea isn't developed. One could read *Strategy Maps* and come away with the idea that every company had a single strategy. No one seems to consider organizations with four different business units producing four different product lines. Perhaps we are to assume that Strategy Maps are only developed for lines of business and that everything shown in the internal perspective always refers to a single value chain. If that's the case, it is not made explicit in *Strategy Maps*.

The fact that process is on one level and the customer is on another is a further source of confusion. When one thinks of a value chain, there is a close relationship between the value chain, the product or service produced and the customer. To isolate these into different levels may be convenient for those oriented to functional or departmental organizations, but it is a major source of confusion for those who are focused on processes.

Overall, the strategic perspective that Kaplan and Norton have developed is a step forward. Before Kaplan and Norton, most academic strategy courses were dominated by the thinking of Michael Porter, who began by emphasizing the "Five Forces Model" that suggested what external, environmental factors would change an organization's competitive situation, and then focused on improving the value chain. By contrast, Kaplan and Norton have put a lot more emphasis on measures and alignment, which has certainly led to a more comprehensive approach to strategy. But their approach stops short of defining a truly process-oriented perspective.

We have described the 1990s as primarily concerned with horizontal alignment. Companies tried to eliminate operational and managerial problems that arose from silo thinking and see how a value chain linked all activities, from the supplier to the customer. Today, most companies seem to have moved on to vertical alignment and are trying to structure the way strategies align with measures and how processes align to the resources that implement them. In the shift, we believe that something very valuable from the horizontal perspective has been lost. Kaplan and Norton put too much emphasis on vertical alignment and risk losing the insights that derive from focusing on value chains and horizontal alignment.

We're sure that this is not the intent of Kaplan and Norton, and that they would argue that their process layer was designed to assure that horizontal alignment was maintained. To us, however, the fact that they don't mention value chains, and define their internal perspective themes in such an unsophisticated way, from the perspective of someone who is used to working on business process architectures, indicates that they have, in fact, failed to incorporate a sophisticated understanding of process in their methodology. We suspect that the problem is that they start at the top and ask senior executives to identify strategic objectives and then define measures associated with them. In our opinion, this isn't something that can be done in isolation. Value chains have their own logic, and the very act of defining a major process generates measures that must be incorporated into any measurement system.

Most large U.S. companies have embraced the Balanced Scorecard system, and have implemented one or another version of the methodology. Fewer, we suspect, have embraced Strategy Maps, but the number will probably grow, since the Maps are associated with the Scorecard system which is so popular. We think, overall, that this is a good thing. Most organizations need better tools to use in aligning strategies and managerial measures, and the Balanced Scorecard methodology forces people to think more clearly about the process and has, in many cases, resulted in much better managerial measurement systems.

For those engaged in developing business strategies, or developing corporate performance systems, the Kaplan and Norton *HBR* article is critical reading.[1] Those who want to create process-centric organizations, however, will need to extend the Kaplan and Norton approach.

Summary

We urge readers to study Porter's *Competitive Advantage*. In helping companies improve their business processes, we have often encountered clients who worried about revising entire processes and suggested instead that standard ERP modules be employed. Some clients worried that we were advocating hypercompetition and urging them to begin revisions that their competitors would match, which would then require still another response on their part. It seemed to them it would be easier just to acquire standard modules that were already "best of breed" solutions. Undoubtedly this resulted from our failure to explain our position with sufficient clarity.

We do not advocate making processes efficient for their own sake, nor do we advocate that companies adopt a strategy based strictly on competitive efficiency. Instead, we advocate that companies take strategy seriously and define a unique position that they can occupy and in which they can prosper. We urge companies to analyze and design tightly integrated processes. Creating processes with superior fit is the goal. We try to help managers avoid arbitrarily maximizing the efficiency of specific activities at the expense of the process as a whole.

We certainly believe that companies should constantly scan for threats and opportunities. Moreover, we recommend that companies constantly adjust their strategies when they see opportunities or threats to their existing position. It's important, however, that the position be well defined, and that adjustments be made in order to improve a well-defined position and not simply for their own sake. In the past few years we've watched dozens of companies adopt Internet technologies without a clear idea of how those technologies were going to enhance their corporate position. In effect, these companies threw themselves into an orgy of competitive efficiency, without a clear idea of how it would improve their profitability. We are usually strong advocates of the use of new technology, and especially new software technologies. Over the last few decades IT has been the major source of new products and services, a source of significant increases in productivity, and the most useful approach to improving process fit. We only advocate the adoption of new technology, however, when it contributes to an improvement in a clearly understood corporate position.

We also recommend that companies organize so that any changes in their strategic position or goals can be rapidly driven down through the levels of the organization and result in changes in business processes and activities. Changes in goals without follow-through are worthless. At the same time, as companies get better and better at rapidly driving changes down into processes, subprocesses, and activities, it's important to minimize the disruptive effect of this activity. It's important to focus on the changes that really need to be made and to avoid undertaking process redesign, automation, or improvement projects just to generate changes in the name of efficiency or a new technology that is unrelated to high-priority corporate goals.

To sum up: We don't recommend that companies constantly change their strategic position to match a competitor's latest initiatives. We don't advocate creating a system that will simply increase hypercompetition. Instead, we believe that companies should seek positions that can lead to a long-term competitive advantage and that that can only be accomplished as the result of a carefully conceived and focused corporate strategy. We argue for a system that can constantly tune and refine the fit of processes that are designed and integrated to achieve a well-defined, unique corporate position.

There will always be processes and activities that will be very similar from one company to another within a given industry. Similarly, within a large process there will always be subprocesses or activities that are similar from one company to another. In such cases we support a best practices approach, using ERP modules or by outsourcing. Outsourcing, done with care, can help focus company managers on those core processes that your company actually relies upon and eliminate the distraction of processes that add no value to your core business processes.

At the same time, we are living in a time of rapid technological change. Companies that want to avoid obsolescence need to constantly evaluate new technologies to determine if they can be used to improve their product or service offerings. Thus, we accept that even well-focused companies that avoid hypercompetition will still find themselves faced with a steady need for adjustments in strategy and goals and for process improvement.

Ultimately, however, in this book we want to help managers think about how they can create unique core processes, change them in a systematic manner, and integrate them so that they can serve as the foundation for long-term competitive advantage.

Notes and References

[1] Some strategists have recently argued that Value Chains are too rigid to model the changes that some companies must accommodate. They suggest an alternative that is sometimes termed *Value Nets*. IBM represents this approach with Business Component Models (BCM). This approach treats business processes as independent

entities that can be combined in different ways to solve evolving challenges. Thus, the Value Nets approach abandon's the idea of strategic integration, as Porter defines it, to achieve greater flexibility. The Value Nets and BCM models we have seen simply represent business processes, and don't show how those processes are combined to generate products for customers. We suspect that this new approach will prove useful, but only if it can be combined with the Value Chain approach so that companies can see how they combine their business processes (or components) to achieve specific outcomes. Otherwise, the Value Nets approach will tend to sub-optimize potential value chain integration and tend to reduce things to a set of best practices, with all the accompanying problems that Porter describes when he discusses Operational Effectiveness.

The best book that describes the Value Nets approach is David Bovet and Joseph Martha's *Value Nets* (John Wiley, 2000). The best paper on IBM's variation on this approach is *Component Business Models: Making Specialization Real* by George Pohle, Peter Korsten, and Shanker Ramamurthy published by IBM Institute for Business Value (IBM Business Consulting Services). The paper is available on the IBM Developer Web site.

Porter, Michael E., *Competitive Strategy: Techniques for Analyzing Industries and Competitors*, The Free Press, 1980. The best-selling book on strategy throughout the past two decades. The must-read book for anyone interested in business strategy.

Porter, Michael E., *Competitive Advantage: Creating and Sustaining Superior Performance*, The Free Press, 1985. This book focuses on the idea of competitive advantage and discusses how companies obtain and maintain it. One of the key techniques Porter stresses is an emphasis on value chains and creating integrated business processes that are difficult for competitors to duplicate.

Porter, Michael E., "What Is Strategy?", *Harvard Business Review*. November–December 1996. Reprint no. 96608. This is a great summary of Porter's *Competitive Advantage*. It's available from *www.amazon.com*.

Porter, Michael E., "Strategy and the Internet," *Harvard Business Review*, March 2001. Reprint no. R0103D. In this HBR article, Porter applies his ideas on strategy and value chains to Internet companies with telling effect. An article everyone interested in e-business should study.

Treacy, Michael and Fred Wiersema, *The Discipline of Market Leaders: Choose Your Customers, Narrow Your Focus, and Dominate Your Market,* Addison-Wesley, 1995. This book was extremely popular in the late 1990s and is still worthwhile. It provides some key insights into company cultures and how they affect positioning and the customers you should target.

Kaplan, Robert S. and David P. Norton, "Having Trouble with Your Strategy? Then Map It," *Harvard Business Review,*. Sept–Oct 2000. This article is available from *www.amazon.com.*

Kaplan, Robert S. and David P. Norton, *Strategy Maps: Converting Intangible Assets into Tangible Outcomes,* Harvard Business School Press, 2004. The Kaplan-Norton model often confuses the relationship between process and measures, but it also provides lots of good insights. Read it for insights, but don't take their specific approach too seriously, or your process focus will tend to get lost. Kaplan and Norton's previous book on the Balanced Scorecard approach to strategy was *The Strategy Focused Organization,* which was published by the Harvard Business School press in 2001, and it's also worth a read.

3

Understanding the Enterprise

I N T H I S C H A P T E R we will develop an overview of the various types of business process concerns companies deal with at the enterprise level. Companies approach enterprise
level activities in many different ways. Some, for example, use the Balanced Scorecard
approach to help with the alignment of corporate goals and the evaluation of managers, but do not tie that program to business processes in any rigorous way. Others have
a business process architecture, but do not tie their architectural models to their ongoing business performance evaluations. For historical reasons, companies have begun
the enterprise level journey from many different starting points.

The BPTrends Enterprise Methodology

To organize our discussion of enterprise level concerns, we will begin by considering
the enterprise methodology taught by BPTrends. This isn't the only possible approach,
but it is one possible approach, and it provides a good starting point for our discussion of how we might systematically address concerns at the enterprise level. Figure
3.1 provides an overview of the BPTrends Process Change Methodology. In this figure
we actually picture two complementary methodologies: one for enterprise change and
one for business process change projects. The BPTrends enterprise methodology, at
the top of the figure, defines the activities companies go through to create and use
enterprise level process tools. The BPTrends process redesign methodology, at the bottom of the figure, defines the steps that a process team would go through to redesign
or improve a specific business process. The enterprise methodology is concerned with

creating the tools that a company can use to organize and manage all its process work. This methodology does not so much define a project as an ongoing effort on the part of management to create and maintain the tools they need to function as a process-centric organization. The process level methodology is similar to many other methodologies designed to facilitate process change projects and is used over and over again. The two methodologies are connected, in practice, because it is the tools created by the enterprise methodology that enable an organization to define, prioritize, and manage, at the enterprise level, all of their ongoing business process change efforts. In Part I of this book we will focus on the concerns defined by the enterprise methodology. In Part II of this book we will consider specific business process change methodologies.

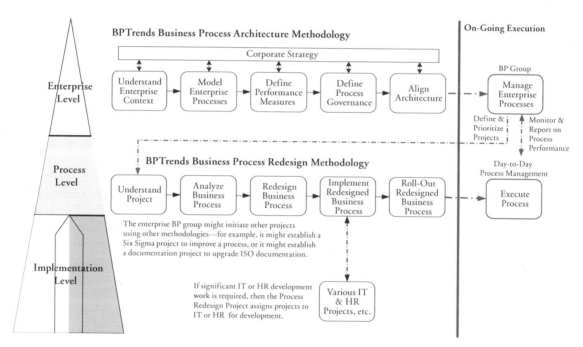

Figure 3.1 The BPTrends Process Change Methodology.

We show corporate strategy in a box above the three boxes in the enterprise model that describe the major phases involved in developing enterprise process management tools. This is to suggest that enterprise process work is constantly interacting with the strategies of the organization.

Understanding the Enterprise. The first phase in the BPTrends enterprise methodology focuses on understanding the enterprise as a whole. This phase often involves the executive committee and the senior executives of the company. It is absolutely critical that everyone understands and agrees on the basic value-chain processes the company supports and the strategic goals each value chain is responsible for achieving.

This phase begins with the creation of a series of organization diagrams that define the business and its key relationships and gradually refine everyone's understanding of the organization and its stakeholders, including stockholders, customers, suppliers, distributors, and various governmental entities. In the course of this phase, the value chains of the organization are defined. The goals of each value chain and the relationship between core processes and managerial and support processes are also specified. Thus, a specific business process architecture is developed for each individual value chain. As a result of this phase, everyone agrees on the basic value chains and the organization is in a position to proceed to define architectures for each value chain.

Defining a Business Process Architecture. Phase II begins with the selection of a specific value chain and the commitment to create a business process architecture for that value chain. At a minimum, each value chain is defined by elucidating the core business processes and subprocesses in the value chain. Then, using the business processes defined in the architecture, the team proceeds to define how each process will be monitored and measured. Depending on the needs of the organization, resources can then be aligned to the processes in the process architecture. Some companies will want to align policies and business rules with their processes. Some will want to align IT resources, like software applications and databases. Others will want to align human resources, including jobs, skill requirements, training programs, and knowledge management programs.

There are different approaches to the creation of a business process architecture. Historically, the most popular way to define a company's processes has been to put a group of managers in a room and discuss how things get done. Usually, following a lot of discussion, the group arrives at a high-level overview of the company's major processes. Today that activity, and the associated activity of defining process measures, can be considerably accelerated by using a business process framework. The BPTrends enterprise methodology usually relies on using the extended version of a business process framework to help managers develop a basic business process architecture and measurement system with a minimum fuss.

Refine Process Governance. Once the business process architecture is in place and measures are defined for each of the major processes, the team should move on to the development of a plan to manage their organization's business processes. Different organizations take various approaches. Some rely primarily on a functional (departmental) organization. A few rely on a process-oriented management organization. Most end up with some kind of matrix that includes both functional and process managers. We will consider the options in Chapter 5. At the same time the enterprise process team will want to consider how to measure and monitor the performance of process managers. Many companies rely on a Balanced Scorecard-oriented approach, either using a portion of each manager's scorecard to track his or her performance as a process manager, or creating a dual scorecard system with one set of scorecards monitoring process work and another monitoring functional responsibilities.

During this same phase the team will probably also create a BPM Group (or BPM Center of Excellence) to provide the staff to help senior executives monitor processes, maintain the architecture tools, and to undertake ongoing responsibilities such as prioritizing project change projects.

Keep in mind that these phases will need to be adjusted to the individual organization. One organization, for example, might already have an existing BPM Center of Excellence. In this case, it would probably be the BPM Center of Excellence that creates the architecture. In other cases an ad hoc group will be established to create the architecture and then to create the BPM group to maintain it. When attempting to change the way things are organized at the enterprise level, one always starts with what is already in place and moves forward from there.

The Day-to-Day Management of Enterprise Processes. The BPTrends enterprise methodology focuses on helping an organization develop the basic tools needed to create and manage a process-centric organization. Once the basic tools are in place and a BPM Group is established, the on-going maintenance and use of the tools becomes a matter of execution. We will discuss what the day-to-day governance of a process-centric organization entails and provide a case study to show how a process-centric organization functions.

Strategy and Enterprise BPM

Everything should begin with a corporate strategy. In most cases the corporate strategy has already been developed by an executive committee, or a group whose major responsibility is the creation and review of strategy. Thus, in most cases, the business process team that is charged with developing enterprise level process tools for the company will simply establish a working relationship with the strategy group. In fact, in most large companies, strategy work occurs on many levels. There is an enterprise strategy, strategies for specific value chains, and, in many cases, strategies for major business processes. It is not uncommon to speak of a supply chain strategy or a marketing strategy. Thus, even if a corporate group creates the company strategy, the business process group may be heavily involved in assuring that the corporate strategy is reflected in the specific strategies of the individual business processes.

Figure 3.2 illustrates one way of thinking about the relationship between the work of a process group and a strategy group. The ongoing work of the strategy group is described in the upper box. They may spend a good bit of their time considering what the competition is doing or how customer tastes are changing, but, ultimately, to determine if the current strategy is working, they need some kind of performance measures. Specifically, they need to know which activities are generating what type of results. If there were no process group, the strategy group would need to generate some kind of map of the organization and figure out how to associate metrics and performance outcomes with the entities on their map. Put a different way, the strategy group needs some tools and they need a constant flow of data.

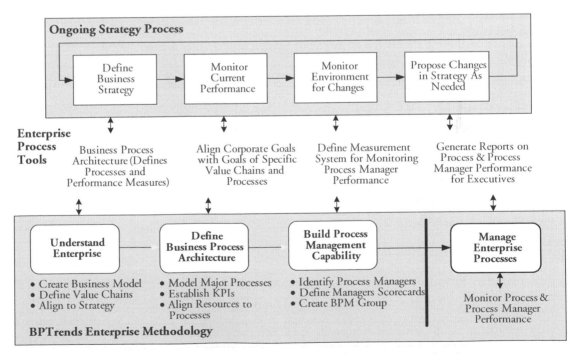

Figure 3.2 Enterprise process managers and those in strategy need a common set of tools.

Managers and the BPM Group need information about how the organization is divided into value chains, processes and subprocesses, how specific processes are measured and managed, and they also need to keep track of changes in performance. In essence, an enterprise process methodology is just a systematic plan for generating the tools that managers, the strategy group, and the BPM group need to do their work. The creation of a BPM Group is simply an efficient way of assuring that the needed tools are maintained and the needed data is gathered and distributed to those who need it in a timely manner.

In the past most organizations have undertaken strategy efforts without the availability of good process tools. Since the 1980s, relying on Michael Porter's work on value chains, there has been a significant shift. Strategy no longer depends on data drawn primarily from functional units. Today, strategy depends on processes, how processes interact with each other, how process performance is measured, and a deep understanding of how processes interface with customers. Thus, with or without a formal enterprise process enterprise, organizations are engaged in defining enterprise level tools that will provide the structure and the data needed to make important day-to-day decisions and to support key initiatives like the entry into new markets, mergers, acquisitions, or outsourcing. As we have already suggested, a business process enterprise methodology simply provides a systematic way to achieve that goal.

Understand the Enterprise

The BPTrends enterprise methodology begins with a phase that focuses on understanding the enterprise. During that phase we develop a generic diagram of the enterprise, define value chains and identify stakeholders. This chapter focuses on understanding enterprises.

The Traditional View of an Organization's Structure

In *Improving Performance*, Rummler and Brache provided a nice example of the distinction between the thinking of those who rely on organization charts and those who focus on processes. When asked to describe their organizations, most managers will draw something like the traditional organization chart shown in Figure 3.3. In some cases they will simply give the various groups or departments names: marketing, production, and so forth. In other cases, they will detail who manages each department and to whom they report. This kind of information is often useful, of course. But it's important to notice what kinds of information a traditional organization chart doesn't provide.

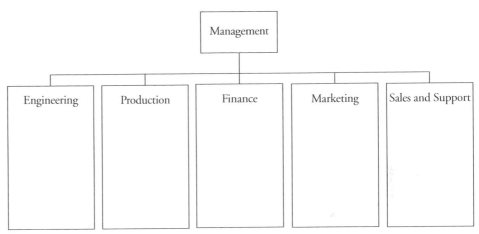

Figure 3.3 A traditional organization chart.

First, an organization chart doesn't show the customers. Equally important, it doesn't show the products and services the company provides to customers, or where the resources needed to create the products and services come from in the first place. It certainly doesn't show how work flows from one activity to another before ultimately being delivered to a customer.

A manager might reply that an organization chart isn't expected to show such things, and we'd agree. Then we'd ask our manager to show us whatever charts he or she uses that do show those things. Most managers aren't prepared to create or show diagrams that provide a systems or process-oriented view of their organizations.

Traditional organizational charts are often described as a vertical view of the organization. The departments or functional groups within a department are referred to as "silos," similar to the tall, windowless grain silos one sees in farming regions. When managers conceptualize their organizations as vertical organizations, they tend to manage in a vertical manner. They focus on who reports to whom, and set goals for each group independent of the others. At the same time, *silo thinking* leads managers to focus on making their departments as efficient as possible, without much regard to what's going on in other silos. When cross-departmental issues arise, they tend to get bounced up the reporting chain till they reach a manager who is responsible for the work done in both departments. That, in turn, guarantees that senior managers spend a lot of time resolving cross-functional or interdepartmental problems that could have been better resolved at a lower level by people with a much better grasp of the specific problem. And, of course, the time that senior managers use for resolving these cross-functional disputes is time they don't have to focus on customer concerns, creating new strategies, or improving productivity.

This problem has been widely discussed since the late 1980s. Many books have been written about the problem. Silo thinking tends to lead to departmental or functional sub-optimization. This often occurs at the expense of the whole organization. An obvious example would be a sales department that gets praised for selling products that production can't deliver in time to meet the delivery dates promised by the salespeople. Or it could be an engineering department that creates a product that is very efficient to manufacture, but doesn't quite have the feature set that marketing has promised or that salespeople can most readily sell. In essence, sub-optimization occurs when one process within one silo is improved at the expense of other processes in other silos, or at the expense of the value chain as a whole.

Managers, like all people, tend to think in terms of their models. Physicians have a saying that, during diagnosis, physicians only find what they are looking for. Managers are the same. To think of organizations as wholes, managers need to learn to visualize their organizations with diagrams that provide insight into how their organizations actually work, as a whole. They need to think in terms of organizational systems and value chains rather than thinking primarily in terms of divisions, departments, or their own functional unit.

The Systems View of an Organization

One alternative to conceptualizing an organization in terms of its departments and reporting relationships is to imagine an organization as a system that responds to inputs and generates outputs. This view is often referred to as a *horizontal* or *systems view* of the organization. Figure 3.4 illustrates a horizontal view of an organization. In this case we provide a very high-level systems view of a hypothetical restaurant, called San Francisco Seafood (SF Seafood).

The organization illustrated in Figure 3.4 is at such a high level of abstraction that it could be any organization. Much that could have been added has been omitted to simplify this diagram. The important thing to note is that this view provides us

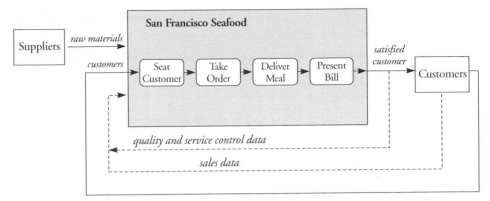

Figure 3.4 A systems view of the SF Seafood company.

with lots of information that we don't get from an organization chart. First, it shows customers, products, and suppliers. Second, it shows how work actually occurs. And, third, it gives us an idea of how things are connected and flow from one thing to another—how raw materials flow to meals and how data about customer satisfaction flows back to the organization.

A systems view emphasizes process and connections, and ultimately adaptation. What would happen if the bar was closed for a period of time? You'd need to stop some supplies. You'd lose some customers. A systems diagram provides a snapshot of how the key elements of your organization work together to achieve its goals.

Models and Diagrams

In this book we will use two broad classes of diagrams: *organization diagrams* and *process diagrams.* In this chapter we will focus on the basic notation used for organization diagrams.[1]

---

[1] Throughout the book we will use the terms *diagram* and *model* interchangeably to refer to graphical collections of boxes and arrows that convey an image of an organization or a process. Strictly speaking, a diagram is an informal collection of boxes and arrows, while a model is something more formal. A model ought to relate things in such a way that we can test assumptions about how the relationships would function in specific instances. We will see later that some diagrams can be assigned values, and simulations can be run to determine how the process will function under certain circumstances. Thus, a simulation is both a diagram and a model that we can test. In the remainder of this chapter and the next, however, we ask our readers to ignore this distinction and allow us to use both terms interchangeably to refer to pictures of graphical elements and relationships that illustrate organizations or process.

As we have suggested, many different groups are involved in business process modeling. Predictably, different groups use different types of diagrams. Even within a relatively well-defined community, like workflow software vendors, a dozen different notations are used. Some of the notations are very different from one another, stressing very different ways to view organizations or processes. Some notations differ on such trivial matters as whether a process should be represented as a rectangle or a rectangle with rounded corners.

The key thing to think about in selecting any notation is who is going to use it. We assume that the diagrams described in this book will be used by managers. They may also be used by software developers, but software developers are not our primary audience. Hence, we have constrained the types of things we describe in diagrams to the things most managers are interested in, and omitted notation that is only used to describe software conventions. Further, although we recommend the use of software diagramming tools for some purposes, we assume that many managers will create diagrams of their organizations and processes on drawing pads, blackboards, or relatively simple diagramming tools, like Visio or PowerPoint. Hence, we have made every effort to use simple, easy-to-understand conventions.

Our goal was to arrive at a way of describing organizations and business processes that is as easy to understand as possible, while still making it possible to describe all of the basics that need to be described. In this chapter, as we describe the notation, we will not consider how it might be implemented in a software tool. Several tools, however, implement notations very similar to the one we use, and thus, in later chapters we will show how software tools can be used in process redesign to simplify the creation of organization and business process diagrams. At this point, however, we only want to provide readers with the basic notational elements necessary to draw models of their organizations and business processes. We will begin by explaining the basic elements of an organization diagram. Then we will proceed to show how this type of diagram can be used to define an organization's value chains, specific value chains, stakeholders, and high-level organizational concerns.

Organization Diagrams

Organization diagrams are an extension of systems diagrams that are modified so that they can be used to describe the basic structure of an organization, the relationship of the organization to its external environment, and the relationships among the departmental units within the organization. In some cases they may also show the basic processes used by the organization and how those processes relate to the basic departmental units.

Figure 3.5 provides a high-level picture of an organization. Rummler and Brache refer to this diagram as a supersystem diagram to emphasize that it focuses on what happens outside the organization rather than on what occurs inside. This is the kind of diagram a strategy committee might use to picture the relationships between your organization and those it depends upon.

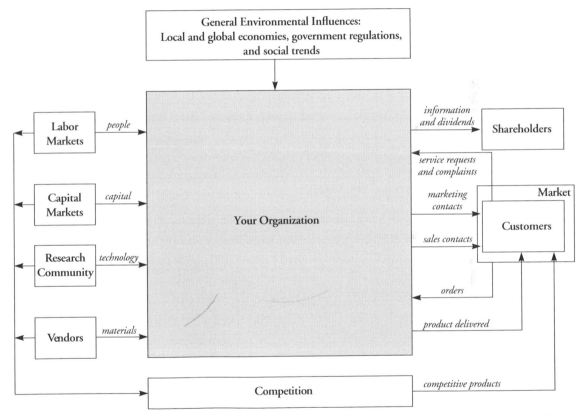

Figure 3.5 An organization diagram that emphasizes external relationships. (Modified after Rummler-Brache.)

The shaded square in the center represents the organization. In this initial version of the diagram, we don't show any internal detail, since we want to focus on the inputs and outputs of the organization.

Suppliers of all kinds, including vendors who supply materials, research organizations that supply new technology, capital markets that supply money, and labor markets that supply employees, are shown on the left of the business. In later diagrams, to simply things, we will often just have a single tall rectangle to the left of the organization box, and label it *Resources* or *Suppliers.*

Customers and shareholders are listed on the right. Customers order and receive products and services. Shareholders buy stock and receive information and dividends. In other versions of the organization diagram, we will often place a single rectangle to the right of the organization box and label it *Customers* or *Market* to further simplify the diagram.

Below the company box, we have a rectangle for competitors, companies that compete with the organization for inputs from suppliers and for customers. If the organization we are describing has one or a few major competitors, we may list them in separate boxes to help focus everyone on the nature of the competition.

Above the company box we have a rectangle that includes more generic environmental impacts on the business. These could include government regulations, changes in the economy, or changes in popular taste.

The detail one provides on this diagram depends on the purpose it is being used for. In strategy discussions, it is often important to show specific types of customers, specific suppliers, and even particular competitors. Later, when one is primarily focused on the relationships between departments and on analyzing internal processes, the external details can be removed to better focus the discussion.

We believe that the organization diagram shown in Figure 3.3 can be used to describe every possible type of organization, including monopolies and government entities. Indeed, we have used these diagrams during consulting engagements with all of these types of organizations. The names may change a little, but all organizations are systems, and they must all obtain supplies and generate products or services, just as they all have some kind of competition and operate under some type of environmental constraints.

Organizations and Value Chains

We defined an idea of a value chain in Chapter 1 (See Figure 1.4.) and referred to it again in Chapter 2. It's a powerful concept and should be used to focus attention on the fact that all the processes that go into making and selling a product line ought to be considered as parts of a whole. Unfortunately, it is easier to talk about a value chain than to define it in many specific contexts.

To begin with, there are always arguments between the "lumpers" and the "splitters." The lumpers want to combine everything that's even vaguely similar and arrive at one or a very few value chains. The splitters want to focus on the differences between different products and different groups of customers and usually end up generating a rather longer list of value chains. Consider whether General Motors supports one value chain, or several. It would be possible to argue that each line of cars represents a different value chain with a different group of customers. Or, perhaps you might argue that all cars are very similar and represent one value chain, while trucks are rather different and represent a second value chain. Most analysts would probably separate the manufacture of automobiles and trucks from GM's financial operations, and argue that one is a manufacturing value chain while the other is a financial value chain. In fact, however, GM often uses its financial group to support auto sales, offering auto loans without interest for a period of time to encourage sales. Thus, it would be possible to argue that even GM's financial group is a process within a broader autos value chain. The goal of a value chain analysis is to assure that all of the processes involved in the creation of a product line are all considered together. Each company will need to determine, for itself, exactly how broadly or narrowly they want to use the term value chain. There is no right answer. The answer usually emerges from a discussion among senior managers.

Another source of confusion derives from the growing use of outsourcing. Figure 3.6 provides one way of thinking about how Dell's laptop value chain is organized. Dell focuses on designing new laptop computers as components become available, marketing its computers and selling computers, on line, via their Web site. Once a laptop is actually ordered, Dell transmits the order to an outsourcer in China who assembles the actual computer and ships it to the customer. If the computer subsequently requires service, the customer calls an outsourcer who diagnoses the problem and schedules a pick-up. An outsourcer picks up the computer and delivers it to a warehouse run by another outsourcer that makes the needed repair and returns it to the customer.

One could argue that Dell is simply a design and marketing organization and that laptop manufacturing is not one of its core processes, but Dell is generally classified as a computer equipment manufacturer, and Dell exerts significant control over the processes it has outsourced. On the other hand, Dell does not have a laptop manufac-

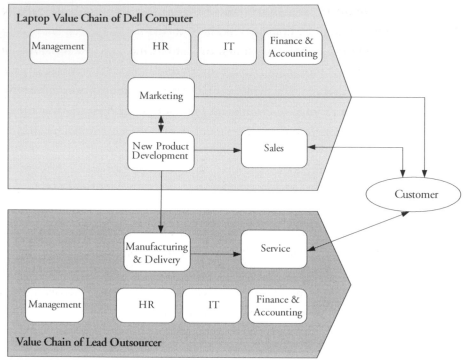

Figure 3.6 The Dell laptop value chain.

turing function or a VP of laptop manufacturing with day-to-day control of computer assembly. That role is performed by an individual working for an outsourcer. More and more companies are trying to think about how a value chain works if significant operational processes are controlled by external organizations. Put a different way, organizations are beginning to talk about value chains that extend beyond the traditional boundaries of the organization.

Another aspect of the value chain concept that many companies find difficult is the requirement that overhead, management, and support processes be combined with primary or core processes. Porter suggests that a company should be able to isolate all of the support activities that are used in a single value chain. Most companies find it easier to organize their management and support processes independent of specific sets of core processes and then use some overhead formula to assign a portion of the cost of the management and support processes to each independent value chain. Some companies outsource their HR or IT processes. In this case, one organization's support process is another organization's core process.

In the 1990s, most companies focused on improving their core processes. In recent years, a lot more attention has been focused on management and support processes, but most companies still find it easier to define their value chains only in terms of core processes and to exclude management and support processes. Some organizations use the term *value stream* as a way of emphasizing that they only focus on core processes. (Other firms use the terms *value chain* and *value stream* as synonyms, so one needs to be sure how a company is using the term before drawing any conclusions.) Throughout the rest of this book, we will use value chain and value stream as synonyms and use them to refer to either a process that includes only core processes or a process that includes both core processes and management and support processes. This accurately reflects the flexibility that we encounter as we move from one company to the next.

However the concept is defined, each company needs to determine how many value chains it has. A business process architecture describes a single value chain. It's simply too complex to try to analyze more than one value chain simultaneously. Thus, one begins by defining the value chains in a company and then, thereafter, one always focuses on one specific value chain at a time.

Figure 3.7 illustrates an organization diagram that shows that a given company has two value chains. In this diagram we have pictured the company organization chart in gray and superimposed the two value chains on top to emphasize that the value chains cross departmental lines and run from supplier inputs to products and services provided to customers. This diagram is something we would only prepare to illustrate a report. Once we have prepared this diagram to provide everyone with an overview of the organization, we shift gears and only focus on one value chain at a time in subsequent organization diagrams.

To be more concrete, let us assume that the organization pictured in Figure 3.7 (we will call it Organization X) has two rather separate lines of business. Organization X produces and sells widgets and it consults with other companies about manufacturing practices. Thus one value chain focuses on manufacturing while the other focuses on providing consulting services.

Once we have defined our value chains, we can use the organization diagram to define a value chain in more detail. There are different ways to do this. One good way is to divide a value chain into a few core processes. It's popular to start with three: create new products, market and sell products, and make and deliver products. Figure 3.8 shows that we have labeled the organization box with both the name of the organiza-

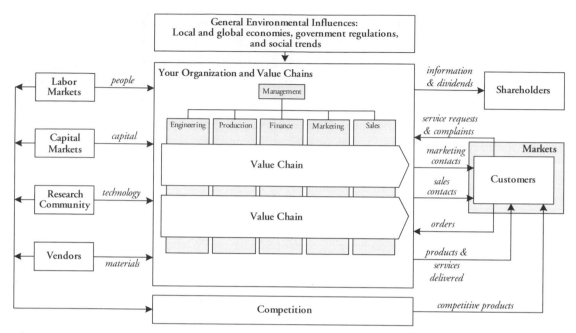

Figure 3.7 An organization diagram of a company with two value chains.

tion and the specific value chain we are focused on, and we have entered the three core processes and begun to link those core processes to external elements (stakeholders) in the diagram.

Some analysts would take this one step further and identify some of the subprocesses within the three core processes we have shown in Figure 3.7. In some cases this may be useful, but in most instances, we find the level of analysis shown in Figure 3.7 to be sufficient. The goal of an organization diagram isn't to define processes in detail, but to get an overview of the whole organization and to help the team think about customers, value chains, and major stakeholders. We have better techniques for analyzing and picturing processes and subprocesses.

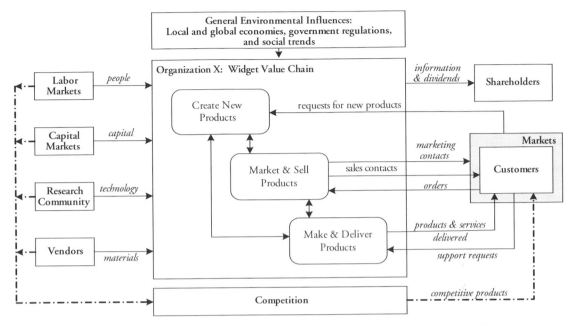

Figure 3.8 An organization diagram for a specific value chain with three core processes identified.

Systems and Processes

We began our discussion of how managers understand the enterprise by considering the kind of model that a manager might provide if asked to explain the organization he or she managed. The traditional organization chart that we guessed our manager might provide is a pretty static way of looking at an organization, and it doesn't provide a very good way of thinking about how things are related. It leads to silo thinking.

In this book we urge *systems thinking* and *process thinking*. As organizations become more complex, effective managers need an overview that allows each one to see how their work fits within the larger whole. Peter Senge wrote a popular book a few years ago that called systems thinking the "Fifth Discipline" and argued that every manager should cultivate this perspective. We believe that the organization diagrams that we have presented here provide an important first step toward developing a systems overview. We know that anyone involved in trying to implement an enterprise strategy needs this kind of perspective. The alternative is to try to figure out how to assign strategic goals to departments without a clear idea of how the departments work together to achieve the desired outcomes.

Process thinking is just a subset of systems thinking. Systems thinking puts the emphasis on understanding the organization as a whole. Process thinking stresses thinking about a portion of the system that produces a specific set of results. The key, again, is to think of the entire process, to understand how a specific process fits within the larger process and ultimately within the value chain. Remember, departments don't produce profits; value chains and processes produce profits. An excellent department may not result in a great process or significant profits. Indeed, in many cases, maximizing departmental efficiency actually reduces the efficiency of the whole process. To avoid this, organizations need to focus on the flows and relationships that actually add value and produce products for customers. Older perspectives need to be subordinated to these newer perspectives if your organization is to prosper.

Notes and References

This chapter has been the subject of several discussions between Roger Burlton and I as we have worked on the BPTrends curriculum that we offer at Boston University, and I have benefited from several of Roger Burlton's insights.

Rummler, Geary, and Alan Brache, *Improving Performance: Managing the White Space on the Organization Chart*, Jossey-Bass, 1990. The book is out of date in the sense that diagramming elements are defined in ways that are pre-UML and BPMN and we have changed various diagrams to bring the Rummler-Brache diagrams into line with current practice.

Geary Rummler is now with the Performance Design Lab (PDL) and gives workshops on advanced process analysis and design issues. For more information, check *www.performancedesignlab.com*. Those who have taken a Rummler workshop know that he makes extensive use of a set of organization and process diagrams of a Fine Times Restaurant he has created. In effect, our SF Seafood restaurant is a West Coast branch of Fine Times and owes much to the original in Tucson.

Magretta, Joan, "The Power of Virtual Integration: An Interview with Dell Computer's Michael Dell," A Harvard Business School Case Study and Commentary, March, 1998. Available from *www.hbsp.harvard.edu*.

Senge, Peter M., *The Fifth Discipline: The Art and Practice of the Learning Organization*, Currency Doubleday, 1994. Senge is also at the Sloan School of Management at MIT, and is a student of Forrester. Senge has created a more popular approach to systems dynamics that puts the emphasis on people and the use of models and feedback to facilitate organizational development. In the introduction we described mature process organizations as organizations that totally involved people in constantly improving the process. Senge would describe such an organization as a learning organization.

chapter

4

Process Architecture and Organizational Alignment

T HE SECOND PHASE of the BPTrends enterprise methodology focuses on creating a business process architecture for the organization. As we have already suggested, we create a separate enterprise architecture for each value chain, so, in effect, we are really talking about creating a business process architecture for a value chain.

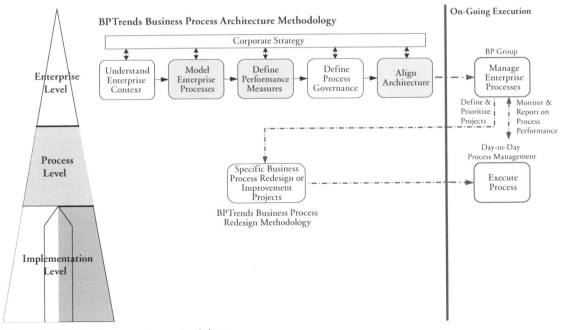

Figure 4.1 BPTrends enterprise methodology.

Different authors and different companies use the term *business process architecture* in diverse ways. In this book, we will use this term to refer to a body of knowledge about the business processes that comprise a value chain. The knowledge is organized by a hierarchical decomposition of the processes that make up the value chain. The processes, in turn, organize information about the performance measures, process managers and organizational resources used by the various processes. The entire business process architecture is hierarchically organized so that executives can see how specific processes are aligned to support the organization's strategic goals, how process measures are aligned and what resources are required for what processes and vice versa.

Process Hierarchies

A value chain is the largest process we normally talk about. It defines a process that begins when the company decides to create a new product or service, or when a customer orders a product, and concludes when the customer has and is satisfied with the product or service. Today, some companies talk about value chains that extend across several companies, but that kind of multicompany process is still relatively rare. The value chain is usually termed the Level 0 process. The major operational processes within a value chain are usually processes like Design New Products, Sell Products to Customers, and Create and Deliver Products to Customers (i.e., Supply Chain). Any one of these Level 1 processes can be subdivided into several Level 2 processes. Thus, the Supply Chain Council's SCOR framework divides the Level 2 operational Supply Chain process into: Source, Make, Deliver and Return.

The use of terms like superprocess and subprocess depends upon where you start. From any arbitrary process, the larger process that contains it is its superprocess. Similarly, the processes contained in the arbitrary process are termed its subprocesses.

There is no technical limit to the subdivision of processes. It's common to see processes divided into three or four levels. It is rare to see a process divided into more than seven or eight levels. For our purposes, the smallest process we diagram is called an activity. We do this simply because process standards like UML and BPMN arbitrarily define a process as made up of activities. That said, it is common to have subdivisions that don't get diagrammed and are defined by outlines or other textual definitions. Thus, we use the terms *steps*, *tasks* and *procedures* either loosely, or to describe the subelements of an activity.

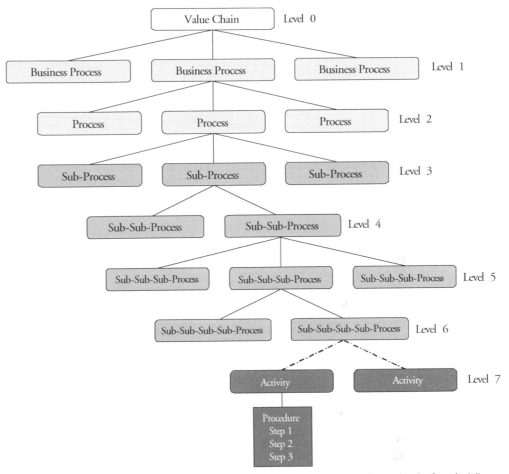

Figure 4.2 A hierarchical decomposition of a value chain, suggesting how "level of analysis" corresponds to process level.

Other authors define these terms in alternate ways and there is, of course, no definitive way of naming process levels. The important thing is simply to keep in mind that processes can be hierarchically arranged and that you need to know, when you consider a project, whether you are going to be analyzing a relatively large process, like a supply chain; a midsized process, like applying for a loan or returning an item; or a small process, like obtaining a credit card approval, or checking a loan application for completeness.

Defining a Business Process Architecture

A business process architecture can be created on paper. To illustrate the basic concepts and relationships, we will use worksheets to explain the process. Any large company, however, will want to use software tools to create and maintain their business process architecture. The relationships involved and the amount of data involved quickly become so complex and extensive that a database is required to manage the architecture.

The key steps involved in creating a business process architecture are as follows:

▶ Identify a specific value chain.
▶ Determine the specific strategic goals the value chain is to achieve.
▶ Determine how you will measure whether or not the value chain achieves its goals.
▶ Subdivide the value chain into its major processes (Level 1 processes). Subdivide the major processes (Level 1 processes) into their subprocesses (Level 2 processes). If appropriate, subdivide the Level 2 processes into their subprocesses (Level 3 processes).
▶ Use a worksheet. For each Level 1 process, determine how the Level 1 process will be measured. Determine who will be responsible for the process. Determine what resources are linked to each Level 1 process.
▶ Repeat this procedure, using new worksheets, for each Level 2 process, and so forth.

Figure 4.3 illustrates the top half of an architecture analysis worksheet and indicates the information that should be included.

Architecture Analysis Worksheet – Level 1 Processes			
Value Chain:	Value Chain Process Manager		
Strategic Goals for Value Chain:			
Level 1 Processes	Process Manager	Level 1 Goals/Process Metrics	Level 1 Resources

Figure 4.3 A Level 1 architecture analysis worksheet.

In Chapter 3 we ended up describing a value chain in terms of three major subprocesses, as pictured in Figure 4.4.

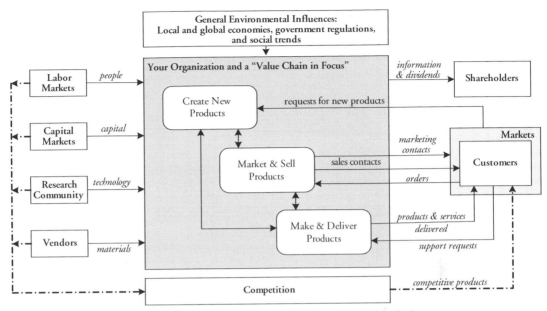

Figure 4.4 An organization diagram showing the major processes in a value chain.

Once we begin to try to analyze a large number of processes and subprocesses, it is often easier to switch to a horizontal process decomposition diagram like the one shown in Figure 4.5. In this case we have broken a Widget Value Chain into three core

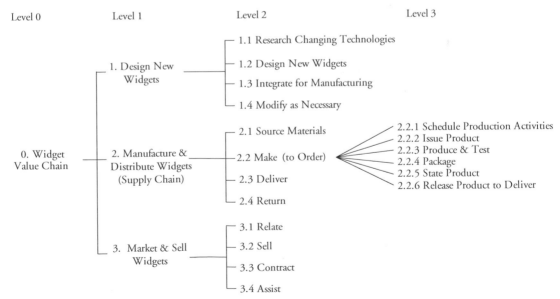

Figure 4.5 Horizontal decomposition of a value chain into three process levels.

processes, then subdivided each of those into subprocesses and subdivided one of the Level 2 processes into a further set of subprocesses.

There are different ways of developing a comprehensive decomposition of a value chain. One can begin with a room full of senior executives and a white board and simply ask: "OK, how do you produce widgets? Where do you begin? What happens next?" This is the traditional approach and, although it's time consuming, it's effective, and it often surfaces lots of concerns about how specific things are done. In many cases, executives do not realize, before they sit down and try to describe it, just how confusing and redundant some of their processes really are. Often, each has only focused on one or another portion of the process and never tried to create a diagram that showed how it all fit together into a value chain.

Increasingly today, managers are approaching the analysis of process architectures in a different way. They are using process frameworks—generic models of all the processes in a value chain, or in a part of a value chain—to provide them with a complete description. Starting with a framework, the executives tailor it to provide a description of their particular value chain. The process framework-based approach works because, at level 1 and 2, most companies do things in a very similar manner, even though they use very different words to describe their processes. Thus, whatever you call them, everyone has some kind of new product/service development process, some kind of product/service development process with an associated procurement process, and some kind of marketing and sales process. We'll look at process frameworks in more detail in a moment; meantime, if you look again at the horizontal value chain decomposition diagram pictured in Figure 4.5, you can see how we move from a process description to worksheets. Worksheet 1 provides space to describe the attributes and resources that support the Level 1 processes in a value chain. The various Level 2 Worksheets allow the analysts to drill down into each specific Level 1 process to identify the attributes and resources used by the Level 2 processes.

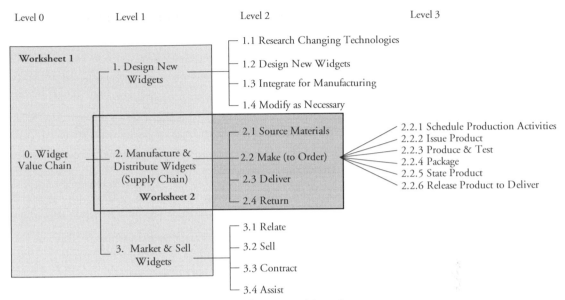

Figure 4.6 Architecture analysis worksheets and a process hierarchy.

Completing a Worksheet

Working across the Level 1 worksheet shown in Figure 4.3, you can see that the top of the worksheet provides a space for the name of the value chain and for a description of how that value chain supports the corporate strategy and how it will be measured. In some cases this discussion will be brief. In other cases the discussion will take time and involve senior managers in very serious discussions of exactly what the supply chain should aim to achieve. Some might see the value chain contributing to the profit of the company. Others might feel that the specific value chain was being undertaken to support the image of the company or to generate ideas for future business ventures. The goals of the value chain must be concisely defined and measures must be developed that everyone agrees will accurately reflect the success or failure of the value chain.

Next, the architecture group should define the Level 1 processes that comprise the value chain. The trick is to keep them simple and general and to limit them to about three to seven processes. Most generic frameworks focus on three level 1 processes—a design process, a product/service development/delivery process, and a sales/marketing/service process.

Core, Support and Management Processes

So far, we have focused on core or operational processes. These are processes that add value to the product or service that the organization is producing for its customers. When Michael Porter defined the value chain, he distinguished between core and support processes. Core processes generate products or services. Support processes do not add value, but are necessary to assure that the core processes continue to function. Thus, in a manufacturing organization, accounting is a support process. We maintain the books to let management know how much manufacturing is costing and to enable them to report to stockholders. Similarly, IT is a support process that generates and maintains the software and systems that manufacturing needs to control its production-line machinery. Today, it is popular to divide support processes between processes that directly support the core processes and more generic management processes that plan, organize, communicate, monitor and control the activities of the organization. Support processes are sometimes called enabling processes.

Figure 4.7 provides one way of thinking about the distinction. In this case, we have a core set of processes that generates a product. Separately, we have a support process—the Stock Reorder Process—that resupplies a core assembly process. We also

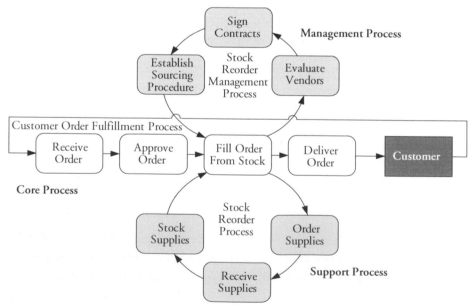

Figure 4.7 Three types of processes: Core, Management and Support processes.

have a management process that determines which suppliers the company will use and establishes and maintains relationships with the suppliers. Obviously, this management process could be an activity undertaken by procurement, but it might also be a process undertaken by finance.

Should we include support or enabling processes in our business process architecture, and, if so, how should we represent them? One approach would be to divide all support processes and organize the support processes under the core processes they enable. This is conceptually clean, but it isn't, in fact, very realistic. In most cases, a company conceptualizes its IT group as a department. In the best case the IT group is managed as a matrix organization, and has some managers responsible for generic IT functions like new product development and ongoing software maintenance, and other managers responsible for IT support for the Supply Chain and IT support for Sales and Marketing. The key here, however, is that IT has a core set of functions, like the company network and good maintenance practices, that apply to all processes or departments it supports; thus, there is a very strong argument for treating IT as an independent department.

An alternative approach, which is increasingly popular, is to treat IT as an independent organization, a cost center, or an independent value chain. This reflects what happens when IT is outsourced. In essence, IT becomes a separate company—a value chain that produces software and services that it sells to the parent company's core processes. Whether your company outsources IT or keeps it in house, if you regard it as its own value chain, and create an independent business process architecture to describe IT's core, support and management processes, you will find that it makes everything easier to understand. Obviously, the same logic can be applied to the other main support processes, including human resources, facilities, and accounting. If you follow this approach, then you will leave support processes off the business process architecture worksheets you create for your core value chains and describe each major support process as an independent architecture with its own worksheets.

Handling management processes is trickier, because the whole idea of management processes has not been very well thought out. To begin with, we need to discriminate between two basic types of "management processes." In one case, we have the processes or activities that are performed by the individuals that actually manage processes on a day-to-day basis. Thus, if we consider Figure 4.7, there is some individual who is responsible for managing the Fill Order From Stock process. That individual plans, organizes, communicates, monitors and controls the Fill Order From Stock process each hour of each day. He or she interacts with the employees that undertake the tasks that we associate with the Fill Order From Stock process, communicates new targets as they occur, and provides feedback when employees do their work in an outstanding or an unacceptable manner. It isn't useful to treat the day-to-day process management directly associated with the core process as a separate process. When you seek to redesign or improve the process, you need to consider both the activities of the employees assigned to the process and, simultaneously, the activities of the manager who is in charge of the process. Insofar as it's useful to discriminate these day-to-day process management processes, it's done to define standard or best-practice procedures that process managers should follow. We'll consider standard process management practices later, when we consider process management and the establishment of BPM support groups. At this point, however, we will simply ignore these day-to-day management processes. They are so closely associated with core processes that they don't need an independent representation on our business process architecture.

There remain some general management processes that perform enterprise planning, organizing, communication or monitoring functions. In essence, if the organization has a business rules group that works to define company policies and to dictate the business rules that specific processes should implement, that group and the processes it implements constitute a kind of management process. Similarly, the team that defines corporate strategy follows a process and the BPM group implements a set of processes. These are true management processes that are independent of the core processes in a normal value chain. Sophisticated companies will want to analyze these management processes to assure that they function as efficiently and effectively as possible. Thus, we should define them and document how they function. The question is where to include them. Unlike the standard support processes, like IT and HR, it is hard to think of these "management processes" as a cost center or an independent company. It's easier to simply think of them as activities undertaken by senior managers. At the moment, it is probably best to simply think of all the "management processes" that are independent of specific operational processes as their own "management value chain" and document them on their own worksheets. It's not a very elegant solution, but it's probably better than trying to associate them with a conventional value chain.

Aligning Managers, Measures and Resources

As processes are identified, the group can determine who is responsible for managing that process. If the company is functionally oriented, then at the highest level it will often be the case that there is no clear manager for Level 1 processes. Instead, the processes will be divided among multiple departments, with no one responsible for overall coordination. We are going to skip any further discussion of process management at this point and delay it until we reach Chapter 5. Suffice it to say that if the team has trouble assigning managers to processes, that should stimulate a discussion of how processes are managed in the organization.

Next, the team should define the goal of each Level 1 process and consider how the success of each of the Level 1 processes should be measured. As with management, we'll delay a discussion of measurement until we reach the next chapter.

The final column on the worksheet asks the architecture team to list resources that are required to support each Level 1 process. This emphasizes that the development of a business process architecture is a long-term undertaking. Obviously, the architecture team could not identify the jobs or the software systems associated with each Level 1 process in the course of a day or a week. In fact, most organizations skip resource alignment during the first pass, and leave it till the entire architecture is better understood. As time passes, the organization and those concerned with processes will find that it would be useful to determine how different resources are aligned, and they will then proceed to capture information about the alignment of those resources. Many organizations create an architecture, and then add detailed resource information to it as the organization undertakes business process change projects. In this case, no one sets out to list every ERP application that every process uses, but as processes are redesigned, information about ERP support is captured and added to the architecture database.

Some of the types of resources that organizations might seek to align with Level 1 or Level 2 processes include:

▶ **Alignment with corporate strategies and goals.** Some organizations list information about specific Level 1 strategies and stakeholders and note how the specific strategies support corporate strategies. Others list all the stakeholders that are interested in each specific Level 1 process.

▶ **Alignment with other processes.** So far we have emphasized core or operational processes. Once the operational processes are defined, some companies proceed to describe management and support processes and indicate just which core or operational processes depend on which management or support processes. We'll consider this in more detail in the next chapter when we discuss management. Many companies are interested in identifying specific subprocesses or activities that are repeated in different Level 1 or 2 processes. Assume, for example, that a Level 1 process includes a Level 3 or 4 subprocess that is called: Determine Customer Credit. Imagine, further, that the determination of customer credit occurred in several Level 1 and 2 processes, and that in some cases it was done by employees and in other cases it was done using an ERP module. It would be nice to know everywhere customer credit was determined, so that the activity could be standardized and the same software could be used whenever possible. Thus, simply listing subprocesses and activities that occur in multiple Level 1 processes can be very useful.

▶ **Alignment with policies and rules.** Many organizations list the corporate policies that apply to specific Level 1 or 2 processes. As the analysis becomes more comprehensive, organizations may list the specific business rules that are used in specific subprocesses, and then check to see that policies and rules are being consistently applied.

▶ **Alignment with IT resources.** Lots of organization indicate which software applications or which databases are used by which processes. If the effort to correlate IT resources with specific business processes becomes very elaborate, it is often termed an enterprise architecture. If a company uses ERP applications, the process architecture is often driven or supported by process architectures suggested by ERP vendors.

▶ **Alignment with HR resources.** Many organizations define which roles or jobs are associated with which Level 2 or 3 processes. If this is carried further, job descriptions associated with processes may be defined, or job competencies may be defined. Similarly, some organizations list the employee documents and the training programs that are given in support of each specific process.

▶ **Alignment with Sarbanes-Oxley, ISO 9000 and various risk management standards.** Organizations are increasingly responsible for gathering and maintaining information about the decisions and the risks involved in specific processes. This information can naturally be placed in the business process architecture database. As time passes and more information is gathered, organizations with comprehensive business process architectures find themselves reversing the process and using the architecture database to generate information required by external agencies.

A business process architecture is a management tool. Once it is defined and then populated with up-to-date data, it can be used, like other databases, to answer ad hoc questions that executives need answered. It can be used to support those engaged in developing corporate strategies and it can be used by a BPM group to identify processes that aren't meeting their goals and that need to be redesigned. The information placed in the business process architecture database will depend on how the company uses it. Most companies that have created architectures find that they make it easier for managers to conceptualize their organizations in terms of processes, which leads to requests for more and more information about the processes that company supports.

Defining a Business Process Architecture

One creates a business process architecture by decomposing a value chain into processes and subprocesses. As we noted earlier, increasingly high-level process analysis efforts are being supported by the use of process frameworks. At this point, we want to look at process frameworks in a little more detail.

The Supply Chain Council's SCOR Framework

The Supply Chain Council (SCC) was established as a nonprofit consortium in 1996. Today, it is a worldwide organization with over 700 members. The Council conducts meetings that allow companies to gather together to discuss supply chain problems and opportunities. In addition, it has been working on a standard supply chain framework or reference model, SCOR.

Before considering SCOR itself, let's consider why the SCC membership was motivated to develop the framework in the first place. Increasingly, companies are creating supply chain systems that cross company boundaries. Thus, it is not uncommon for ten or twenty companies to sit down to figure out how their companies will work together to move materials to manufacturers and then to distributors and, ultimately, to customers. If each team had to begin by trying to straighten out what terms they used to describe what processes, the effort would take a lot more time. Instead, the Supply Chain Council decided to define a high-level set of supply chain process names that everyone could use. Each company could continue to use whatever particular process names they chose, but in conversations with the other companies, each could use the standard vocabulary defined by SCOR. Later, the SCOR model was extended so that it not only defines core processes, but also defines management and support processes and provides precisely defined performance measures for each process. Using the performance information, companies can define who will pass what to whom and when, in an unambiguous manner. Having once established the system, the SCC members then proceeded to provide performance information to an external benchmarking organization that provides general information in return. Thus, an individual company can determine how its delivery processes compare with other members of the SCC, or, more specifically, with others in the same industry. Thus, SCOR began as an effort to facilitate efficient communication and modeling and evolved into a general methodology that can be used to quickly define a supply chain architecture complete with benchmarked measures.

Let's begin with a more detailed look at the SCOR architecture. The SCC speaks of SCOR as being comprised of three levels. They ignore the fact that the supply chain is only one of the major business processes that make up the entire value chain. To clarify this, we will always refer to the value chain as Level 0. Then we will refer to the supply chain as a Level 1 process. To make things even more complex, SCOR subdivides the supply chain into three "levels" but, in fact, one of the levels is not a decomposition of the higher level, but instead requires the modeler to define the higher-level process in terms of one of three variations. Either the Level 1 source process is concerned with Stocked Products or it is concerned with Made-to-Order products, or with Engineered-to-Order products. To simplify things, we will consistently speak of SCOR as having three levels. Level 1 is the supply chain. Level 2 consists of the high-level processes that make up a supply chain, including Source, Make, Deliver and Return. Plan is an additional SCOR process that describes management planning. These Level 2 processes are first defined. Then their variation is specified, and then they are decomposed into a set of Level 3 subprocesses, as pictured in Figure 4.8.

The SCOR reference manual defines each Level 2 and Level 3 subprocess and also indicates what planning and support processes are typically linked to each process or subprocess. The SCC does not define a fourth level, leaving the specification of Level 4 activities to individual companies. In other words, SCOR defines a supply chain architecture and all of the high-level processes and leaves the technical implementation of the Level 4 processes to the individual members.

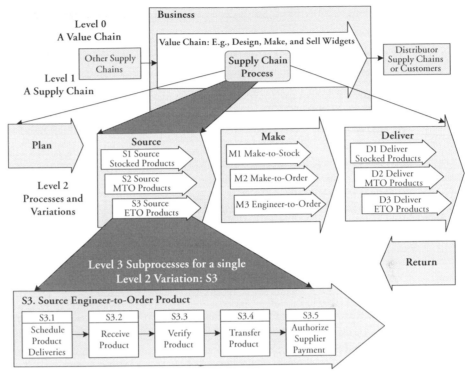

Figure 4.8 The three levels of a SCOR architecture.

Developing a Supply Chain Architecture with SCOR

Using SCOR, a company can quickly characterize its supply chain architecture. Figure 4.9 illustrates a map that SCOR architects usually draw to show where materials originate and how they are moved to assembly points and then distributed to customers.

Once the supply chain is described by means of a map, it is then redrawn using the SCOR diagramming convention illustrated in Figure 4.10. The SCC refers to the diagram as a *thread diagram*. In this diagram, each Level 2 process in the supply chain is illustrated with a small arrowhead. The bold lines separate companies and the dashed line separates divisions within a company. Notice that two suppliers are feeding the Alpha company supply chain. The letters indicate that a process is either a Source (S) process, a Make (M) process, or a Deliver (D) process. The numbers indicate the variation. Thus, an S1 is a Source process that relies on continuously Stocked products, while an M2 process is a Make process that relies on providing products that

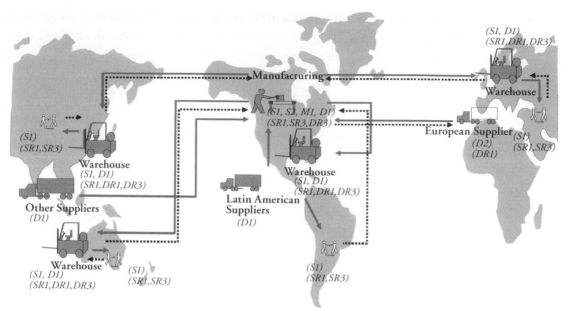

Figure 4.9 An As-Is Geography Map of a Company's Supply Chain.

are Made-to-Order. (Refer to Figure 4.6 for the designations.) A thread diagram can be quite a bit more complex if the supply chain involves multiple columns of suppliers and columns of distributors. Similarly, in more complete diagrams, the Plan processes are also entered. In effect, as Plan refers to a process management effort. For every core process shown on the thread diagram, there is also a Plan process.

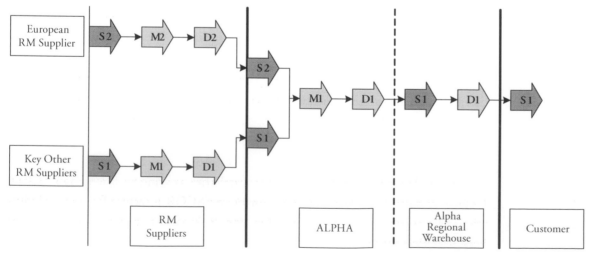

Figure 4.10 A SCOR thread diagram of a simple supply chain process.

The Supply Chain Council provides members with a reference manual that defines every supply chain process and subprocess. In addition, the manual describes performance measures that are appropriate to each process at each level. The SCC divides all performance measures into five general categories, which are then clustered into either external or customer facing metrics or internal facing metrics. Figure 4.11 provides a high-level overview of the measures that are defined for the supply chain as a whole (the Level 1 process). We won't go into measures any further here, but suffice it to say that one can use the SCOR metrics to quickly generate an interlocking list of metrics for an entire supply chain architecture.

	Performance Attribute	Performance Attribute Definition	Level 1 Metric
Customer Facing Attributes	Supply Chain Delivery Reliability	The performance of the supply chain in delivering: the correct product, to the correct place, at the correct time, in the correct condition and packaging, in the correct quantity, with the correct documentation, to the correct customer.	Delivery Performance
			Fill Rates
			Perfect Order Fulfillment
	Supply Chain Responsiveness	The velocity at which a supply chain provides products to the customer.	Order Fulfillment Lead Times
	Supply Chain Flexibility	The agility of a supply chain in responding to marketplace changes to gain or maintain competitive advantage.	Supply Chain Response Time
			Production Flexibility
Internal Facing Attributes	Supply Chain Costs	The costs associated with operating the supply chain.	Cost of Goods Sold
			Total Supply Chain Management Costs
			Value-Added Productivity
			Warranty / Returns Processing Costs
	Supply Chain Asset Management Efficiency	The effectiveness of an organization in managing assets to support demand satisfaction. This includes the management of all assets: fixed and working capital.	Cash-to-Cash Cycle Time
			Inventory Days of Supply
			Asset Turns

Figure 4.11 SCOR performance attributes and Level 1 metrics.

Several organizations that track benchmarks are working with the Supply Chain Council and can provide generic benchmarks for SCOR measures for specific industries. If a company wants specific benchmark data, it needs to contract with one of the benchmarking groups.

In Figure 4.12, we illustrate what SCOR refers to as a SCORcard. It shows the performance attributes, a set of historical data, and the benchmark data for a hypothetical company's supply chain. In the right-hand column, the team has made some "guestimates" about what kind of value Alpha might achieve, assuming it could move its supply chain process closer to the average for its industry. SCOR terms the comparison of the company's actual, historical performance with the benchmarks for the company's industry as a gap analysis, and uses it to determine if redesign or improvements in the As-Is supply chain will really justify an investment.

Supply Chain SCORcard				Performance Versus Competitive Population			
	Overview Metrics	SCOR Level 1 Metrics	Actual	Parity	Advantage	Superior	Value from Improvements
EXTERNAL	Supply Chain Reliability	Delivery Performance to Commit Date	50%	85%	90%	95%	
		Fill Rates	63%	94%	96%	98%	
		Perfect Order Fulfillment	0%	80%	85%	90%	$30M Revenue
	Responsiveness	Order Fulfillment Lead times	35 days	7 days	5 days	3 days	$30M Revenue
	Flexibility	Supply Chain Response Time	97 days	82 days	55 days	13 days	Key enabler to cost and asset improvements
		Production Flexibility	45 days	30 days	25 days	20 days	
INTERNAL	Cost	Total SCM Management Cost	19%	13%	8%	3%	$30M Indirect Cost
		Warranty Cost	NA	NA	NA	NA	NA
		Value Added Employee Productivity	NA	$156K	$306K	$460K	NA
	Assets	Inventory Days of Supply	119 days	55 days	38 days	22 days	NA
		Cash-to-Cash Cycle Time	196 days	80 days	46 days	28 days	$7 M Capital Charge
		Net Asset Turns (Working Capital)	2.2 turns	8 turns	12 turns	19 turns	NA

Figure 4.12 A SCORcard with actual and benchmark data, and some guesses about the value that might be achieved by redesigning the supply chain being analyzed.

Once the SCOR team has examined the Level 1, and in some cases the Level 2, As-Is historical data, it is in a position to decide if the supply chain should be changed. In effect, it is now ready to review the organization's existing approach to its supply chain and, if necessary, define a new supply chain strategy and to set targets, priorities and a budget for any redesign effort. The use of the SCORcard provides a nice illustration of the power of the architecture approach. Once a company has a complete overview of all its processes and solid performance data, it is positioned to consider how each of the processes are performing, compare them with benchmarks and then decide which possible intervention would produce the most significant result. This illustrates the sense in which an architecture is a tool for management.

The Extension of SCOR

The next part of the SCOR story is closely associated with Joseph Francis and the Hewlett-Packard-Compaq merger. The HP-Compaq merger was announced in September of 2001. The previous two years had witnessed a major slump in sales, which had forced many IT companies to reevaluate their strategies. The proposed merger of two leading IT companies—the largest IT merger to date—represented a major strategic initiative on the part of the management teams at both companies to change the overall dynamics of the IT market.

HP was a leading player in mid-range servers, in PCs and laptops, and in printers. It was also a leader in integration services and outsourcing and had a worldwide reputation for cutting-edge technology. At the same time, however, HP wasn't large enough to compete for the largest service contracts, which typically went to larger competitors like IBM. Moreover, HP's marketing prowess had declined in recent years. In 2001, for example, HP had some 6,000 people in marketing, while similar-size competitors managed with one-third as many. Compaq was even stronger than HP in PC and laptop sales, but lacked HP's strength in all other areas. Compaq had acquired Tandem Computers and Digital Equipment in the late 1990s in an effort to diversify, but had never managed to utilize Tandem or Digital's strengths in mid-range computers, technology, or consulting to achieve the market presence it had hoped to obtain when it made those acquisitions. On the other hand, Compaq was known for its aggressive marketing capabilities.

The merger of the two companies would result in a significantly larger company. Together, HP and Compaq would be in a position to dominate the market for PC, laptop, server, and printer sales. At the same time, the combined company would be nearly as large as IBM and would thus be well positioned to compete on an equal footing for the largest service and outsourcing contracts. The new company would also be in the position to require suppliers to offer it the largest possible discounts. Moreover, since there was considerable overlap in the PC area, the two companies hoped to squeeze out some $2.5 billion in annual savings while simultaneously creating a leaner, more aggressive organization.

From the beginning, the proposed merger was controversial. The arguments about the wisdom of the merger and the proxy fight that followed have been extensively reported on in the popular press. Ultimately, in fact, the actual merger went smoother than most anticipated and resulted in greater savings than those who planned the merger had hoped for. As even the merger's strongest opponents admitted, the planning that preceded the merger was excellent.

What is of interest to us is the planning process that helped make the merger successful. Specifically, we want to consider the activities of the merger planning team that planned for the integration of the HP-Compaq supply chain processes. As soon as the merger was formally announced, a new organization was set up to plan for the merger. This merger organization ultimately included some 1,000 employees drawn from the two companies. The employees met in what was referred to as a clean-room environment. In effect, they were separated from the day-to-day work of both HP and Compaq, placed in an isolated setting, provided detailed information about both companies, and asked to develop a merger plan.

The merger organization was headed by an executive committee that made high-level strategic decisions and, ultimately, approved all the detailed recommendations of the more specialized teams. Reporting to the executive committee were eight teams that focused on specific areas of concern. There were teams for IT Infrastructure, Supply Chain, Sales/Orders, Product Design, Communications/ Marketing, Finance, Human Resources, and Services/Support.

Some of the teams lacked any overarching framework and had to create a new, common vocabulary and a standard way of identifying existing processes. Luckily, HP and Compaq managers who were members of the Supply Chain team were familiar with the work of the Supply Chain Council (SCC). The HP-Compaq Supply Chain team realized that they could use SCOR to greatly simplify their task. SCOR provided a standard approach that they could use to rapidly characterize and measure the supply chain processes at both HP and Compaq.

By agreeing in advance to map both companies' processes to the SCOR model and to use SCOR's standard vocabulary and measures, the HP-Compaq team was able to accomplish in a month what might otherwise have taken many months.

SCOR's ease of use was critical for the work undertaken by the Supply Chain IT team during the merger. SCOR made it possible for the team to quickly analyze all of the HP and Compaq supply chains for all regions and product lines. This analysis, in turn, made it possible for the Supply Chain IT team to accurately compare a Compaq process with an HP process for similar product lines, to determine what each process actually accomplished.

The HP-Compaq Supply Chain group was able to define all their supply chains quickly, by simply relying on SCOR's Level 1 definitions. In effect, all supply chains were quickly divided into Sourcing processes, Make processes and Deliver processes, as well as some additional planning and enabling processes. Once this was done, high-level software applications that supported each of these processes were identified.

SCOR provides a well-defined set of measures for each of the Level 1 processes. Those measures are tied to established financial measures that both companies have tracked for years. Thus, in most cases, one simply used the SCOR Level 1 measures to compare two regional lines to determine which line was the more efficient and cost effective. If one line was clearly more efficient than the other, then the Supply Chain IT group tended to simply select the applications that supported the more efficient process.

Those familiar with how technical people can disagree about the virtues of competing software applications can easily imagine that the Supply Chain IT group could have become an arena for intense arguments among the HP and Compaq advocates of alternative software applications. The Supply Chain IT team knew that if they allowed the discussion to become focused on specific technical features they would never accomplish their assignment. Moreover, a technical discussion wouldn't assure that the application chosen would be aligned with corporate goals. Instead, the group knew that it was important that their work focus on the value that the various applications delivered to the company. In effect, the group decided to select those applications that supported the most efficient processes, without regard to which company currently supported the application, or which departments were involved.

Some of the measures focus on external results and some focus on internal efficiencies. In each case the SCC has defined precise definitions for the measures. No organization would want to apply all of these measures to a given SCOR process or subprocess. Instead, the SCC has a methodology that helps practitioners align the measures they consider with the strategic goals the company is trying to achieve with a given supply chain process. Consider the goal of a given product line. If the company wanted to compete in the market for that product line as the low-cost provider, it would focus on keeping a minimal amount of inventory, since low inventory is one of the ways to keep costs down. On the other hand, if the company was committed to service and wanted to assure that customers could always get what they wanted, it would need to accept higher inventory costs and would focus, instead, on satisfying customer requests. Different strategies require different measures. The Supply Chain business group made most of the decisions about marketing strategies for the combined product lines and the Supply Chain IT group then selected appropriate measures and used them to compare how the existing HP and Compaq product lines performed.

In a few cases, two competing regional lines would appear to be equally efficient and effective when analyzed with Level 1 measures. In those cases, the Supply Chain IT team would expand their effort and model the processes to SCOR Level 2 or even, in a very few cases, to Level 3.

About 20% of the total time used by the Supply Chain team was used in modeling processes, measuring them, applying criteria, and making judgments as to which applications to save and which to discard.

Once the Supply Chain group had identified product lines to maintain, modeling the processes, and then evaluated and selected applications to maintain, it was possible to step back from the specific supply chain processes being evaluated and to identify a generic supply chain architecture for the combined company. In effect, this architecture identified common supply processes, derived from SCOR, and common applications that the merged company could eventually standardize on, worldwide. The applications identified were not new applications that the merged company would acquire, but applications already being used with successful product lines that the company would standardize on and migrate to in order to minimize the number of applications the new HP would need to support.

At the end of this phase, the Supply Chain IT group had identified all of the product lines that were to be supported in the merged company, had identified all of the applications that were to be maintained and those to be dropped, and identified a set of overall architectural standards that the company would move toward as soon as possible.

Other HP-Compaq teams made their recommendations, but the Supply Chain team's recommendations stood out because they were based on an analysis of the processes involved and hard numbers on the performance of the processes. The Supply Chain team's recommendations to use specific software applications were justified by the performance of the processes that had used those applications. The business logic behind the Supply Chain team's work led to the appointment of the team's leader, Joe Francis, to the head of the new HP's business process improvement program.

The Extension of SCOR at HP

Joe Francis was impressed with how the SCOR framework had facilitated their analysis of existing supply chain processes. Since his new job required that he look at other processes in HP, he assembled a team and began to develop frameworks, like SCOR, for marketing, sales, new product development, and for various support processes. In 2003, partly because of the work he had done during the HP-Compaq merger, Joe Francis was elected chair of the SCC's board of directors.

By 2003 HP had developed several frameworks. Unlike the SCOR framework, however, these new frameworks had only been developed by HP personnel and there were no benchmarks available to use with them. To remedy this, Joe Francis persuaded HP to offer the frameworks they had developed to the SCC to encourage the SCC to expand beyond its focus on the supply chain and eventually offer an entire value chain framework. Today, the SCC is moving beyond SCOR and has created initial standards for a DCOR (design chain) model and a CCOR (customer chain) model. Thus, in the course of the next few years, as SCC members use these new frameworks and report their results, benchmarks should become available for all of the core processes of a typical supply chain. This, in turn, means that it will be possible for a company to rapidly characterize an entire architecture using standard, benchmarked processes.

Other Approaches

Around the same time that the SCC decided to launch its extension of SCOR, a separate group of former SCC members created a new group to extend SCOR into a complete value chain framework. This group, the Value-Chain Council (VCC), has created its own model, the Value Reference Model (VRM)[1], which is similar to SCOR but in some ways better integrated. Obviously, with SCOR so well established, the SCC's effort has focused on adding new processes while leaving the existing SCOR model untouched. The Value-Chain Council was able to start from scratch and made some changes in SCOR to simplify the overall framework. Figure 4.13 illustrates the VRM approach.

---

[1] The VCC's Value Reference Model was originally called VCOR, but the name was changed in early 2007 to VRM.

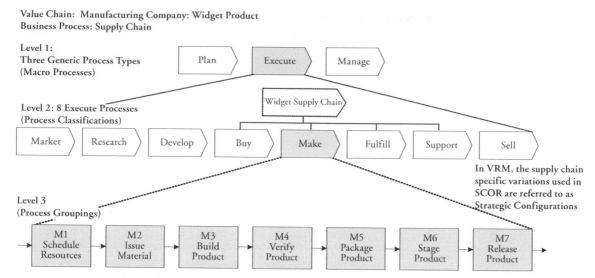

Figure 4.13 The Value Chain Council's VRM framework.

Notice that the VRM model does not discriminate the supply chain as a process—we've shown where it could be inserted between VRM levels 1 and 2—but simply treats SCOR's four Level 2 processes Source (Buy), Make, Deliver (Fulfill) and Return (Support), as four of eight core processes. At the top level, VRM discriminates between Planning processes (we'd call them Management processes), Execution processes (we'd call them Core processes) and Manage processes (which we'd call support processes). The details of the evolving VRM model aren't too important. What is important is that VCC is working on a complete value chain framework. Just as SCOR has processes and measures, VRM includes both a process framework and a performance measurement schema.

Figure 4.14 suggests how Plan and Manage processes support the basic Execute process.

The SCC has 700 members, an established annual budget, and a lot of momentum. On the other hand, their membership has historically been composed of supply chain managers and many of those members have resisted the SCC's efforts to expand into other process areas. The VCC is new and has only a few members. It has the advantage of starting from scratch and taking advantage of everything the SCC has learned, but it has the challenge of recruiting members and then building a database of reliable benchmarks. At the moment, the two organizations are competing and each

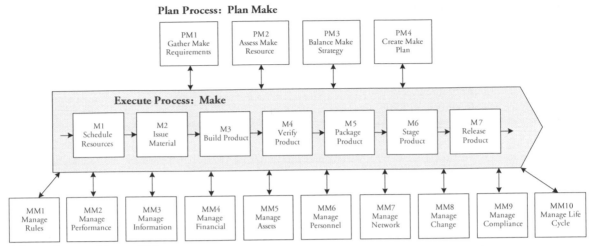

Figure 4.14 The Plan and Manage Processes that are associated with the Execute Make Process.

stimulating the other's efforts. With luck, in a few years a merger will take place and result in a value chain framework that combines the best of the two approaches.

The TeleManagement Forum's eTOM Framework

Another approach to a complete value chain framework is provided by the TeleManagement Forum, a consortium of telecom companies. Their framework is highly tailored to the needs of telecom companies. Thus, it can't be used by non-telecoms, but it does provide a comprehensive approach for telecom companies.

One group within the TeleManagement Forum has spent several years developing a process architecture for telecom companies. It is assumed that no specific company will have exactly the same processes identified by the TeleManagement Forum, and that they will probably use different names for the various processes. Thus, this is a reference architecture rather than an architecture of a specific business. It is assumed as time passes that most members will move toward this process architecture and that, during the same period, vendors will tailor products to implement many of the processes defined by the model.

The architecture we describe is the third iteration that the TeleManagement Forum has developed. This latest iteration, called the eBusiness Telecom Operations

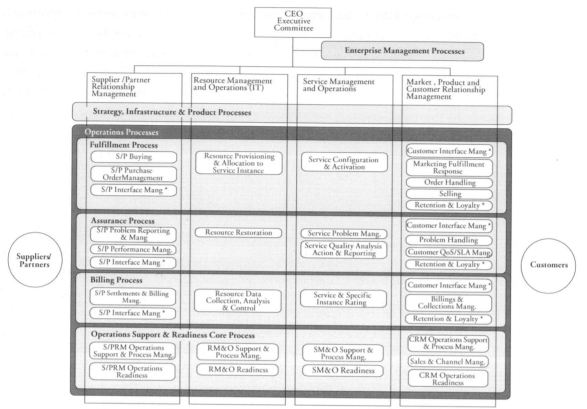

Figure 4.15 The TeleManagement Forum's eTOM reference architecture.

Map (eTOM), is based on earlier work that only sought to define the operations processes within telecom companies. As the companies began to implement e-business applications, however, they discovered that processes included in general and enterprise management had to be added to the architecture. One of the major advantages of e-business systems is that they integrate management and operations, and it's important that everyone have a clear overview of all the processes if they are to see how integration might occur.

Figure 4.15 shows a version of the eTOM framework, rearranged so that it matches the format that we use in this book. In effect, we rotated the basic eTOM diagram 90 degrees to the right. The *customer* was moved to the right side of the diagram so that *processes* now flow from left to right and functional units flow down, as organization charts typically do.

Figure 4.15 provides an idea of how a telecommunications company is organized. In essence, a telecom sells time on its network to customers. Since the time is sold and monitored by means of computers that track phone access, Service and Resource are important functions. Since almost all long-distance phone calls cross multiple networks, arrangements with other telecom companies—partners—are very important. We suspect that actual phone companies might subdivide their departments somewhat differently, placing marketing and service in separate departments, but remember that most phone sales and service requests come in through a common call center, so this high-level grouping works reasonably well. In any case, Figure 4.15 provides an idea of how a group of telecom managers felt they could represent their organizations.

When you look at the modified version of the eTOM diagram, it's clear that the three shaded blocks are groups of business processes. Within each group, there are subprocesses. By splitting up the processes in the way they have, it's unclear if Operations represents a value chain or not. The key would be if one could add the costs of all of the processes within the Operations box to determine the total cost and the profit margin on a product line—in this case, phone service. If you could, that would mean that everything in the lower two shaded boxes could be grouped together as overhead and assigned to a single value chain—Phone Operations.

The important thing isn't the notation, however, but the fact that either Figure 4.14 would provide a telecom process architecture committee with an overview of the company. Every business process architecture committee needs something like Figure 4.15 if they are to have a standard way to describe their company's processes and identify processes that require changes when new strategies and goals are announced.

Notice that some subprocesses occur within multiple processes. These subprocesses are marked with an asterisk to highlight the fact. Thus, the Customer Interface Management—presumably a set of customer portal management activities—is shared by the Fulfillment, Assurance, and Billing processes. Similarly, a Supplier/Partner Interface Management subprocess is shared by these same processes.

If you are not a telecom executive, you might not be familiar with some of the terms used to describe the various subprocesses. The key thing is that this business process architecture illustrates a framework that is detailed enough that a telecom process architecture committee that was familiar with its own organization could be reasonably efficient in determining just which processes or subprocesses would need to be changed to achieve specific changes in company strategy and goals. One could easily imagine an accompanying document that provided short written descriptions of each of the subprocesses.

Figure 4.15 raises two issues that we will consider in more detail later in this book. First, it suggests the possibility of a matrix management system. Someone is usually responsible for complete processes like Fulfillment. That person thinks about how all the subprocesses in Fulfillment work together to deliver services to the customer in a smooth and efficient manner. Someone else is probably responsible for Service Management and Operations. The employees that work on the Service Configuration and Activation subprocess probably report to the Service Management and Operations manager. Thus, one manager works to assure that the complete process works efficiently. Another is responsible for employees that perform some of the subprocesses within the Fulfillment process, and within other processes as well.

The other issue that is obvious when we begin to discuss a framework like eTOM is how many times the word *process* appears. When the chart is as simple as the one in Figure 4.15, we can live with groups of processes, processes, and subprocesses. We have already seen how the ultimate process is a value chain. Most organizations only have a few value chains. We suspect that the entire eTOM framework really only pictures one value chain that delivers telecommunication services to customers.

Other Frameworks

We have hardly considered all the existing architecture frameworks available. The U.S. government has one and several government agencies have others. The insurance industry consortium, ACORD, is working on a framework for the insurance industry, and there are probably others we haven't heard of yet. The point, however, is that companies undertaking the development of a business process architecture are, today, in a position to greatly accelerate the process by beginning with one of the available frameworks and then tailoring it for their specific needs.

From Strategy Statements to a Process Architecture

We began with an overview of how one goes about developing a business process architecture. We saw that one could use a process description to organize the collection and alignment of data about the processes. Then we considered how an actual process architecture development team can use a process framework like SCOR, VRM, or eTOM to speed the architectural development process. The frameworks don't provide a management strategy, or suggest specific alignments, but they provide a systematic decomposition of the high-level processes and suggest performance measures that can be used for all of the processes in an architecture. One can use a framework to quickly fill out worksheets or populate a business process database and then tailor it and begin aligning resource information. Thus, in a very short time, a company can begin to benefit from the kind of analysis and project prioritization that one can derive from having an effective process architecture.

Notes and References

Once again, many of the ideas incorporated in the BPTrends methodology are derived from conversations Roger Burlton and I have had.

The organization diagram figures derive from figures originally developed by Geary Rummler.

The discussion of the Supply Chain Council's SCOR methodology and some of the figures came from the SCC's beginning workshop on SCOR or from other SCC publications. More information on the SCC is available from *www.supply-chain.org*.

A good general overview of the SCOR methodology is available on *www.bptrends. com*. Search: Harmon, *An Introduction to the Supply Chain Council's SCOR Methodology*, Jan. 2003.

Bolstorff, Peter and Robert Rosenbaum, *Supply Chain Excellence: A Handbook for Dramatic Improvement Using the SCOR Model,* AMACOM, 2003. A good book that presents a specific approach for implementing SCOR at a company.

I am particularly indebted to Joseph Francis for his comments and insights on SCOR and the evolution of SCOR+ at Hewlett-Packard. Joe was, for awhile, the BPM manager at HP and is currently the CTO of the Supply Chain Council. He also runs his own consulting company and helps companies with framework issues. See *www.pcor.com*.

For information on the VRM approach, check *www.value-chain.org*.

Information about the TeleManagement Forum and eTOM can be obtained from their Web site: *www.tmforum.com*. You can download publications from their site, including the specification for their eTOM framework.

TeleManagement Forum, *eTOM: The Business Process Framework: For the Information and Communications Services Industry*, Public Evaluation Version 2.5, December 2001, Document GB921. This document describes the current state of the eTOM specification and is available from the TeleManagement Forum Web site.

For a paper on how the eTOM framework is being used in conjunction with other frameworks, go to *www.bptrends.com* and search for: Huang, TMF White.

For information on ACORD's Insurance Framework, go to *www.acord.org*.

Proforma Corporation has a detailed version of the eTOM model, created in their ProVision Workbench tool that I studied before developing my own models. For more information, contact Proforma about their Telecommunications Industry Model at *www.proformacorp.com*.

chapter

5

Process Management

THIS CHAPTER focuses on how companies organize their managers to assure that the organization's processes are accomplished. In this chapter we will only focus on enterprise level management issues. We will begin by considering the nature of management and how companies structure their managers. Then we will consider how management processes might be represented in a company's business process architecture.

We introduced the BPTrends Enterprise Methodology in Chapter 3. In Chapter 4 we discussed a business process architecture and saw how the process hierarchy can be used to organize corporate information by, among other things, identifying the managers and measures associated with business processes. Logically, we might have discussed management and measurement right after discussing process levels and introducing the business process architecture worksheets. In fact, we put off discussing process management until this chapter so we would be able to discuss management issues in a more general way and place process management in a broader context. We will do the same with measurement in the next chapter. At the end of the next chapter, we will return to the architecture worksheets and see how management and measurement information can be recorded.

The division between the process architecture and management and measurement issues also reflects a practical consideration. Companies often consider the issues separately. Thus, companies that have not yet begun a process architecture may already have a Balanced Scorecard system which they use to evaluate managerial performance. Or a company may already have a performance evaluation system that is based on functional goals and only tangentially related to processes. Thus, it's usually easier to lay out the basic process hierarchy and align resources and get agreement on that in one step and then go back and add measurements and managerial responsibilities at a later time, and this is just what we do when we work with companies using the BPTrends Enterprise Methodology. (See Figure 5.1.)

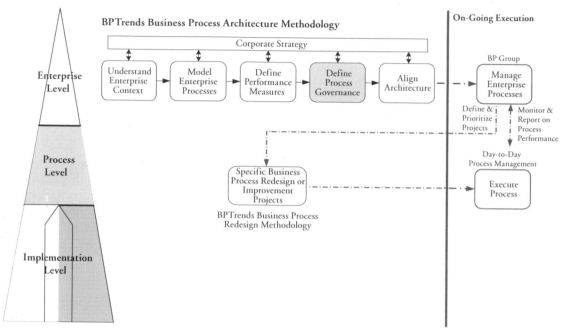

Figure 5.1 An overview of the BPTrends Enterprise Methodology.

We will first consider the general issues that companies need to address and then zero in on the specifics that companies need to define a business process architecture.

What Is Management?

Many books have been written about management. This book is about improving business processes, so we will consider how management can be organized to support effective business processes. Before we get into specifics, however, we need to start with some definitions. In the discussion that follows we are talking about roles and not about jobs or individuals. A single individual can fulfill more than one role. Thus, for example, one individual could perform two different managerial roles in two different situations—managing a functional department, but also serving as the manager of a special project team. Similarly, a job can be made up of multiple roles.

Broadly, there are two types of managerial roles: *operational management* and *project management*. Operational managers have ongoing responsibilities. Project managers are assigned to manage projects that are limited in time. Thus, a project manager might be asked to redesign the Widget process, or to conduct an audit of the company's bonus system. The head of a division, a department head, or the process manager in charge of the day-to-day performance of the Widget process all function as operational managers. In the rest of this chapter we will focus on operational management. We will consider project management when we consider what's involved in managing a business process change project.

Operational management can be subdivided in a number of ways. One distinction is between managers who are responsible for functional units, like Sales or Accounting, and managers who are responsible for processes, like the Widget process.

Functional or Unit Managers

Most companies are organized into functional units. Smaller companies tend to structure their organizations into departments. Larger organizations often divide their functional units into divisions and then divide the divisions into departments. The definition of a division varies from company to company. In some cases, a division is focused on the production of one product line or service line. In that case, the division manager can come very close to functioning as a process manager. In other cases, divisions represent geographical units, like the European division, which may represent only a part of a process, or even parts of multiple processes that happen to fall in that geographical area. At the same time, there are usually some enterprise-wide departments like IT or Finance. Thus, in a large company it is not uncommon to have a mix of divisional and departmental units.

Figure 5.2 illustrates a typical organization chart for a midsize company. The managers reporting to the CEO include both divisional managers (SVP Widget division) and departmental managers (CIO, CFO). Some of the departmental managers might be responsible for core processes, but it is more likely they are responsible for support processes.

An organization chart like the one illustrated in Figure 5.2 is designed to show which managers are responsible for what functions and to indicate reporting relationships. In Figure 5.2, it's clear that the Widget Manager of Production reports to the VP of Widget Manufacturing. This probably means that the VP of Widget

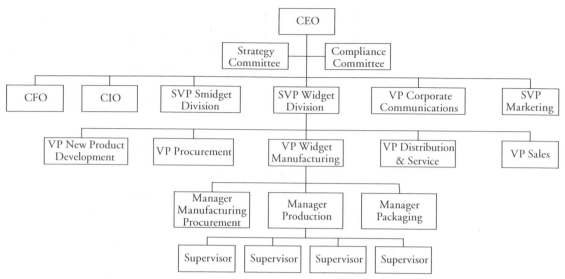

Figure 5.2 An organization chart describing the reporting relationships of unit managers.

Manufacturing sets the Manager of Production's salary, with some guidance from Human Resources, evaluates the manager's performance, approves his or her budget, and is the ultimate authority on policies or decisions related to Widget production.

In most organizations, midlevel functional managers wear two hats and serve as both a functional manager and a process manager. Consider the managers shown in Figure 5.3. In this simple example, a value chain is made up of a sales, manufacturing and a delivery process. Each of these processes is managed by an individual who works within a functional unit and reports to the head of the functional unit. Thus, the same manager—the sales supervisor, for example—is both the functional and the process manager of the Widget Sales process.

This situation shown in Figure 5.3 is very common. If problems arise they occur because functional units often defend their territory and resist cooperating with other functional units. What happens if the Manufacturing process doesn't get the sales information it needs to configure Widgets for shipment? Does the Manufacturing Supervisor work with the Sales Supervisor, as one process manager to another, to resolve the problem, or does the Manufacturing Supervisor "kick the problem upstairs" and complain to his or her superior? It's possible that the VPs of Sales, Manufacturing and Delivery all sit on a Widget process committee and meet regularly to sort out problems. It's more likely, unfortunately, that the VP of Sales manages sales activities

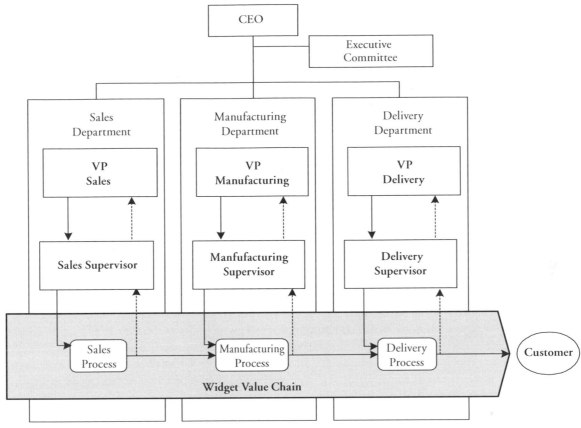

Figure 5.3 Functional managers who are also process managers.

in multiple value chains and is more concerned with sales issues than he or she is with Widget process issues. In the worst case, we have a situation in which the issue between the two Widget activities becomes a political issue that is fought out at the VP level with little consideration for the practical problems faced by the activity-level supervisors. This kind of silo thinking has lead many organizations to question the overreliance on functional organization structures.

Before considering shifting to an alternative approach, however, we need to be clear about the value of the functional approach. As a strong generalization, departmental managers are primarily concerned with standards and best practices that apply to their particular department or function. In most cases, a manager was hired to fulfill a junior position within a department—say Sales or Accounting—and has spent the last twenty years specializing in that functional area. He or she is a member of professional sales or accounting organizations, reads books on sales or accounting and attends conferences to discuss the latest practices in sales or accounting with peers from other companies. In other words, the individual has spent years mastering the details and best practices of sales or accounting by the time he or she is appointed a VP. Such an individual naturally feels that he or she should focus on what they know and not get involved in activities they have never focused on before. This type of specialization is a very valuable feature of the functional approach. Thus, for example, bookkeepers in an organization ought to follow accepted accounting practices. Moreover, they ought to follow the specific policies of the company with regard to credit, handling certain types of transactions, etc. The CFO is responsible to the CEO for assuring that appropriate standards and practices are followed. In a similar way, the head of sales follows standard practices in hiring and motivating the sales force. Moreover, the head of sales is well positioned to recognize that a Widget sales supervisor is due a promotion and conclude that she is ready to become the new sales supervisor of the Smidget sales process when the current guy retires. Functional management preserves valuable corporate knowledge and brings experience to the supervision of specialized tasks. Sometimes, however, it results in senior managers who are very territorial and prefer to focus on their special area of expertise while ignoring other areas.

Process Managers

Since we are primarily concerned with process management, we'll consider the role of a process manager in a little more detail. Figure 5.3 provides a very general overview of the role of a process manager. This model could easily be generalized to serve as a high-level description of the job of any operational manager. This model could describe the job of the Sales Supervisor in Figure 5.3, for example. We'll talk about it, however, to provide a description of the various managerial functions as they relate to a process. The key point to consider is that an organization is made up of processes and, for each process, there must be someone who is responsible for the day-to-day functioning of that process. At lower levels within an organization, the individual who is responsible might very well be a functional manager who is also wearing a process manager's hat. At higher levels in the organization, wearing two hats is harder, because value chains and even large processes like new product development and supply chain often cut across functional boundaries.

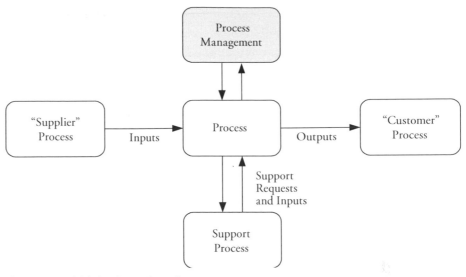

Figure 5.4 A high-level overview of process management.

Ignoring organizational issues for a moment, let's just consider what any process manager needs to accomplish. The process manager is responsible for what happens as the process is executed. He or she is also responsible for working with suppliers, customers and support processes to assure that the process he or she manages has the resources and support it needs to produce the product or service the process's customer wants. When one approaches process management in this way, it is often unclear whether one is talking about a role, a process or an individual. When you undertake specific process redesign projects, you will often find yourself analyzing whether or not a specific process manager is performing in a reasonable manner. Things the specific individual does or doesn't do may result in process inefficiencies. When you focus on organization charts and managerial responsibilities, you are usually focused on the role and seek to define who a specific manager would report to, without concerning yourself with the specific individual who might perform the role. Finally, when you focus on the competencies that a process manager should have to function effectively, you are focusing on the managerial processes that successful individuals need to master if they are to perform the role effectively.

In Figure 5.5 we have expanded the Process Management box from Figure 5.4, and inserted some typical managerial processes. Different managerial theorists would divide or clump the activities that we have placed in the four managerial processes in different ways. Our particular approach is simply one alternative. We divide the process management process into four generic subprocesses: one that plans, schedules and budgets the work of the process, one that organizes the workflow of the process, arranges for needed resources and defines jobs and success criteria; one that communicates with employees and others about the process; and one that monitors the work and takes action to assure that the work meets established quality criteria. We have added a few arrows to suggest some of the main relations between the four management processes just described and the elements of the process that is being managed.

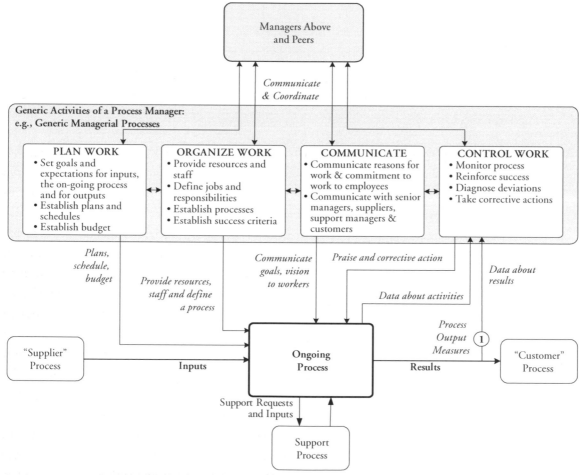

Figure 5.5 An overview of the generic process management processes and subprocesses.

Most process managers are assigned to manage an existing process that is already organized and functioning. Thus, their assignment does not require them to organize the process from scratch, but, if they are wise, they will immediately check the process to assure that it is well organized and functioning smoothly. Similarly, if they inherit the process, they will probably also inherit the quality and output measures established by their predecessor. If the new manager is smart, he or she will reexamine all of the assumptions to assure that the process is, in fact, well organized, functioning smoothly, and generating the expected outcomes. If there is room for improvement, the new manager should make a plan to improve the process. Once satisfied with the process, the manager has some managerial activities that need to be performed on a day-to-day basis and others that need to be performed on a weekly, monthly or quarterly basis. And then, of course, there are all the specific tasks that occur when one has to deal with the problems involved in hiring a new employee, firing an incompetent employee, and so forth.

We'll consider the specific activities involved in process management in a later chapter when we consider how one approaches the analysis of process problems. At the enterprise level, we will be more concerned with how companies establish process managers, how process managers relate to unit or functional managers, and how processes and process managers are evaluated.

Process managers, especially at the enterprise level, have a responsibility to see that all of the processes in the organization work together to assure that the value chain functions as efficiently as possible. While a functional manager would prefer to have all of the processes within his or her department operate as efficiently as possible, a process manager is more concerned that all the processes in the value chain work well together, and would, in some cases, allow the processes within one functional area to function in a suboptimal way to assure that the value chain functions more efficiently. Thus, for example, there is a trade-off between an efficient inventory system and a store that has in stock anything the customer might request. To keep inventory costs down, the inventory manager wants to minimize inventory. If that's done, then it follows that customers are occasionally be disappointed when they ask for specific items. There is no technical way to resolve this conflict. It comes down to the strategy the company is pursuing. If the company is going to be the low-cost seller, they have to keep their inventory costs down. If, on the other hand, the company wants to position itself as the place to come when you want it now, they will have to charge a premium price and accept higher inventory costs. The process manager needs to understand the strategy the company is pursuing and then control the processes in the value chain to assure the desired result. In most cases, this will involve sub-optimizing some departmental processes to make others perform as desired. This sets up a natural conflict between functional and process managers and can create problems when one manager tries to perform both roles.

If we had to choose the one thing that distinguishes a process manager from a functional manager, it would be the process manager's concern for the way his or her process fits with other processes and contributes to the overall efficiency of the value chain. This is especially marked by the process manager's concern with the inputs to his or her process and with assuring that the outputs of his or her process are what the downstream or "customer" process needs.

Functional or Process Management?

As we have already seen, at lower levels in the organization, it's quite common for a single manager to function as both a unit and a process manager. At higher levels, however, it becomes harder to combine the two roles. Thus, when an organization considers its overall management organizational structure, the organization often debates the relative advantages of an emphasis on functional or process management. Figure 5.6 illustrates a simple organization that has two value chains, one that produces and sells Widgets and another that sells a totally different type of product, Smidgets. This makes it easy to see how the concerns of functional managers differ from process managers. The head of the sales department is interested in maintaining a sales organization. He or she hires salespeople according to sales criteria, trains sales people, and evaluates them. Broadly, from the perspective of the head of sales, selling Widgets and selling Smidgets is the same process, and he wants to be sure that the selling process is implemented as efficiently as possible. The VP for the Widget process, on the other hand, is concerned with the entire Widget value chain and is primarily concerned that the Widget sales and service processes work together smoothly to provide value to Widget customers. The Widget process manager would be happy to change the way the sales process functions if it would, in conjunction with the other Widget processes, combine to provide better service to Widget customers.

Thus, although it's possible for one individual to serve as both a unit and a process manager, it's a strain. Without some outside support from someone who emphasizes process, it's almost impossible.

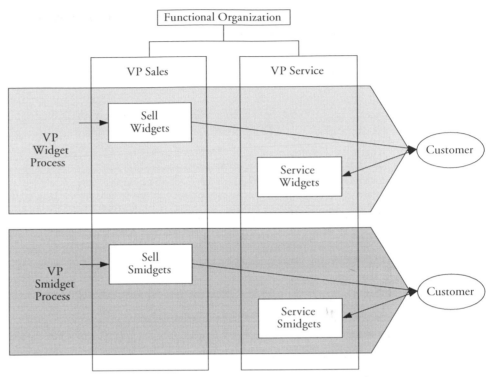

Figure 5.6 The different concerns of functional and process managers.

Matrix Management

Having defined functional and process management, let's consider how an organization might combine the strengths of the two approaches at the top of the organization. Recently, leading organizations have begun to establish some kind of process management hierarchy that, at least at the upper level, is independent of the organization's functional hierarchy. The top position in a process hierarchy is a manager who is responsible for an entire value chain. Depending on the complexity of the organization, the value chain manager might have other process managers reporting to him or her. This approach typically results in a matrix organization like the one pictured in Figure 5.7.

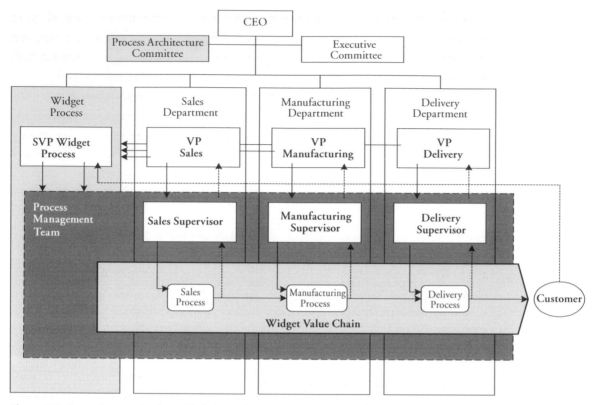

Figure 5.7 A matrix organization with independent senior functional and process managers.

In Figure 5.7 we show a company like the one pictured earlier with three functional units. In this case, however, another senior manager has been added and this individual is responsible for the success of the Widget value chain. Different organizations allocate authority in different ways. For example, the Widget process manager may only function in an advisory capacity. In this case, he or she would convene meetings to discuss the flow of the Widget value chain. In such a situation the sales supervisor would still owe his or her primary allegiance to the VP of sales and that individual would still be responsible for paying, evaluating and promoting the sales supervisor. The key to making this approach work is to think of the management of the Widget value chain as a team effort. In effect, each supervisor with management responsibility for a process that falls inside the Widget value chain is a member of the Widget value chain management team.

Other companies give the Widget value chain manager more responsibility. In that case, the sales supervisor might report to both the Widget value chain manager and to the VP of sales. Each senior manager might contribute to the sales supervisor's evaluations and each might contribute to the individual's bonus, and so forth.

Figure 5.8 provides a continuum that is modified from one developed by the Project Management Institute (PMI). PMI proposed this continuum to contrast organizations that focused on functional structures and those that emphasized projects. We use it to compare functional and process organizations. In either case, the area between the extremes describes the type of matrix organization the company has instituted.

Figure 5.8 Types of organizational structure (modified from the Project Management Institute's classification of five organization types).

The type of matrix an organization has is determined by examining the authority and the resources that senior management allocates to specific managers. For example, in a weak matrix organization, functional managers might actually "own" the employees, have full control over all budgets and employee incentives, and deal with all support organizations. In this situation the process manager would be little more than the team leader of a team that gets together to talk about problems and would try to resolve problems by means of persuasion.

In the opposite extreme, the process manager might "own" the employees and control their salaries and incentives. In the middle, which is more typical, the departmental head would "own" the employees and have a budget for them. The process manager might have control of the budget for support processes, like IT, and have money to provide incentives for employees. In this case, employee evaluations would be undertaken by both the departmental and the project manager, each using their own criteria.

Most organizations seem to be trying to establish a position in the middle of the continuum. They keep the functional or departmental units in order to oversee professional standards within disciplines, and to manage personnel matters. Thus, the

VP of sales is probably responsible for hiring the sales supervisor shown in Figure 5.7 and for evaluating his or her performance and assigning raises and bonuses. The VP of sales is responsible for maintaining high sales standards within the organization. On the other hand, the ultimate evaluation of the sales supervisor comes from the SVP of the widget process. The sales supervisor is responsible for achieving results from the widget sales process and that is the ultimate basis for his or her evaluation. In a sense, the heads of departments meet with the SVP of the widget process and form a high-level process management team.

The Management of Outsourced Processes

The organization of managers is being complicated in many companies by outsourcing. Reconsider Figure 3.6 in which we described how Dell divides its core processes from those it outsources. Dell currently designs new computers that can be manufactured by readily available components. It markets its computers in a variety of ways and sells them by means of a Web site that lets users configure their own specific models. Once a customer has placed an order, Dell transfers the information to an outsourcer in Asia. The components, created by still other outsourcers, are available in a warehouse, owned and operated by the outsourcer, and the computers are assembled and then delivered by the outsourcer. If, after deliver, the computer needs repairs, it is picked up by an outsourced delivery service and repaired in a warehouse operated by the outsourcer, then returned to the owner.

Leaving aside the issues involved in describing a value chain that are raised when a company outsources what have traditionally been considered core processes—Dell, after all, is usually classified as a computer equipment manufacturer—consider the management issues raised by this model. Dell isn't doing the manufacturing or the distribution. The outsourcer is managing both those processes and presumably has its own management organization. On the other hand, Dell certainly needs to indirectly manage those processes, since its overall success depends on providing a customer with a computer within 2–3 days of taking the customer's order. In effect, Dell does not need to manage the traditional functional aspects of its PC/Desktop manufacturing process, but it does need to manage the process, as a whole. This situation, and many variations on this theme, is driving the transition to more robust process management.

Value Chains and Process Standardization

One other trend in process management needs to be considered. When we discussed the types of alignment that companies might seek to document, we mentioned that the identification of standard processes was a popular goal. In effect, if a company is doing the same activity in many different locations, it should consider doing them in the same way. A trivial example would be obtaining a credit card approval. This occurs when a customer submits a credit card and the salesperson proceeds to swipe it through a "reader" and then waits for approval and a sales slip to be printed. The flow we described depends on software that transmits information about the credit card to the credit card approval agency and returns the information needed to generate the sales slip. Doing this process in a standard way reduces employee training, simplifies reporting requirements, and makes it easier to move employees between different operations, all things that make the company more agile and efficient. Doing it with the same software reduces the need to develop or buy new software. If a packaged software (ERP) application is used, then a standardized process reduces the cost of updating the ERP module and assures that the same ERP module can be used everywhere credit card approval is undertaken.

Many companies installed ERP applications without first standardizing processes. This resulted in ERP modules that were tailored in different ways to support different specific processes. When the basic ERP module is updated, this means that the new module has to be tailored, again, for each different specific process that it supports. If all the processes are standardized, this will greatly reduce the cost of developing and maintaining the organization's ERP applications. Thus, several large companies have launched programs designed to identify and standardize processes throughout the organizations.

Most companies, when they set about standardizing their processes, structure the effort by establishing a process management organizational structure. Thus, they create a matrix organization and assign individuals to manage "standard process areas." These individuals (process managers) are then asked to look across all the departments in the firm and identify all the places where activities are undertaken that might be standardized. Figure 5.9 shows the matrix developed in the course of one such effort.

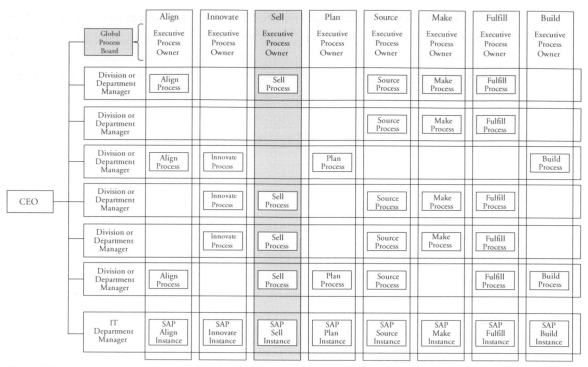

Figure 5.9 A matrix organization.

	Align	Innovate	Sell	Plan	Source	Make	Fulfill	Build
Global Process Board	Executive Process Owner	Executive Process Owner	Executive Process Owner	Executive Process Owner	Executive Process Owner	Executive Process Owner	Executive Process Owner	Executive Process Owner
Division or Department Manager	Align Process		Sell Process		Source Process	Make Process	Fulfill Process	
Division or Department Manager					Source Process	Make Process	Fulfill Process	
Division or Department Manager	Align Process	Innovate Process		Plan Process				Build Process
Division or Department Manager		Innovate Process	Sell Process		Source Process	Make Process	Fulfill Process	
Division or Department Manager		Innovate Process	Sell Process		Source Process	Make Process	Fulfill Process	
Division or Department Manager	Align Process		Sell Process	Plan Process	Source Process		Fulfill Process	Build Process
IT Department Manager	SAP Align Instance	SAP Innovate Instance	SAP Sell Instance	SAP Plan Instance	SAP Source Instance	SAP Make Instance	SAP Fulfill Instance	SAP Build Instance

(CEO is shown at the left, connected to the Global Process Board and the seven Division or Department Managers and the IT Department Manager.)

In Figure 5.9 we have turned the traditional functional organization on its side, so that the company's divisions and departments run from left to right. Across the top we picture the process managers and show how their concerns cut across all the divisions and departments. At first glance, this might seem like a matrix organization that organizes around functional units and processes. Consider, however, that the company has more than one value chain. One division sells commodity items to hospitals while another builds refinery plants, which it then sells to other organizations. These activities are so different that they have to be separate value chains. If we are to follow Porter and Rummler, we will seek to integrate all the processes within a single value chain around a single strategy to assure that the value chain, as a whole, is as efficient as possible. To achieve this, the ultimate process manager is the manager responsible for the entire value chain. In the example shown in Figure 5.10, the division manager responsible for the Customer Refinery Engineering division is better positioned to pursue that goal than the Sales Process manager. Similarly, the division manager responsible for Hospital Products is better positioned to optimize the Hospital Product value chain than the Sales Process manager.

The Sales Process manager in Figure 5.9 is well positioned to examine all of the sales processes in all the divisions and departments and find common processes. The company's goal in creating this matrix was to standardize their ERP applications. If the "process manager" is careful and focuses on lower-level processes, like credit card approval, then he or she will probably be able to identify several processes that can be usefully standardized. On the other hand, if the "sales process manager" seeks to standardize the overall sales processes, he or she runs the risk of suboptimizing all of the value chains. It's to avoid this situation that we recommend beginning by identifying the organization's value chains and then organizing process work around specific value chains. We certainly understand the value in identifying standard processes that can be automated by standard software modules, but it is an effort that needs to be subordinated to the goal of optimizing and integrating the organization's value chains. Otherwise this becomes an exercise in what Porter terms operational effectiveness—a variation on the best practices approach—that seeks to improve specific activities without worrying about how they fit together with other activities to create a value chain that will give the company a long-term competitive advantage.

Setting Goals and Establishing Rewards for Managers

Managers, like everyone else, need to have goals to focus their efforts. Moreover, in business situations, predictably, managers will try to accomplish the goals they are rewarded for achieving. Rewards can take many forms: being told that you did a good job, getting a raise, knowing you are likely to get promoted, or receiving a significant bonus. The key point, however, is that a well-run organization sets clear goals for its managers and rewards effective performance. If the goals aren't clear, or if a given manager is asked to simultaneously pursue multiple, conflicting goals then suboptimal performance will invariably result. In examining defective processes, it is common to find that the manager is being rewarded for activities that are detrimental to the success of the process. This sounds absurd, but it is so common that experienced process analysts always check for it.

Does the organization really want more sales, and motivate the sales manager in every way it can? Or does it want sales reports turned in on time, and reward the sales manager who always gets his or her reports in on time while criticizing the sales manager who achieves more sales for failing to submit the reports? We remember working on a call center process where the management wanted the agents to try to cross-sell hotel stays to people who called to ask about airline flights. One group worried that, in spite of training and posters in the call center, few hotel stays were being sold. A closer examination showed that the call center supervisor was rewarded for keeping the number of operators at a minimum. That was achieved by keeping each phone call at a minimum. The time operators talked to customers was carefully recorded and operators that handled more calls in any given period were rewarded and praised. Those who spent more time on their calls—trying to sell hotel stays, for example—were criticized. There were no compensating rewards for selling hotel stays so, predictably, no hotel stays were being sold.

When we consider the analysis of specific processes, we will see that it is important to carefully analyze each manager's goals and motivation. If a process is to succeed, then we need to be sure the manager's goals and rewards are in line with the goals of the process. Thus, just as it is important to have a management system that focuses on integrating and managing processes, it is important to see that there is a system for aligning the goals and rewards of specific managers with the goals of the processes that they manage. We'll consider performance measurement and then return to a discussion of how an organization can align measurement and manager evaluation.

Management Processes

A company could analyze each manager's work from scratch, using our generic management model. Increasingly, however, companies find it more efficient to rely on one or more generic models that help analysts identify the specific management processes that effective process managers need to master. Let's quickly review some of the frameworks and maturity models that are currently popular. We'll start with the Project Management Institute's (PMI) Project Management Maturity Model and then consider the Software Engineering Institute's (SEI) CMMI model, the Supply Chain Council's (SCC) SCOR business framework, and the IT Governance Institute's (ITGI) COBIT framework.

The PMI Project Management Maturity Model

PMI distinguishes between operations management (ongoing) and project management (done in a limited timeframe). They describe a body of knowledge about project management (PMBOK) and an Organizational Project Management Maturity Model

(OPM3) that organizations can use to (1) evaluate their current sophistication in managing projects and then to (2) use as a methodology for introducing more sophisticated project management skills. In their PMBOK and in the OPM3, they assume that there are five management processes that every project manager must learn. They include: (1) initiating, (2) planning, (3) executing, (4) monitoring and controlling, and (5) closing. Figure 5.10 suggests how the skills involved in each of these processes map to our general overview of management.

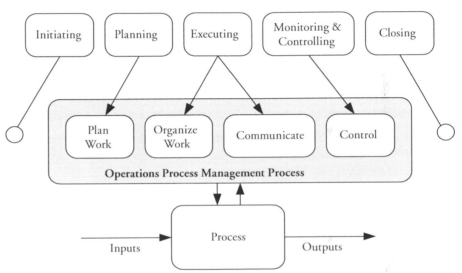

Figure 5.10 How PMI's management processes map to the BPTrends process management model.

Our general model pictures an operational management role and describes the activities that a process manager must perform. Project extends that by adding a process for defining the nature of the specific project to be managed (Initiating) and another that critiques the project and pulls together things that were learned in the course of the project (Closing).

The SEI's CMMI Model

The best known of all maturity models is the Software Engineering Institute's Capability Maturity Model Integrated (CMMI), which we discussed in some detail in the Introduction. Although CMM was originally developed to evaluate IT departments, the extended version, CMMI, is designed to help companies evaluate and improve any type of business process. CMMI supports two ways of organizing your effort. You can either analyze the capabilities of a given department or group of practitioners or you can focus on the overall maturity of an organization. The first, which focuses on Capability Levels, looks to see what skills are present and then focuses on teaching managers or process practitioners the skills that are missing. The second, which focuses on Maturity Levels, assumes that organizations become more process savvy in a systematic, staged manner and focuses on identifying the state the organization is at now and then providing the skills the organization needs to move to the next higher stage. Obviously, if you focus on organizational maturity, then CMMI functions as an enterprise process improvement methodology that provides a prescription for a sequence of process training courses designed to provide process managers with the skills they need to manage their process more effectively. If you focus on the individual work unit and emphasize capabilities, then CMMI provides a set of criteria to use to evaluate how sophisticated specific process managers are and to determine what management processes they need to master to more effectively manage the specific process you are trying to improve.

No matter which approach you use, once the basic evaluation is complete, the focus is on either the management processes that need to be acquired by the organization's managers or on the activities needed by individuals who are responsible for improving the organization's existing processes..

Although CMMI doesn't place as much emphasis on types of management as we might, one way they organize their processes is based on the type of manager who will need to master the process. Thus, they define some management processes for operations managers (which they term process management), a second set of processes for project managers, and a third set for engineering and support managers who manage enabling or support processes. Figure 5.11 shows how CMMI would define the various management processes and shows at what organizational maturity level company managers would normally require the ability to use those processes. It will help to understand the CMMI classification if you keep in mind that day-to-day operational managers need to manage routine improvements in processes, but that major changes are undertaken as projects, and that a BPM group that maintained an architecture or provided Black Belts to a specific project effort would be a support group. Put a different way, CMMI's focus is on improving processes, but their major assumption is that processes are improved as they are defined, executed consistently, measured and, as a result of measurement, systematically improved. Ultimately, putting these elements in place and executing them on a day-to-day basis is the responsibility of the individual who is managing the process.

Process Areas That Support CMMI Maturity Levels	Four Management Areas Defined by CMMI			
	Project Management Project Mang.	Process Management Operations Mang.	Engineering Support Proc. Mang.	Support Support Proc. Mang.
Level 5. Optimizing *Focus on process improvement.*		OID-Organizational Innovation & Deployment		CAR-Causal Analysis & Resolution
Level 4. Managed *Process measured and controlled.*	QPM-Quantitative Project Management	OPP-Organizational Process Performance		
Level 3. Defined *Process characterized for the organization and is proactive.*	RSKM-Risk Management IPPD-Integrated Project Management	OT-Organizational Training OPF-Organizational Process Focus OPD-Organizational Process Definition	VAL-Validation VER-Verification PI-Product Integration TS-Technical Solution RD-Requirements Development	DAR-Decision Analysis & Resolution
Level 2. Repeatable *Process characterized for projects and is often reactive.*	SAM-Supplier Agreement Management PMC-Project Monitoring & Control PP-Project Planning		RM-Requirements Management	MA-Measurement & Analysis PPQA-Process & Product Quality Assurance CM-Configuration Management
Level 1. Initial *Processes unpredictable, poorly controlled, and reactive.*				
	Project Management	Process Management	Engineering	Support

Figure 5.11 CMMI's management processes, arranged by management type and by organizational maturity levels.

Here are the definitions that CMMI provides for its process management "process areas."

▶ *OPD—Organizational Process Definitions process.* Establish and maintain a usable set of organization process assets and work environment standards.

▶ *OPF—Organizational Process Focus process.* Plan, implement, and deploy organizational process improvements based on a thorough understanding of the current strengths and weaknesses of the organization's processes and process assets.

▶ *OT—Organizational Training process.* Provide employees with the skills and knowledge needed to perform their roles effectively and efficiently. It includes: identifying the training needed by the organization, obtaining and providing training to address those needs, establishing and maintaining training capability, establishing and maintaining training records, and assessing training effectiveness.

▶ *OPP—Organizational Process Performance process.* Establish and maintain quantitative understanding of the performance of the organization's set of standard processes in support of quality and process-performance objectives, and to provide the process-performance data, baselines and models to quantitatively manage the organization's projects.

▶ *OID—Organizational Innovation and Deployment process.* Select and deploy incremental and innovative improvements that measurably improve the organization's processes and technologies.

If we were to map this particular subset of operational management processes to our general management model, it would look something like what we picture in Figure 5.12. We placed numbers in front of the processes to suggest that at maturity level 3 a manager would be expected to have the capabilities identified as (3). As the individual or organization matured and reached level 4, you would assume the manager had mastered the (4) processes and at level 5 he or she would have mastered the (5) processes.

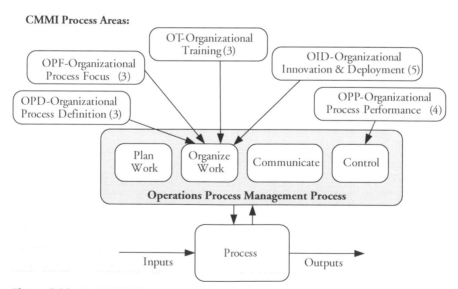

Figure 5.12 How CMMI's management processes map to the BPTrends Process Management Model.

As this book is being completed, the Object Management Group is considering adopting a standard Business Process Maturity Model (BPMM), which is a variation on the CMMI approach.

The SCC's SCOR Framework

The Supply Chain Council is primarily focused on defining the core processes that make up a supply chain system. At the same time, however, they have a generic process called Plan. For each supply chain process, like Source, Make, Deliver, or Return, they require the modeler to add a Plan process. In fact they require a hierarchy of Plan processes, in effect creating a picture of the process management effort required for a supply chain process. Figure 5.13 shows how SCOR analysts would model a simple supply chain. To simplify things, we only show Plan processes for the top row of processes. Within Alpha there are two departments, which are separated by the dashed line. Within each department there are Source, Make and Deliver processes. There is one Plan process for each. In addition, there is one Plan process for all of the Plan Source, Plan Make and Plan Deliver processes within a given department.

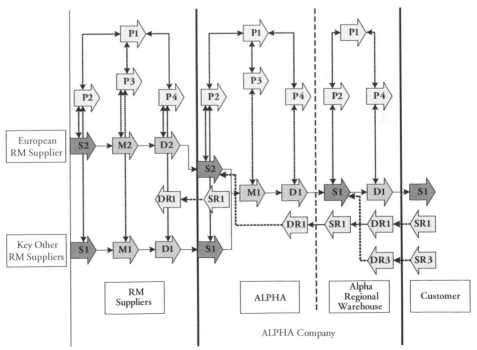

Figure 5.13 A SCOR thread diagram showing the operational and management processes in a supply chain.

The SCC defines four subprocesses for their Plan process, which vary slightly, depending on the core process they are supporting. The Plan Make subprocesses include:

▶ PM1. Identify, Prioritize and Aggregate Production Requirements
▶ PM2. Identify, Assess and Assign Production Resources
▶ PM3. Balance Product Resources and Requirements
▶ PM4. Establish Production Plans

Although they don't picture the processes on their thread diagrams, the SCC's SCOR framework also defines an Enable process and then defines Enable subprocesses. Here are the eight Enable Make subprocesses:

▶ EM1 Manage Production Rules
▶ EM2 Manage Production Performance
▶ EM3 Manage Production Data
▶ EM4 Manage In-Process Production Inventory
▶ EM5 Manage Equipment and Facilities
▶ EM6 Manage Make Transportation
▶ EM7 Manage Production Network
▶ EM8 Manage Production Regulatory Compliance

The subprocess list reflects the more specialized role of the supply chain manager. In addition, while a lower-level Make process manager might not be concerned with some of these subprocesses, higher-level supply chain managers would and this reflects the fact that SCOR describes not only the work of the immediate managers of a process but also considers the work that the manager's boss will need to do.

The SCC decided to focus on management processes that are more knowledge intensive and thus didn't include things like assigning people to tasks, monitoring output or providing employees with feedback. An overview of how the SCOR management processes map to our general model is presented in Figure 5.14.

Although we haven't tried to show it in Figure 5.14, the SCOR management processes are a little subtler, since the SCOR developers knew exactly what core process each set of Plan and Enable processes would end up supporting. Thus, we might have tried to show how specific SCOR Plan and Enable subprocesses, in fact, support the planning for inputs to Make or seek to manage the relationship between Make and support processes.

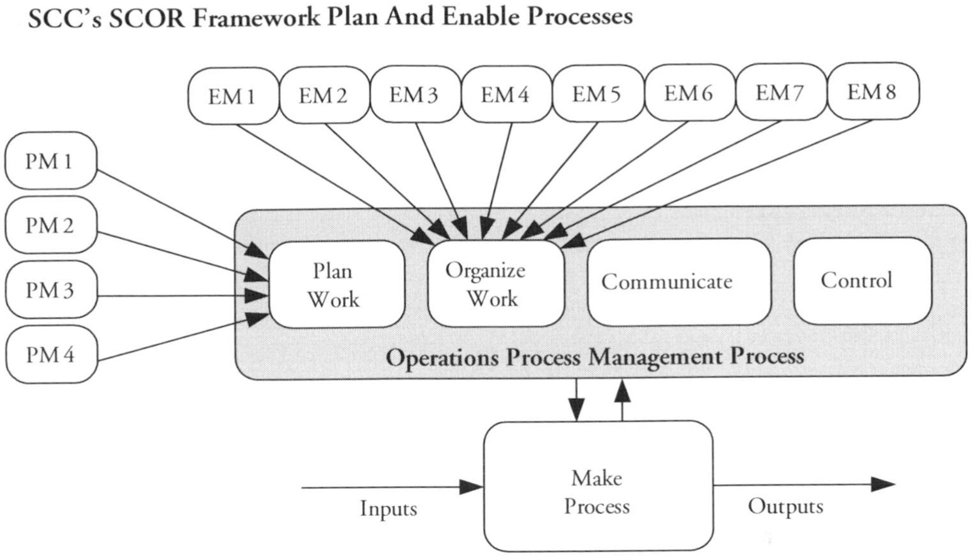

SCC's SCOR Framework Plan And Enable Processes

Figure 5.14 How the SCOR Plan and Enable management processes for the Make process map to the BPTrends Process Management Model.

The ITGI's COBIT Framework

The IT Governance Institute (ITGI) developed their process framework to organize the management of IT processes. Their high level IT management processes map easily to our general management model. (See Figure 5.15.)

The ITGI has defined subprocesses for each of their processes and the subprocesses also reflect our general model. Thus, for example, the ITGI subprocesses for Plan and Organize (PO) include:

▶ PO1 Define a Strategic IT Plan
▶ PO2 Define an IT Architecture
▶ PO3 Define Technical Direction
▶ PO4 Define IT Processes, Organization and Relationships
▶ PO5 Manage IT Investment
▶ PO6 Communicate Management Aims and Directions
▶ PO7 Manage IT Human Resources
▶ PO8 Manage Quality
▶ PO9 Manage Projects

ITGI's COBIT Framework

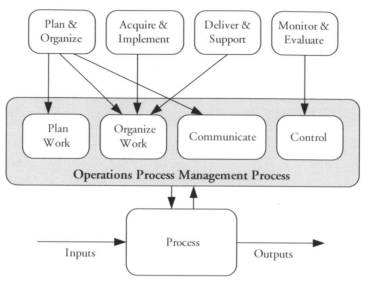

Figure 5.15 How ITIG's COBIT management processes map to the BPTrends Process Management Model.

As we look at the subprocesses we realize that the COBIT management processes are more appropriate for a CIO or a senior IT manager and not for the manager of the Maintain ERP Applications, let alone the manager of the process to Maintain ERP for Accounting.

On the other hand, a review of the COBIT documentation shows that COBIT not only defines high-level IT management processes, but defines goals for the IT organization as a whole, and then shows how different IT management processes can be linked to IT goals and proceeds to define metrics for each management process.

We have not gone into any of the various process management frameworks in any detail. For our purposes, it suffices that readers should know that lots of different groups are working to define the processes that managers use when they manage specific processes. Some groups have focused on the activities, skills and processes that a manager would need to manage an ongoing process, and others have focused on the activities, skills and processes a manager would need to manage a project. Some have focused on the activities of senior process managers and others have focused on managers who are responsible for very specific core processes. As we suggested earlier, defining process management is hard. Different people have pursued alternative approaches. Some simply diagnose what specific managers are doing wrong as they look for ways to improve the performance of a defective process. Others focus on the actual processes and activities that effective managers need to master to plan, organize, communicate and monitor and control the process they are responsible for managing. Organizations that focus on managerial processes usually tend to establish process management training programs to help their managers acquire the skills they need to perform better.

Documenting Management Processes in an Architecture

Most organizations do not document management process in their formal business process architecture. If you think of every operational process as always having an associated management process, then it seems unnecessary to document the management processes. If the day-to-day management processes are documented, they are usually documented as generic, standard processes that it is assumed every manager will use. If this is the company approach, then using one of the frameworks described as a source of information and definitions is a reasonable way to proceed. Most organizations identify high-level management processes that are independent of any specific value chain, and document them independently. Thus, an organization might document the strategy formulation process or the processes of a business process management support group. Others treat these specialized processes as support processes and document them in the same way they document other support processes. However your company decides to approach documentation, the management processes describe sets of activities that process managers ought to master, and thus they should provide a good basis for a process manager training program.

Completing the Business Process Architecture Worksheet

Recall that the Level 1 Architecture Analysis worksheet provides a space at the top for the name of the manager of the value chain (see Figure 4.2). Then, below, you were asked to enter each Level 1 process, and identify the manager for each of the Level 1 processes. Then you were asked to complete a worksheet for each Level 1 process on which you listed the Level 2 processes that make up the Level 1 process, and you were asked to identify the managers responsible for each Level 2 process. In our experience, most companies can identify the managers of their Level 2 or Level 3 processes without too much trouble. They have problems with identifying the managers responsible for the value chains and for the Level 1 processes. If you recall our sales supervisor in Figure 5.7, that individual was both a unit manager and a process manager, and he or she would be easy to identify in most organizations. It's the process manager who is responsible for processes that cross the traditional boundaries that are harder to identify. In many cases, they don't exist. Yet they are the only managers who can assure that your organization's large-scale processes work as they should. They are the managers who focus on integrating the entire value chain and aligning the value chain with your organization's strategy. They are the managers who are really focused on the value chain's external measures and satisfying the customer. Most organizations are just beginning to sort through how they will manage processes at the higher levels of the organization, yet it is at these levels that huge gains are to be made and that competitive advantage is to be achieved. Ultimately, this is the work of the senior executives of your organization. If they believe in process, then this is a challenge they must address.

Notes and References

Once again, many of the ideas incorporated in the BPTrends methodology are derived from conversations Roger Burlton and I have had. And most of my ideas on the relationship between process managers and processes derive from even earlier conversations with Geary Rummler.

There are so many ways of classifying the basic tasks a manager must perform. I worked for awhile for Louis Allen and became very familiar with his system. I've certainly studied Drucker, and my personal favorite is Mintzberg. And, of course, I've studied Geary Rummler's papers on process management. They all segment the tasks slightly differently, but the key point is that managers undertake activities to facilitate and control the work of others.

Drucker, Peter F., *Management: Tasks, Responsibilities, Practices,* Collins, 1993.

Allen, Louis A., *Principles of Professional Management,* Louis Allen Associates (2nd), 1978. In the mid-1970s I worked briefly for Louis A. Allen, a then-popular management consultant. As far as I know, his books are no longer in print, but he introduced me to the idea that managers must plan, organize, lead, and control. I've simplified that in this chapter to planning and controlling.

Mintzberg, Henry, *The Nature of Managerial Work,* Prentice Hall, 1973.

A lot of companies tried matrix management in the 1970s and found it too difficult to coordinate, and dropped it. Most companies are doing it today—individual managers are reporting to more than one boss— but no one seems to want to call it matrix management. But there doesn't seem to be any other popular name for the practice, so I've termed it matrix management.

The Project Management Institute (PMI) has developed an excellent framework for project management. We rely on them for their description of organizational structure, which they suggest ranges from functional to project management, with stages of matrix management in between. And we also discuss their PMI Management Maturity Model. For more information, check their Web site: *www.pmi.org.* The best book for a general description of their maturity model is:

Bolles, Dennis L. and Darrel G. Hubbard, *The Power of Enterprise-Wide Project Management,* AMACOM, 2007.

Ahern, Dennis M., Aaron Clouse, and Richard Turner, *CMMI Distilled (2nd Ed.): A Practical Introduction to Integrated Process Improvement,* Addison-Wesley, 2004. The best general introduction to CMMI management processes. For more information on CMMI, visit *www.sei.cmu.edu.*

Information about how the Supply Chain Council's SCOR defines Plan and Enable processes is available from *www.supply-chain.org.*

Information about IT Governance Institute's COBIT framework is available from *www.itgi.org.*

Other business process theorists have also focused on improving the management of processes:

Champy, James, *Reengineering Management,* HarperBusiness, 1995. As with the original reengineering book, this is more about why you should do it than how to do it.

Hammer, Michael, *Beyond Reengineering: How the Process-Centered Organization Is Changing Our Work and Our Lives,* HarperBusiness, 1997. Similar to the Champy book. Lots of inspiring stories.

Spanyi, Andrew, *More for Less: The Power of Process Management*, Meghan-Kiffer, 2006. This is a good, up-to-date discussion of the issues involved in managing processes from an enterprise perspective.

Information on the Chevron process management improvement effort is documented in a white paper: "Strategic Planning Helps Chevron's E&P Optimize Its Assets," which is available from the Pritchett Web site: *www.pritchettnet.com/COmp/PI/CaseStudies/chevroncase.htm.*

6

Measuring Process Performance

THIS CHAPTER FOCUSES on process performance measurement. Every organization keeps track of its performance. Some have very elaborate performance measurement systems that allow them to determine what is taking place in real time, while most track a wide variety of measures and review them at the end of each week or month. It is widely held that performance information is a key differentiator and that organizations that can obtain and use information about their markets and their processes in a timely manner can perform better. Thus, it is not surprising that companies are investing large amounts of money in developing new and more elaborate performance monitoring systems.

Historically, there was a rather large disconnect between what executives were concerned with and what operational managers focused on. As a generalization, executives were interested in financial reports and in the performance of the company's stock. Everyone agrees that these are key performance indicators, but problems arise when the organization tries to translate these measures into more concrete measures that can be applied to marketing, manufacturing or accounting. Functional units were established, historically, because they represent logical ways to divide the work and manage the specialized skills that companies need to accomplish their goals. There is no clear relationship, however, between the departmental units that exist in most companies and the outcomes and measures that most executives track most carefully. This is one reason for the shift to divisional and product line managers and for installing process managers who are responsible for entire value chains. When one looks at an entire product line or a complete value chain, one is in a much better position to see how changes in the work result in increased or decreased costs or sales.

What Is Measurement?

We'll start with a few definitions of popular measurement terms, and then proceed to a discussion of how processes can be measured.

Goals, Metrics, Measures and KPIs

Most companies begin their strategy work with a vision statement. Then they write a more detailed document that describes their strategy. This statement is still pretty general. Next, most organizations translate their strategy statement into a number of goals. The goals define specific things the company will have to do to realize its strategy. These strategic goals are often called critical success factors. Thus, for example, the strategy may call for market growth. A specific goal may call for a 15% increase in sales in the fiscal coming year. Once an organization has its strategic goals, it needs to create a hierarchy of more specific goals. These specific goals are usually called metrics or measures. (We will use the two terms as synonyms.) Thus, our general goal—a 15% increase in sales—might get passed on to the head of the Widget Division sales team, and be restated: The Widget sales team will increase the sale of Widgets by 15% in the coming fiscal year.

We have already mentioned the fact that there is often a problem translating strategic goals into functional goals. A 15% increase in sales is a relatively easy goal to align, but it still requires some thought. For example, if we are to increase Widget sales by 15%, we are going to have to manufacture 15% more Widgets to fulfill the orders, and that means we will need to procure 15% more parts for Widget assembly. It may also mean that the Widget's finance group must be prepared to fund a larger inventory for awhile. In other words we need to be sure we align goals across the entire value chain. Consider what would happen if one goal called for a 15% increase in sales and another called for a 10% reduction in costs in manufacturing. Worst case, the manufacturing group might decide to cut back on inventory, which is always expensive, and find that it is unable to meet a sharp increase in Widget sales at the end of the quarter when all the new sales orders arrived.

Most organizations begin with a number of strategic goals and then generate lots of additional goals and measures. These are often supplemented by another whole set of measures that the functional units have tracked for years. Thus, the sales department may have a number of different measures it uses to determine if salespeople are doing their job in the manner prescribed by the department's sales procedures manual.

Tracking measures costs money and takes time and ultimately too much information is as confusing as too little. Most companies have some way to discriminate between all their routine measures and those that are really important. The important measures are sometimes called the *key performance indicators* (KPIs). It's important to consider a wide variety of different measures and then settle on a few KPIs to watch really closely.

Finally, it is critical that executives understand that they will usually get what they decide to measure. Managers and employees both know what numbers senior executives think most important. Everyone who wants to get ahead will focus on "making the numbers." If a measure is poorly chosen or if it has unintended side effects, then corporate performance will suffer. Thus, time spent developing and selecting good measures and aligning them with corporate goals is usually time well spent.

Internal and External Measures

There are many, many different ways of talking about metrics and measures. We want to start with a critical distinction, and use simple terms to assure that the distinction is clear. *External measures* tell you about the results achieved by a process or value chain. *Internal measures* tell you about the results achieved by subprocesses, or activities within the process or value chain. Figure 6.1 provides an overview of the distinction. Note that the emphasis is on the value chain, and not on processes in general. Process C in the value chain shown in Figure 6.1 has an output. We could measure the output of Process C, separate from any measures we might establish with regard to Process C's internal activities, but that output measure is not an external measure as we are using the term here.

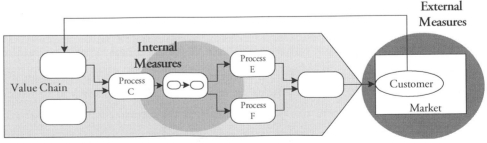

Figure 6.1 External and internal measures of process performance.

If we are focused on the organization, then the customer is outside the organization. We can apply this same concept inside an organization, if we simply regard any process that receives another process's outputs as its customer. Thus, in Figure 6.2, we see that processes can be both the supplier of one process and the customer of another. In this case Process D has two external customers, Processes E and F. Before the manager of Process D should consider examining whatever internal measures are used to evaluate Process D, he or she should be sure that Process D's outputs are satisfying its customers, Process E and Process F. The logic here is the same as it is on the enterprise level. It doesn't make any sense to decrease the cost or to increase the productivity of Process D if, as a result, the process is no longer able to deliver the products or services it provides to Processes E and F. Once the external measures are defined and it's clear that Process D can consistently meet its external commitments, then, while keeping its external measures constant, the process manager should focus on improving internal measures.

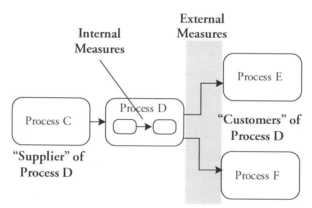

Figure 6.2 Internal "customers" are external to the processes that supply them.

External measures are the ultimate measures of whether your company or process is succeeding. Focusing on the company for the moment, examples of measures we might want to examine include:

▶ External Measures
  – Income measures
  – Measures of customer satisfaction
  – Market growth measures

- Stockholder satisfaction or other external measures of the stock market's confidence in what the company is doing

▶ **Internal Measures**
  - Efficiency and effectiveness of specific functions or subprocesses
  - Costs of producing the product or service
  - Quality of internal outputs

It's usually easier to define or measure internal metrics than to measure external results. Moreover, most functional units tend to focus on internal measures. In fact, as we will see in a moment, one often focuses on internal measures because they are leading indicators and provide managers with valuable information. Ultimately, however, to effectively evaluate the performance of an organization, you must focus on the external measures. Once you "lock down" the external measures, then you can begin to focus on improving your internal measures, confident that any efficiency you achieve will result in a real benefit to the organization. If you fail to lock down the external measures first, however, you run the risk that you will improve internal efficiency or reduce production costs at the expense of customer satisfaction, market growth, or the organization's share price. We know of a company that did exactly that. They announced that bonuses would depend on a 20% cut in costs. Costs dropped and customer complaints soared. Products were delivered late, they had more defects and service became harder to obtain. The company quickly halted its drive for cost cuts and instituted a program that measured customer satisfaction. Once that program was in place and managers were getting monthly reports on customer satisfaction, the company reinstated the cost-cutting drive, making it clear that customer satisfaction was first, and cost cuts were desirable, but the bonuses would only be given for units that cut costs while maintaining customer satisfaction.

Leading and Lagging Indicators

Another way to think about metrics and measures is to focus on whether they measure something that can suggest action, or whether they simply report on a situation that one can do nothing about. This focus is on using performance measures to help managers make decisions. Leading indicators are measures that report on situations that are causally related to outcomes that you desire. Lagging indicators describe situations that can't be changed.

Imagine you are a sales manager for Widgets, Inc. The executive board adopts a strategy that calls for the expansion of Widget's presence in the market. This is translated into a specific goal: The company will increase its sales by 15% each quarter of the year. You can wait till the end of the quarter and then determine how many Widgets you sold. That measure, however, is a lagging indicator. Once the quarter is over, you won't be able to do anything about the number of sales you made during the quarter. You'll know if you achieved your goal or not, but you won't be in any position to change the results. Now let us assume you have been tracking your Widget sales for some time and know that about 10% of your leads normally result in qualified prospects, and that your salespeople can typically arrange calls with half of the qualified prospects. You also know that your salespeople sell Widgets to 20% of the customers they call on. Figure 6.3 illustrates the Widget sales cycle we just described.

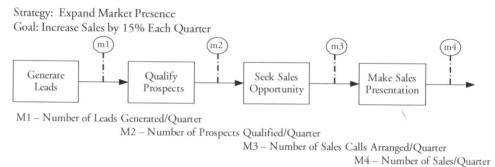

Strategy: Expand Market Presence
Goal: Increase Sales by 15% Each Quarter

M1 – Number of Leads Generated/Quarter
M2 – Number of Prospects Qualified/Quarter
M3 – Number of Sales Calls Arranged/Quarter
M4 – Number of Sales/Quarter

Figure 6.3 A simple sales cycle with three leading and one lagging measure.

If you know that your salespeople are scheduled to make 100 sales calls this quarter, you can predict that you will be making about 20 sales. Thus, sales calls scheduled is a leading indicator of successful sales. It comes rather late in the sales cycle, however, and may not give you much time to make corrections. The best leading indicator, in this case, would be to track leads. A quick calculation shows that you get one sale for each 100 leads. Or, to look at it a little differently, to increase your sales by 15% in a quarter, you will need to increase your leads by 15%. If you track leads per month, you will know at the end of the first month in the quarter if you are on track. If you aren't, you will need to sharply increase the effectiveness of your lead-generation process in the second month or you will be unlikely to meet your goal.

As a generalization, whenever possible it is good to monitor leading indicators that provide managers with the ability to take corrective action. Ultimately, of course, you are also going to want to know exactly how many sales you made in the quarter, so you will end up measuring both leads and sales, but the leading indicator will be more useful to the process manager who wants to use the measure to help achieve his or her goals.

Balanced Scorecard and Process Measures

We already discussed Kaplan and Norton's Balanced Scorecard approach when we considered how Balanced Scorecard could be used to define an organization's strategy. The approach is even more popular as a tool to define managerial responsibilities and to align the goals and measures used to evaluate the performance of managers.

The basic idea is very straightforward. Kaplan and Norton began by arguing that, "What you measure is what you get," and that, "An organization's measurement system strongly affects the behavior of managers and employees." They go on to say that, "Traditional financial accounting measures, like return-on-investment and earnings-per-share, can give misleading signals for continuous improvement and innovation…" To counter the tendency to rely too heavily on financial accounting measures, Kaplan and Norton argued that senior executives should establish a scorecard that took multiple measures into account. They proposed a Balanced Scorecard that considered four types of measures:

- ▶ Financial Measures: How Do We Look to Shareholders?
- ▶ Internal Business Measures: What Must We Excel At?
- ▶ Innovation and Learning Measures: Can We Continue to Improve and Create Value?
- ▶ Customer Measures: How Do Customers See Us?

Figure 6.4 illustrates a scorecard of a hypothetical company discussed in Kaplan and Norton's Jan/Feb, 1992 article in Electronic Circuits Inc (ECI).

The initial book on the Balanced Scorecard methodology appeared just as business process reengineering was taking off in the early 1990s. Subsequent articles emphasized important ideas, like linking processes to customer concerns and linking measures to strategies. Many of the early business process theorists emphasized the importance of measurement, but didn't provide specifics about how to accomplish it. It became popular for business process gurus to mention the Balanced Scorecard when asked to explain how to align strategies, processes and measures. The Balanced Scorecard approach has

ECI's Balanced Business Scorecard			
Financial Perspective		**Internal Business Perspective**	
Goals	Measures	Goals	Measures
Survive	Cash flow	Technology capability	Manufacturing geometry vs. competition
Succeed	Quarterly sales growth & operating income by division	Manufacturing experience	Cycle time, Unit cost, Yield
Prosper	Increased market share and ROI	Design productivity	Silicon efficiency, Engineering efficiency
		New product introduction	Actual introduction schedule vs. plan
Innovation & Learning Perspective		**Customer Perspective**	
Goals	Measures	Goals	Measures
Technology leadership	Time to develop next generation	New products	Percent of sales from new products, Percent of sales from proprietary products
Manufacturing learning	Process time to maturity	Response supply	On-time delivery (defined by customer)
Product focus	Percent of products that equal 80% sales	Preferred supplier	Share of key accounts' purchases, Ranking by key accounts
Time to market	New product introduction vs. competition	Customer partnership	Number of cooperative engineering efforts

Figure 6.4 ECI's Balanced Business Scorecard (after a figure in Kaplan and Norton's *The Balanced Scorecard—Measures that Drive Performance*).

grown in popularity and today a large number of companies implement it, in either the original way advocated by Kaplan or Norton, or in some more tailored manner. Indeed, it has become so popular that many people use the term Balanced Scorecard to refer to any approach to organizing management performance measures, although most stick with the basic principles laid out by Norton and Kaplan.

In their Sept/Oct 1993 HBR article titled *Putting the Balanced Scorecard to Work*, Kaplan and Norton offered an overview of how one could link the balanced scorecard to corporate strategies. Figure 6.5 provides an overview of the approach they proposed. The overall pattern is familiar to anyone who has worked in strategy and measurement and we have already described it when we introduced measurement. The particular aspect that reflects Kaplan and Norton's contribution is the emphasis on defining four different types of strategies and generating four different types of measures.

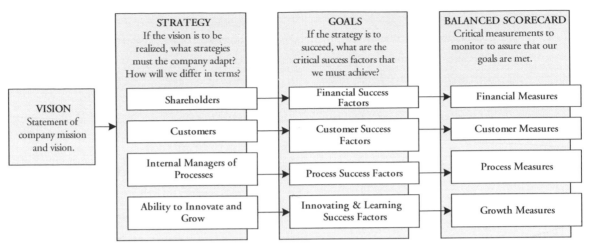

Figure 6.5 Linking strategies to Balanced Scorecard measures.

The Balanced Scorecard has proved popular for many reasons. The most important reason was simply that it served as a wake-up call in the mid-1990s. Many senior managers were relying too heavily on financial measures, and a tidy model that suggested how they might rely on other measures, including process measures and customer satisfaction, proved popular.

In 2000 Kaplan and Norton came out with a new book and another *HBR* article, *Having Trouble with Your Strategy? Then Map It* (*HBR*, Sept–Oct, 2000). The new article expanded their description of how one aligned measures and strategic goals. They suggest what they term "Balanced Scorecard Strategy Maps." In essence, they introduce a hierarchical model that suggests that some measures contribute to others and are summed up in shareholder value. Figure 6.5 summarizes the idea behind the Balanced Scorecard Strategy Maps.

One problem we have with Figure 6.5 is that it seems like it's moving back to where Kaplan and Norton began in the 1990s. We have gone from the idea that senior managers should not rely exclusively on financial measures, but on four balanced sets of measures, to the idea that there is a hierarchy of measures and that financial measures are on the top. It's easy to imagine that some executives will look at Figure 6.5 and conclude that they can simply monitor the financial measures, and leave the rest to lower-level managers. In our opinion, the basic Balanced Scorecard idea is very useful, but it should be more closely tied to a process view of the organization. From a process perspective, activities are directly linked to customer satisfaction. Breaking

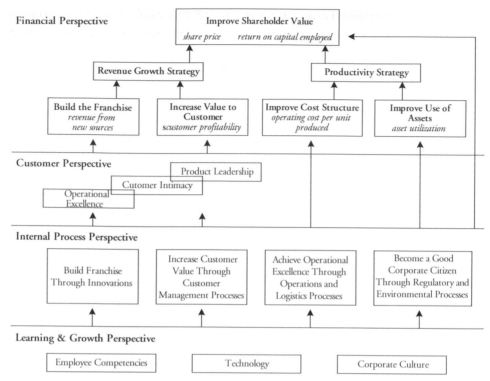

Figure 6.6 Balanced Scorecard Strategy Maps (modified from figure in HBR, Sept/Oct 2000 article).

them up and arranging them in a hierarchical fashion reflects a functional or departmental mentality. We'll come back to this point later and suggest how we would deal with the problem. In the meantime, it is worth noting that many organizations that have embraced the Balanced Scorecard approach usually do so by conceptualizing the different boxes in the scorecard as being the responsibility of different functional units. Thus, sales and marketing generate the goals and measures for the customer perspective while operations, manufacturing usually generate the goals and measures for the internal business (or process) perspective. Table 6.1 illustrates some typical functional and process measures.

Most organizations that use the Balanced Scorecard to assign goals to managers start by generating a corporate scorecard. Then each department derives its own scorecard that emphasizes the goals and measures they think their department can effect. The process is then driven down from the head of the department to his or her reports and then to their reports, as pictured in Figure 6.7. If too much emphasis is placed on functional units, then the card is actually divided as it goes down and different quadrants become the primary responsibility of different functional units.

Table 6.1 A comparison of some functional and process measures.

Department or function	Typical departmental measures	Typical process measures
Sales department	▶ Cost of sales ▶ Revenue ($)	▶ Timely and accurate submission of orders ▶ Timely and accurate entry of new orders ▶ Cost of processing orders
Production department	▶ Cost of inventory ▶ Cost of labor ▶ Cost of materials ▶ Cost of shipping	▶ Timely order scheduling ▶ Timely and accurate production of orders ▶ Timely shipment of orders ▶ Cost of unit production and shipping costs
Finance department	▶ Percent of bad debt ▶ Mean labor budget	▶ Timely and accurate invoice preparation ▶ Timely and accurate credit checks for new accounts ▶ Cost of processing an invoice
External organizational measures	▶ Gross revenue ▶ Cost of sales ▶ Growth of customer base ▶ Price of stock	▶ Percent of on-time delivery ▶ Percent of rejects ▶ Customer satisfaction as measured on survey or index

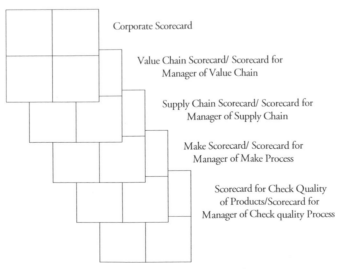

Figure 6.7 A hierarchy for a functional chain of managers.

Unfortunately, used as it is in most companies, the Balanced Scorecard system tends to support and entrench functional specialization. Recently, process-oriented organizations have begun to explore the use of the Balanced Scorecard in matrix organizations. Obviously this approach assumes that a single manager is being evaluated by and accountable to both a process and a functional manager. This requires that the same manager have two scorecards, or one scorecard with two parts to each perspective area, as you prefer. One part of each perspective area reflects the concerns of the functional unit. The other part of the area reflects the concerns of the process or value chain manager. Figure 6.8 illustrates how this works when applied to our Widget sales manager who reports to both the head of the sales department and to the manager of the Widget process. This approach is a bit confusing at first glance, but it forces senior management to think hard about what goals and measures it will assign to the process manager and what goals and measures will be used to manage the success of the functional unit.

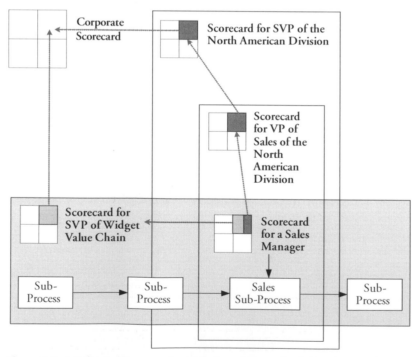

Figure 6.8 A Balanced Scorecard system that supports both functions and processes.

The advantage of the approach pictured in Figure 6.8 is that it clearly delineates a set of measures that are related to the value chain, as a whole, and are not the responsibility of any specific functional unit. Once an organization begins to divide up performance measures in this manner, the organization is in a much better position to decide what kinds of goals and responsibilities a manager must achieve to fulfill his role as a process manager and what goals and responsibilities the manager must fulfill in his or her role as a unit manager. Once clarity is achieved regarding this distinction, then a bonus system and rewards can be tailored to support superior process performance.

Aligning Process Measures

Now let's consider an entirely different approach to aligning process goals and measures. In this case we are dealing with an organization that is totally committed to process. At a minimum, the organization has a division that is focused on producing a specific product line. Or it might be a company that is organized around undertaking projects. The specific example we will look at involves an aerospace company that undertook a project to create and deliver a set number of highly specialized aircraft to the U.S. Air Force. The company was Boeing, and the contract (project) was undertaken by the Boeing Global Mobility Systems (GMS) unit. Specifically the contract was undertaken to deliver the C-17, a giant aircraft than can transport military tanks, trucks and heavy equipment. Imagine the project described as a very general process, as illustrated in Figure 6.9. The output of the project is C-17 aircraft. The customer is the U.S. Air Force. The quality and the cycle time for the project are precisely specified. Each plane is carefully evaluated by the Air Force and either accepted or rejected. Thus, the ultimate external measure is the acceptance or rejection of C-17 aircraft, coupled with supplying the required number of aircraft on time, as specified in the contract.

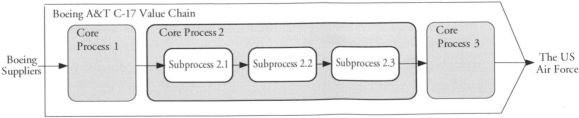

Figure 6.9 An overview of a Boeing value chain that produces C-17 aircraft for the U.S. Air Force.

Using a diagram like the one shown in Figure 6.9 we can align our process measures by "backing" into the process and writing "contracts" that define the relationships between each of the processes and subprocesses in the value chain. Figure 6.10 shows how we might decompose the processes pictured in Figure 6.9, which may make the discussion easier to follow. At the highest level, Boeing has a contract with its single customer, the U.S. Air Force. Boeing has agreed to deliver a set number of C-17 aircraft for an agreed-upon price within a given time and of a set quality. This external contract is represented by the top gray circle in Figure 6.10.

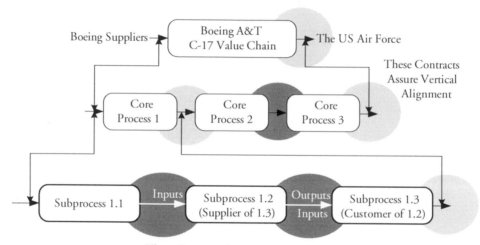

Figure 6.10 An overview of a Boeing value chain that produces C-17 aircraft for the U.S. Air Force, decomposed into levels.

The value chain is made up of three core processes, 1, 2, and 3. Since core process 3 actually generates the product that is delivered to the Air Force, in effect the contract between the Air Force and core process 3 is exactly the same as Boeing's overall contract. Now we back up and ask the manager of core process 3 what he or she will need to meet the contract with the Air Force. The manager on core process 3 must consider what's involved in core process 3 and then negotiate a contract with the manager of core process 2. This is represented by the dark circle between core processes 2 and 3. In essence, the manager of core process 3 agrees that he or she can meet their contract with the Air Force, IF core process 2 meets its contract with core process 3.

This alignment process can be driven down to any arbitrary level in the process hierarchy. Thus, for example, core process 1 is made up of three subprocesses. The final subprocess in core process 1 must meet the contract that is established between the managers of core process 1 and 2. To assure alignment, the manager of subprocess 1.3 must write a contract with the manager of subprocess 1.2 that defines what subprocess 1.3 will need if it, in turn, is to meet its contract with core process 2. In a similar way, this obligation can be passed by other contracts back from subprocess 1.2 to 1.1. Thus, eventually, an entire value chain and all its processes and subprocesses can be linked by sets of contracts that define what each operational process must do to assure that the downstream or "customer" process succeeds. We don't picture it on this diagram, but other contracts can be written by process managers to define what support they require to meet their output agreements.

This is a very process-oriented way of thinking about outcomes and measures. It largely ignores functional concerns and puts all the emphasis on assuring that each process and subprocess manager knows exactly what is required and generates output ("external") measures for each process and subprocess. Any process (or process manager) that fails to meet its contract can be instantly identified and corrective action initiated.

Not all organizations can embrace an approach that puts as much emphasis on process as Boeing GMS does. When it is done, however, it makes it possible to create a very rigorous system of measures, all carefully aligned. And, of course, it makes it possible to establish performance criteria for process managers with an equal degree of rigor.

Deriving Measures from Business Process Frameworks

In the last chapter, when we discussed business process frameworks, we mentioned the fact that both SCOR and VRM provide measures for each of their processes. Figure 6.11 provides an overview of the measures for the SCOR supply chain process. The five high-level SCOR measures are divided between external (customer-facing) and internal measures.

If a company uses a framework like SCOR to structure its business process hierarchy, then it can proceed to derive appropriate measures from the SCOR reference materials. The manual contains the definitions for all processes included in the SCOR framework, the metrics appropriate for evaluating each process at each level, and definitions of how each measure is to be calculated. The following extract from Version 7.0 of the SCOR reference manual gives an overview of a sample of the metrics available.

	Performance Attribute	Performance Attribute Definition	Level 1 Metric
Customer Facing Attributes	Supply Chain Delivery Reliability	The performance of the supply chain in delivering: the correct product, to the correct place, at the correct time, in the correct condition and packaging, in the correct quantity, with the correct documentation, to the correct customer.	Delivery Performance
			Fill Rates
			Perfect Order Fulfillment
	Supply Chain Responsiveness	The velocity at which a supply chain provides products to the customer.	Order Fulfillment Lead Times
	Supply Chain Flexibility	The agility of a supply chain in responding to marketplace changes to gain or maintain c ompetitive advantage.	Supply Chain Response Time
			Production Flexibility
Internal Facing Attribute	Supply Chain Costs	The costs associated with operating the supply chain.	Cost of Goods Sold
			Total Supply Chain Management Costs
			Value-Added Productivity
			Warranty / Returns Processing Costs
	Supply Chain Asset Management Efficiency	The effectiveness of an organization in managing assets to support demand satisfaction. This includes the management of all assets: fixed and working capital.	Cash-to-Cash Cycle Time
			Inventory Days of Supply
			Asset Turns

Figure 6.11 Level 1 measures defined for the SCOR framework. (After SCOR Reference Manual.)

In this case we are looking at the reference material provided for a specific Level 2 process—Make (Variation: Make-to-Order), and then for one Level 3 process within that Make process. In the body of the reference manual, measures are referred to by name. In an appendix of the manual each measure is precisely defined. We give the measures appropriate to the processes first, and then the definitions of specific measures.

SCOR defines five generic performance attributes and then suggests appropriate metrics for each attribute. Different companies will choose different metrics as KPIs, depending on the nature of the industry, the supply chain, and the performance that the company seeks to monitor and improve.

Level 2. Make Process — Variation: Make-to-Order: M2

Process Definition: The process of manufacturing in a make to order environment adds value to products through mixing, separating, forming, machining, and chemical processes. A make to order environment is one in which products are completed after receipt of a customer order and are built or configured only in response to a customer order.

Performance Attributes	Appropriate Metrics
Reliability	Perfect Order Fulfillment
Responsiveness	Make Cycle Time
Flexibility	Upside Make Flexibility Downside Make Adaptability Upside Make Adaptability
Cost	Plant Operating Cost per Hour Indirect to Direct Headcount Ratio Cost\unit Indirect To Direct Process Cost Ratio Product Losses (Sourced/In-Process/Finished)
Assets	Cash to Cash Cycle Time Inventory Aging Return on Supply Chain Fixed Assets

Two examples of Level 3 subprocesses of the Make (M2) process follow:

Level 3. Schedule Production Subprocess — Variation: Schedule Production Activities for Make-to-Order: M2.1

Subprocess Definition: Given plans for the production of specific parts, products, or formulations in specific quantities and planned availability of required sourced products, the scheduling of the operations to be preformed in accordance with these plans. Scheduling includes sequencing, and, depending on the factory layout, any standards for setup and run. In general intermediate production activities are coordinated prior to the scheduling of the operations to be preformed in producing a finished product.

Performance Attributes	Appropriate Metrics
Reliability	Percent of orders scheduled to customer request date Schedule achievement
Responsiveness	Schedule Production Activities Cycle Time
Flexibility	None Identified
Cost	WIP inventory days of supply Scheduling resource costs as % of Make costs Plant level order management costs
Assets	Capacity utilization

Level 3. Issue Sourced/In-Process Subprocess — Variation: Issue Sourced/In-Process Activities for Make-to-Order: M2.2

Subprocess Definition: The selection and physical movement of sourced/in-process products (e.g., raw materials, fabricated components, subassemblies, required ingredients or intermediate formulations) from a stocking location (e.g., stockroom, a location on the production floor, a supplier) to a specific point of use location. Issuing product includes the corresponding system transaction. The Bill of Materials/routing information or recipe/production instructions will determine the products to be issued to support the production operation(s).

Performance Attributes	Appropriate Metrics
Reliability	Inventory accuracy % Parts received at point of use
Responsiveness	Issue Sourced/In-Process Product Cycle Time
Flexibility	None Identified
Cost	Inventory obsolescence Inventory days of Supply
Assets	None Identified

An example of a Metric Definition, for the Reliability Metric for the Level 2 process is as follows:

Level 2 Metric: Perfect Order Fulfillment

Metric Definition: The percentage of orders meeting delivery performance with complete and accurate documentation and no delivery damage. Components include all items and quantities on-time using customer's definition of on-time, and documentation - packing slips, bills of lading, invoices, etc.

- A product is considered perfect if the product ordered is the product provided.
- A quantity is considered perfect if the product ordered is provided in the ordered quantity.
- A delivery is considered perfect if the location and delivery time ordered is met upon receipt.
- A customer is considered perfect if the product is delivered to the specified entity.
- Documentation supporting the order line is considered perfect if it is all accurate, complete, and on time.
- The product condition is considered perfect if the product is delivered / faultlessly installed (as applicable) according to specifications with no damage, customer ready, and is accepted by the customer. Faultlessly installed (as applicable), correct configuration, customer-ready, no damage, on specification.

Calculation: [Total Perfect Orders] / [Total Number of Orders]

The Supply Chain Council not only provides a comprehensive set of measures for the processes included in their Supply Chain, Design Chain and Sales and Marketing frameworks, but they also work with an outside benchmarking agency so that companies using the Supply Chain Council's measures can get benchmark information on the same measures. To use the Supply Chain Council's framework, measures and benchmarks, an organization needs to join the Supply Chain Council. Once that is done, however, the company has free access to a comprehensive process measurement system that it can use to rapidly develop its own business process architecture.

Putting It All Together

As we suggested at the beginning, most companies are still experimenting with process management and with the specification of process-based performance measures. Most companies tend to have measures defined at the lower process levels, but they don't have performance measures at the value chain level. Moreover, they rarely have their measures tightly integrated with their strategic goals. Companies that have done work in this area tend to do it within the scope of the Balanced Scorecard framework and this approach, while useful, often obscures the role of processes and overemphasizes the functional approach.

A few companies, like Boeing GMS, are far ahead of others, and have a rigorous process measurement system that runs from the top right down to the smallest process in the organization. Using contracts, the Boeing GMS system lines everything up and makes a rigorous traceability possible.

A few companies have begun to explore the integration of frameworks, with their well-defined systems of measures, and the Balanced Scorecard. Figure 6.12 illustrates how we can align the high-level financial measures of the Balanced Scorecard system with lower-level measures provided by the SCOR framework.

Figure 6.12 also suggests how we can get around the layered nature of the Balanced Scorecard strategy model. Instead of thinking of customers as forming a layer, we think of customers as those who receive the output of a process. Thus, any problem with customer satisfaction can be traced to products and services, which can, in turn, be traced to the process that produced the specific products or services. Learning and growth issues, in turn, are conceptualized as resources used by specific processes to produce results. This approach provides a much more process-oriented set of measures and shifts the Balanced Scorecard bias to process and away from functional units.

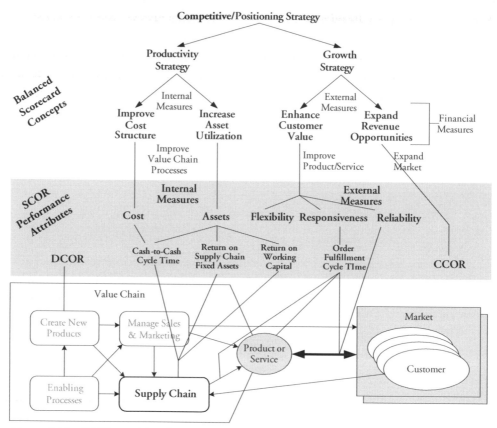

Figure 6.12 SCOR provides the process measures to support high-level Balanced Scorecard measures.

Using SCOR in conjunction with a Balanced Scorecard system that relies on both process and functional unit scorecards provides an organization with the means required to create a much more rigorous process performance measurement system and to align the evaluation of the performance of process managers with the overall evaluation of organizational performance.

Completing the Business Process Architecture Worksheet

Now that we've reviewed some of the management and measurement issues that any company interested in developing a business process architecture will need to address, let's return to the business process architecture analysis worksheet that we first considered in Chapter 4. We began by structuring all the worksheets with operational processes. The Level 1 worksheets allow us to define the Level 1 operational processes that make up a value chain. The Level 2 worksheets focus on specific Level 1 processes and allow us to define Level 2 operational processes for each Level 1 process. In each case, once we have defined the processes, we should identify the manager who will be responsible for each specific process and we should define the metrics or measures that we will use to determine if the process is accomplishing its goals and if the manager is doing his or her job effectively.

Architecture Analysis Worksheet – Level 2 Processes			
Value Chain: *The Widget Value Chain*		Level 1 Process: *Widget Supply Chain*	

Goals and Measures for Level 1 Process:
   Increase customer satisfaction (Reduce complaints by 50%)
   Reduce costs (by 15% per year)			

Level 2 Processes	Process Manager	Level 2 Goals/Process Metrics	Level 2 Resources

Make Process	*Artie Kahn*	Reliability
		  Perfect Order Fulfillment
		Responsiveness
		  Make Cycle Time
		Flexibility
		  Upside Make Flexibility
		  Downside Make Adaptability
		  Upside Make Adaptability
		Cost
		  Plant Operating Cost per Hour
		  Indirect to Direct Headcount Ratio
		  Cost\unit
		  Indirect to Direct Process Cost Ratio
		  Product Losses (Sources/In-Process/Finished)
		Assets
		  Cash to Cash Cycle Time
		  Inventory Aging
		  Return on Supply Chain Fixed Assets
			ERP Modules Used
			
			Business Rules Used
			
			Employee Training Courses Used

Deliver Process			

Figure 6.13 A Level 2 architecture analysis worksheet.

Figure 6.13 illustrates a Level 2 worksheet with two Level 2 processes, and information on who will manage and what metrics will be used to evaluate the Level 2 Make process. We only hint at some of the resources that might be aligned with the Level 2 Make Process.

Notes and References

Once again, many of the ideas incorporated in the BPTrends methodology are derived from conversations Roger Burlton and I have had. And most of my ideas on the relationship between process managers and processes derive from even earlier conversations with Geary Rummler.

Rummler, Geary and Alan Brache, *Improving Performance: How to Manage the White Space on the Organization Chart (2nd Ed.),* Jossey-Bass, 1995. Still the best introduction to measuring business processes.

Spitzer, Dean R., *Transforming Performance Measurement: Rethinking the Way We Measure and Drive Organizational Success,* AMACOM, 2007. A very nice introduction to the latest ideas on organizing performance measurement.

Lynch, Richard L. and Kelvin F. Cross, *Measure Up! Yardsticks for Continuous Improvement,* Blackwell, 1991. An older book with lots of good ideas on process measurement.

Balanced Scorecard is a popular approach to measuring corporate and managerial performance. The term was coined by Robert S. Kaplan (a Harvard Business School accounting professor) and David P. Norton (a consultant) in an article titled "The Balanced Scorecard—Measures that Drive Performance," that appeared in the Jan/Feb 1992 issue of the *Harvard Business Review.*

Kaplan, Robert S., and David P. Norton, *The Balanced Scorecard: Translating Strategy into Action*, Harvard Business School Press, 1996. Kaplan and Norton describe a popular approach to tying measures to organization strategies. It's good in that it gets executives thinking of a variety of measures. It's bad if it's used alone, as a measurement solution, and not incorporated into a total business process management strategy. If you want, you can easily think of the collection of measures that accumulate as a process is analyzed as a score-card of measures.

Kaplan, Robert S. and David P. Norton, "Having Trouble with Your Strategy? Then Map It," *Harvard Business Review,* Sept–Oct 2000. This article describes how the authors link strategy to Balanced Scorecard measures. It is available from *www.amazon.com.*

Kaplan, Robert S. and David P. Norton, *Strategy Maps: Converting Intangible Assets into Tangible Outcomes*, Harvard Business School Press, 2004. The Kaplan-Norton model often confuses the relationship between process and measures, but it also provides lots of good insights. Read it for insights, but don't take their specific approach too seriously, or your process focus will tend to get lost. Kaplan and Norton's previous book on the Balanced Scorecard approach to strategy was *The Strategy Focused Organization* which was published by the Harvard Business School press in 2001 and its also worth a read.

Kaplan and Norton's books are still available and are as good as any of the many other books on the Balanced Scorecard we have seen. If you just want the basic idea, however, we suggest you buy the original Harvard Business Review article that can be bought and downloaded from *www.amazon.com.*

Smith, Ralph, *Business Process Management and the Balanced Scorecard,* Wiley, 2007. This is a recent book that describes the challenges of using the Balanced Scorecard with BPM.

Most of the material on aligning processes from the top-down derives from the work at Boeing GMS (formerly called Boeing A&T). The best article describing this effort is Pamela Garretson's "How Boeing A&T Manages Business Processes," which is available on *www.bptrends.com.* Search on Pam Garretson.

Information on the Supply Chain Council's measurement systems is from a number of SCC publications. The specific information about Make-to-Order process measures is from the SCOR manual. All SCC information is available from *www.supply-chain.org.*

7

An Executive Level BPM Group

ORGANIZATIONS HAVE DIFFERENT ways of managing their business process efforts and there is no one best way. It largely depends on how an organization is already structured. Some organizations have a group charged with working on enterprise strategy. Others have an executive committee that defines enterprise strategy. Others treat it as a special project headed by the CEO. In a similar way, different organizations handle the overall management of their process work in different ways. In a survey, BPTrends found that about 34% of the companies surveyed did not have a formal BPM group; 20% had BPM groups that were located within divisions or reported to department managers; 18% had a BPM group that reported at the executive level; and 14% had a BPM group located in their IT organization. Obviously, the location of a BPM group or center of excellence says a lot about the goals of the organization and their interest in business process. Organizations that think of business process management as an automation initiative would be more likely to delegate it to the IT organization. Organizations that are focused on the redesign or improvement of specific business processes are more likely to locate their process groups in divisions or departments. Organizations that are focused on enterprise issues and think of processes and process management as strategic resources that need to be aligned with corporate strategy and company-wide performance measures will tend to locate their BPM group at the enterprise level, just as they locate their strategy group at the enterprise level. In a similar way, the name that companies apply to the group tends to reflect their objectives. A BPM group reflects an emphasis on management. A Process Excellence group suggests process redesign and improvement projects, and a Business Process Automation group suggests an IT emphasis.

In this chapter we will focus on the types of activities that an enterprise BPM group might manage. Then, we will consider how Boeing GMS has organized an entire business unit around processes and see how the Process Management Group at Boeing GMS plays a key, coordinating role.

What Does a BPM Group Do?

Different companies assign different sorts of responsibilities to their BPM groups. In Figure 7.1 we provide an overview of the various types of activities that a BPM group might be responsible for creating, managing, or maintaining. We suggest inputs to the various BPM group's processes on the left and outputs the group might generate on the right. Most BPM groups will support fewer processes and almost all will have the processes subdivided into different processes, but this will provide a basis for a discussion of the kinds of things that a BPM group might do. We'll consider each BPM group process in turn.

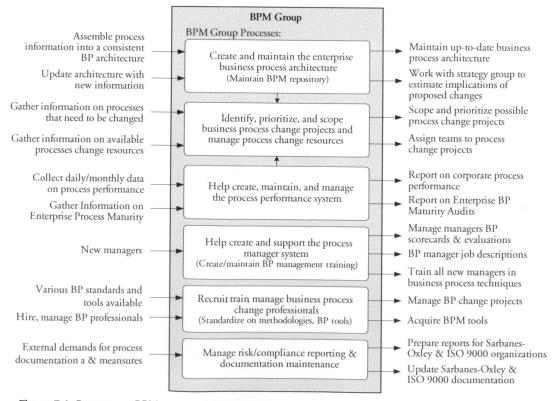

Figure 7.1 Processes a BPM group might manage.

Create and Maintain the Enterprise Business Process Architecture

Any organization that wants to exert a systematic, ongoing control over its processes needs to understand exactly what processes it has. We have already discussed this in Chapter 3. The business process architecture in question can be a minimal architecture that simply identifies the major value chains and key processes and the relationships between them, or it can be a more detailed architecture that defines processes, managers, measures, links to strategies and policies, links to IT resources, links to training resources, and so forth. The more elaborate the process architecture, the more valuable it will be as a senior management tool, but only if it is up to date. Any organization that is serious about maintaining a large detailed business process architecture will need to maintain it in a database (or repository) that will make it easy to maintain a large amount of information, to identify linkages among the architectural elements, and, very importantly, to constantly update the information.

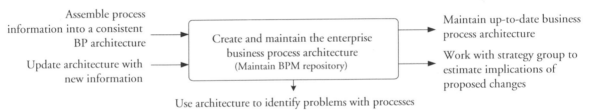

Figure 7.2 The "create and maintain a business process architecture" process.

A BPM group with an up-to-date business process architecture, stored in a repository, is well positioned to provide a variety of management support tasks. For example, the U.S. government, via the Sarbanes-Oxley legislation, recently asked all U.S. firms to submit reports proving they could monitor key financial decision points. Companies without a business process architecture spent anywhere from a year to three years struggling to analyze their decision flows and developing the means to comply with the required Sarbanes-Oxley reporting. Leading firms with an existing business process architecture simply created a Sarbanes-Oxley reporting form and used their existing business process repository to populate the form they needed to submit. In other words, companies with comprehensive business process architectures already understood their processes and had the data required and it was only a matter of creating a report-generation procedure to pull the data from the repository and put it into the form the U.S. government required.

An up-to-date business process architecture allows the members of a BPM group to quickly define the impact of proposed changes. Since a well-defined architecture defines the relationships between processes and subprocesses and between processes and IT resources and training resources, among other things, the BPM group can quickly project what a specific business process change will require in the way of changes to IT or training. Thus, the creation of a business process architecture provides the organization with a key tool to assure the organization's continuing agility and its ability to deal with change in a rapid and efficient manner. The BPM group should maintain a close relationship with the organization's strategy group, providing it with process performance data and advice on the opportunities or problems involved in adapting to new strategic directions. If the architecture is well defined and up to date, the BPM group ought to be able to quickly define all of the core and support processes that would need to be changed to implement any specific strategic change.

Finally, an up-to-date business process architecture becomes the central tool that a process-oriented company uses to identify needs for process changes.

Identify, Prioritize and Scope Business Process Change Projects

Using inputs from operations managers, from the strategy committee, from those working with the business process architecture and those maintaining the process performance system, the BPM group is in a position to determine what processes need to be changed. In most large organizations there are more processes requiring change than resources to undertake process change projects. In many organizations, process change projects are initiated by different groups without coordination. A major advantage of a BPM group ought to be oversight and prioritization of all process change projects. This will only occur if senior management requires everyone to work with the BPM group to schedule a process change project.

Even in a large organization, there is a limit on the amount of disruption the organization can handle at any one time. Thus, usually an organization should only attempt one or two really major redesign projects at any given time. The same organization might still undertake several midsize projects and is quite capable of undertaking a large number of small process improvement projects at the same time.

The BPM group should maintain an overview of all processes that require changes, and define the project scope for each possible change project. (We will consider how to scope a process change project in Chapter 8 in more detail.) This document should allow the BPM group to determine the overall scope of the effort and to determine what resources will be required. By maintaining a close relationship with the strategy group and with senior management, the BPM groups should be able to assign a priority to any specific process change project.

Obviously the priorities and the schedule need to be reviewed on a monthly basis and changes made to reflect changes in the organization's goals. Figure 7.3 provides a high-level description of a process that analyzes process problems and available resources and defines, prioritizes and assigns business process change projects.

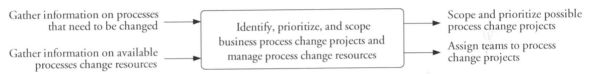

Gather information on processes that need to be changed

Gather information on available processes change resources

Identify, prioritize, and scope business process change projects and manage process change resources

Scope and prioritize possible process change projects

Assign teams to process change projects

Figure 7.3 The "identify, prioritize and scope BP change projects" process.

Figure 7.4 provides one way that a BPM group might begin to develop an overview of the opportunities the organization had for process improvement. In this case the BPM group has used an organization diagram that shows how the organization relates to the outside environment. As the team has examined the various relationships, probably in conjunction with the strategy team, they have noticed various threats or opportunities that need to be addressed. Using this or a similar technique, the BPM group can maintain an enterprise-wide overview of major process change opportunities.

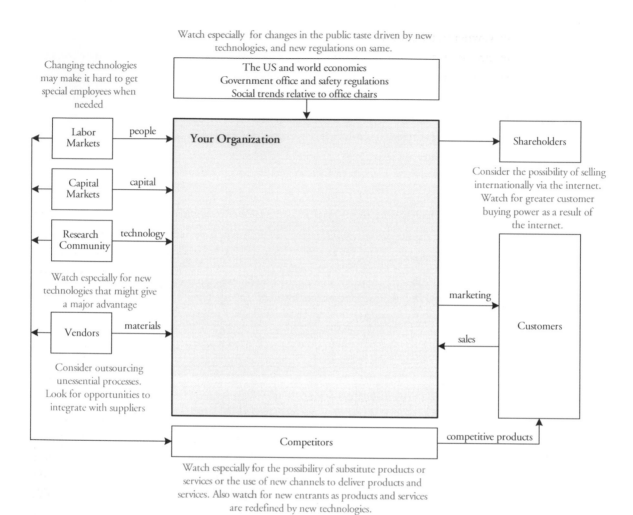

Watch especially for changes in the public taste driven by new technologies, and new regulations on same.

Changing technologies may make it hard to get special employees when needed

The US and world economies
Government office and safety regulations
Social trends relative to office chairs

Labor Markets   people   Your Organization

Shareholders

Consider the possibility of selling internationally via the internet. Watch for greater customer buying power as a result of the internet.

Capital Markets   capital

Research Community   technology

Watch especially for new technologies that might give a major advantage

Vendors   materials

Consider outsourcing unessential processes. Look for opportunities to integrate with suppliers

marketing

Customers

sales

Competitors   competitive products

Watch especially for the possibility of substitute products or services or the use of new channels to deliver products and services. Also watch for new entrants as products and services are redefined by new technologies.

Figure 7.4 Analysis of organization threats and opportunities using an organization diagram.

Figure 7.5 shows how an organization diagram could be used to review the various stakeholders who have an interest in an organization. Stakeholders are simply people who care about and exert influence over the company, its processes, and its products. Value chains have stakeholders, and specific processes have stakeholders. One can assume that the goal of a process is to satisfy the customers of the process. As a first approximation, that's true, since the customers of processes are usually the major stakeholders. Other obvious stakeholders include:

▶ Owners (shareholders)
▶ Employees
▶ Managers
▶ Partners
▶ Suppliers
▶ Government (legal, regulatory)
▶ Public
▶ Competitors

When you want to determine if a process is functioning correctly, you should develop a list of stakeholders and check what each one expects from the process and how the process would need to be changed to satisfy that particular stakeholder. In Figure 7.5, we are looking at an entire value chain, and have highlighted three possible stakeholders for the generic value chain pictured within the organization box.

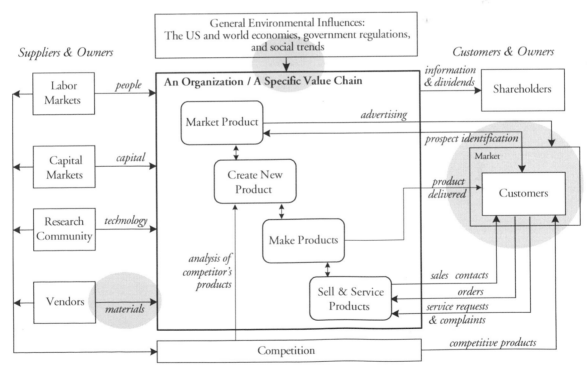

Figure 7.5 An organization diagram with some key stakeholder relationships highlighted.

Most BPM groups that are prioritizing processes will work with the business process architecture team to be sure they know everything they can about a process before determining if the process needs to be changed, and, if it does, what priority should be assigned to a particular process change.

Assuming that the BPM group controls or coordinates the various process change resources in the organization, it is also in a good position to determine what resources are available and to schedule specific process change projects. Today, there are lots of different approaches one can take to improve the performance of a company's business processes. Without trying to exhaust the list, here are some of the major options:

▶ *Redesign.* This is a major analysis of the existing process followed by a redesign effort that should significantly improve the process. This kind of effort typically results in changed job descriptions and the introduction of some automation. This type of effort is usually undertaken by business process redesign consultants from inside or outside the company.

▶ *Automation.* This can be used in conjunction with process redesign, or it can be an independent effort to automate a specific process or activity. This type of effort is usually undertaken by the IT group within the organization or by an outside IT group. There are different techniques available, including packaged applications (ERP, CRM), or software specially developed by an internal or external IT group.

▶ *Improvement.* This is a more focused effort aimed at incrementally improving an existing process. This can be an effort a process manager undertakes, or an effort undertaken by a Lean or Six Sigma improvement team.

▶ *Management.* Rather than focusing on changing a process as such, one can focus on changing the way managers plan, organize, measure and control their process. This usually requires the introduction of a process-oriented management structure and systematic training for company managers.

▶ *Outsourcing.* Organizations are increasingly willing to subcontract the execution and management of processes to an organization that specializes in performing that kind of process.

Companies establish different criteria for determining process change priorities. Figure 7.6 suggests one general way of thinking about the process change projects. Using this approach, a BPM group can rank projects according to two criteria. On one axis of the matrix, we consider the complexity and dynamics of the process, and on the other we consider the strategic importance of the process.

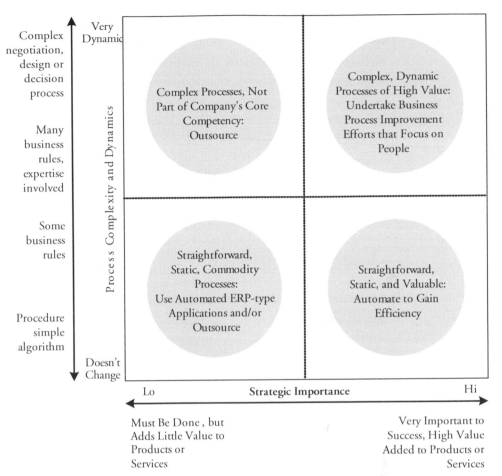

Figure 7.6 An analysis based on the complexity and the strategic importance of a process.

When we speak of process complexity and dynamics, we ask what types of tasks are involved in the process. Are we talking about something like sorting the mail, which is a reasonably straightforward procedure, with perhaps a few rules for handling cases when employees have left or work at home? Or are we talking about an international delivery process that involves lots of rules for dealing with different country policies, tariffs, and address systems? Or, are we talking about a process that includes negotiating terms for international credit lines with Fortune 1000 companies? (To simplify things, when you think about complexity, don't ask if it could be automated, but only ask what would be involved if a human were to do the job.) We also ask how often the rules change. Dynamics refers to the fact that some processes don't change very often, while others keep changing rapidly in response to changes in the market or regulations. Imagine, for example, being a member of an international bank loan team, whose process includes an activity that assigns risk premiums.

On the horizontal axis, we simply ask how much value the process contributes to the products or services the company sells. Is the process a core competency of your company, or simply an enabling process that needs to be accomplished to assure that you can do something else that really makes you money?

Now consider the kinds of processes we find in the four quadrants defined by our two axes. In the lower left, we have processes that must be done, but add little value, and are basically straightforward procedures. These are tasks that we usually want to automate in the most efficient possible way.

Processes that fall in the lower-right quadrant are high-value processes that are straightforward. An assembly process may be straightforward and involve few decisions, but the process results in the product that the company sells, and hence is very important. You want to automate these, if possible, to reduce costs and to gain efficiency. In any case, you want to improve these processes, making them as efficient and consistent as possible.

Processes that lie in the upper-left quadrant are complex processes that have to be done, but don't add much direct value to your company's product or services. They just cause problems if they aren't done, and they are complex enough that they may be hard to automate. In most cases, these are processes that you should probably consider outsourcing to another company that specializes in doing this type of process.

Finally there are the processes at the top right that are high value and complex. They often involve human expertise—processes like new product design or negotiating partnerships—and are hard to automate.

Obviously, one company's strategic process is another company's routine process. Company A may only worry about manufacturing the best widgets. For Company A, shipping is simply a process that needs to occur to assure that widgets get to customers in a timely manner. For Company B, a shipping company, their core competency is efficient, on-time deliveries. That's how they make their money. For Company B, delivery operations are a strategic process.

In Figure 7.7 we show some of the solutions we have just proposed. If the BPM group is to prioritize and schedule the organization's process change resources, it either has to manage or at least coordinate the groups that provide the services described in Figure 7.7. Thus, for example, the BPM group might directly control the company's process redesign teams. It might control or coordinate the company's Six Sigma efforts. It would probably not control strategy, but should work closely with them, especially when they, or the company's executives, are considering process outsourcing. Similarly, the BPM group should probably coordinate with IT in selecting processes for automation. It should also coordinate with any department or divisional managers who are considering installing ERP or CRM software applications. If the BPM group is properly empowered and situated, then it should be well positioned to bring order to the company's business process change efforts.

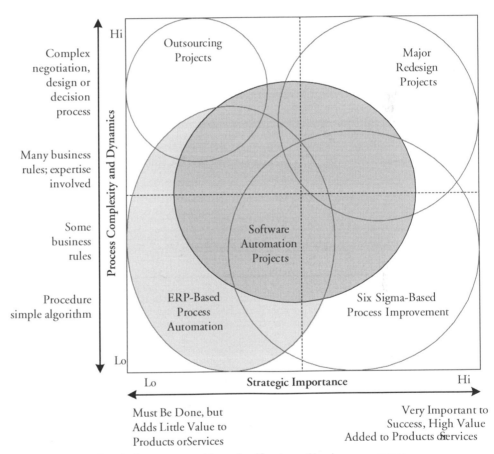

Figure 7.7 Generic solutions suggested by a classification of business processes.

Help Create, Maintain, and Manage the Process Performance System

Some organizations maintain a business process architecture, but conceptualize it as something quite separate from their overall performance management system. This is especially true if they maintain an independent Balanced Scorecard group and if the organization focuses primarily on KPIs and performance measures that focus on divisional and departmental performance. As companies shift and begin to track value chain and process performance more carefully, they tend to associate performance with processes and it becomes natural to delegate the management of the process performance reporting to the BPM group.

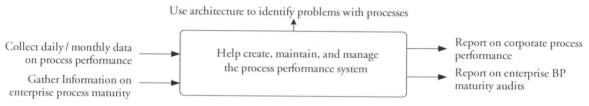

Figure 7.8 The "create and maintain a process performance system" process.

As a general principle, a BPM group with an efficient repository and with a process management system will track a wide variety of different measures. It will use some measures to evaluate the performance of business process managers and it will report other measures (KPIs) to senior management.

Often the BPM group will spearhead an effort to automate the reporting of process performance data to management, resulting in the creation of management dashboards that provide on-line information to executives. There is a lot of talk about executive dashboards today and there is a huge difference between what is on offer. Some of the dashboards overwhelm. Others report departmental data that is unrelated to processes' performance. The best of them, from a process perspective, are carefully organized around processes so that senior managers can quickly determine how each value chain is performing, using a few KPIs. Then, as desired, senior managers can click on process diagrams or models and drill down to determine the causes of any unexpected results. These process performance systems need to be carefully aligned with a well-defined business process architecture and represent one of the most interesting outcomes of the current corporate emphasis on business process work.

A growing number of companies use some kind of capability maturity audit to determine how well their organization is handling processes. The most popular of these is the Software Engineering Institute's CMMI audit. CMMI postulates five levels of maturity and assigns an organization to one of those levels. An organization's assignment describes what the organization has already accomplished and suggests what tasks it should focus on next. As we saw in Chapter 5, SEI's approach is mostly built around managerial activities that are or are not present and, thus, many organizations associate CMMI audits with the process management training. Some organizations use less formal auditing systems. A few simply ask their managers to rate their own maturity based on a questionnaire that can be tabulated to suggest the level of the organization. However it's done, establishing a maturity level and then organizing to achieve the next level can be a powerful way of organizing a company's process efforts.

Help Create and Support the Process Manager System

In Chapter 5 we considered different ways organizations might structure process management. However it's done, companies are increasingly emphasizing the role that managers play in assuring that business processes perform as they should. In Chapter 5 we considered several of the process frameworks that have defined management processes that company managers should master. Some, like CMMI, have defined a evolutionary path that companies can follow to evolve the skills of their managers. We have recommended that organizations create Balanced Scorecard systems that evaluate managers on their ability to manage processes in an effective manner. Whatever path companies take, it is clear that most will want to provide their process managers with training.

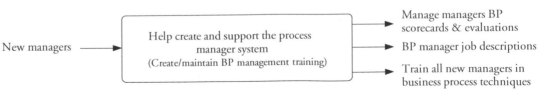

Figure 7.9 The "create and support the process manager" process.

Process manager training can take many forms. In some cases companies will provide Six Sigma training for managers to provide them the skills they need to continuously improve their processes. Other companies are documenting processes with process flow models and provide training to assure that each manager can read process diagrams. Still other organizations provide an entire curriculum in process management. In most cases, when process management training is provided, the BPM group organizes and coordinates the training.

Recruit, Train and Manage Business Process Change Professionals

Many organizations expect their BPM groups to function as a "Center of Excellence" and provide support for managers or other groups that are working on process re-design or improvement projects. Typically, the BPM group will have a few process change professionals who work directly for the BPM group and consult with or mentor other groups or project teams. At the same time, it is common for the BPM group to offer training to other company employees engaged in process work.

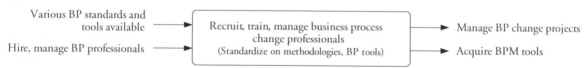

Figure 7.10 The "provide BP professional training and support" process.

The most organized version of this particular process is usually found in organizations that have embraced Six Sigma. In these companies there is a well-established training program that generates individuals needed for process work. Typical titles include: Master Black Belt (individuals who are very skilled and consult with others), Black Belt (individuals who lead large process improvement projects), and Green Belts (individuals whose normal function is to work in a unit, but who temporarily join a process improvement team). In these organizations the Master Black Belts remain in the BPM group and are assigned to projects as needed. In some cases, Black Belts are also supported by the BPM group. In nearly all cases this same group is responsible for training new Black and Green belts—although the actual training is often contracted to an outside firm.

Similarly, it's common for organizations that are involved in large-scale process redesign projects to maintain a core of process redesign experts in a central group.

This process can easily overlap with the process management training process, and that's quite useful, but there is a subtle difference between the two processes. One aims at training operational managers to manage processes on a day-to-day basis. The other aims at providing managers and others with the skills they need to take part in a business process redesign or improvement project.

Manage Risk/Compliance Reporting and Documentation

Every large organization today has to comply with several government regulations that are process oriented. The best example in the U.S. is Sarbanes-Oxley, a law passed to assure, among other things, that executives can demonstrate that they understand where and how financial decisions are made in their organizations. The law requires that companies document their process decision points. In a similar way, most organizations that do business in Europe need to obtain ISO 9000 certification. This International Standards Organization (ISO) certification is meant to demonstrate that the companies understand their business processes and have quality control standards in place. Organizations respond to initiatives like Sarbanes-Oxley and ISO 9000 in very different ways. Some integrate these initiatives into their overall process architecture, while others simply hire an outside consulting company to a project to generate the required documentation.

Figure 7.11 The "manage risk and standards reporting" process.

However companies create the initial documentation for Sarbanes-Oxley, ISO 9000, or any of the other risk and compliance requirements, the documentation has to be maintained. Processes change and the documentation has to be kept up to date. This can either be a boring, tedious job, or it can be integrated with a business process architecture initiative, maintained in a repository, and become an active part of the effort that provides management with useful tools.

A Case Study: Boeing's GMS Division

So far we've considered a number of issues, more or less independent of each other. Now we want to describe an organization that has integrated all of these ideas. The organization is the Boeing Global Mobility Systems (GMS) division. In the course of the 1990s, Boeing GMS changed itself from an organization in trouble to a world-class performer that has become one of the outstanding examples of the power of a comprehensive commitment to business process management through the organization of its day-to-day management system around business processes.

Boeing GMS is a group within Boeing's Air Force Systems business segment, which, in turn, is a part of Boeing's Integrated Defense Systems (IDS) organization. One of the primary products produced by Boeing GMS is the C-17 Globemaster III Cargo Plane—a huge airplane capable of carrying a payload in excess of 32 tons. The primary customer of Boeing GMS is the U.S. Air Force. The program employs over 7,000 people distributed between facilities located at Long Beach, California; Macon, Georgia; Seattle, Washington; and St. Louis, Missouri.

Senior Management's Commitment

The key to any serious process-based governance program is the support of senior management. Senior executives at most companies are willing to support a wide variety of process improvement programs, but are usually reluctant to provide the kind of ongoing, in-depth commitment a company needs to really change the way the organization does business. Senior management commitment happened at Boeing GMS because the company does most of its work for a single client, the U.S. Air Force. In the early 1990s, that client was very upset with the work the C-17 program was doing. The program was over budget and behind schedule, and the Air Force was threatening to stop purchasing aircraft. This threat focused senior management on the need to alter significantly the way the C-17 program was managing its business.

This management transition began with an executive leadership team that focused on how the C-17 program might be changed to improve its management practices and products. In essence, the C-17 program, and, later, all of Boeing GMS, committed itself to implementing a management framework based on the Malcolm Baldrige National Quality Award criteria, which emphasizes six areas, including leadership, strategic planning, customer focus, information management, human resources focus, and the management and integration of processes, in addition to results. The Baldrige criteria are embedded in a quality management program that is managed by the U.S. Department of Commerce and that recognizes outstanding U.S. companies with an annual quality award. [1]

As part of the deployment of the Baldrige criteria, [2] the C-17 program's focus on process management and integration spawned the *process-based management* (PBM) approach. The PBM approach starts by defining the organization as a series of processes and by assigning process management oversight responsibilities to senior executive process owners who, in turn, drive PBM downward by assigning process responsibilities to subordinate process owners. Thus, a wide cross-section of the management structure within the C-17 program, and now within Boeing GMS, has process management responsibilities. In the mid-90s, senior executives not only supported the organization's transition to PBM but assumed leading roles, serving as training role models and participating in joint reviews of processes with the government customer. Today, ongoing, active commitment of senior executives continues as part of day-to-day process management.

Starting with a Vision and a Plan

Integral to the C-17 program's successful deployment of not only the PBM approach but the overall implementation of the Malcolm Baldrige criteria was the implementation of a vision that focused on improving performance and quality as well as on customer satisfaction. As the PBM approach was developed and deployed, the Air Force customer participated jointly in the identification and management of key processes.

The C-17 program's process focus began when there was considerable interest in process reengineering but less emphasis on process management. Although there were some trials and errors along the way, the C-17 program eventually created the PBM methodology to guide its ongoing efforts. Boeing GMS defines PBM as follows:

> *Process-Based Management (PBM) is a management approach that defines an organization as a collection of processes focused on customer satisfaction and waste reduction by defining measures, and stabilizing and improving processes.*

Boeing GMS goes on to define the characteristics of a process-based organization as one that:

▶ Views business as a collection of processes
▶ Uses strategic plans to drive processes
▶ Understands the precise relationship between processes and key business results and goals
▶ Focuses on key customer-driven processes
▶ Uses work teams to implement processes
▶ Uses process reports to determine the health of processes
▶ Manages by data
▶ Has the patience to work via processes
▶ Emphasizes sustainable improvements
▶ Demands improvement in processes across the entire business
▶ Integrates processes with other initiatives
▶ Uses common processes and standardization whenever possible

Modeling the Company and Its Processes

The Boeing C-17 program management team began its process work by defining the program's core processes and its major support or enabling processes and documenting them in an enterprise process model. Over time, the processes were modified as necessary to adapt to the current Boeing GMS organization. Figure 7.12 provides an overview of the major processes identified in the GMS enterprise process model.

The five tall, light-gray processes that run through the middle of the value chain are the five core processes. The two long processes above and the one below include management and support processes that help lead or enable the core processes. We've highlighted one process in the top box and made it larger. This is the process for process management itself—Boeing's BPM group—that helps define, deploy, and monitor all the other processes.

The process owners of the top-level core and support processes are called executive process owners. Collectively, they make up the Integration Board at the GMS level and the Process Council at the C-17 level, both of which are tasked with overseeing the deployment and health of the entire PBM effort, in conjunction with the process management integration group.

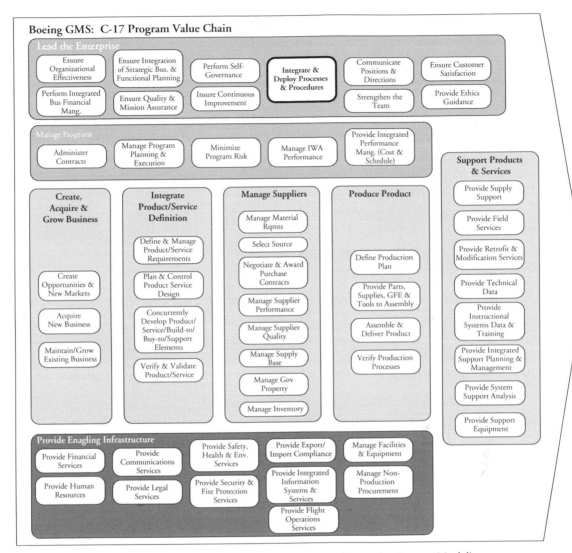

Figure 7.12 Boeing GMS program's core and support processes (Enterprise Process Model).

When PBM was first established, the methodology was used by senior executives to define the core processes in the company. Then those executives deployed it in a top-down manner, to define subprocesses and sub-subprocesses (Figure 7.13). This effort continued until all of the processes were defined.

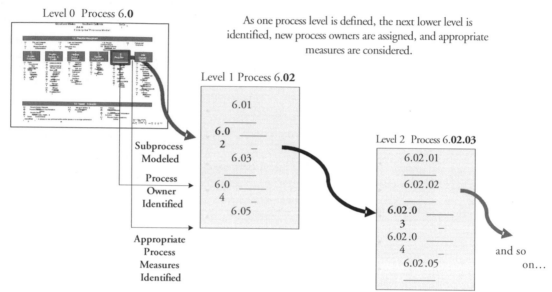

Figure 7.13 The iterative, top-down definition of processes.

A few complex processes—within production and engineering, for example—have been decomposed into as many as five levels of subprocess. Ultimately, a total of slightly more than 300 processes have been identified. Each process has a manager. (Boeing calls them process owners.) One individual can be the manager of more than one process, and some individuals manage as many as six or seven processes. Thus, the GMS group currently has slightly fewer than 300 process managers.

Today, with the overall process structure in place, the BPM group uses the PBM methodology is used both to train new process owners in their responsibilities and to deal with changes that require the addition of processes or major revisions to existing processes.

Figure 7.14 provides an overview of the seven steps in Boeing GMS's PBM methodology—which is very much a process improvement methodology. The key to the PBM approach is that every process in the enterprise process model is documented and has a responsible process manager. Those processes determined to be most critical to operational performance are additionally measured, managed, and reported on by the process manager. Moreover, process performance measures are aligned from the top to the bottom of the model using the approach described in Figure 6.10. Whenever a process fails to meet its goals, the process manager develops a plan to improve the process. The improvements are implemented, and the cycle continues with further measurements and, if necessary, further improvements.

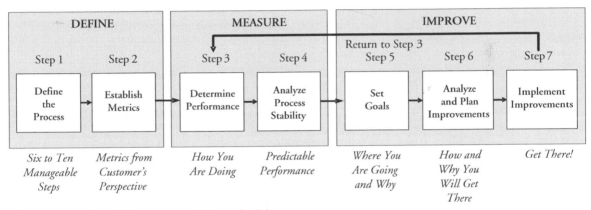

Figure 7.14 Boeing GMS seven-step PBM methodology.

Processes are modeled using a popular swim-lane flow diagram like the one shown in Figure 7.15. The top-down, iterative nature of process analysis at Boeing GMS does not require a given process owner to define his or her process in minute detail. Instead, it requires a general description of the process like the one shown in Figure 7.15, in addition to a process definition form that provides more detail on supplying and receiving process linkages. Major activity boxes in one process owner's diagram may become the boundaries of subprocesses that are defined, in turn, by other process owners assigned to those subprocesses.

All processes are defined and documented by the responsible process owners and stored in a repository maintained by the BPM group that manages the "Integrate and Deploy Processes and Procedures" process. This group maintains a complete picture of all the processes within Boeing GMS.

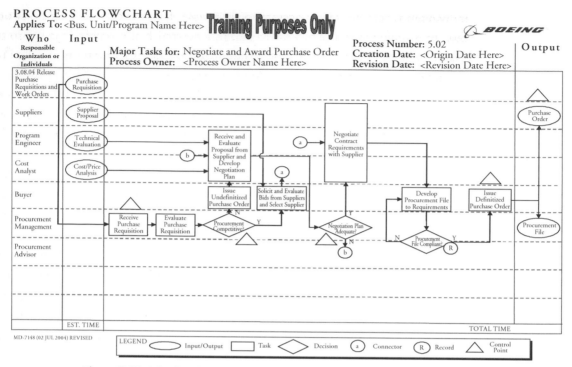

Figure 7.15 A Boeing GMS Process Flow Chart.

Process Owners

A process owner may or may not be a regular manager. The owners of some lower-level or technical processes are *subject matter experts*. The owner is familiar with the working of the process and is responsible for the planning, modeling, measurement, and improvement of the process if it is determined that the process should progress to the measurement step. The process owner most often works with a team of individuals to model, measure, and improve the process.

When an individual becomes a process owner, he or she is provided with eight hours of training in process management and a set of tools to help perform the job. If it is determined that the process will go beyond definition into measurement, the owner is also responsible for negotiating an agreement with the customer of the process to assure that the customer concurs with the output of the process. Customers may include external government customers in addition to internal customers, i.e., individuals within another process who are recipients of the outputs of the first process. In a similar way, the process owner, as a customer of a process further up the chain, must negotiate with one or more process suppliers to assure that his or her process will get the inputs it needs. (See Figure 6.10.)

The process owner is responsible for ensuring that the process adheres to all requirements and that the output meets the quality agreed to with the process's customer. When it is determined that a process must undergo measurement and improvement, the process owner must also report on agreed-upon metrics each month. The report is made via computer, using the PBM system Boeing has developed, which is discussed later in this chapter. Process owners also attend process review meetings to assure that the larger process of which their specific process is an element is functioning smoothly.

Executive process owners not only oversee their processes and monitor performance, but they also actively work to support the process owners who are responsible for the processes that make up their high-level processes. Each month, for example, executives are measured on how they provide recognition for at least 1% of their process owners, and on their attendance at process review meetings with their process owners.

Defining Process Measures

Once a process is defined and a process owner assigned, specific measures are determined for the process. Boeing wants to maintain the vertical and horizontal alignment of process measures, which means that many a subprocess defines its measures in ways that indicate how the outcomes of that process will contribute to the achievement of the desired outcomes of its superprocess.

Figure 7.16 provides an overview of the four general categories of key performance indicators (KPIs), or metric categories that Boeing GMS uses. Quality and timeliness tend to be external measures usually determined by reference to the customer of the process. Efficiency and cycle time tend to be internal measures and are pursued to assure that the process does what it does in the most cost-efficient possible manner.

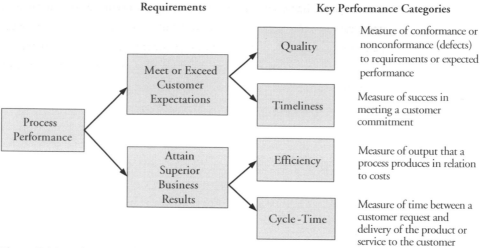

Figure 7.16 Basic Types of Process Measures.

Most process owners strive to track all four metric categories but some track more or less depending on the nature and needs of the individual process. The key is to ensure that the KPIs take into account the goals of the customer and that there is a balanced set of measures, to preclude too strong an emphasis in one performance area that would compromise performance in another.

The Boeing GMS Process-Based Management System (PBMS)

Boeing GMS's Information Technology group (a functional unit, not a process) created and maintains the Process-Based Management System (PBMS). PBMS is a set of software tools and a repository that helps process owners document processes and measures, that gathers and summarizes process performance data, and that stores all process information. Boeing had experimented with a variety of modeling and reporting tools but eventually decided to build its own system to assure that everything was integrated to support PBM.

PBMS is available to every process owner. Initial process descriptions and process models are documented using PBMS tools. Process measures are specified and monthly reports are prepared via PBMS to allow an analysis of the performance of each process that is being measured.

Figure 7.17 illustrates metric reports delivered by Boeing GMS's PBMS program. The bars represent monthly performance on process measures. The lower line that crosses both bar charts is what the process owner and the customer have agreed is acceptable performance. The higher dotted bold line is the actual process goal—that is, the level of performance that both owner and customer agree would be ideal. Any time a bar falls below the lower line, it indicates that the output of the process is below the minimum acceptable level.

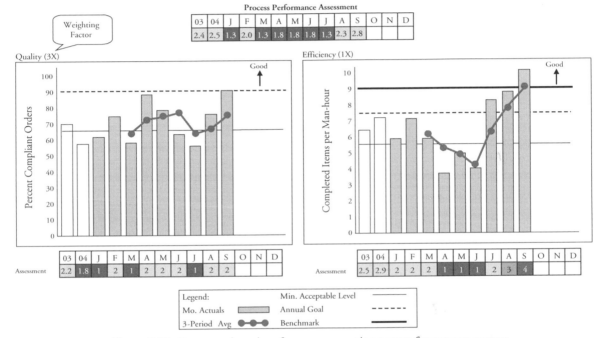

Figure 7.17 Computer-based performance reporting system for process owners.

The overall performance of all of the metric panels is summarized in the matrix bar above the two charts. In this case, colors of red, yellow, green, and blue are used to suggest a process is performing below par, is in need of improvement, or is meeting or exceeding goal.

Whenever a process owner has a process that is performing below par, he or she is required to coordinate and submit a plan to improve the process. The performance of processes and the review of process improvement plans are monitored by the process management integration group, which offers technical support when needed. For example, if a process improvement plan requires extensive changes to achieve quality goals, this "process management" process team may facilitate assignment of a Six Sigma Black Belt to assist the process owner.

During the initial deployment of PBM, considerable time was spent defining and modeling processes and determining appropriate measures. This effort continues on an annual basis, when each process owner validates with his or her customer that the process and its measures are still accurate and effective. When a new process is developed, it often requires months of data analysis to identify just the right measures to track on a monthly basis.

As in any organization, there is turnover among managers and other personnel, and new process owners always need to be trained. In a similar way, existing process owners receive refresher training on a regular basis, as enhancements to PBM and PBMS are continually made.

PBM, Process Redesign, Six Sigma, Lean, and Balanced Scorecard

Most companies embrace a variety of process improvement programs. In some cases, the IT department has a process redesign group that looks for automation opportunities. The same company may also have Six Sigma practitioners spread throughout the company and a Balanced Scorecard group working to define management objectives. Unfortunately, in most cases these groups operate in isolation, often duplicating efforts, and, in the worst case, contradicting each other.

Boeing's GMS program has individuals trained in each of these disciplines. Unlike most companies, however, these groups are not working independently to define tasks for themselves. Instead, they come together in support of PBM. As specific process owners encounter problems achieving their process objectives, they coordinate with the PBM process team to determine how to improve their performance. In most cases, the individual process owner proposes a solution that a team from the specific process can execute. When they need help, the PBM process team provides it, drawing on specifically trained process change practitioners, as needed.

ISO 9000, CMMI, and Sarbanes-Oxley

During the past two years, publicly held U.S. companies have been struggling to define where and how financial decisions occur within their organizations. They have done this to comply with the requirements of the U.S. government's Sarbanes-Oxley Act, which Congress passed in the aftermath of several accounting scandals. Implementation of the requirements was complicated and, while it was difficult at best to define the requirements, Boeing GMS already had related processes defined. The applicable process owner and process team studied the Sarbanes-Oxley documentation, and then worked through the process diagrams, identifying every activity and decision required by the legislation. Once the initial documentation was finished, the group checked with other specific process owners to assure that their understanding matched the understanding of all the owners involved, and then generated the required documentation. Boeing GMS has built the Sarbanes-Oxley information into its basic process models and can therefore update it whenever the Sarbanes-Oxley requirements change, as a byproduct of routinely updating process changes.

Dealing with Sarbanes-Oxley went relatively smoothly for Boeing GMS, in part because it has undertaken several similar exercises. Several years ago, the Boeing process team used its process modeling and measurement system to rapidly generate ISO 9001 documentation. It was accomplished by creating a map to show where each item in ISO is related to the Boeing PBM structure. Process owners were then assigned to ensure that their process documentation and related procedural documentation were in compliance with the ISO requirements.

Later, the Boeing GMS process owners did something similar to prove to an audit team that the C-17 program within Boeing GMS was operating at CMMI Level 5.

Most companies face significant challenges when asked to document their ISO, CMMI, or Sarbanes-Oxley compliance because they don't have the detailed data required by these various systems, or at least they can't organize it in any cohesive format. Boeing GMS, on the other hand, has detailed and precise division-wide data that maps to all the requirements that the various standards expect, and it has its data organized according to a comprehensive process hierarchy. Thus, Boeing GMS will be prepared to conform to any future standard that requires that an organization document how its processes are organized and how they are performing.

The Success of the Transition to Process-Based Management

Figure 7.18 provides a summary of the problems Boeing GMS faced and the impressive turn around it has achieved as a result of its implementation of the Baldrige framework in general and process management in particular since its launch in 1994. Pre-1994, Boeing GMS was failing to meet its agreements with the Air Force. This forced the shift that began in 1994. It took about four years for the BMS group to completely turn itself around, but in the end the division was one of the best-performing manufacturing organizations in the world. Boeing GMS won the Malcolm Baldrige National Quality Award in 1998 and the California state version of the Baldrige Award, the California Awards for Performance Excellence (CAPE) Gold, and the California Governor's Award, in 2002. A glance at the figures will show that Boeing GMS has continued to improve ever since. (Some of the numbers seem to drop a bit in 2000, but that reflects a major increase in the units being processed and not a drop in overall quality.)

Performance Factor	'92	'93	'94	'95	'96	'97	'98	'99	'00	'01	Awards
			Collier	CalQED	Daedalian	Baldrige			IW Finalist		
				5 X	7.5 X	17 X	18 X	31 X	50X+		RONA
			120 Aircraft Decison	Largest Multi-year Contract	Flex Sustainment	C32/C40	15 C-17 add-on +60 appropriation	UK Order	UK1-4 Deliveries		Milestones
		+10 Days	+25 Days	+40 Days	+20 Days	+60 Days	+100 Days	+204 Days	+107 Days*		Schedule
		442 Days	380 Days	374 Days	349 Days	286 Days	268 Days	223 Days	208 Days		Span Time
		5.0M	4.0M	2.5M	1.8M	1.4M	866K	707 K	644 K	535 K	Rework / Repair $
		4.2%	4.3%	2.9%	2.5%	2.2%	1.9%	1.4%	1.4%	1.1%	COQ
		100	80	50	17	12	8	6	10	15	Delivery Waivers
	58%	58%	67%	100%	92%	100%	100%	100%	100%	100%	Systems
	1.7	1.6	2.3	2.9	3.3	3.4	4.1	4.2	4.1	4.2	CPAR
	'92	'93	'94	'95	'96	'97	'98	'99	'00	'01	KEY

*Days ahead of schedule to USAF decreased due to an insertion of four UK planes into the 2001 schedule

Figure 7.18 Boeing GMS achievements from 1996 to 2005.

Following the success of Boeing GMS, other businesses within Boeing have adopted the Baldrige criteria and launched their own PBM programs. Boeing's Logistics Support Systems (formerly Aerospace Support) adopted the PBM methodology as well as the Malcolm Baldrige criteria and was recipient of the 2003 Malcolm Baldrige National Quality Award. In March of 2004, Boeing's IDS organization formally adopted the Malcolm Baldrige Criteria for Performance Excellence as the framework for its business model company-wide. Boeing is also embarking on a company-wide process management methodology for all its businesses, which will enable all its programs to operate and report within a common process framework. Meanwhile, IDS is now deploying an automated process management system that will eventually incorporate the Boeing GMS process data currently residing in PBMS.

Summary

Lots of people today are talking about business process management. For most, the phrase refers to isolated efforts or, at most, an organization-wide commitment to Six Sigma, performance measurement, or a Balanced Scorecard. Few companies have had the vision and the commitment to organize their entire management effort around processes and to create the infrastructure necessary to integrate and consistently manage all their business process efforts on a day-to-day basis. Boeing's GMS group is one of the rare exceptions that has not only embraced the vision but followed through and demonstrated the power of the approach.

When one examines the various components of Boeing GMS, one finds elements that are used by hundreds of companies. The difference, however, is that Boeing GMS has pulled them all together into a complete system, and they have placed their business managers, operating as process owners, at the center of the system. Boeing's GMS PBM program isn't something that a BP group runs. It's simply the way that Boeing's managers run their day-to-day business, as they have for the past 10 years.

Today, Boeing GMS is one of the best organized and managed business organizations in the world, and its performance and quality continue to be maintained on a day-to-day basis by its process owners.

The BPM Group

BPM groups undertake different tasks, depending on the organization of the company. In some cases they are established to help a management team create a business process architecture. In other cases they are created after the initial architecture is complete and are charged with maintaining it. In some cases the group is started from scratch. In other cases the group was originally a Balanced Scorecard group or a Six Sigma group. In other cases these functions are incorporated. Increasingly, the BPM group is being asked to coordinate all process work and that means that the group needs to either directly control or at least coordinate the resources of all of the company's process groups or initiatives. The alternative is competition among process initiatives, a lack of coordination, and inefficiencies. If the BPM group is established and given a proper role, it can help create and maintain the company's enterprise-level process management tools, report on process performance to managers, and prioritize and coordinate a company's process efforts. In this case, it will represent a major step toward creating a true process-centric organization that is able to use process to manage and change to meet challenges and to seize opportunities.

Notes and References

Once again, many of the ideas incorporated in the BPTrends methodology are derived from conversations Roger Burlton and I have had.

Most of the material on aligning processes from the top down derives from the work at Boeing GMS (formerly called Boeing A&T). The best article describing this effort is Pamela Garretson's "How Boeing A&T Manages Business Processes," which is available on *www.bptrends.com*. Search on Pam Garretson.

[1] The Baldrige Award is a U.S. government program managed by the U.S. Commerce Department. Information on the Baldrige program is available at *http://www.quality.nist.gov*. The Baldrige Awards are given annually to acknowledge superior companies. They are based on a series of evaluations that consider candidate performance in seven performance categories. The questions about process management are derived from Category 6.

[2] The Baldrige Criteria questions for Category 6, Process Management, include the following concepts:

- ▶ **Establishment**: What are your key value creations and key support processes and how does your organization determine them?
- ▶ **Requirements**: How do you determine requirements for your key value creation processes, incorporating input from customers, suppliers, and partners?
- ▶ **Measures**: What are your key indicators or performance measures to control and improve these processes?
- ▶ **Prevention**: How do you prevent rework and defects in these processes?
- ▶ **Improvement**: How do you improve these processes?
- ▶ **Learning**: How do you share lessons learned?

[3] The **Integrate and Deploy Processes and Procedures process** is one of Boeing GMS's processes, managed by their BPM group. In effect this is the process that helps Boeing GMS maintain its process health and deployment. Individuals involved in activities that fall within this process perform tasks that one would associate with a PBM support group in another organization, and the process owner of this group functions as the Boeing GMS Chief Process Officer. This process is responsible for overseeing the deployment of PBM, training new process managers, monitoring the performance of other processes, assisting process owners who need help, reporting on the process health of the enterprise, and providing other services to the organization. This "process for process management" falls organizationally within the GMS Business Excellence function that is additionally responsible for activities such as GMS Strategic Planning, the GMS Vision Support Plan (a version of a Balanced Scorecard), and the GMS Malcolm Baldrige assessment process.

In the fall of 2006 BPTrends did a survey of companies who had undertaken business process change projects. One of the interesting correlations we found was between companies that had BPM groups (or Centers of Excellence) and companies that had success on their BPM projects. Companies with BPM groups reported being much more successful. For more information on this survey go to *www.bptrends.com* click on Surveys, and then check the survey authored by Nathaniel Palmer and published in early 2007.

PART II

PROCESS LEVEL CONCERNS

I N PART II we will consider what's involved in analyzing processes and in undertaking process redesign and improvement projects. We will begin, in Chapter 8, by discussing the nature of business process problems and discussing how a process redesign or improvement team can begin to understand and scope a new process problem.

In Chapter 9 we will consider basic business process flow diagrams. We will introduce a general approach to flow diagramming that is based on a combination of Rummler-Brache, UML Activity Diagrams, and BPMN and consider how flow diagrams can be used by process analysts.

In Chapter 10 we will drill down and consider techniques that can be used for task analysis, and consider what's involved in defining the knowledge that workers require to perform tasks. We will also discuss the role of business rules in process analysis.

In Chapter 11 we will describe the role that managers play in the day-to-day success of business processes and consider what's involved in analyzing and improving the managerial activities associated with problem processes. And we'll consider the use of business rules in a little more detail.

In Chapter 12 we will describe the methodology that Six Sigma practitioners apply to the improvement of business processes. We will also look at Lean and, briefly, at TRIZ.

In Chapter 13 we will step through the activities defined by the BPTrends Process Redesign Methodology that synthesizes many different techniques while also emphasizing the importance of process management, information gathering, communication, and change management for any successful project.

chapter

8

Understanding and Scoping Process Problems

I N A FEW LEADING COMPANIES a corporate BPM group will use a business process architecture and associated performance measures to define and scope new process redesign or improvement projects. Most organizations are less mature. In those organizations it is usually a senior manager who decides there is a problem and creates a team to determine what can be done. In this situation, the team begins by gathering information in an effort to understand the nature of the problem that concerns the manager who initiated the effort. In such an informal situation, one cannot assume that the manager who ititiated the project really understands the problem. The manager knows something is wrong, but he or she may not know exactly what activities are causing the problem or have a clear idea about the nature of the changes that will be necessary to resolve the problem. In essence, the first task of any process team is to be sure that it has a good definition of the nature and scope of the problem. Once the team understands the problem, it needs to consider, in a very general way, what kinds of changes might make a difference. In some cases the team should be prepared to tell the manager that the problem can't be solved within the time or the budget that the manager has suggested. In other words, the first phase of any process change project is to define the project itself, consider possible solutions, and then make a recommendation about what level of effort and budget will be needed to solve the problem.

In this chapter we want to consider the nature of business process problems and suggest some smart approaches to scoping a process redesign or improvement project. We'll begin with a general discussion of the nature of processes to establish a common vocabulary and then we'll proceed to consider the nature of the process problems that teams are likely to encounter. We'll end with a discussion of techniques for scoping problems.

What Is a Process?

A process is a bounded set of activities that are undertaken, in response to some event, in order to generate an output. Processes can be very simple or extremely complex. One example of a process might be a software application that is initiated by a salesperson swiping a credit card across a reader. The software application would proceed to transmit information to a credit card center mainframe to determine if the card is valid and the amount is acceptable. Upon receipt of an approval, the application might trigger a printer to print out a purchase slip for the customer to sign. (See Figure 8.1.)

Figure 8.1 An example of a simple process.

Another process might be initiated by a call from a taxpayer for help in determining what tax form to use. In this case the call would be answered by a person who would ask questions and then tell the taxpayer what form to use. We can imagine a general description of the Answer Taxpayer Inquiry process, and hundred of instances of it as particular tax clerks answer phones and undertake the process with different taxpayers. Still another process might be a corporate supply chain that responds to customer orders by generating and delivering products to customers. The supply chain process at any large company is complex and could easily be subdivided into subprocesses that contain hundreds of activities and thousands of business rules and are implemented by employees located throughout the world.

We understand that our initial definition is a little vague, but we prefer to use the word "process" informally, as the term is normally used, and then refine our understanding with some adjectives.

One important distinction to consider, when thinking about a process is whether it functions as a core or operational process, a management process, or an enabling or support process. We discussed this in Chapter 4 when we considered process architectures and you should review Figure 4.6 if you are unclear about the distinction.

Process Levels and Levels of Analysis

Another key concept is the idea of a process hierarchy and the use of levels to describe the subdivision of processes. This was also discussed in Chapter 4. We reproduce the figure we used there as Figure 8.3 and have added notes on the left to suggest how a process analysis effort will tend to vary, depending on whether we are dealing with very large processes, midlevel processes, or specific activities or tasks.

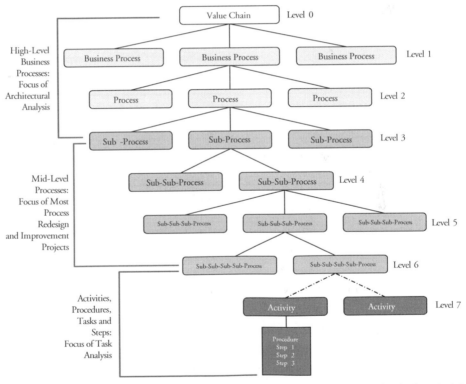

Figure 8.2 A hierarchical decomposition of a value chain, suggesting how "level of analysis" corresponds to process level.

As a generalization, we can usually divide the process hierarchy into three parts and associate problems and analysis techniques with specific levels. Broadly, one set of process analysis techniques are used to redesign or improve higher-level processes. Another set is used on the types of process problems we find in the middle of the process hierarchy. Still another set of techniques is appropriate for processes at the bottom of the hierarchy. Figure 8.3 provides an overview of this three-part distinction.

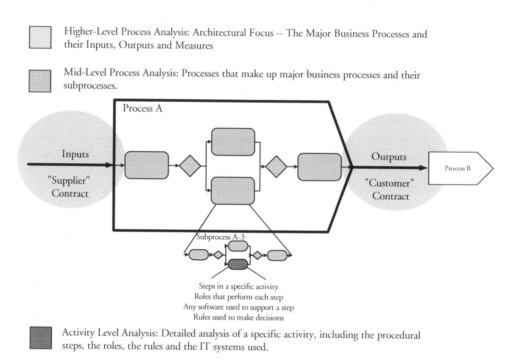

Higher-Level Process Analysis: Architectural Focus -- The Major Business Processes and their Inputs, Outputs and Measures

Mid-Level Process Analysis: Processes that make up major business processes and their subprocesses.

Activity Level Analysis: Detailed analysis of a specific activity, including the procedural steps, the roles, the rules and the IT systems used.

Figure 8.3 An overview of the different levels of process analysis.

Thus, the top part of the process hierarchy is usually associated with architecture problems and with problems of coordination between departments or functional units. In this case, we focus on aligning inputs and outputs and write contracts to specify what Process A will need to deliver to its "customer," Process B.

Mid-size problems usually occur in processes managed within a single department. The problems often require that the processes be simplified or the sequences rearranged. Non-value adding processes need to be removed; some activities need to be automated.

Low-level problems usually involve individual performers or software systems. They usually require a detailed task analysis. In some cases, the business rules used by the performers or the systems need to be specified. Often training programs and job descriptions need to be developed.

Simple and Complex Processes

Another way to begin the analysis of a process is to consider the overall complexity of the process you are going to analyze. Simple processes usually follow a consistent, well-defined sequence of steps with clearly defined rules. Each step or task can be precisely defined and the sequence lacks branches or exceptions.

More complex processes involve branches and exceptions, usually draw on many rules and tend to be slightly less well-defined. They require more initiative on the part of human performers. Really complex processes demand still more initiative and creativity on the part of human performers. They are usually processes that cannot be automated using current technologies. We usually don't train people to do these tasks, but hire people who have already demonstrated the creative or analytic skills required. These processes are less well defined, change often and evolve as time passes. Successful performance usually requires that the performer study an evolving body of knowledge in order to be prepared to perform the tasks required to create successful results. Figure 8.5 illustrates the continuum that ranges from simple, procedural processes through more complex processes to very complex processes.

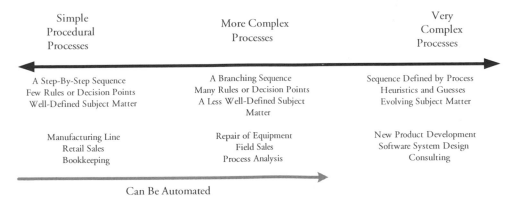

Figure 8.4 A continuum suggesting how processes vary as to their complexity.

It is popular today to suggest that the nature of work has changed in advanced economies. In the past, workers were more likely to be engaged in the type of procedural tasks one still finds in production-line manufacturing and in some clerical tasks. Increasingly, however, today's workers are engaged in tasks that require more knowledge and many writers refer to them as *knowledge workers*. For some, this implies that the workers use computers to acquire or manipulate the information they need to do their jobs, but for others it simply refers to the fact that the workers perform in more complex processes.

Figure 8.5 pictures the space that results when we cross levels of analysis with process complexity. On the horizontal axis we place the task complexity continuum. To the left we have simple, repetitive tasks. In the middle we have tasks that require more skill and flexibility. On the extreme right we have tasks that are very complex and require considerable creativity. On the vertical axis, we have placed a continuum that ranges from high-level, very abstract processes at the top to low-level, very concrete activities and tasks at the bottom.

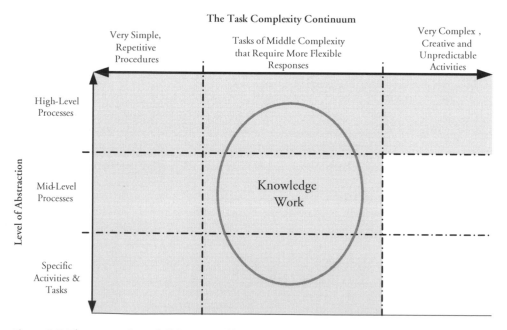

Figure 8.5 The space of possibilities created by crossing levels of analysis with process complexity.

As long as we are only trying to provide a very high-level overview of the processes involved, we aren't concerned with the specific nature of the task. At the architectural level it is possible to describe both procedural and complex processes with equal ease, since we aren't concerned with details, but only with abstractions. Thus, for example, a supply chain is a very large process that contains some procedural subprocesses and some very complex planning subprocesses. At the level of abstraction that we work at when creating a business process architecture and defining major process performance measures, we simply don't care about the numerous and various specific tasks that make up the high-level processes. The real supply chain may involve numerous loops and feedback cycles, but at the high level we are simply concerned with defining major processes that will need to be managed and measured and defining handoff points that will need to be coordinated. For this, conventional modeling with a workflow notation like SCOR or BPMN will serve very well.

Extending our analysis, we can analyze and describe mid- and low-level procedural processes without too much difficulty. It becomes more difficult as we try to analyze mid- and low-level processes of moderate complexity, and it becomes very difficult to analyze mid- or low-level processes of great complexity. Consider one example—the various activities of the CEO of a large corporation. It might be possible to specify that all CEOs are concerned with several general processes like defining company strategy, finding a successor, and maintaining relationships with senior government officials. Beyond such generalizations, however, it wouldn't be valuable to try to analyze exactly how the CEO went about defining strategy, let alone how he or she managed the very specific tasks, like conducting interviews or handling luncheon meetings. Companies don't try to specify exactly how their CEOs, their creative marketing directors, or their lead software architects should do their jobs.

Most process analysts today are focused on defining and improving processes that involve knowledge workers. Analyzing the activities of these individuals is complex enough and the analysis techniques we will focus on in the remainder of this chapter are mostly used to define mid-level processes of moderate complexity. That's where the interesting challenges in analysis and design lie today.

Business Process Problems

Projects begin with problems. The challenge is to figure out the nature of the problem, and then to consider what kind of intervention might be required to resolve the problem. Let's formalize this a bit with a model of problem solving—which we refer to as the Gap Model—which we've illustrated in Figure 8.6. Formally, a problem is the difference between what exists now and what we desire. We represent that with two boxes. The left-hand box is labeled the Existing or As-Is Process. The right-hand box is labeled the Redesigned or To-Be Process.

We can talk about the existing and the To-Be process in either of two ways. We can speak of measures that describe the performance of the process, or we can describe how the As-Is or the To-Be process works. The manager who assigns the project, for example, might simply say that the output of the process needs to be doubled, or he or she might say that defective outputs need to be cut in half. Similarly, the manager might say that competitors have automated similar processes and we need to automate our own process. Depending on the situation, the project team usually ends up working back and forth between descriptions of what is and what might be and between measures that define how the process works today and proposed activities that describe how the process ought to perform once it is "improved."

We refer to the difference between measures of the performance of the As-Is process and the To-Be process as the performance gap. We refer to descriptions of the difference between how things are done now and how they could or should be performed in the redesigned process as the capabilities gap.

One problem that any project team will encounter is the difference between descriptions of actual problems and descriptions of causes or consequences. Figure 8.8 suggests some of the different types of statements you might encounter. The project team is forced to ask, often several times: "Why do you think this happens?" or "Why is this a problem?" until the team is satisfied that they can clearly define the actual problem. Often measures or statistics cited by management will be measures of consequences and the team will need to work backwards to determine what problem they will need to eliminate to improve the measure that management is concerned with changing.

If we extend the Gap Model, we can see that it also provides a framework for thinking about the kinds of analytic techniques we might want to use to define the problem and can even suggest the redesign techniques we might use to resolve the problem. Figure 8.8 illustrates the relationship between the problem gap and analytic and redesign techniques and illustrates the use of the model with an actual project.

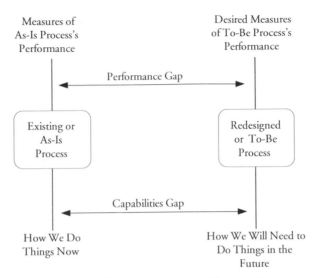

Figure 8.7 Some relationships between causes, problems, and consequences.

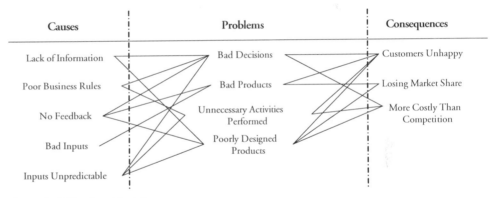

Figure 8.6 The Gap Model.

In the example illustrated in Figure 8.8 the manager assigning the project stated that the goal of the project was to produce outputs in half the time currently required. Thus, presumably, the project team gathered data on the time required by the current process and then projected how much time they would have to eliminate to achieve the project goal. Since the essence of the problem involved the time the project takes, the team used a time study technique, which involved determining the time each step takes and the time that elapses between each step. They relied on Lean techniques to examine each step to determine what could be eliminated or streamlined. In other words, the nature of the Capability Gap often suggests the project approach, analysis data to gather and the process redesign or improvement techniques that will be most useful.

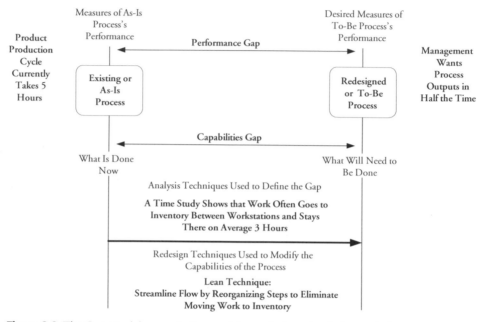

Figure 8.8 The Gap Model suggests the need for analysis and redesign techniques.

The Initial Cut: What is the Process?

At some point during the scoping process, you will need to work up a good overview of the existing or As-Is process. Most teams begin by asking management about the nature of the process. What is it called, for example? Let's assume, for the purposes of our discussion, that the management of a pizza company, with several different stores, asks you to help improve their pizza delivery process. From the very beginning, you assume that the process being discussed is the Pizza Delivery process. (It is usually best to define a process with a verb-noun phrase, so we mentally turn "Pizza Delivery" process into "Deliver Pizzas.")

At some point we usually acquire more information. At a minimum, we define the inputs that trigger the process and the outputs that signal that the process has successfully concluded. At the same time, we usually define the major substeps in the

Figure 8.9 A very general overview of the process we are asked to study.

overall process. Thus, in the case of our pizza delivery problem, we determine that the process begins when customers call to order pizzas. Their calls are managed by a phone system that takes calls for the entire city and then routes them to the appropriate store. The actual process, within a given store, begins when they are notified of an order. They proceed to cook the pizza. Meanwhile, the delivery manager schedules the delivery, grouping orders so that each delivery run will be as efficient as possible. If business is brisk, the area around each store is divided into regions and deliverys are organized according to region so that the delivery trucks travel the minimum distance and the pizzas are delivered warm. When a delivery vehicle becomes available and a set of orders is assembled, delivery takes place. Comments made by managers about the availability of delivery trucks leads us to add that activity to our overview, although we are uncertain, at this point, if it's to be included in our project or not. If some measure, like the time required per delivery, is mentioned, we often make a note on our diagram to suggest what we will want to measure. All this results in a very simple diagram that captures the overall process, the major inputs and outputs, and any important subprocesses or measures, as illustrated in Figure 8.10. We are not defining a formal notation or a vocabulary for this type of diagram. The key here is to simply get a rough but useful overview of the elements in the process, as it is currently understood.

As the high-level diagram of the process is developed, it is shared with everyone involved in the project, and management is asked: Does this describe the process we are to improve? Should we consider the maintenance of delivery trucks? Should we look at problems with the phone system? Should we consider the food preparation process, or only the delivery scheduling and delivery activities? Our goal at this point is not to get into any detail, but simply to determine what management wants us to study.

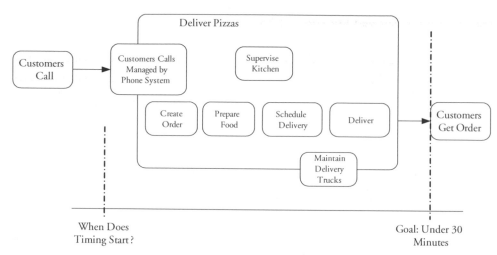

Figure 8.10 A diagram of the Deliver Pizzas process that includes some detail.

Keep in mind that management might not have considered all the implications of their request. They may assume that the problem is in the scheduling of deliveries, and not realize that it is the frequent lack of available vehicles that makes scheduling so inefficient. We start by determining what management *thinks* the problem is and then we proceed to gather more information to determine if their understanding is probably correct, or if it will make sense for us to suggest changing the scope of the project in some way. Once we have an initial description of the problem, we talk with people involved with the process to refine our understanding of the process and to identify likely problems. In all cases we are seeking to refine our understanding of the measures of the As-Is process, of the actual inputs, steps and outputs of the process, the causes of whatever specific problem that management has asked us to eliminate, and of any other problems that prevent the process from functioning as well as it might.

Stakeholders

As you gather information from senior management about the process to be changed, you should also be developing a list of all the stakeholders who have an interest in the process. Stakeholders will include customers, suppliers, managers, employees, and anyone managing a process that interacts with the process you are going to try to change. During the analysis phase of the project, you will want to interview all of the stakeholders (or at least representatives) to assure that you understand how they view the process and its problems.

Refining an Initial Process Description

Once you have a basic description of the problem process, represented as either one process that needs to be changed or as a process with 4–5 subprocesses that need to be improved, you are ready to refine your understanding of the process, the scope of the problem, and specific nature of the problems you will need to deal with.

Now you are ready to interview a number of different stakeholders, including customers, employees, and day-to-day managers.

At this early stage we often find it useful to create a project scoping diagram. Later, once we understand the problem better and as we begin to refine our analysis of the problem, we usually move to a process flow diagram. (See Figure 8.11.)

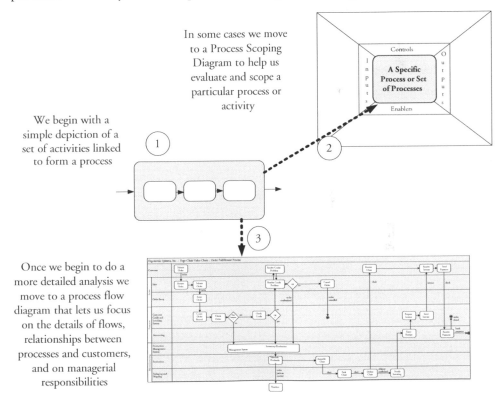

Figure 8.11 Moving from an initial, informal process diagram to a project scoping diagram or a process flow diagram.

In this chapter we'll consider project scoping diagrams in some detail. In the next chapter we will move on to process flow diagrams. The basic ideas behind the project scoping diagram originated with the structured software analysis modeling technique, called IDEF (Integrated DEFinition language), which was originally developed by the U.S. Air Force and which proved popular with CASE (computer-assisted software engineering) tool vendors in the late 1980s. Most of the elements in IDEF are too technical to be of interest to business modelers, although elements of other IDEF diagrams are still used by software engineers. The idea of analyzing and scoping a process within a "box," however, has been developed and popularized by Roger Burlton and his associates at the Process Renewal Group (PRG) and is quite useful in business analysis.

The basic diagram is referred to, in the IDEF literature, as a function box. Burlton refers to it as an IGOE (inputs, guides, outputs and enablers) diagram. We'll refer to it, more generically, as a project scoping diagram and develop it somewhat beyond its use by either IDEF or PRG. In essence, we create a diagram, like the one shown in the upper right of Figure 8.11, and then place the process or processes we intend to analyze in the center of the space, which we call the process area. The area to the left of the process area is reserved for information about inputs to the process or processes in the problem area. The area to the right of the process area is reserved for outputs from the process or processes in the problem area. The inputs and outputs can link the process(es) in the process area to individuals, documents, products, or other processes. The area above the process area is for guides or controls, which can be individuals, documents or processes that manage, constrain, or control the activities of the processes in the process area. The area below the process area is where we enter information about the support or enabling processes that support the execution of the processes in the process area. It sometimes helps to remember that the inputs are consumed by the processes, modified, and turned into outputs. The controls and the enabling processes, on the other hand, are reusable resources. Figure 8.12 provides a more detailed look at the kinds of issues that we are concerned with when we create a project scoping diagram.

Readers more familiar with cause-effect diagrams (which are also called Ishikawa or fishbone diagrams) might prefer to do their project scoping with a cause-effect diagram, which can represent the same information. (See Figure 8.13.) We prefer the project scoping diagram partly because it seems to provide more space in which to record information and also because it lets us show how we might change the scope of the project. In our experience, cause-effect diagrams work better for smaller problems,

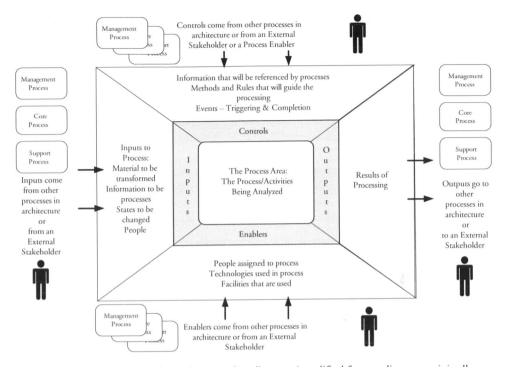

Figure 8.12 The elements of a project scoping diagram (modified from a diagram originally developed by Process Renewal Group).

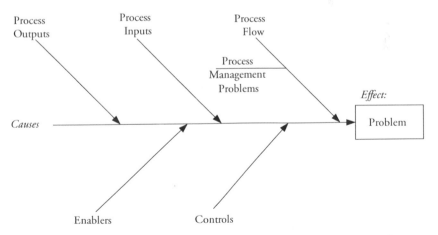

Figure 8.13 A cause-effect figure with prespecified cause categories for scoping.

and larger problems require more space simply because there are more problems and more opportunities to make improvements. But it is obviously a matter of personal taste and many prefer to scope with cause-effect diagrams.

If we were to use a process scoping diagram to analyze the Deliver Pizzas process, we would begin by placing the rough process diagram of the Deliver Pizzas process in the process area. Then we would begin to make notes in the process area or in the areas surrounding the process area. These notes would reflect things we found out about the process when we interviewed individuals involved with the process. In essence, the process scoping diagram reminds us of the types of problems we might encounter in analyzing any process and provides us with space to make notes about actual problems we encounter. Thus, the diagram provides room for information about relationships between the process-in-scope (in the process area), other processes, documents or individuals, or what flows between them. At the same time, considering these relationships, we are able to focus on the five generic types of process problems we typically encounter, including:

▶ Process Flow and Day-to-Day Management Problems
▶ Output Problems
▶ Input Problems
▶ Problems with Controls
▶ Problems with Enablers

Process Flow and Day-to-Day Management Problems

The place to begin with any initial process analysis effort is to assure that you understand the process that is being described. This area is more complex because there are two things to consider. There are the activities that make up the process itself, and then there is the day-to-day process management issues. In essence, every process or activity should have someone who is responsible for assuring that the process or activity is accomplished. This process manager may be a team leader, a supervisor, or a manager who is responsible for several other activities including this one. It is the manager who is responsible for assuring that the process has the resources it needs, that employees know and perform their jobs, and that employees get feedback when they succeed or when they fail to perform correctly. It's just as likely that a process is broken because the manager isn't doing his or her job as it is that the process is broken because of the flow of activities or the work of the employees.

We begin with the process itself and consider its subprocesses or activities, and we ask everyone involved in the process a number of questions to explore the following possibilities.

1.1 Flow Problems

1.1.1 Problems with Logical Completeness

▶ Some activities are not connected to other, related activities

▶ Some outputs have no place to go

▶ Some inputs have no place to go

1.1.2 Sequencing and Duplication Problems

▶ Some activities are performed in the wrong order

▶ Some activities are performed sequentially that could be performed in parallel

▶ Work is done and then put into inventory until needed

▶ Some activities are performed more than once

▶ There are no rules for determining or prioritizing flows between certain activities or individuals

1.1.3 Subprocess Inputs and Outputs

▶ The inputs and outputs of subprocesses are wrong or inadequately specified

▶ Subprocess inputs or outputs can be of inadequate quality, insufficient quantity or untimely

▶ Subprocesses get inputs or make outputs that are unnecessary

▶ Some subprocesses do things that make for more work for other subprocesses

1.1.4 Process Decision-Making

▶ The process-in-scope, or one of its subprocesses, is called upon to make decisions without adequate or necessary information

▶ The process-in-scope, or one of its subprocesses, is required to make decisions without adequate or complete guidance from the value chain or organization. E.g., decisions must be made without stated policies or without specific business rules

1.1.5 Subprocess Measures

▶ There are inadequate or no measures for the quality, quantity or timeliness of subprocess outputs

▶ Subprocess measures are lagging measures and don't provide the process manager or other employees with the ability to anticipate or plan for changes in pace or flow volume

Keep in mind that we will explore all of these issues in greater detail as we proceed with our process analysis effort. During the initial scoping phase we are simply trying to get an overview of what could be wrong with the process. At this point we are looking for problems that stand out and that will clearly have to be addressed if we are to eliminate the gap between the existing process and the process that management desires. Figure 8.14 shows our process scoping diagram with the provide delivery service process, subdivided into five activities, pictured in the process area.

Figure 8.15 depicts the same processes as we pictured in Figure 8.14, but in this case we have explicitly pictured the management process associated with each subprocess in the Deliver Pizzas process. In fact, we would rarely draw such a diagram. When doing a quick, early analysis, we simply assume that each operational process has an associated day-to-day management process. To illustrate this idea, however, we have added each of the management processes in Figure 8.15 to suggest that we need to consider how the management processes work at the same time that we consider the flow of the basic processes.

Some of the questions we ask when we consider if there are problems with the day-to-day management processes include:

1.2 Day-to-Day Management Problems
1.2.1 Planning and Resource Allocation Problems
▶ The process manager working on the process-in-scope is given lagging data, but no leading data that he or she can use to anticipate work, plans, schedule, etc.

1.2.2 Monitoring, Feedback and Control Problems
▶ Employees working on the process-in-scope are not held responsible for achieving one or more key process goals
▶ The employees working on the process-in-scope are punished for pursuing one or more key process goals
▶ The employees working on the process-in-scope are not given adequate information about the performance of the process he/she is responsible for managing
▶ The employees working on the process-in-scope are given lagging data, but no leading data that they can use to anticipate work, plans, schedule, etc.
▶ The employees working on the process-in-scope are either not rewarded for achieving key process goals or they are punished for achieving key process goals e.g., the employee who works the hardest to assure that the process-in-scope meets a deadline is given more work to do

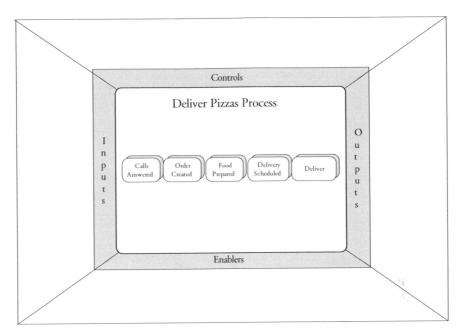

Figure 8.14 A process scoping diagram with the process area filled in.

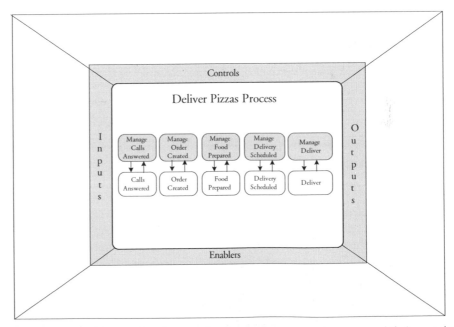

Figure 8.15 Project scoping diagram showing both processes in scope and their associated day-to-day management processes.

1.2.3 Manager's Goals and Incentives Conflicted

▶ The process manager is trying to achieve functional/departmental goals that are incompatible with the goals of the process-in-scope

▶ The process manager does not have the authority, budget or resources required to effectively manage the process-in-scope

1.2.4 Manager Accountability

▶ The process manager is not held responsible for achieving one or more key process goals

▶ The process manager is punished for pursuing one or more key process goals

▶ The process manager is not given adequate information about the performance of the process he/she is responsible for managing

There is an important distinction between day-to-day process management and the more generic, higher-level management processes that are included under controls. Thus, for example, a day-to-day manager is responsible for assuring that employees know and apply the business rules that apply to a given process. In most cases that manager is not responsible for creating, maintaining or changing the business rules. If the business rules aren't being applied, we focus on the day-to-day process manager. If the business rules are wrong or should be changed, we are probably going to have to look at the higher-level management process that sets policy and defines business rules.

Output Problems

Output problems result when the "customer" of the process isn't getting what is needed. It's possible the outputs are unrealistic or unnecessary and should be changed, but as things stand, if the quality, quantity or timeliness of the outputs of the process-in-scope aren't satisfying your customers, you have problems. Keep in mind that "customers" can be other processes.

Similarly, there can be other stakeholders that have an interest in the outputs of a process. Thus, for example, local government regulators might be interested in outputs that don't meet local food service laws. Similarly, delivery service employees might be stakeholders if the delivery schedule required them to exceed speed laws to make the required deliveries in the time allowed. Outputs can take different forms, including physical entities, information or data, or decisions/approvals.

2.1 Quality of Output
▶ Output is rejected by a quality control process downstream (number, ratio of rejects)
▶ Downstream process refuses to accept output of process-in-scope
▶ Output is returned (ratio of returns to output)

2.2 Quantity of Output
▶ Process does not produce number of outputs required
▶ Process cannot scale down quickly when a decreased number of outputs is required
▶ Process cannot scale up quickly when an increased number of outputs is required

2.3 Timeliness of Output
▶ Some or all of the needed outputs are not produced when required

In the case of our pizza example, the obvious customers are the individuals ordering pizzas.

Input Problems

This type of problem results because the "suppliers" of the process-in-scope aren't producing what's needed by the process-in-scope. Suppliers can include companies, individuals or other processes and "inputs" can include things, information, money or even temporary employees. As with output, inputs to the process-in-scope can be deficient in quality, quantity, or timeliness. Similarly, inputs can take different forms, including physical entities, information or data, or decisions/approvals.

3.1 Quality on Inputs
▶ Inputs are rejected because they don't meet quality standards of process-in-scope
▶ Inputs must be returned to upstream process or supplier (Ratio of returns to input)

3.2 Quantity of Input
▶ Supplier does not produce number of inputs required
▶ Supplier can not scale down quickly when a decreased number of inputs are required

▶ Supplier can not scale up quickly when an increased number of inputs are required

3.3 Timeliness of Inputs

▶ Some or all of the needed inputs do not arrive when needed

▶ Inputs arrive in batches and must be stored till needed

Figure 8.16 shows a project scoping diagram for the Deliver Pizzas process with some basic inputs and outputs.

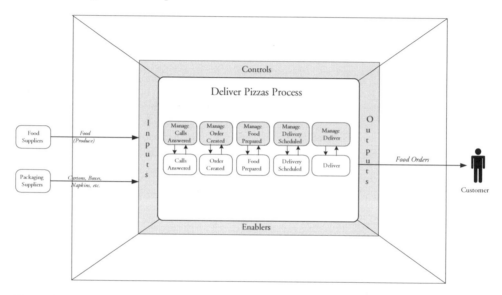

Figure 8.16 A project scoping diagram with some inputs and outputs shown.

So far we are only describing some of the people and processes that generate inputs or accept outputs. Later we will list some of the specific problems that might occur in each section of the diagram.

Problems with Controls

Controls define or constrain how a process is performed. In most cases, controls are created by higher-level management processes and then released to the managers and employees of the process-in-scope. Thus, for example, a high-level management process generates a company strategy. Then higher-level managers define policies and goals that are passed down to the day-to-day managers responsible for specific processes. Broadly, there are four general types of control problems: Problems with the goals of the process-in-scope, problems with policies and business rules, problems with documentation, manuals and other formal sources of control information, and problems with external management processes that either don't support the day-to-day managers or don't supply data, or require outputs that are incompatible with the nature of the process-in-scope.

4.1 Process-In-Scope Not Aligned to Organization or Value Chain Strategy

Processes implement strategies just as organizations do. An organization might decide to pursue a low-cost-provider strategy. A given process, however, for whatever reason, might be doing things that assure that its outputs are anything but low cost. This is a strategy alignment problem. Similarly, some processes pursue strategies that are incompatible with the value chain of which they are a part. The assumption is that organization strategy trumps value chain strategy and that value chain strategy preempts process strategy. Process strategies should be changed to assure they actually implement organizational and value chain strategies.

▶ Organization strategy, with regard to the process-in-scope, is unclear

▶ Process is pursuing a strategy incompatible with stated organization strategy

▶ The value chain strategy is unclear and two or more processes are pursuing un-coordinated or incompatible strategies. E.g., one process is doing something to save money that is costing another process more money.

4.2 Problems with Policies or Business Rules

Policies are statements of how an organization intends to do business. Business rules are more specific statements that define how specific situations are to be handled. Logically, business rules should be derived from and align with organizational policies.

▶ Full implementation of stated policies would make it impossible for the process-in-scope to function

▶ The process-in-scope consistently ignores one or more organizational policies

▶ The process-in-scope consistently ignores one or more specific business rules

▶ Individual employees working in the process-in-scope ignore one or more specific policies or business rules

▶ The process-in-scope is tasked to implement incompatible goals or policies

▶ The priority of goals or policies that the process-in-scope is tasked to implement is unclear

▶ The priority of goals or policies that the process-in-scope is tasked to implement can shift rapidly and the process is unable to make the switch quickly or
completely enough

4.3 Problems with Documentation, Manuals, etc.

Problems in this area are closely related to problem category 4.2. They usually arise
because documentation is out of date, and policies or rules in the documentation
are wrong or because two or more sources of information are incompatible.

▶ Documentation is incomplete, out-of-date, or wrong

▶ Documentation is obscure and hard to read or understand

▶ Documentation is written in the wrong language

▶ Documentation is unavailable to people who need it, when they need it

4.4 Problems with External Management Processes

This type of problem results from information provided by or required by a
management process that is not in the scope of the analysis effort. In essence,
these are situations that usually have to be lived-with or worked around, as they
can't be changed.

▶ External management process require information that the process-in-scope is
unable to provide

▶ External management processes input information or directions that the process-in-scope in unable to use or implement

In the case of our pizza process, we know that there are a number of federal, state
and local laws that govern any business and many particular laws that regulate food
preparation. All of these laws must be obeyed and any management policy or business
rules that contradict these external laws creates an immediate problem. In addition,
the company we are considering runs a number of different pizza stores, so we can be
sure there are company-wide policies, manuals and rules that define or constrain what
local store managers can do. There are also, undoubtedly, goals set for local managers
by the company management which can generate a variety of problems.

Problems with Enablers

Problems with enabling or support processes arise when those processes fail to provide or maintain the resources needed by the process-in-scope. Support processes and
problems can be divided into three or four broad categories. Information Technology

(IT), Human Resources (HR), and Facility, equipment and location problems are the most obvious. Some would also include problems with the gathering or production of accounting and financial data in this area, but others would consider it a control problem. It doesn't make too much difference where you consider accounting problems, as long as they are handled consistently on your Project Scoping Diagrams.

5.1 Employee Problems

▶ The process-in-scope is understaffed. HR can't find or hire enough employees to adequately staff the process-in-scope

▶ The jobs or roles defined for employees assigned to the process do not match the needs/requirements of the process-in-scope

▶ Employees lack the skills needed to perform the work required to accomplish the process-in-scope

▶ The employees have never been told who is responsible for various tasks that are part of the process-in-scope

▶ Employees need training

▶ Training provided is inadequate or offered at the wrong times

▶ Manuals or other documentation do not offer complete or adequate guidance

▶ The rewards or incentives provided for employees do not support the performance required by the process-in-scope. Worse, they actively discourage the correct employee performance. For example, the salespeople get bonuses for selling widgets, but get nothing if they spend time trying to sell the products generated by the process-in-scope

▶ The employees lack the time, space or tools required for the performance of some of the tasks involved in the process-in-scope

▶ The employees working on the process-in-scope are given lagging data, but no leading data that they can use to anticipate work, plans, schedule, etc.

▶ The employees believe that some or all of the performance required by the process-in-scope is unnecessary, not properly part of their job, or should not be performed for whatever reason

5.2 IT Problems

▶ IT applications require inputs or generate outputs that are out of sync with the actual flow and activities of the process-in-scope

▶ Data is required or is generated that is out of sync with the actual flow and activities of the process-in-scope

▶ IT applications or tools require inputs or make outputs that are hard to impossible to interpret and thus inadequate user interfaces lead to inefficiencies or errors

▶ IT applications or tools support normal processing but do not adequately support exception handling, which is a special problem whenever the number of exceptions spikes

▶ Activates are performed manually that could be more efficiently performed by a software application

▶ Data must be input more than once because the software applications being used do not share the relevant data

▶ Data or reports provided to employees is inadequate, incomplete, or out of date

5.3 Facilities, Equipment and Location Problems

▶ Resources or tools required by the process-in-scope are unavailable when they are needed

▶ The facilities are inadequate

▶ The equipment is inadequate

▶ The process-in-scope is geographically distributed and this causes inefficiencies

5.4 Accounting and Bookkeeping Problems

▶ Bookkeeping requirements impose heavy burdens on the process-in-scope

▶ Accounting information needed for decisions in the process-in-scope isn't available or isn't available in the form needed for the decisions.

Figure 8.17 illustrates a project scoping diagram with some controls and support processes defined.

At this point we've suggested the five major types of problems one can encounter and suggested some of the processes and individuals that might be associated with the Deliver Pizzas process. To further develop the example, in Figure 8.18 we've included a Process Analysis Worksheet we prepared while talking with stakeholders in the Deliver Pizzas Process. The worksheet lists some of the problems that we encountered. Figure 8.19 shows how we transferred the notes from our worksheet to the project scoping diagram. We then went on to indicate how critical we thought different problems were. Obviously problem criticality depends on the goals of the project. Something that can be ignored in one project might become the central issue in a different project.

State and County Food Health Regulations

Manuals and Policies Defined by Fast Food Inc.

Figure 8.17 A project scoping diagram with some controls and enablers defined.

Provide Delivery Service					
Subprocess	Nature of Activity	Manager	Employees	Measure of Success	Problems ?
Calls Answered	Answering system answers calls and asks customer to wait for an available operator	Order Supervisor	(Phone System)	(System answers each call within 10 seconds.)	System can tell customers of specials, but Supervisors often don't program system with new specials
Order Created	Operator answers next call on queue, takes order, and asks how customer will pay (credit card or cash). If credit card, information taken and checked. Operator puts paper order on kitchen "rotator."	Order Supervisor	From 1 to 5 phone order takers who sit at a phone with a head set and take orders.	Each order taken within 3 minutes of call. Each order written down correctly. Only valid credit card orders processed.	Supervisors don't have enough order takers. Customers sometimes have to wait 4-5 minutes and some hang up.
Food Prepared	Food prep person takes next order from "rotator" and cooks or assembles food and then places it in a bag. Bag is placed in Delivery "window."	Kitchen Supervisor	From 2 to 5 cooks	Every order processes within 4 minutes of receipt. Each order prepared and packaged correctly. Food packaged so it stays warm.	"Continuously available items (e.g., French Fries) are re-set-up often enough and delays result while new batches need to be prepared. Some order mistakes made. Key supplies sometimes run out.
Delivery Scheduled	Delivery supervisor looks at order on each bag placed in "window," and determines location, prepares route sheets and groups deliveries in boxes, which are assigned to delivery people.	Delivery Supervisor	(no employees)	Orders clustered into routes that can be run in under 30 minutes.	Sometimes there aren't enough delivery people available when orders "surge." Some routes take more than 30 minutes.
Delivery Undertaken	Delivery person takes route sheet assigned, loads boxes in truck and makes deliveries. Collects from all cash orders. Returns to store with cash and accounts with delivery supervisor.	Delivery Supervisor	From 2 to 8 delivery people	Routes run in 30 minutes. Cash collected from all cash customers. Delivery people are polite to customers. All cash correctly accounted.	Some routes take more than 30 minutes. Some food delivered cold. Some delivery people "brisk." Cash is sometimes not properly accounted.

Figure 8.18 A worksheet with information gathered about the Deliver Pizza process.

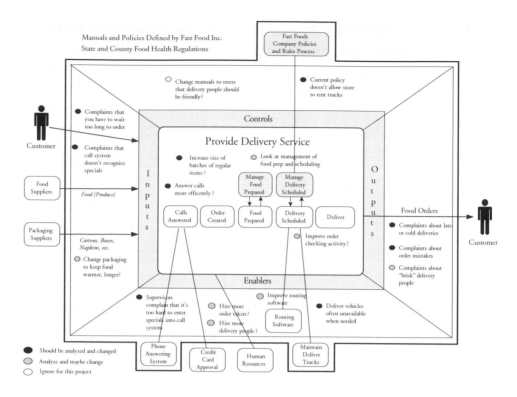

Figure 8.19 A project scoping diagram with problems indicated and with a bold line to suggest additional processes that should be included in the scope of the project to maximize the odds of a successful outcome.

Finally, we added a bold line to the project scoping diagram to suggest a revised scope for our project. Keep in mind that the initial scope was the process or processes and their associated day-to-day management processes that we placed in the process area of our initial diagram. In many cases that remains the scope when we finish the project scoping diagram, and the diagram simply documents the relationships and the problems with the process-in-scope. In other cases, however, we may decide that a successful project requires that we expand our scope and analyze and redesign processes that lie outside the original scope and the project scoping diagram helps us document and explain why we would like to expand the scope of the project. Obviously an expanded scope will invariably require the consent of the manager who initiated the project and may require asking other managers who are responsible for other processes to become involved in the project. In some cases, for practical or political reasons, the scope of the project can't be expanded. In those cases, however, it helps if everyone understands, at the beginning of the project, what limits are being imposed on the scope of the process change we will attempt. In a few cases, the inability to expand the scope of a project strongly suggests that the project probably can't be successfully undertaken and should not be pursued.

Different practitioners use project scoping diagrams in slightly different ways. Some practitioners like to simply mention problem areas and then use bullets to suggest if there are problems in that area. Others do as we do here and suggest specific fixes to be considered. Some would list lots of additional processes that might be related to the Deliver Pizza process. They important thing about the project scoping diagram is its informality. It provides a way to gather and record information about all of the possible problems you might encounter without requiring a formal definition about how processes are related or how policies are created or manuals are maintained. It's a very useful diagram when you are first trying to decide what will be included in a project and what kind of problems you might encounter. In the next chapter we will begin to examine process flow diagrams. They provide a much more precise and detailed way to approach the analysis of processes and activities, but they also require a lot more time to assure that they are accurate. The project scoping diagram is useful precisely because it doesn't require precision, while simultaneously allowing the project team to capture all of the different problems that might impact a project. And they provide a nice way of underlining when the scope of a project will probably need to be enlarged to assure that the project team can meet the project goals established by management.

Redesign, Improvement and Lean Six Sigma

We have discussed process analysis in this chapter without regard to redesign, improvement or any particular methodology. Those familiar with Lean or Six Sigma might react one of two ways. They might already consider all of the issues we have discussed as appropriate topics for a Lean or Six Sigma project. In that case, they are among the more flexible Lean and Six Sigma practitioners. Many Lean and Six Sigma practitioners will find our discussion of management, human performance, and scoping issues beyond what they normally consider when they approach a process improvement project. Hopefully they will be challenged by the idea that they can add new dimensions to their practice and will see ways to combine this material with the concepts and techniques they are already using. This book reflects the growing synthesis that is taking place among all those who are working to redesign and improve business processes. Today, everyone is borrowing from everyone else and a richer set of process tools is rapidly emerging.

Creating a Business Case for a Process Change Project

To wrap up our discussion, let's consider what is involved in creating a business case for a business process change project. Different companies have different forms or approaches, but the essence of the task reflects the Gap Model that we discussed at the beginning of this chapter and the scoping effort we undertook when we developed the project scoping diagram.

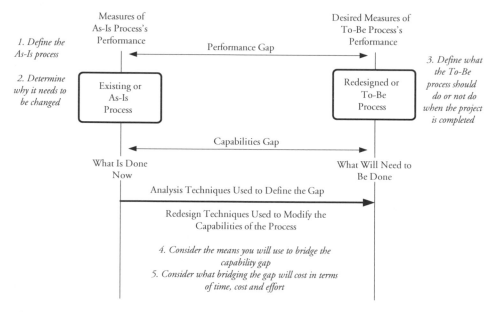

Figure 8.20 The Gap Model provides an overview of a business case.

One begins with a statement of the problem, as defined by management. Next one refines the statement of the problem and describes the performance gap. One discusses measures that describe the current or As-Is process and one considers measures that would define an acceptable redesigned process. Then the business case ought to describe the capability gap, characterizing the current process and suggesting what kind of changes will be required to create a new process that will be able to generate the desired To-Be measures. One goes further and considers how one might study the gap and hints at the redesign techniques that might be used to eliminate the performance and capability gaps.

At the end of the first phase of a project, one can usually only define the capability gap in a general way and only suggest possible redesign options. The detailed study of the capability gap is the focus of the analysis phase of the project and the definition of possible redesigns is the work of the redesign phase. Even during the understanding phase, however, the project team has an obligation to try to define the likely changes that will be required. In some cases, even at an early point, the team can see where the effort is going to cost a lot more money or take a lot more time than management expects, and they have a responsibility to suggest this possibility. In such cases, management might decide, after the initial phase of the project, that the project should be discontinued, at least for the present.

In a similar way, the business case produced at the end of the initial phase cannot be very precise, but the team should do the best they can to "guesstimate" the possible redesign possibilities and to assign some costs to each to provide management with an initial business case.

The steps in defining a preliminary business case include:

1. Define the As-Is process (what's in and out of scope).
2. Determine what the As-Is process is or isn't doing now (concrete measures).
3. Define what the To-Be process should or should not do when it's completed (the goal of the project).
4. Consider the means you will use to bridge the capability gap.
5. Then consider what bridging the gap will cost in terms of time, cost, and effort.
6. Finally, consider the risks and the "politics" and revise if needed.

Here are some guidelines and an outline for a business case proposal:

▶ Keep it simple.
▶ State clearly: What is the problem?
　　– What process do we want to change?
　　– Why do we want to change it?
　　– Describe measures of the current situation.
▶ What is the objective or goal of the project?
　　– What would the new process be like?
　　– What measures would we expect of the new process?

▶ What is involved in creating the new process?
  – Analysis and Design.
  – Implementation.
  – Roll-out.
▶ What resources, time and cost will be required to solve this problem?
▶ What risks or opportunity costs will be required?
▶ What results and what return should we expect from this effort?

The worksheets pictured as Figure 8.21 provide one way to structure the development of an initial business case. More detailed business cases are developed by following the same outline. When you finish the analysis and design phases, however, you will know much more about the specifics of the process and what it will cost to implement various changes and you will be in a much better position to recommend some changes and not others. At this point, however, you simply want to establish the overall scope and suggest what might be involved, best and worst case.

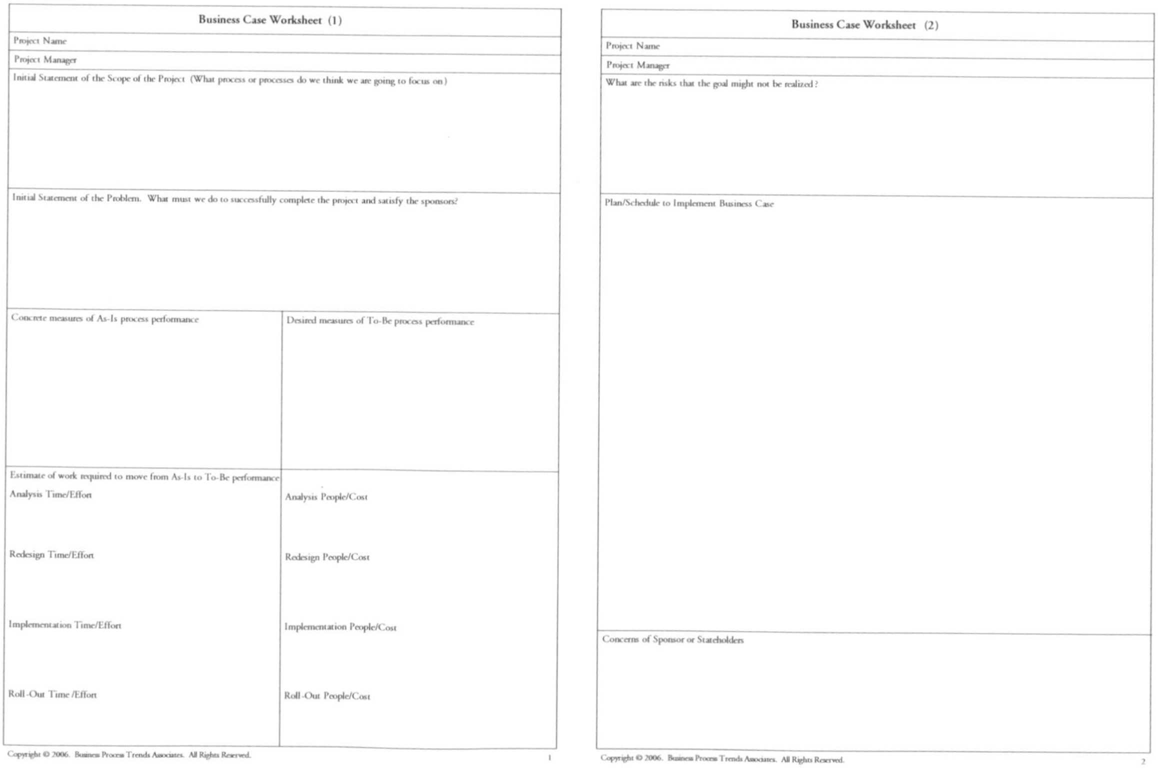

Figure 8.21 Worksheets for the development of an initial process change project business case.

Notes and References

In this chapter I have not only drawn on ideas developed in discussions with Roger Burlton, Artie Mahal and Sandra Foster as we have worked on the BPTrends methodology, but I have also used some ideas that were initially developed by Process Renewal Group (PRG), Roger Burlton's company before we began to work on the BPTrends methodology.

Burlton, Roger T., *Business Process Management: Profiting From Process,* (SAMS, 2001). This is the book that Roger Burlton published in 2001 that contains many of the ideas used by PRG.

PRG's IGOE diagram was originally derived from work done in the early 1990s for the U.S. Air Force. The software development methodology developed at that time included a business analysis methodology, usually termed IDEF0. In December 1993, the Computer Systems Laboratory of the National Institute of Standards and Technology (NIST) released IDEFØ as a standard for Function Modeling in FIPS Publication 183. Two books that describe IDEF0 are:

Marca, David A., and Clement L. McGowan, *IDEF0/SADT: Business Process and Enterprise Modeling.* Electic Solutions, 1988.

Feldmann, Clarence G., *The Practical Guide to Business Process Reengineering Using IDEF0,* Dorset House Publishing, 1998.

chapter

9

Modeling Processes

I N CHAPTER 4 we considered how we might model all of the high-level processes in an organization and store that information as a business process architecture. Once an organization has created a business process architecture, then any specific process change project becomes a matter of redefining or elaborating on a well-defined portion of the business process architecture. If a company has not created a business process architecture, it often needs to model specific processes from scratch. In Chapter 8 we considered how you might begin such a effort by creating an informal model of a process to determine the scope of a business process project. In this chapter we are going to consider how one creates a formal model of a business process. We will consider techniques that can be used to model anything from a very small process to a very complex value chain.

Formal process diagrams are often called process maps, activity diagrams, or workflow diagrams. Historically, process analysts have used a wide variety of different diagramming notations to describe processes. This isn't surprising when you consider all of the different groups that do process diagramming. In some cases business managers create diagrams just to figure out how a complex process works. In other cases a Six Sigma team will create a diagram as they prepare to focus on improving a specific process. In still other cases, an IT group will create a process diagram as the first step in a project to automate a process.

The most important practical distinction in process modeling is between the relatively informal diagrams that business managers use to help them understand processes and the relatively formal diagrams that IT software developers use to specify exactly how a software program might implement the process. IT software diagrams

231

can be very complex and include details that business people aren't interested in. At the same time, IT people rarely consider large processes, like a corporate supply chain, that includes lots of tasks that employees perform. We believe that companies that are serious about business process change need to create architectures and store information about processes in business process repositories. To do this, everyone in the organization needs to adopt a standard notation and use it consistently. Most companies adopt the notation of the business process modeling tool that they use to manage their business process repository. Business process modeling tools can support a variety of different notations, including tailored variations to accommodate the special needs or preferences of individual companies. It isn't so important what notation is used, but it is important that whatever notation is used is used consistently.

In the past few years, a consensus on business process notation has begun to emerge. It began with diagrams introduced by Geary Rummler and Alan Brache in their popular 1990 book, *Improving Performance*. The notation introduced in *Improving Performance* is usually called Rummler-Brache notation. The Rummler-Brache notation was further formalized in an IBM notation called LOVEM. Then some Rummler-Brache concepts were incorporated into the Object Management Group's UML Activity Diagrams. In 2004 the Business Process Management Initiative (BPMI) group brought most of the major business process modeling tool vendors together to create a new notation—the Business Process Modeling Notation (BPMN)—which is very close to the OMG's Activity Diagram notation. In 2005 the BPMI organization merged with the OMG and the OMG is now working to assure that BPMN and UML Activity Diagrams work smoothly together. Both UML Activity Diagrams and BPMN diagrams have large sets of symbols and can represent very complex processes so precisely that the diagrams can be used to generate software code. This level of detail would overwhelm most business process modelers. UML Activity Diagrams and BPMN, however, support a core set of diagramming elements and these core elements represent the emerging consensus and is rapidly becoming the standard notation supported by business process tools and by business process authors. We use the core BPMN notation throughout this book whenever we diagram complex processes, as we do in this chapter. In Appendix I we describe the core BPMN notation, and show some of the extensions that one can use with the core elements to create more complex diagrams.

The only major alternative to the approach we use here is represented by the ARIS diagrams that are widely used by those who model processes in conjunction with ERP efforts. Most business people find ARIS diagrams difficult to understand, since they rely too heavily on concepts that are relevant for software development but irrelevant for most process redesign or improvement efforts.

Business people model to simplify, highlight, clarify, and communicate. Thus, any notation that makes things too complex is counterproductive. At the same time, we want to enable different individuals within the same organization to read common process diagrams, and so, we need to agree to a minimum set of conventions. We believe that the core set of BPMN notational elements provides the best that's currently available. On the other hand, when we find we want to express something that's not easily expressed in BPMN, we feel free to informally extend BPMN to be sure we make our point as clearly as possible.

Process Diagram Basics

Figure 9.1 illustrates the basic elements in any process notation. A process is a set of activities that receives and transforms one or more inputs and generates one or more outputs. For the purposes of this discussion, we are using process, subprocess and activity almost as if they were synonyms. In creating diagrams we commonly decompose a process into its subprocesses. Then we refer to those subprocesses as processes for further decomposition. And, informally, we speak of the processes making up any larger process as the activities of the larger process.

In UML and BPMN a process or an activity is represented by a rectangular box with rounded corners. To simply our explanations, we'll refer to this as a "process rectangle" or an "activity rectangle" which is a little simpler than referring to a "rectangle with rounded corners." In Figure 9.1 we show three process rectangles, one in the center, one upstream, that generates the inputs for center process, and one downstream, that receives the outputs of the center process.

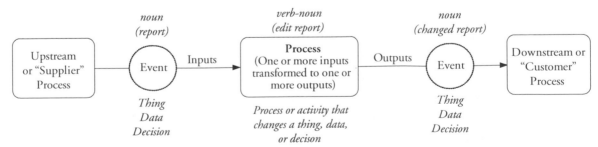

Figure 9.1 The basic elements in a process or workflow diagram.

A process takes time. An event, on the other hand, is simply a point in time. Specifically, it's the moment in time when one process has concluded and generated an output. Or, looked at from downstream, it's the point in time at which an input becomes available for use by the downstream process. In some cases we say that events "trigger processes"—as when a customer calls to request service. Events are represented by circles. We often represent the initial event that triggers a process as a circle and we usually include another circle to show that a process has concluded. We usually don't include events between activities within a process flow, although some analysts do.

In the real world, processes are occasionally arranged so that a series of processes follow one another without any time elapsing between them. In other situations one process will conclude and place its output in a bin where it may wait for hours or days until it is removed by the subsequent process. Events are often described with names that describe the artifact that passes between two processes. Imagine the upstream process in Figure 9.1 assembles a set of documents, puts them in a tray and sets it where the center process can get them. We might term the upstream process "Assemble Documents." And we might term the output of that process "Assembled Documents." By the same token, the inputs of the center process would be "Assembled Documents." Assume the center process reviewed the assembled documents and determined to make a loan or to refuse a loan. The output of the center process, in this case, would be "Approved/Disapproved Loan." Another output might be "Documents to File." We represent the flow of artifacts and decisions between processes with arrows. If we need to describe the artifacts or decisions, we can write labels above or below the arrows. If we really needed to record a lot of data about the artifacts or decisions that occurred in a particular process, we could insert an event circle between two process rectangles, although this is an uncommon convention.

Software systems that monitor human or other software processes usually store data when events occur. Thus, if the people working in the upstream process are using computers, they will most likely assemble the documents into a software file, and hit some key to "pass" the file to the next process. The software system monitoring the work will update its records as a file is moved from one process to another. Most business managers create models to understand processes. For their purposes, process rectangles and arrows are important. Similarly, the nature of the artifact or decision being made may be important. Events are more important to software modelers who need to know when databases will be updated.

Figure 9.2 illustrates the basic format of a BPMN process diagram. In this instance we are focusing on a single, high-level order fulfillment process that begins when a customer places an order and ends when the product is delivered. Thus, the largest process is represented by the diagram itself. The example we use is a very high-level view of a process and isn't interesting in itself. It is only used to provide a starting point for our discussion of a process diagram.

Let's consider the notation used in Figure 9.2. We have written the name of the process just above the BPMN diagram. In this case we are told that the diagram describes the Ergo Chair value chain, and the order fulfillment process. We already know that we can represent the subprocesses of the Order Fulfillment Process with process rectangles. Processes are either labeled with abstract titles, like Manufacturing Process, or they are given specific names that normally begin with a verb, such as Manage Leads, Determine Needs, or Ship Product.

In our figures, all the text that would normally appear on a BPMN process diagram is printed in the Times Roman font. Some of the text is used to point out features of the diagram. We have put those explanatory notes in Arial to make it clear that they are only notes.

Ergo Chair Value Chain: Order Fulfillment Process

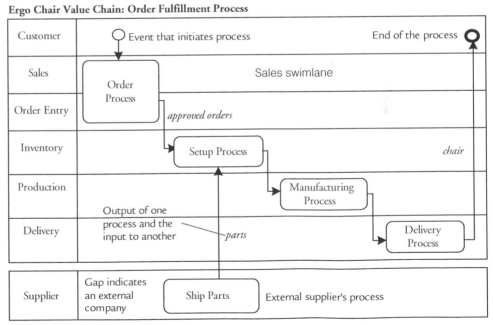

Figure 9.2 A process diagram.

The process diagram shown in Figure 9.2 is divided into a series of horizontal rows, which are called swimlanes. Although there are exceptions, as a strong generalization, as you move from left to right on a diagram you move through time. Thus, a process begins on the left-hand side of the diagram and proceeds to the right, and activities on the left take place before activities on the right.

The top swimlane is always reserved for the customer of the process being described. If the process links to the outside world, then it is a real, external customer of the company. Otherwise the top lane is reserved for whatever entity or process initiates the processes shown on the diagram. In most cases this will be the downstream or "customer" process. If there is more than one "customer" you can insert multiple "customer" swimlanes at the top of the diagram. Or you may want to show a "supplier" and a "customer" as two top swimlanes. If the diagram pictures a lower-level process, it's common to omit the customer swimlane and simply insert a circle to represent the trigger that initiates the process in the same swimlane as the first activity.

Sometimes we represent the initial event that starts the process as an activity performed by the customer. At other times we simply represent the initial event as a circle, as we do in Figure 9.2. We use activity rectangles whenever we want to be more specific about what the customer does. We'll return to this later when we consider another diagram.

All of the activities that occur within the same organization are represented as adjacent swimlanes. If the process being described is linked to an external activity—like the Ship Parts activity that is performed by a Supplier in Figure 9.2—the external activity is placed in its own swimlane, which is separated from the company's process. In this case we refer to the company activities as all occurring in the same pool of swimlanes, while the Supplier's activity occurs in a single swimlane in a separate pool.

In some organizations, a diagram similar to the one shown in Figure 9.2 might be called a workflow diagram. In a typical workflow diagram, however, we would simply represent all of the activities, connected by arrows, but without swimlanes. In Figure 9.2, however, we want to show the functional or organizational units responsible for each of the activities. Thus, the organizational departments or functional units are represented as swimlanes. In some cases a swimlane will represent a department, in some cases it will represent a subsidiary unit within a department, and in some cases it will represent the process manager who is responsible for the activities within the given swimlane. Figure 9.2 shows that there is an Inventory Department and that the Inventory Department is responsible for the Setup Process. Put a different way, some manager or supervisor within the reporting hierarchy of the Inventory Department is responsible for the Setup Process. If the process being described is a high-level process, we usually just show departments. As we drill down and focus on more specific processes or even on very specific activities, we tend to get more specific about who is responsible for the subprocess or activity.

A formal process diagram, as we will use the term, is a workflow diagram with swimlanes. As far as we know, this approach to process diagramming was originated by Geary Rummler and Alan Brache, but it has since been adopted by a wide variety of business process modelers, including the OMG, which uses swimlanes with both UML activity diagrams and BPMN diagrams.

If we analyze large-scale processes, as we are doing in Figure 9.2, it's possible that a process will be the responsibility of more than one functional group. Thus, both Sales and Order Entry are responsible for activities that occur within the Order process. If we analyze the Order process in more detail, however, we will need to determine just which activities Sales is responsible for and which activities the Order Entry group performs. We allow ourselves to spread a given activity across more than one swimlane when we create high-level diagrams, but confine activities to a single lane as we refine our understanding of the process.

As you can see by glancing at Figure 9.2, we can either label arrows or not, depending on whether we think the information useful.

We usually do not represent three levels of processes on the same diagram. The diagram itself is one process and we use process rectangles to show the major subprocesses of the single process represented by the diagram itself. In other words, we do not include process rectangles inside other process rectangles. It can certainly be done, and it's sometimes useful when you are trying to analyze processes at a very high level of abstraction, but it is usually too confusing. Instead, we represent a number of processes or activities that are all at more or less the same level of granularity. We usually analyze very high-level processes on an organization diagram and then create a diagram, like Figure 9.2, to define the major subprocesses within one process we identified on the organization diagram. The key point, however, is that if you want to know what goes on inside the Order process, you create a second process diagram with the Order process on the title line and subprocesses within the swimlanes.

As we drill down, the functional groups listed on the swimlanes keep getting more specific. In effect, we are moving down the organizational chart. Initially we label swimlanes with department names. At a finer level of detail, we may only show two departments, but subdivide each of the departments into several functional units. If we continue to drill down, ultimately we arrive at swimlanes that represent specific managers or specific employee roles.

Figure 9.3 provides an overview of the way in which someone might drill down into a process. This figure shows how we use organization diagrams and charts as a

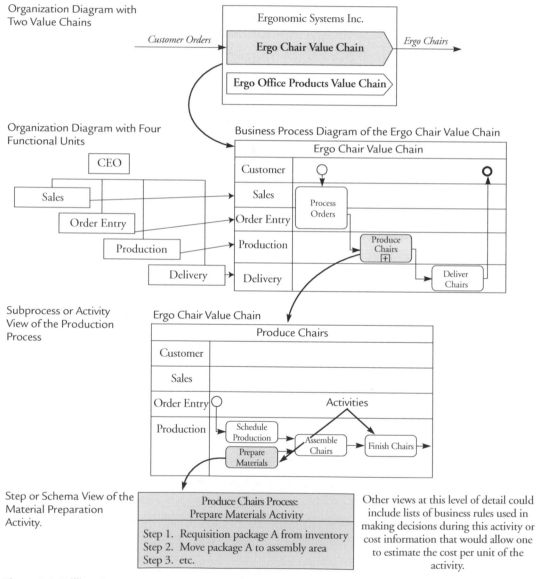

Figure 9.3 Drilling down into a process to examine more specific levels of processes.

way of gathering the information that we later use when we create process diagrams. In effect, the departments identified in the organization chart become the swimlanes for a process diagram while the organization diagram suggests which processes we might want to analyze further.

On the initial process diagram, we show one process, Production process, which we subsequently define in more detail. The plus in a box at the bottom center of the Production process rectangle is placed there to remind viewers that a more detailed subprocess diagram is available for the Produce Chairs process.

In Figure 9.3 we arbitrarily assume that Prepare Materials is an atomic activity. In other words, for the purposes of our analysis, we are not going to diagram anything that occurs within the activity box labeled Prepare Materials. That is not to say that we won't gather additional information about that activity. We simply aren't going to create a diagram to describe the sequence of steps that occur within Prepare Materials. Instead, we might create a textual description of the materials preparation activity. If we want a finer definition of the process, we might type out a list of steps that occur during the accomplishment of the activity. We will certainly want to know if the activity is performed by humans or by computers or machines, or some combination of them. Similarly, if we are planning on doing simulation, we might accumulate information on the units processed in the activity, the costs per unit, time per unit, and so forth. If you are doing this by hand, you could simply write out the information on a sheet of paper and attach it to the diagram.

Later, we will provide an activity worksheet that you can use to prompt yourself in accumulating data you might need to record for an activity. If you are using a sophisticated software tool, when you click on an activity box, it opens and provides you with a worksheet in a window, and you can type in the information on your computer.

More Process Notation

In addition to the symbols we have already introduced, there are a few more symbols a manager must know in order to read process diagrams. Figure 9.4 illustrates another simple process. In this figure we are looking at a process that describes how a retail book company receives orders by phone and ships books to customers. This company doesn't manufacture books; it simply takes them from its inventory and sends them to customers.

Books-By-Mail: Order Fulfillment Process

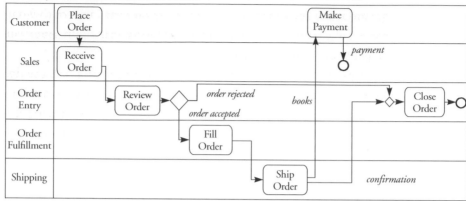

Figure 9.4 Another simple process diagram.

Some of the symbols in Figure 9.4 are new, and others are simply variations. For example, instead of starting with a circle, we placed information inside a box that indicates that the customer placed an order. We aren't concerned with what process the customer goes through in deciding to order the book, although we might be and will return to the concept of a customer process in a bit. From our perspective, the placement of the order is an event or stimulus that triggers the book order fulfillment process. Hence, the customer's action is handled in a special way.

Some activities are well-defined procedures, while others involve the application of rules and decisions. Review Order is an example of a process or activity that requires a decision. If the decision process is complex, we record the decision criteria as business rules and put them on a separate piece of paper, or record them in a software tool that associates them with the activity.

Business rules take this generic form:
IF < something is the case >
AND < something else is also the case >
THEN < do this >
ELSE < do something else >

For example, we might have a rule that said:
IF the order is from a customer we don't know
AND the order is over $50
THEN check the credit card number for approval
OR wait till the check clears our bank.

Complex decision processes can involve lots of rules. In the extreme cases, there are too many rules to analyze, and we rely on human experts who understand how to solve the problem. We'll consider this entire topic in more detail when we discuss how activities are analyzed in Chapter 10.

In some cases, as in the example shown in Figure 9.4, the decision is relatively simple and different activities follow, depending upon the decision. In this case, we often place a diamond or gateway after the activity that leads to the decision. We indicate the alternative outcomes as arrows leading from the diamond to other activities. In the example shown in Figure 9.4, the order can either be:

▶ *rejected*, in which case the order is terminated, or
▶ *accepted*, in which case the order is passed on to shipping and invoicing.

In most cases, a small diamond is sufficient, and outcomes are simply written by the arrows leading from the decision point.

In some cases, you may want to describe the decision point in more detail. In that case, you can expand the diamond into a hexagon, as follows:

Are All Books Available?

Figure 9.5 is a slightly more complex version of Figure 9.4. In this case we have three arrows coming from the first gateway. Notice that we show one arrow running *backward in time* in Figure 9.5, as it goes from the decision point, back to the Receive Order activity. This shouldn't happen too often because it runs counter to the basic idea that a process diagram flows from left to right. On the other hand, it's sometimes very useful to show *loops or iterations* like this rather than making the diagram much larger. We refer to it as a "loop," since we assume that once the salesperson has called the customer and completed the order, it will proceed back to the Review Order activity just as it did in the first instance. Most business analysts ignore the "exceptions" when they prepare their initial diagrams. Most business people don't need this level of detail, although software systems analysts do need to understand all possible outcomes. Some analysts prepare tables to describe decision situations and list all the possible outcomes. For example, what if an order form arrives and the company name is misspelled, or a signature is left off?

Books-by-Mail: Order Fulfillment Process

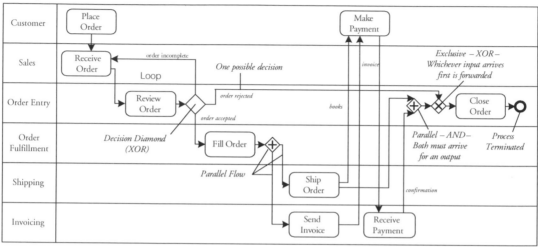

Figure 9.5 Another simple process diagram.

Notice the second use of a decision diamond on the right side of Figure 9.5. In this case the diamond has two inputs and only one output. In effect, the diamond says in this instance that EITHER the order is going to be closed because the order was rejected OR because the order was shipped and paid for. The diamond, in this second case, is simply a graphical way of saying there are two different possible inputs to Close Order. The Close Order activity takes place whenever either one of the inputs arrives.

At this point we need to decide just how much information we need to record in this diagram. BPMN defines a core set of symbols, and then defines elaborations. To make it possible to use the same diagram to show either a simple overview or to include more complex information, BPMN extends its core symbols. Thus, for example, any event can be represented by a circle. A circle drawn with a line of average width that appears at the beginning of a sequence, however, represents a trigger that starts a process. A circle drawn with a bold line represents the end of a process. By putting various symbols inside the circle, it can be refined to represent a variety of different event types. Similarly, we can use a simple diamond to represent any of a number of different gateway or decision situations. Without any special notation, the diamond simply shows that the flow is diverging or converging. With adornments, the diamond can represent different flow conditions.

 Gateway or Decision Diamond

 Exclusive (XOr)
Multiple input paths but the actual inputs comes via only one path
Multiple output paths but only one is actually taken

 Inclusive (Or)
All inputs go to all outputs

 Parallel   (And)
All inputs go to all outputs, but only when all inputs
are ready to go together

Some analysts will find these refinements useful, and we may use them later in special cases, but in general we stick with the core notation and simply use a diamond. In Figure 9.5 we use two parallel diamonds and two decision diamonds, but only mark the parallel diamonds.

In effect, diamonds allow analysts to indicate the basic logic of business flows. In most cases, when you are creating an early draft of a workflow, you avoid such logical subtitles. Thus, for example, we could have shown the flow from Fill Order to Ship Order and Send Invoice, as shown in Figure 9.4.

These two alternatives don't tell us anything about the logic of the flow. It might be sufficient if the information from Fill Order only arrived at Ship Order, for example. It might be that different forms were sent to Ship Order and to Send Invoice. If the second, we would probably label the arrows to tell us what went where. The point, however, is that you can define processes informally at first, and then refine the flow to capture business rules or procedural logic as you refine the diagram.

Consider the two arrows leaving Ship Order in Figure 9.5. In one case the arrow represents an object or thing—books. In the second case the arrow represents information—a confirmation—sent to the person responsible for closing orders. Some analysts use different arrows to denote the flow of information and things. We don't and prefer to simply label the arrows. This usually works well enough for simple business diagrams.

Finally, from the Close Order activity, an arrow leads to a terminal event—a bold circle. This symbol indicates that the process ends at this point. Sometimes we also use the end point to indicate that we don't wish to pursue a given workflow any further. Thus, for example, rather than use the second diamond and create that complex bit of logic just before the Close Order activity, we might have simply let the arrow labeled [*order rejected*] lead to an end point. If we did, it would be because we thought that what happened next was obvious and we didn't want to clutter the diagram by showing the flow of that output of Review Order. (BPMN uses a double circle, one inside the other, to indicate that a flow is incomplete and continued elsewhere.)

Figure 9.6 introduces some additional symbols that you may find useful. In this case we are considering a simple process that involves letting customers order books via the Web. Thus, the two swimlanes below the customer swimlane describe an auto-

Books-OnLine: Order Fulfillment Process

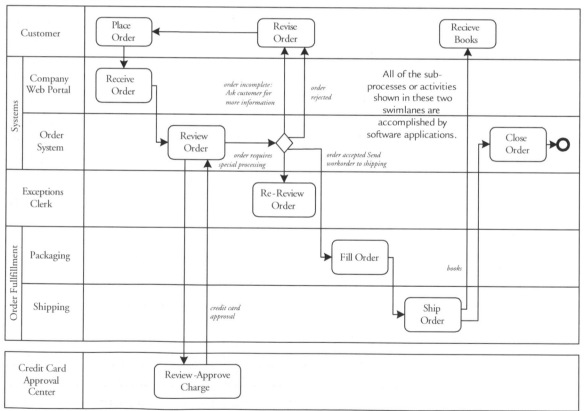

Figure 9.6 Some additional process diagramming techniques.

mated process. In this case, other than clearly labeling them as software applications, there is no essential difference between activities performed by an employee and activities performed by a soft application. Indeed, in initially analyzing a process it's best to ignore how the process will be performed and focus instead on defining what needs to be done. Later, as you focus on how specific processes will be done, you will probably introduce variations to better accommodate the employees or the system, but at a high level of abstraction, it's simply work that needs to be done to satisfy customers.

We have also used two types of labels to identify some of the swimlanes. Both the Web portal and the order system are systems. (We are avoiding the issue of whether this is a departmental-based IT group or the enterprise IT organization at this point.) Both the packaging group and the shipping group report to the Order Fulfillment department at Books-OnLine. By representing it as we have, we show some of the departmental structure or the management reporting relationships.

Most analysts make distinctions between individuals, jobs, and roles. In most cases when we speak of an activity, we speak of a role. It's something one or more people do. It may or may not be a complete job. Imagine that there are six Exceptions Clerks. There is one job description for Exception Clerk and six individuals have been hired to do the job. Next, imagine that there are 10 different activities, or roles, that are included in the Exception Clerk job description. One of the activities or roles is to re-review orders that are listed on the special processing report generated by the order system in conjunction with the Web orders. Another role might be to handle errors generated by an accounting system. In other words, the job of the Exceptions Clerk is larger than the Re-Review Order activity. Thus, we speak of the abstract unit of work required by the Re-Review Order activity, which could be done by any one of the six Exception Clerks as a role.

Similarly, we might have a process that includes an activity that requires the approval of the VP of marketing. We might show the VP of marketing on a swimlane. Again, we wouldn't be referring to an individual because the person holding the job might change. We would simply be referring to the job or role.

Notice that Figure 9.6 shows that the Exception Clerk handles orders that require special processing. In this case, we didn't want to follow the various flows that might come from the Re-Review Order box. If we did, we would have inserted a small box with a plus in the activity rectangle and then developed another process diagram to capture the details. You can ignore this in some cases, but it's very useful to remind readers that they can go to another diagram to obtain more detail.

Figure 9.7 provides a few more variations. In this case we are looking at a small part of an auto claims process. Here we don't show the customer, but simply begin with a claims agent submitting a claim.

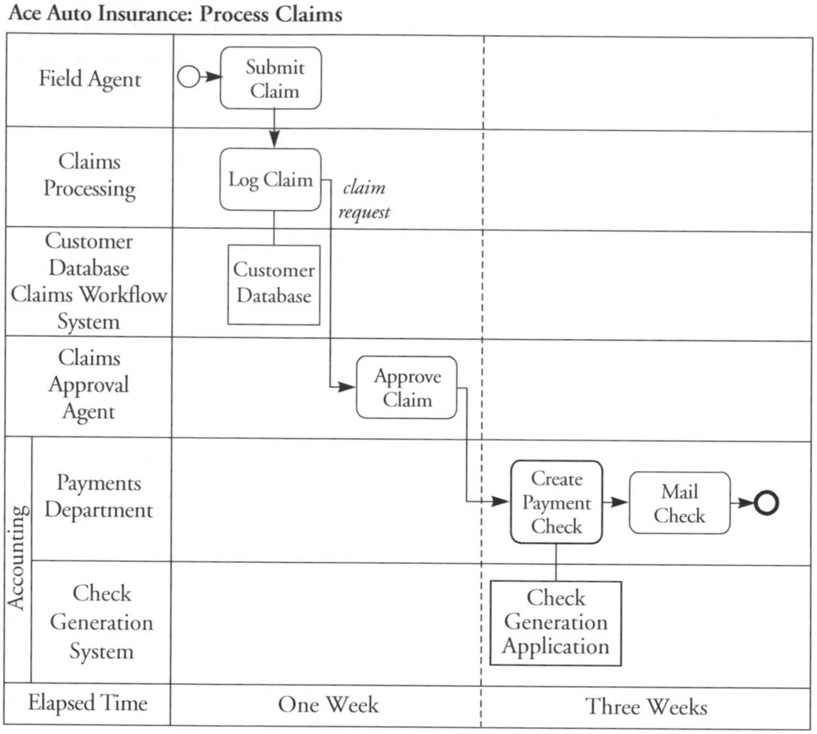

Ace Auto Insurance: Process Claims

Figure 9.7 Additional symbols.

When the claim arrives, a Claims Processing clerk enters the claim into the customer database. We show a software application/database in a swimlane representing the unit that owns or maintains the database—probably the IT group. We picture the application itself as a square-cornered box and connect it to the activity box with a line without an arrowhead. The application is not an activity, as such, but a tool—like a file cabinet—used by the Log Claim activity. Because it is often important to keep track of software applications and databases, however, we frequently represent them on our process diagrams. In a similar way, the employees in the payments department use a check generation application to actually generate the checks they mail to customers.

We added a special row at the bottom of the process diagram shown in Figure 9.7 to indicate the time involved. In this example, we assume that the company wants to get all claims processed within one week of receipt and that it wants to pay accepted claims within three weeks of claim acceptance. We usually don't indicate times for specific processes or activities, but it is occasionally useful to provide elapsed times for groups of activities, especially when the project is focused on reducing the time the process takes.

So far, we've always shown process diagrams whose swimlanes run horizontally across the page. Some analysts prefer to have the swimlanes run vertically. If you do this, then the Customer lane should be the leftmost lane and non-company functions should be shown on the right-hand side of the page. In Figure 9.8 we show the same information we pictured in Figure 9.7, arranged with vertical swimlanes. Obviously, in this case, time will accumulate from the top downward.

Ace Auto Insurance: Claims Process

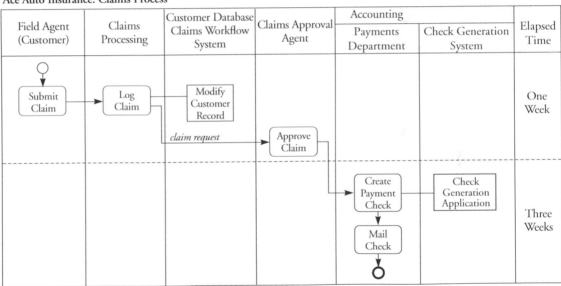

Figure 9.8 An auto insurance claims process with vertical swimlanes.

We have always found it much easier to picture the flow of activities and to fit the information into process diagrams with horizontal swimlanes, and we will use them throughout this book. But, ultimately, this is just a matter of personal preference, and readers can just as well draw process diagrams with vertical swimlanes if that orientation works better for them.

As-Is, Could-Be and To-Be Process Diagrams

In analyzing a specific business process, we usually begin with an analysis of what is currently being done. We usually refer to the process diagram that documents the existing process as the *As-Is process diagram.* Once we understand what is currently being done, we often generate alternative workflows and compare them. When we are creating speculative alternative diagrams, we usually call them *Could-Be process diagrams.* When we finally arrive at the new process, we term that a *To-Be process diagram.*

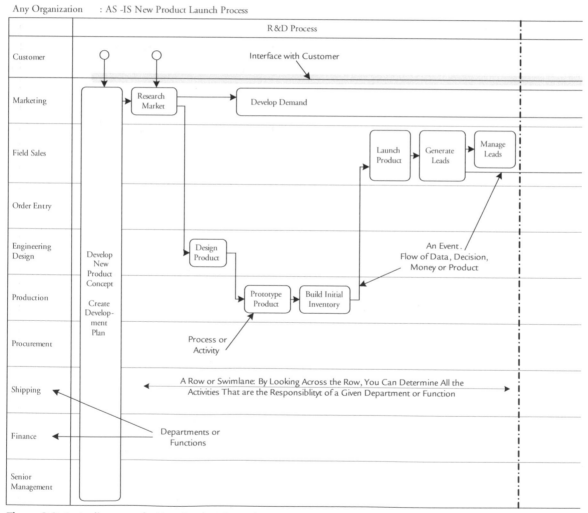

Figure 9.9 As-Is diagram of a New Product Launch process.

Figure 9.9 provides an example of a typical As-Is process diagram. In this case we actually are showing three layers of process. The entire diagram represents the Product Launch process. The three labels across the top, the R&D process, the Sales and Marketing process, and the Manufacturing and Order Fulfillment process, define the Level 2 decomposition. The process rectangles shown in the swimlanes represent a third level of decomposition.

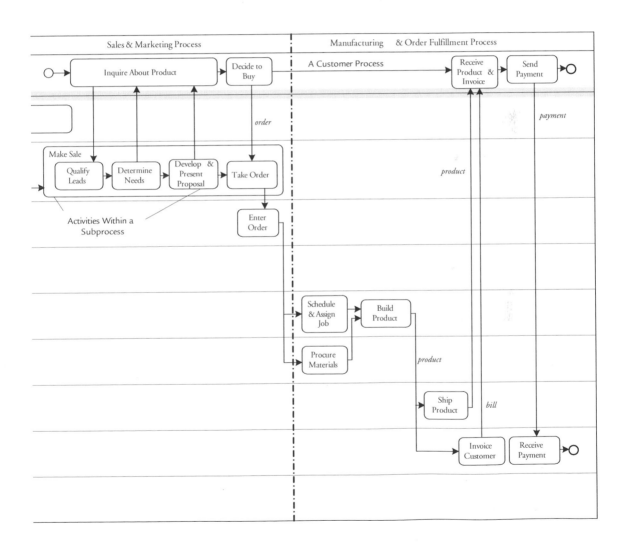

Any Organization : To -Be New Product Launch Process

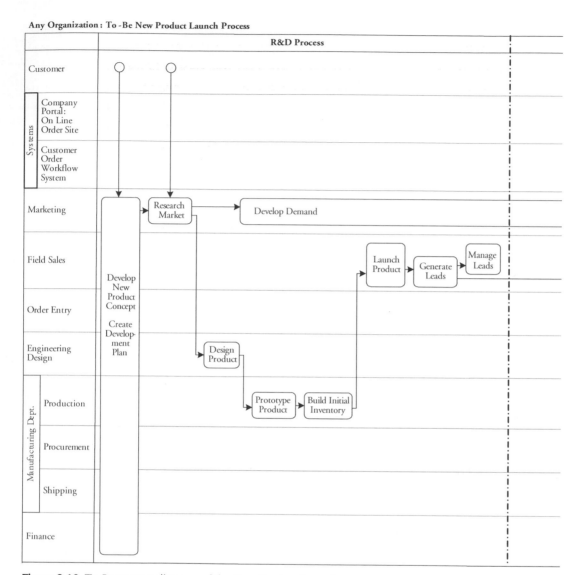

Figure 9.10 To-Be process diagram of the New Product Launch process.

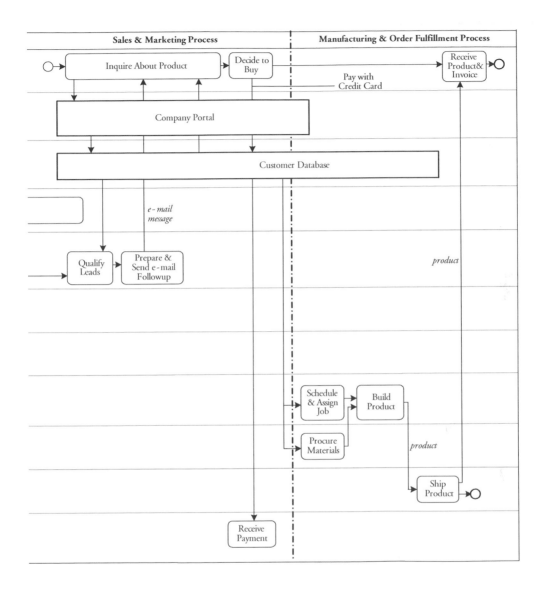

In addition, we have introduced something else that's new in Figure 9.8—a customer process. Notice that the customer activities shown in the customer swimlane are connected and begin with a trigger event and end with an end-of-process event. In most diagrams, we simply represent customer activities and don't link them together, simply because we are normally focused on the company's process. In some cases, however, it is useful to think about what a customer goes through to interact with your company. In effect, you create a customer process and then ask how you could improve it. If you can improve it, in essence, you are creating a better experience for your customer. Keep in mind when you study the customer process that the customer doesn't care about any processes that he or she does not interact with. The customer only cares about the steps he or she has to go through to accomplish the goals of their process. Imagine that you bought a laptop and now find that you need to replace a battery. You don't care what's going on inside the vendor's company—you only focus on the activities you have to go through to get the battery replaced. If your company makes it a lot harder and more complex to buy a product than your competitors, don't be surprised to find that you are losing customers.

In the mid-1990s, IBM promoted a business process methodology called LOVEM (Line of Vision Enterprise Methodology) that used diagrams much like the ones used in this book. The "line of vision" referred to in the IBM methodology was the line between the organization and the customer, which we have highlighted in gray. Swimlane diagrams with the customer swimlane at the top provides everyone with a quick way of checking how and when your organization is interacting with its customers.

Figure 9.10 illustrates a To-Be diagram. It suggests how a team has decided to improve the New Product Launch process. In essence, the team decided to create a Web site and let the customers interact with the company via the Web. Thus, when the customer interacts with the company now, he or she is interacting with a software application and information is going directly into the customer database. The customer can now access, online, in the course of a single sitting, a variety of information that would otherwise have required separate inquiries. Similarly, if the customer decides to purchase the product, the company now asks the customer to provide his or her credit card information, thereby arranging payment before the product is shipped. Notice how much these changes in the company's processes have simplified the customer's process.

A quick glance back at Figure 9.9 will indicate that we have removed sales activities and an order entry activity. When software is introduced into business processes, lots of specific activities that were formerly done by individuals at specific points in time are done on a continuous basis by the software system. It usually isn't worth maintaining the information on the process diagram. What is important is that you show when information is put into the software process and when information is given to workers by the software application. If you need to track what goes on within the software process box, it's usually best to prepare a separate process diagram that just shows what happens within the software process. And since that gets technical and depends on the company's hardware and software architecture, it's usually best to leave that diagramming effort to software specialists.

In other words, in most cases, you should focus on inputs and outputs to software processes and ignore the internal workings. If you want to assure that everyone knows that the customer database is expected to maintain all information on customer contacts and orders, you can write that and other system requirements on a separate note and attach it to the diagram.

We have represented some processes with long rectangles to suggest that they run while other processes are taking place. This occurs because, in effect, a workflow application or a database runs constantly, taking outputs from the processes shown on the diagram and using them to update the database from which it subsequently withdraws the data to pass to subsequent activities.

If we were really going to try to automate the New Product Launch process, there are lots of additional things we could do. We could add a production system, for example, to automatically handle scheduling and job assignments. We might also outsource the shipping operation, for example. An accounting system could automatically prepare bills. In addition, there are lots of activities we didn't show. For example, we would probably add a third major software system to automate and control most of the accounting. New orders could be checked against the customer database as soon as they were entered, and credit checks could be handled before the order was ever transmitted to finance. An accounting system could automatically prepare invoices when it was notified that the order was shipped. Better, since it's an online system, we could ask the customer to pay in advance, or provide information on an account that could be automatically debited when the product was shipped. In this case, the customer database system would probably automatically contact an external financial institution to check the source of funds or the credit line to be debited later. In other words, we could automate this process quite a bit more. For our purposes here, however, it's enough that we've introduced the basic concepts and notation we will use when we discuss organizations, functions, and processes later in this book.

Notes and References

This chapter draws heavily on ideas introduced by Geary Rummler and Alan Brache in their book *Performance Improving: Managing the White Space on the Organization Chart*. (Jossey-Bass, 1995.)

This chapter relies on a loose interpretation of BPMN. We have used the notation, but added extensions occasionally to clarify things. We have included a formal description of the core BPMN notation as Appendix I.

The official source of the BPMN specification is the Object Management Group (OMG). You can go to their Web site and download the complete specification. Similarly, you can obtain the UML Activity Diagram notation at the OMG site as well.

By far the best introduction to BPMN is provided by two papers written by Stephen White which are available on the BPTrends site. White was the chair of the BPMN task force that created the notation. Go to *www.bptrends.com* and search on Stephen White.

In "Introduction to BPMN" (July 2004) White presents the basic BPMN notation.

In "Process Modeling Notations and Workflow Patterns" (March, 2004) White shows how BPMN and UML would each model the workflow patterns that were described by Wil van der Aalst in *Workflow Management: Models, Methods, and Systems* (MIT Press, 2002). The patterns Aalst describes provide a good benchmark to the kinds of software situations that any comprehensive workflow tool should be able to model, and thus provide the process notation with a reasonable workout.

There has been quite a bit of discussion in the business and IT communities about the nature of business rules. Some business rules only specify policy actions. If X happens, then do Y. Other rules specify actions in more detail, so that the rules can be programmed into software. For our purposes in this book, we suggest that managers only focus on high-level rules that define policies and specify how decisions should be handled. Leave more precise rules for those that develop software. We'll consider the business rules literature in more detail in the notes following Chapter 10.

chapter

10

Task Analysis, Knowledge Workers and Business Rules

IN THIS CHAPTER we will focus on activities. Activities are the smallest processes we choose to model in any given analysis effort. Activity level analysis is the most detailed analysis we undertake. (Recall Figure 8.3 for an overview of different levels of process analysis.) We said earlier that the work of a business is ultimately done by the processes that make up the business. In a similar way, the actual work done by any process is ultimately done by the activities that make up the process.

In one sense, an activity is just a process, and we show activities on process diagrams. In another sense, however, when we try to say what occurs within an activity, we cross the line between describing process and entering into describing human behavior or the behavior of a software system. Our goal in this book, of course, is not to go deeply into the technologies used in the analysis of employee behavior or systems analysis. Business managers who specify process changes are not normally expected to develop training materials or to program software. To complete a process description, however, they are expected to describe activities in enough detail so that others can write the job descriptions, create the training, or design the software needed to assure that the activity will be properly performed. Thus, in this section and in subsequent chapters on automation, we will describe techniques that business managers can use to assure that they understand and can communicate what must be done to perform any given activity.

Since an activity is of arbitrary size, any given activity could contain lots of different steps. In some cases, hundreds of people might be employed in the accomplishment of a specific activity—say, picking grapes in a vineyard. Or an activity might be a meeting of a bank corporate loan committee in which several different people participate and discuss some complex decision.

If we are redesigning an important process, we usually refine our models to the point where each activity represents a fairly discrete set of behaviors. In some cases, we will want to run simulations. In those instances we will need to be very precise about what happens in each activity.

Analyzing a Specific Activity

Let's start with an activity that is performed by a single person. To simplify things further, let's assume that the employee works full-time on the single activity. Imagine, for example, that the activity involves the entry of expense report information into a ledger. We hope no one does something like this without using a computer system today, but let's imagine that this activity is an entirely manual operation. In other words, there is a job description, describing the work of an Expense Report Entry Clerk, and there is a one-to-one relationship between the job description and the work done in the *Enter Expense Reports* activity. We might diagram the activity as shown in Figure 10.1.

If we were going to analyze this activity, we would begin by obtaining copies of *expense reports* and a correctly updated *expense report ledger.* Then we'd sit down with a skilled Expense Report Entry Clerk and watch him or her do the job. We would take notes to describe the steps and actions taken by the clerk as he or she received the reports and then created the updated ledger. We assume the clerks would do things like stamp the incoming expense report with a date, and then examine it to see that it was complete. If it was complete, the clerk would probably proceed to copy information from various locations on the expense report to other locations on the ledger. In some cases, numbers would be added and sums would be entered. After the entry was complete, the original report would probably be filed, and the ledger numbers added or subtracted to reflect a change in various balances. If the original report was incomplete, we assume the clerk would follow some alternative path. For example, the report might be returned to the sender with a note pointing out that additional information was required.

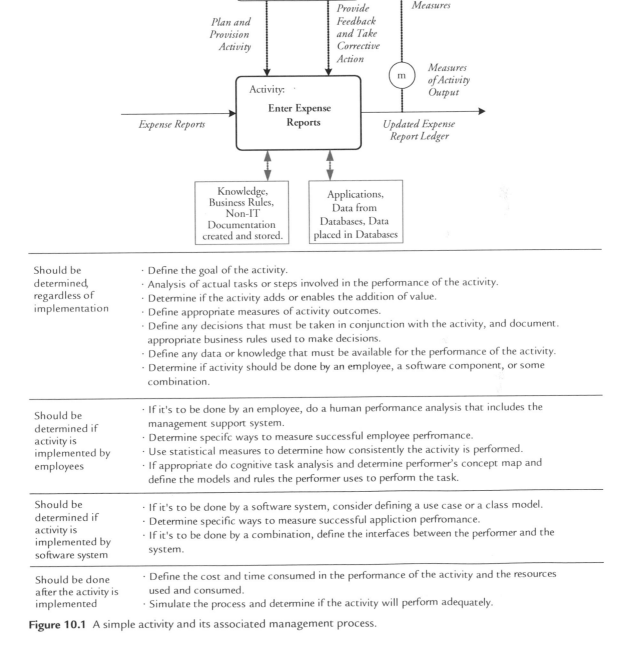

Figure 10.1 A simple activity and its associated management process.

Should be determined, regardless of implementation	· Define the goal of the activity. · Analysis of actual tasks or steps involved in the performance of the activity. · Determine if the activity adds or enables the addition of value. · Define appropriate measures of activity outcomes. · Define any decisions that must be taken in conjunction with the activity, and document. appropriate business rules used to make decisions. · Define any data or knowledge that must be available for the performance of the activity. · Determine if activity should be done by an employee, a software component, or some combination.
Should be determined if activity is implemented by employees	· If it's to be done by an employee, do a human performance analysis that includes the management support system. · Determine specifc ways to measure successful employee perfromance. · Use statistical measures to determine how consistently the activity is performed. · If appropriate do cognitive task analysis and determine performer's concept map and define the models and rules the performer uses to perform the task.
Should be determined if activity is implemented by software system	· If it's to be done by a software system, consider defining a use case or a class model. · Determine specific ways to measure successful appliction perfromance. · If it's to be done by a combination, define the interfaces between the performer and the system.
Should be done after the activity is implemented	· Define the cost and time consumed in the performance of the activity and the resources used and consumed. · Simulate the process and determine if the activity will perform adequately.

In other words, the activity would be composed of a number of steps or tasks. The steps would be triggered by the receipt of an expense report and terminate when the report was filed and the ledger was completely updated. Obviously, we could create a diagram showing each step and use arrows to show how the clerk moved from one step to the next, and where decisions and branches occurred. In this case, however, the analyst decided he or she didn't need a diagram and that a list of steps would suffice.

There would probably be some rules that helped the clerk make decisions. One rule would state what was required of a complete report and specify that, if reports were incomplete, they should be returned to the submitter with a note about what was missing.

There might be other rules, specifying how to deal with reports submitted over one month late, or reports submitted with or without various types of documentation. Still other rules might deal with how to handle reports that deal with expenses in foreign currencies, or with reports in which the submitter included expenses that were not permitted by the company expense policy. There might also be rules requiring the signature of a senior manager.

In addition to defining the steps in the process and the rules to be followed at each step, we might also document the time required to process an average expense report, the number of reports the clerk typically processed in a day, and the kinds of problems or exceptions that were typically encountered and the frequency of each. We would probably also determine the salary of the clerk so that we could determine the cost of processing an average report, or of handling common exceptions. We might even check on departmental overhead estimates for office space, file space, and such to obtain an even more accurate idea of the total cost of the activity.

We would also probably make some statement about the goal fulfilled by the activity—what value it adds to the production of company products or services. We would also probably gather data on how the ledgers were evaluated by the activity supervisor, and information on the rate and kinds of errors that occurred. Assuming multiple entry clerks were employed, we would develop a statement about the quality and quantity of an average clerk, and about the output typical of the best and worst performers. In other words, we would want to know how consistently the task was performed and what kind of deviation there was.

If the employee or supervisor felt that there were problems with the performance of the activity, we would ask the employee and the supervisor to suggest causes of the problems and gather any data we could to support or refute those suggestions.

In this example, we are looking at a very straightforward job. In most companies, jobs like these are so straightforward that they have been automated. If they aren't, they are elementary enough that they have probably been documented for some time, and new supervisors probably simply inherited the job description and various activity measures when they were made supervisor. On the other hand, there are lots of much more complex jobs that a manager might be made responsible for supervising. The manager of sales must do something similar for his or her salespeople, and the manager of software development must analyze the jobs and performance of programmers. We are discussing a simple set of tasks, but the basic principles are the same.

In this book, to provide readers with a quick way of organizing information you might want to gather about an activity, we will use two activity worksheets: a basic *Activity Analysis Worksheet* and a supplemental *Activity Cost Worksheet.* If you were using a software tool, you would probably simply click on the activity rectangle on a process diagram and be able to enter this information. We've simply used worksheets as a quick way to summarize the kind of information you would want to record.

Figure 10.2 illustrates an Activity Worksheet we prepared for the Enter Expense Reports activity. In this case we listed the basic steps, identified who was responsible for each step, and defined some of the decision rules that control the activity.

We didn't assume the use of computers in the activity described on the Activity Worksheet in Figure 10.2. If we had assumed a computer, then one of the key variables would be the computer screens that the performer used to enter or obtain information from the computer. In that case we would have noted the name or some other reference code to identify the computer screen used in each step. Occasionally, if there are problems, they arise because the user doesn't understand the information as presented on the computer screen or doesn't understand the appropriate response called for by the computer screen, and changes in the layout or text on the computer screen can solve the problem and improve performance.

Activity Analysis Worksheet			
Activity: _Enter Expense Reports_ **Process:** _XYZ Sales Process_			
Activity Performed by (✓) employee, ( ) software, ( ) a combination			
Major Output of Activity: _Updated expense report ledger_			
Measures of Output: _Ledger reflects all reported expenses documented in expense reports filed by sales personnel. Ledger closed at the end of each month._			
Steps in the Activity	Responsibility	Decisions/Rules	Opportunities for Improvement
1. Date-stamp each expense report when it's received. 2. Review expense reports for completeness and accuracy (return if incomplete). 3. Cross-check information on expense report with supporting documentation. 4. Enter information on expense report into ledger. 5. Update ledger. 6. File expense report and supporting documentation.	Expense Report Entry Clerk responsible for work. Work managed by Sales Accounting Supervisor	Rule 1. No expense report is processed before supporting documentation arrives. Rule 2. Incomplete reports are rerouted to submitter for completion. Rule 3. Submitter is notified whenever an item is disallowed. Rule 4. Any sign of a purposeful attempt at fraud should be brought to attention of accounting supervisor. Rule 5. Expense reports must be processed and paid in month submitted. Rule 6. If expense reports are submitted that are over 3 months old, the Sales Accounting Supervisor should be notified to approve processing.	

Figure 10.2 An Activity Worksheet.

If we were interested in doing cost analysis or simulation, we would also need to gather additional information on the activity. We've provided a separate Activity Cost Worksheet for such information, and it's pictured in Figure 10.3.

In Figure 10.3 we've shown the data we gathered on the Enter Expense Reports activity. We marked it IS to indicate that this is the way the activity was performed in the existing process.

Assuming that the Enter Expense Reports activity was performed by an individual, then part of the analysis effort might involve defining or redefining the job of the individual that performed the activity. In most cases this will be beyond the basic scope of the process analysis effort. Typically the process analysis team would

Activity Cost Worksheet				
Process or Subprocess: *XYZ Sales Process*			AS-IS (✓) or TO BE ( ) Analysis	
Activity	Outputs of Activity	Time/Output	Costs/Output	Problems or Decisions
Enter Expense Reports	Updated Expense Report Ledger	15 minutes/report and update, or 4 per hour.	@$24/hr (loaded with overhead) the cost per report is $6.	1 in 20 involves an exception, which takes up to 30 minutes to process.

Figure 10.3 An Activity Cost Worksheet.

simply define the activity and leave specialists from human resources to refine the job description of the individual who performs the job. In some cases, however, if there are problems with this specific activity, process analysts need a general approach to analyzing the performance of manual activities.

Analyzing Human Performance

When an activity is not being performed correctly, we need to analyze the situation to see what could be wrong. The best approach to this is *human performance analysis*, a technology developed by psychologists and performance analysts over the course of the last 50 years. Human performance analysis defines the variables that affect human performance and offers heuristics for analyzing any given human activity. Figure 10.4 provides a version of the human performance model used by Rummler in *Improving Performance*.

Let's consider each of the factors illustrated in Figure 10.4 in more detail.

1. Activity Standards

Do activity standards exist? If measures exist, then one assumes they measure whether the activity meets one or more standards. Obviously if you are a new manager and there are no existing measures or standards in place, then your first job is to create them. It's always useful to check to see if standards are documented and to ask performers how they interpret the standards. It's always possible that someone provided performers with standards, then established measures. Later they might have changed

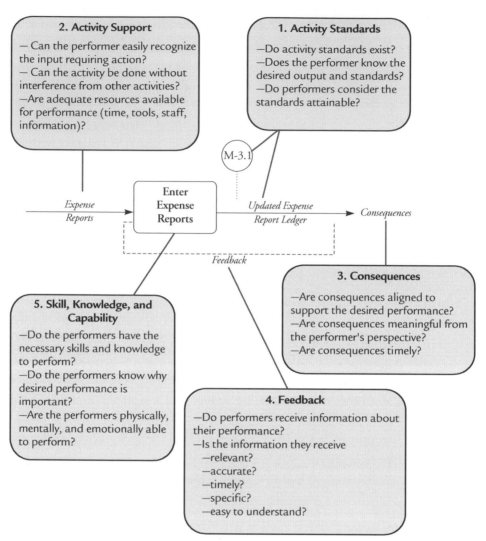

Figure 10.4 Factors affecting the performance of an activity (modified after Rummler and Brache, Improving Performance).

measures without realigning the standards that the employees are using. Similarly, it's worth checking on what standards software developers used when they created any software component used in the activity and assure they are current and aligned.

Does the performer know the desired output and standards? Once the manager knows that standards exist, he or she should next determine that the people or systems performing the activity know what the standards are. Obviously people can't systematically achieve a standard they don't know about. If performers don't know about a standard, it's the manager's job not only to assure that they learn about the standard, but also to devise an arrangement to make sure that they don't forget it and that other, new performers learn of the standard. Moving the standard from a line of text in a manual to a sign posted in the workplace is one way to accomplish this.

Do performers consider the standards attainable? Few people persist in trying to achieve something they can't achieve. When systems designers are asked to create components that are expected to achieve results the designers know they can't achieve, they tend to create components that simply do what can be done. Unattainable standards shouldn't happen, but occasionally they are established by someone who isn't being realistic. A manager needs to check to see that everyone agrees that the standards are, indeed, attainable. If they aren't, either because no one could achieve that standard, or because an existing performer can't, the manager needs to make changes. In the first case, one changes the standard. In the second, one changes the performer or system.

2. Activity Support

Can the performer easily recognize the input requiring action? Consider a situation in which salespeople are wasting their time on unqualified prospects. The manager should begin by determining if the salespeople know what a "qualified prospect" is. If the salespeople don't know the difference, then one step in solving the problem is to teach them how to recognize qualified and unqualified prospects. There are lots of problems that arise from similar causes. Diagnosticians don't check for certain potential problems because they don't recognize the signs that suggest they should make such a check. Developers create systems that respond to one set of inputs but don't build components that respond to other inputs because they don't realize that those situations could occur.

Can the activity be done without interference from other activities? Sometimes one activity will interfere with another. Consider, for example, a salesperson under pressure to obtain more sales and to provide documentation for past sales. These are two separate activities, and in a good situation there would be time for both. Sometimes, however, achieving one activity might preclude the successful completion of another. Or consider that one person may need to answer phones right next to someone who is trying to write a report. The report writer is constantly distracted by the person carrying on phone conversations. Or consider that a given activity may require a forklift, which someone else is always using for some other activity. In an ideal workplace none of these things happen, but in the real world they often do. Managers need to check the environment in which the work is to take place to assure themselves that one activity isn't interfering with the performance of another.

Are adequate resources available for performance (time, tools, staff, information)? Are needed resources available to those performing the activity? Do they have the time required? Do they have the tools needed for the job? If staff support is required, is it available and adequate for the job? If information is needed, is it available? These are obvious sorts of things, but more performance failures can be tracked to environmental problems than to lack of trained employees or employees who willfully choose not to perform some task. This is an extension of budgeting—assuring that employees and systems have the resources needed to perform their jobs.

3. Consequences

Are consequences aligned to support the desired performance? Motivation can be turned into a complex subject. In most cases it's really quite simple. It involves knowledge of the task to be performed, consequences, and feedback. Consequences refer to whatever follows the performance of an activity. Salespeople who make sales usually expect praise and bonuses. Every sales manager knows that a good incentive system gets good results. If people perform and only get complaints that they didn't do even better, in most cases it results in even less adequate performance. Imagine two activities: sales and entering information about sales. Imagine that the salesperson has less time than is needed to perform both tasks well. Further imagine that he or she gets a significant bonus for every sale but only gets complaints at the end of the month if all the system entries haven't been made. Which is the salesperson likely to do? It's always important to not only consider the consequences of each task by itself, but to also consider the effect of asking one individual to do several tasks with different consequences.

Are consequences meaningful from the performer's perspective? Different individuals respond to different types of consequences. It's important that the consequences be appropriate to the individual. Bonuses usually work, but in many situations, a day off will be more appreciated than a small bonus. Some employees look forward to the opportunity to do some travel, and others regard it as punishment. The good manager should have a clear idea about the consequences that will be valued by different employees.

Are consequences timely? Lots of research shows that consequences that immediately follow an activity are more likely to affect performance than those delayed. This doesn't mean that you need to hand salespeople money as soon as they return from a successful sales call. It does mean that the reward system should be clear so that the salesperson can calculate what bonus he or she made on that sales call. Making an effort without knowing if there will be consequences isn't a good practice. Giving someone a big, surprise bonus at the end of the year isn't nearly as good as giving smaller bonuses that are clearly associated with excellent performance. Best is a system that makes the consequences clear so that employees can mentally reward themselves when they succeed. The same thing is true in reverse. Punishment should be closely associated with the action that deserves punishment. Waiting for a yearly evaluation to tell someone he or she is not performing up to snuff is a bad policy.

4. Feedback

Do performers receive information about their performance? Forgetting more explicit rewards, every manager should ask if employees receive information about the outcomes of their work. Assume the manager collects information about the number of chairs that arrive at the distributor's site undamaged versus with defects. As soon as the manager gets such information, he or she should pass it along to the employees involved. If defects go down, employees should learn about it (and receive praise as a consequence). If defects go up, employees should be informed immediately. Similarly, if chairs arrived damaged as a result of poor packaging, the employees in shipping should learn about it immediately, and vice versa. In too many companies, employees try to do their jobs, and month in and month out no one tells them if their work is adequate or not. After awhile, most employees will take a little less care if, as far as they can tell, no one notices or cares if they take more care. This is an area where the process sponsor plays an important role. Often the feedback needed by people in one subprocess isn't immediately available to the functional manager managing that subprocess. Care taken in packing may only pay off in reduced customer complaints, which go to sales and service and never directly to manufacturing or packaging. It's the process sponsor's job to design a process-wide feedback system that assures that subprocess managers have the information they need to provide their people with timely feedback.

Is the information they receive relevant, accurate, timely, specific, and easy to understand? As with consequences, there is more useful and less useful feedback. It's important to tell the packaging people that chairs are getting damaged in transit because chairs aren't properly packed. It's much more useful to tell them exactly how the chairs are being damaged so they will know how to change their packaging process to avoid the problem. Many companies provide managers with accounting data that is summarized in ways only accountants can understand. This isn't useful feedback. (This is one of the reasons for moving to an activity-based costing system to assure that cost information can tell specific employees about whether specific activities and subprocesses are contributing to the value of products or costing the company money.) A manager that yells that a subprocess isn't performing up to snuff without being specific about what's wrong is only creating anxiety and increasing the problems facing the people in that subprocess.

5. Skill, Knowledge, and Capability

Do the performers have the necessary skills and knowledge to perform? In many companies, the solution to all performance problems is to provide more training. For many employees, one of the worst features of a job is having to sit through training courses that drone on about things one already knows. The performance of a task requires specific information and the skills needed to evaluate the information, make decisions, and perform tasks. In most cases the place to begin is to identify the performer who is doing the job right, and then ask what is missing in the case of a performer who isn't doing the job right. If the deficient performer needs to learn specific items of knowledge or specific skills, then some kind of training is appropriate. Before training, however, be sure you really are facing a skill/knowledge problem. If employees have performed correctly in the past, it's very unlikely they have forgotten what they knew. It's much more likely in that case to be an environmental problem or a problem arising from a lack of feedback or consequences.

Do the performers know why desired performance is important? The importance and effort we assign to a task usually reflects our understanding of the importance of the consequences that result. If employees don't realize that some seemingly minor shutdown procedure, if left undone, can, infrequently, cause a major explosion, they might tend to skip the shutdown procedure. On most days, indeed for months or years, there may be no consequence. In these situations it's important that employees have a good overview of what's important and why it's important.

Are the performers physically, mentally, and emotionally able to perform? Finally, it's important to assure that performers can actually perform the tasks assigned. If employees can't reach a shelf or can't read English, there are tasks they simply can't perform. In some cases changes in the environment will help. Steps can be provided or signs can be posted in another language. In some cases, however, an individual simply isn't able to perform a task. In those cases another performer needs to be assigned to the task.

As we suggested earlier, most of these same criteria apply to systems, although in the case of systems, the understanding and the feedback usually involve the person maintaining the software system and not the software itself.

An interesting complement to the approach we have described here is provided by the People Capability Maturity Model (People-CMM). We have already discussed the CMM model in the introduction. It provides an analysis of the process orientation and maturity of organizations based on standards developed by Carnegie-Mellon University. When we spoke of it earlier, we emphasized the transitions organizations go through to become more systematic in their use of a process-oriented approach to management. Bill Curtis and others have created a variation on CMM that emphasizes how organizations support their workforce, and has shown cultural changes that occur in the way people are managed as organizations become more sophisticated in their use and management of processes. The People-CMM approach should be studied by any manager that wants a high-level overview of how effective organizations change their people management practices as they become more mature in their support of processes. We describe a good book on this approach in the Notes and References section at the end of the book.

Managing the Performance of Activities

Broadly, an operational manager is responsible for five things:

1. Identifying goals to be accomplished
2. Organizing activities to accomplish those goals
3. Communicating the goals to the employees
4. Monitoring the output of the activities to assure they meet their assigned goals
5. Diagnosing problems and fixing them when activity output is inadequate

In many if not most cases, defective output is a result of a flaw in the design of the activity or an environmental problem that prevents the correct execution of the activity. In rarer cases, the correction of the defect requires a change in the software system or one or more people assigned to perform the task.

The key, as we have stressed elsewhere, is for operational managers to organize around subprocesses and activities. Managing employees separate from the activities they are expected to perform is always a bad practice. The good manager begins by understanding the process and improves it if he or she can. Only after the process is organized does the manager turn his or her attention to the performers, and then only in the context of successful or inadequate output measures. This approach can go a long way toward taking the blame out of management, and focusing everyone instead on the problems of performing activities in ways that achieve company goals.

Automating the Enter Expense Reports Activity

As we suggested earlier, the entry of expense reports is so straightforward that it has probably been automated at most companies.

In some cases employees enter their travel expense information directly in software programs on their laptop computers and transmit it, via the Internet, to accounting. The expense reports generated in this way may be examined by a clerk or passed electronically to an application that analyzes them, makes calculations, and generates checks for the employees. In most cases, however, an employee examines the forms on a computer screen and approves the claims before they are paid. In any case, the paper documentation for the expenses still has to be mailed in and needs to be filed. Most large companies conduct internal audits to compare documentation with payments.

One way we might represent this situation is illustrated in Figure 10.5. In this case we show that the entry of expense reports by the salespeople is a mixed manual/systems task. (The salesperson is completing a form managed by a software application that he or she accesses via the Internet.) Later, before a payment can be made, the report must be reviewed by an expense report clerk and approved. This is another mixed activity. The report clerk is also using a computer. The sales system sends the report to the clerk's computer and he or she approves it, after comparing it to the salesperson's documentation. After the clerk indicates that the report is approved, the sales system automatically generates the payment to the salesperson and transfers the money to his or her bank account. Meanwhile, the expense report clerk files the documentation.

In Figure 10.4 we assumed that the Enter Expense Reports activity was performed by a clerk. In Figure 10.5 we assume the entry activity is performed by a salesperson.

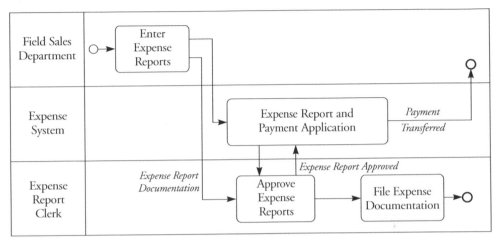

Figure 10.5 An automated expense report system.

In Figure 10.5 the expense clerk has a new job. The forms now arrive by computer, and the clerk approves them online. The inputs would be computer screens rather than forms. The clerk would have to know how to use a computer, access the electronic forms, and approve them. The procedure would be different, and the clerk would need to learn the new sequence. In this case, as with most automated systems, one of the key problems would be consequences and feedback. It's easy to automate the system and forget that the performer may no longer be in a position to know about the consequences of his or her work. If we want the clerk to review and approve 50 reports a day, we might want to provide a counter as part of the software application so the clerk knows how he or she is doing. We might also want to create a way for the clerk to learn when payments are made so he or she will be in a position to tell a salesperson who inquires about the status of a check when it will likely be paid.

In effect, each time an arrow goes from a manual activity to an automated activity, there is a computer interface, made up of one or multiple computer screens that the user needs to master. The salesperson has a set of computer screens that allow him or her to create a new expense report and then fill in expense information. Similarly, the clerk interacts with the expense reports on screen. The clarity and logic of the screen layouts is a major factor in efficient processing.

We haven't shown what happens in the case of various exceptions as, for example, when the documentation is incomplete, or when the clerk needs to move an expense item from one category to another or to disallow it altogether. We might create an Activity Worksheet to document this information. If we were going to ask an IT group to create the Expense Report application, they would need answers to these questions. On the other hand, if we buy the Expense Report application from an outside vendor, they should provide documentation, and the manager and employee will need to study the documentation and redesign their activity to accommodate the new software application.

A More Complex Activity

We considered the expense approval activity because it was simple and provided us with a good overview of what was involved in analyzing an activity. Now, let's consider a more complex activity, like selling. Assume that the same company that employs the Expense Report Entry Clerk also employs salespeople. These salespeople sell the company's products throughout North America by calling on customers, explaining the products, and taking orders. The salespeople are divided into regions managed by regional managers, and so forth. To keep things relatively simple, we are only going to focus on the sales job in its most generic form. In a process diagram, it might simply look like Figure 10.6.

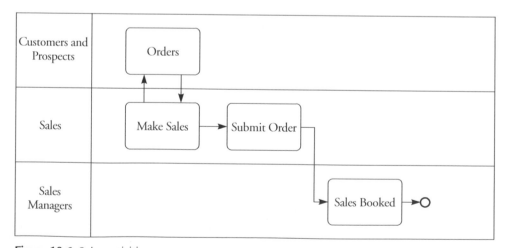

Figure 10.6 Sales activities.

Once again, we could easily analyze the sales activities in much greater detail. For our purposes, however, it might be easier in this case to provide a job description in a text format. Figure 10.7, for example, is an overview of the salesperson's job description.

Sales Activities That Define The Salesperson's Job

Selling Activities
1. Customer-Related Activities
    1.1 Prepare Account Related Paperwork
    1.2 Prepare Cross Selling Proposals
    1.3 Make Maintenance Calls
    1.4 Maintain Customer Contact by Phone or Email
2. Prospect-Related Activities
    2.1 Identify New Prospects
    2.2 Contact and Qualify New Prospects
    2.3 Make Sales Calls
    2.4 Develop Proposals
    2.5 Maintain Prospect Contact by Phone or Email

Overhead Activities
3. Planning and Coordinating Activities
    3.1 Time and Territory Planning
    3.2 Prioritizing Accounts
    3.3 Key Account Strategizing
4. Organizational Activities
    4.1 Meeting with Manager
    4.2 Attending Sales Meetings
    4.3 Accounting for Time and Expenses
    4.4 Preparing Special Reports
5. Product Knowledge
    5.1 Keeping Current on New Products
    5.2 Keeping Current on Competitive Products
    5.3 Maintaining Contacts with In-House Specialists
6. Self-Development and Motivation
    6.1 Keeping Current on General Business Trends
    6.2 Keeping Current on General Selling and Marketing Trends and Practices
    6.3 Arranging a Personal Schedule of Contingencies

Figure 10.7 Job description of a salesperson.

We could go further and write more detailed descriptions of each of these activities and assign measures to each or at least to the more important activities. For example, we could specify how many sales are expected per unit of time, how many prospect calls need to be made each month, or when expense accounts need to be submitted.

In effect, the job description in Figure 10.7 defines the salesperson's job. Assuming we only want to list two activities—Make Sales and Submit Orders—then this job description defines the steps that define those activities.

If you were the sales manager and you decided that sales were inadequate, you would need to define the tasks as we have and measure results to obtain some idea about what could be wrong. Measures of actual sales performance might reveal that most salespeople were performing in an adequate manner, but that a few weren't. In that case the sales manager would need to focus on the salespeople who weren't performing adequately. If most salespeople were performing in about the same manner,

Human Performance Analysis Worksheet

Process or Subprocess: _XYZ Sales Process_   Activity or Job: _XYZ Sales Activity_   AS-IS (✔) or TO BE ( ) Analysis

Tasks Included in Activity	Measures of Task Performance	Potential Performance Problems				
		Activity Specifications	Activity Support	Consequences	Feedback	Skill, Knowledge, and Capability
1. Customer-Related Activities - Preparing account-related paperwork - Preparing cross-selling proposals - Making maintenance calls - Maintaining customer contact	Increase sales to existing customers by 12% per quarter	Does the salesperson know the goals? Does the salesperson consider the goals attainable?	Does salesperson's territory have enough prospects?	Does the current bonus system reflect the effort required?	Does the salesperson get email whenever the company gets a complaint, or a compliment from one of his/her customers?	Does the salesperson understand the new product line? Does the salesperson understand how to demonstrate the new product with his/her laptop?
2. Prospect-Related Actvities - Identifying new prospects - Contacting and qualifying prospects - Making sales calls - Developing proposals - Maintaining prospect contact	Make 20 new sales per month.		Does the salesperson get leads whenever they come to company? Does the salesperson have the new laptops with the new demo loaded?			

Figure 10.8 A partially completed Human Performance Analysis worksheet for the Sales activity.

however, then the manager would need to consider redesigning the sales job or activity to correct a more generic problem.

In either case, the place to begin the analysis would be to analyze the sales tasks and compare them with the human performance model we presented in Figure 10.4. To make this easier, we use a Human Performance Analysis Worksheet, which is pictured as Figure 10.8.

Human Performance Analysis Worksheet (continued)						
Process or Subprocess: _XYZ Sales Process_		Activity or Job: _XYZ Sales Activity_			AS-IS (✓) or TO BE ( ) Analysis	
Tasks Included in Activity	Measures of Task Performance	Potential Performance Problems				
		Activity Standards	Activity Support	Consequences	Feedback	Skill, Knowledge, and Capability
3. Planning and Coordinating Activities - Time and territory planning - Prioritizing accounts - Key account strategizing						
4. Organizational Activities - Meeting with manager - Attending sales meetings - Accounting for time and expenses - Preparing special reports						
5. Product Knowledge - Keeping current on new products - Keeping current on competitive products - Maintaining contacts with in-house specialists						
6. Self-Development and Motivation - Keeping current on general business trends - Keeping current on general selling and marketing trends - Arranging a personal schedule of contingencies						

We haven't filled in the complete worksheet, but we did enter a few questions to suggest how a sales manager might begin to analyze what could be wrong with a deficient sales activity.

To analyze the sales activity, one begins by identifying the measures and examining historical records. The best performer should be compared with the average performer. That provides information on the gap between the best and the average, and provides a measurement of how much improvement could be obtained if everyone performing the activity performed as well as the best performer. Assuming the gap is worth the effort, then you need to examine the performance variables, comparing in each case the best and the average salesperson, to identify just where the differences lie. (We'll speak more of this type of analysis in the next chapter when we consider measurement in more detail.) Once the problems are identified, the supervisor can develop an improvement program.

Analyzing a Completely Automated Activity

The expense clerk's job provided a nice example of a simple job that might involve a mix of manual and computer-aided performance. The sales job is a more complex job that also has computer-aided elements, but is primarily a job performed by a human employee. In addition, the job is complex enough to assure that the manual or procedural aspects of the job are trivial compared with the analysis, decision-making, and human interaction skills required of the performer. The sales job is the kind of job that might require human performance analysts from human resources to help define and to assist in any needed training.

A third possibility is that we define an activity that will be completely automated. During the initial analysis phase of most process redesign projects, it doesn't make any difference whether the activity is performed by a person or a software system running on a computer. In both cases we need to determine the inputs and outputs of the activity, and measures for judging the quality of the outputs. Similarly, we need to determine how the activity relates to other activities in the same process and who will be responsible for managing the activity.

Once we decide the activity will be automated, we usually turn the actual software development task over to an appropriate IT group within the organization. In some cases, we will be asking that an existing application be modified. In other cases, we will be asking for the creation of a new software system. In either case, there usually isn't a one-to-one relationship between activities identified on our process diagrams and the software application to be developed. Recall Figure 10.5, where we indicated that a software application would capture expense reports from salespeople, place reports on the expense report clerk's computer, and later generate payments and transfer them to salespeople's bank accounts. In this case we were treating the software application as a black box. We really don't know or care if the application that automated the sales expense report entry activity is a single application or a combination of applications. That's a software design issue that IT will need to solve. It will depend on existing software applications being used, on the hardware used by various individuals, on the infrastructure already in place, and on the skills and software architectural strategies of the IT organization.

The important thing from our perspective is to define the inputs and outputs, and the performance requirements of the activity, as best we can, and then to turn the task over to IT. Figure 10.9 reproduces a variation of Figure 10.5. In this case we have added small boxes where the arrows from manual activities interface with a software system and labeled them I-1 and I-2, to indicate that there are two interfaces we will need to describe. Depending on the time, we could actually sketch the screens that we imagine would be used at each interface. Similarly, we could create lists of all of the data that is to be captured by each screen. We probably wouldn't go so far as to try to organize or structure the data to be collected, since that is usually done by the individual in IT who creates the database to store expense information. We can, however,

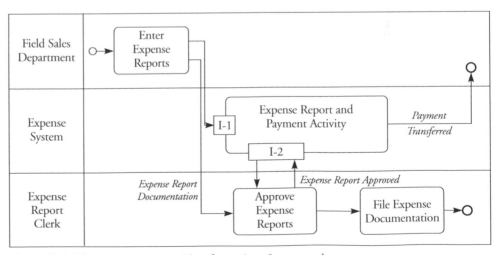

Figure 10.9 The expense system with software interfaces noted.

indicate the data we know we will want to collect. (In the Notes and References at the end of the book, we suggest books on interface or Web form design.)

Predictably, IT will need more information than we will probably provide. We probably won't consider all the exceptions, and an IT analyst will surely want to work with our design team to define more exact requirements. In essence, when we seek to fill the salesperson's job, we hire for a lot of skills, knowledge, and experience. We only have to teach a new salesperson a portion of his or her job. Humans come equipped with lots of common sense and can generalize from common business practices, or ask when they run into problems. Software systems don't come with common sense or the ability to ask when they get in trouble. Hence, we need to be much more precise about defining activities that are to be performed by software systems and anticipate every possible problem that might occur. The key, from the perspective of the process designer, however, is who should do what when. We believe that the process design team should define each activity as if it were being done by an intelligent person. Beyond that, when it turns out that the task is to be performed by a software system, IT analysts should be called in to work with the process design team to define the activity more precisely, and then be allowed to develop the software application in the way that works best. IT may decide that five different activities will be part of a single software application, or should be implemented via two separate software components. The process redesign team shouldn't worry about such details, as long as IT develops a system that functions as specified on the process diagram. In other words, the IT application must take the specified inputs from the designated individuals and make the specified outputs in accordance with measures established by the process redesign team.

In a nutshell, we carefully define the inputs and outputs of activities that are to be performed by software applications and leave the actual development of the software applications to the IT folks.

Knowledge Workers, Cognitive Maps and Business Rules

People are at the heart of any organization. They set the organization's goals, they manage it, they deal with customers, and they work together to produce the organization's products and services. Figure 10.10 describes some of the types of processes and the types of jobs that occur in any company. Simpler processes can be done by individuals that simply follow procedures. More complex jobs require workers who think. In some cases, the workers simply analyze a situation—using established business rules—and decide which of several alternative paths to follow, but in more complex cases, they analyze, diagnose, design, redesign, program, plan or schedule. In some cases, they create new products, new processes or entirely new ways of positioning a product or the company. Very complex jobs require individuals who can analyze and solve very complex problems.

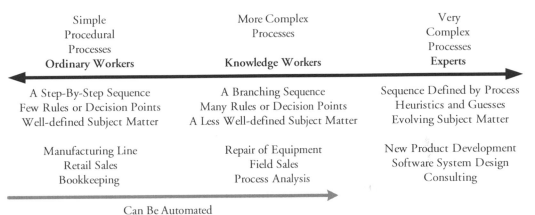

Simple Procedural Processes **Ordinary Workers**	More Complex Processes **Knowledge Workers**	Very Complex Processes **Experts**
A Step-By-Step Sequence Few Rules or Decision Points Well-defined Subject Matter	A Branching Sequence Many Rules or Decision Points A Less Well-defined Subject Matter	Sequence Defined by Process Heuristics and Guesses Evolving Subject Matter
Manufacturing Line Retail Sales Bookkeeping	Repair of Equipment Field Sales Process Analysis	New Product Development Software System Design Consulting

Can Be Automated

Figure 10.10 The process/knowledge continuum.

It's a commonplace to observe that the U.S. has become a service economy that is run by knowledge workers. In other words, many U.S. companies have lots of knowledge workers doing more complex tasks than in the past. One need only think of a software firm that employs hundreds of software architects, designers and programmers, a movie company with all of the specialists required to create a movie—from writers and actors to directors and special effects people—or a financial firm with specialists who help individuals create and manage their financial portfolios. Knowledge workers create special problems for those who must recruit and manage them. Managers need to be especially careful in designing performance reviews and incentive and motivation programs for such individuals. If you think of the CEOs and senior managers in a firm as the ultimate knowledge workers, you can see what kinds of problems boards encounter when they seek to define their goals or motivate them.

Knowledge workers also create special problems for anyone who tries to analyze the processes that employ them. These usually aren't processes one would try to automate, although the processes typically rely on complex software systems that the knowledge workers use, themselves, to perform their work.

Don't misunderstand. It's easy to diagram a supply chain that employs hundreds of knowledge workers and experts. One can easily decompose the analysis from level one processes to level two or three processes and identify just what activities each knowledge worker or expert is expected to accomplish and when it is to be performed. The problem comes when you try to move lower and define the specific procedures that individual knowledge workers or experts are to follow when they perform their daily tasks. That's usually hard and, in some cases, it's impossible. The work involves thought and creativity and we simply don't have good tools to use to capture those kinds of processes.

One problem process analysts face when they seek to define the specific procedures that knowledge workers perform arises from the fact that knowledge keeps evolving. Thus, knowledge workers, to remain useful, need opportunities to learn of new theories, facts, and procedures. They need training and they need to network at conferences and with peers within their organizations.

Many knowledge management (KM) programs are focused on providing ways to facilitate the sharing and accumulation of insights acquired by knowledge workers. Some KM programs provide Web sites where knowledge workers can describe their insights for others facing similar problems. Others provide summaries of new articles or new procedures. Still others simply list individuals with skills so those in need of help or advice know where they can turn.

A related problem is that knowledge workers often need to communicate with others as they solve problems. Email has become one of the most important tools in many companies. Groupware represents an effort to facilitate such interaction, and it will become more important as international companies increasingly build teams that require the participation of knowledge workers from different countries around the world.

As you think about these issues, imagine diagramming a process that includes steps that depend on the exchange of email between dozens of different employees at different locations around the world. High-level diagrams that don't try to capture the details are easy enough to draw, but a diagram that might someday be rendered into BPEL and turned into a BPMS application can be pretty daunting.

It's important to distinguish between knowledge workers and true experts. Experts typically require 10 years to become really expert. Studies have shown that they understand the problems they face by means of very complex networks of cognitive concepts and solve problems by employing thousands of rules. A physician who diagnoses meningitis infections typically employs 10,000 rules to determine what type of meningitis he or she is faced with. Moreover, those rules change and are reorganized each month as the physician reviews new studies being published in the relevant medical journals. It is rarely cost-effective to try to automate the work of a human expert. As expensive as it is to maintain such experts, it is cheaper to hire them and pay them to remain up to date than to try to capture and automate their knowledge.

Knowledge workers, on the other hand, do not employ such complex cognitive networks or use quite so many rules. A knowledge worker often employs a few hundred rules to solve the problems he or she encounters. In many cases, process practitioners are asked to analyze the jobs of knowledge workers. This is particularly true in high-turnover organizations, like the U.S. Army or Air Force, where people need to be rapidly trained to perform complex jobs that they may only occupy for 3–5 years. Similar situations occur in other domains when new technology is introduced and knowledge workers need to rapidly learn to perform in new ways.

This usually entails analysis of the knowledge used by the knowledge worker—and the capture of that knowledge in some form—as well as the development of complex software programs or training programs to pass that knowledge on to new workers. In this case, the process analyst needs to do cognitive task analysis, capture and document knowledge structures and knowledge rules, and then work with others to create training or software systems to deliver the information and skills to the workers who will need them. This isn't something taught in beginning process analysis courses, but these tools will increasingly be required of process professionals as they seek to redesign complex processes.

When I first started analyzing human performance problems, in the late 1960s, the techniques we used were generally termed "behavior task analysis." This term reflected the dominant trend in psychology in the late sixties—behaviorism—which stressed observation of overt activity. Broadly, behaviorism represented a revolt by academic psychologists against the cognitive psychology that had predominated in the late nineteenth century. Nineteenth-century psychology had relied on introspective reports of individuals and had led to Freudian psychoanalysis, which most serious psychologists regarded as unscientific. Behaviorism stressed the systematic observation of behavior and careful measurements. Studies by Watson, Skinner, and others illustrated how the behavior of rats and pigeons could be controlled and predicted by observing the stimuli the animals were subjected to and by the consequences that followed. By the late sixties, behaviorism had made its way into industry and was being used, in a variety of ways, to improve the design and management of human performance. Thus, behavioral task analysis focused on the documentation of stimulus-response sequences, and on designing work procedures that were more efficient.

By the late seventies, however, most academic psychologists had returned to the study of cognition. Using new techniques, derived primarily from work with computers, psychologists began to conceptualize human performers as information-processing systems, and ask questions about the nature of human cognitive processing. The new cognitive psychology put its emphasis on observation and was at least as rigorous as behaviorism. An early classic of cognitive task analysis was Allen Newell and Herbert A. Simon's *Human Problem Solving* (1972). In it, Newell and Simon analyzed a variety of human cognitive tasks, including cryptarithmetic, logic and chess playing, and reached a variety of interesting conclusions that formed the basis for a decade of work in both cognitive psychology and artificial intelligence. Indeed, it could be argued that their work led directly to expert systems—software programs that sought to duplicate expert human performance. The key point to make here, however, is that psychologists and computer scientists spent several years in the early 1980s developing techniques to capture human expertise and embed expert knowledge in software systems. [1]

Those of us working in the behavioral paradigm had largely arrived at the same conclusion by a different route. [2, 3] In the early seventies, most of the processes I worked on involved procedural tasks—on manufacturing lines, for example—that really could be analyzed by observation. You studied the sequence of activities that the employees followed, and developed systems to make the flow as efficient as possible. Most of the problems that we encountered, by the way, involved managers who didn't define the tasks properly, provided inadequate feedback, or reinforced the wrong activities. By the late seventies, however, most of the processes I was working on involved knowledge workers, although we didn't use that term back then. I did a lot of sales analysis, analyzed managerial decision-making in a variety of contexts, and increasingly worked on financial operations that entailed computer interactions. It was common to encounter an activity in which the worker received a batch of information, stared at the computer screen for a few minutes, and then made a decision. Similarly, with sales, a bank salesperson would interview a potential customer and then return to the office and write up a multipage proposal for a complex loan package. In these cases the "behavior" that was important was occurring inside the heads of the employees. They were thinking, analyzing, designing solutions and making decisions—all things that behavior task analysis was unable to capture. It was precisely these types of process problems that led me to investigate cognitive psychology and to get involved in expert systems development.

Ultimately, expert systems have not proven very viable. It turns out that human expertise—if it's worthy of the name—needs to be constantly maintained. Human experts attend conferences, read books and research papers, and constantly interact with peers while trying to solve hard problems. All this leads to their reformulating their knowledge. It is expensive to capture human knowledge for an expert system, but it is much more expensive to maintain that knowledge. In fact, it is so expensive that it turns out to be more cost-effective to just keep using the human experts. They will need to be maintained, in any case, to keep learning and revising the knowledge that is required to make the expert system effective.

This is not to suggest that all the work that went into expert systems development was in vain. We have, for example, developed some rather good ways of representing human knowledge. It turns out that expert decision making can be represented with rules. It is also obvious that human experts rely on cognitive models of the problem domain, which psychologists tend to call "cognitive maps" and which computer scientists usually call "object networks." In essence, the cognitive map allows the human expert to classify and organize the facts in the problem space, and the rules allow the expert to draw inferences and conclusions about how to deal with the problem he or she is facing.

Not many people are building expert systems today, but knowledge of the techniques used to develop expert systems has spread to other domains and found new applications. Thus, today, when business process analysts are faced with tasks involving human knowledge, they are in a good position to draw on some of the techniques developed by cognitive psychologists and expert systems designers in the eighties and nineties.

If you think of a continuum that ranges from nonexperts to experts, knowledge workers lie in the middle. (See Figure 10.10.) A true expert, such as an engineer who could design an M1 battle tank, might have models with many hundreds of objects and use ten or twenty thousand rules. The soldiers who diagnose M1 battle tank problems in the field might only require a hundred objects and five-hundred rules. The trend, in other words, is to ignore true expertise, which is too hard to analyze or maintain, and to focus on analyzing the knowledge that knowledge workers bring to bear on their more circumscribed tasks. The work of knowledge workers is, of course, very important and valuable, and if we can capture significant portions of it, we can share it and use it to design processes that can contribute significantly to the value of our organizations.

There are two tools that cognitive analysts rely on heavily. One is the cognitive map, a diagram that defines the concepts and relationships between concepts that a knowledge worker relies on. The second is the rule that defines what a knowledge worker should do in the presence of a specific situation. Figure 10.11 illustrates a cognitive or knowledge map that describes the conceptual network of an individual who builds cognitive maps.

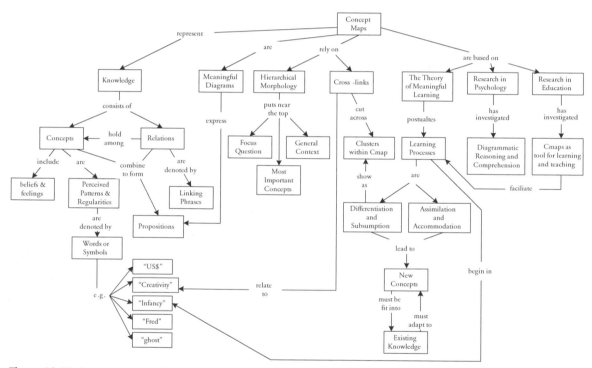

Figure 10.11 A concept map about concept maps (after Crandall, et al., *Working Minds*).

We do not have the space to go into cognitive task analysis or the capture of knowledge and the creation of concept maps in this book, but several books are listed in the Notes and References section for readers who must deal with processes with knowledge workers.

Business Rules and Knowledge Rules

The capture of rules is an even more complex topic. Companies have always had policies and rules to define what should or should not be done. Similarly, business rules have been written down in employee manuals for generations and are currently embedded in many legacy software systems. Today, however, business rules have achieved a new status as assets of a company that ought to be explicitly defined and managed.

A *business rule* is a statement that defines some policy or practice of the business. Business rules, whether implemented by employees or by automated systems, determine that appropriate actions are taken at appropriate times. Changes in company policies or practices invariably are reflected in business rules, and the ability to maintain consistency between policies and the business rules used in business processes, IT applications, and employee practices, especially when changes take place, has become a key characteristic of agile companies.

Today's efforts to formalize the capture and management of business rules originated in four different movements that have waxed and waned over the course of the last two and a half decades. A review of those movements helps explain the current situation in the business rules market.

Business Rules for Software Development

In the late 1980s there were a series of meetings of IBM user group GUIDE at which technologists sought to define the business rules that software applications were written to implement. Programmers realized that different elements of their software applications changed at different rates. The data that a company collected, for example, changed relatively slowly. Business rules, which often incorporated specific business assumptions—information about specific interest rates or types of clients, for example—tended to change much more rapidly. Thus, many software architects began to believe that business rules should be formalized and stored independently of the software applications in which they are used. Properly organized, software applications would simply look up rules as they were needed. This would mean that business managers could change the business rules as needed, without having to reprogram software applications.

Many of those who advocated the formalization of business rules believed that rule formalization should be a top-down effort. Executives ought to define strategies and goals and those should be translated into formal policies. Those policies, in turn, should be translated into high-level business rules, which should then be translated into more specific business rules.

Anyone who has undertaken a rules documentation effort knows that, if one isn't very careful, one soon runs into problems with the specific terms and names one uses in the rules. To create a formal system of rules, one must simultaneously create a formal vocabulary. In other words, everyone in the company must use words like "customer," "account," and "primary account number," in the same way. Thus, one needs a formal vocabulary (or concept map) to assure that a rule that states:

All customers are assigned one and only one primary account number.

will be unambiguous and interpreted in the same way by everyone throughout the company. At a minimum, we need to define "communities" that will use the same words in the same way. Thus, business rule methodologists are usually concerned with the formalization of both business vocabularies—sometimes called an *ontology*—and business rules for companies or for communities within a company.

Most business software products use a repository to store information about rules. In effect, as one writes rules, one is also creating and maintaining an object-attribute network that specifies the terms used and the relationships between terms.

Unfortunately, large companies are usually broken into many divisions and departments that are spread throughout the world. Getting management to spend the time required to formalize a corporate business ontology and then proceed to define formal business rules has proved very difficult. It's a huge undertaking and most companies have been unable to justify the effort. Those that have—several insurance companies, for example—have been companies from industries that were already inclined to think in terms of very precise rules. Others have created rules and an associated ontology for only one division or one group within the company.

Figure 10.12 suggests how someone advocating a comprehensive rule formalization effort might conceive of the effort. In essence, they would start at the enterprise level and work with executives to formalize the company's policies and create a formal ontology and appropriate business rules. Then they would work down through divisions and departments, formalizing their ontologies and business rules, constantly being sure that lower-level ontologies and rules were clearly aligned with high-level rules. Finally, they would reach the implementation level and check to see where business rules appeared, in procedures manuals, training courses, and in software applications and assure that those implementations used rules clearly derived from high-level rules. In the end, if a company persevered, they would have a complete description of all the rules used in the organization. Subsequently, a change in policy would drive changes in high-level rules and those changes, in turn, would work their way down through the entire organization, assuring that all rules were changed to reflect the changes in policy.

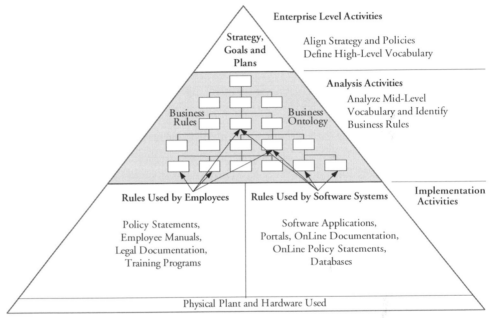

Figure 10.12 A systematic, top-down approach to business rules.

The theory behind such a comprehensive, rule-oriented approach is sound, but the problems involved in actually capturing and maintaining it are significant, and the effort has not been one that most companies have chosen to undertake. One problem that faced anyone considering such an effort in the 1980s was that most of the advocates of this approach were database technologists, and the databases being used at the time were not very well designed to support this approach. Thus, although many people appreciated the power of the "rules approach," it didn't gain much traction until recently, when new tools became available.

Rule-Based Systems for the Capture of Expertise

Another approach to rules was undertaken by the expert systems movement of the mid-eighties. Expert system development, as we mentioned earlier, derived from research in artificial intelligence (AI) and focused on capturing the rules used by experts to analyze and solve very hard problems. For example, systems were developed to analyze readings from geological equipment and to determine constantly changing seat prices for airlines. Expert systems development was facilitated by software tools—expert system-building tools—that stored the rules in a knowledge base and used an inference engine to examine facts and rules when a decision was required and to generate a decision.

As we noted, some of the expert system applications that resulted from these efforts proved very valuable, but most proved too hard to maintain.

In the mid-nineties, as interest in the capture of expert knowledge waned, many of the vendors who had provided expert system-building products repositioned themselves to provide support for those who were interested in capturing and using business rules. Expert rule sets had proved too unstable and hence too difficult to maintain, but business rules tended to be more stable and to change less frequently. The rule tools originally developed to support expert rule sets turned out to be much better for maintaining business rule sets and supporting the types of rule changes that business managers wanted to make. Thus, in the late nineties, the IT rules documentation movement and the expert system-building tool vendors had largely joined forces.

Risk Management and Compliance Issues

Corporate executives have always been concerned with whether employees are, in fact, following corporate policies. Many industries are regulated and there are laws that require that certain types of companies report on compliance. Recently, Sarbanes-Oxley and related regulations have been promulgated that require that companies demonstrate that they are able to track changes in processes that might lead to a compliance failure. The various concerns have placed a new emphasis on both formal business rule systems that can track compliance from policies to high-level rules to specific rules in software programs and employee manuals. At the same time, these same regulations have encouraged companies to develop formal descriptions of key business processes and to show where business rules within those processes assure compliance with government regulations. These legal and management concerns have highlighted the importance of a well-managed business process effort that documents not only processes but business rules.

Business Rules Used in Business Processes

In the 1990s, considerable attention was focused on reengineering major business processes. To understand a business process, analysts usually began by creating a diagram or model that showed the major steps or activities that occur during the process. At the simplest level, business rules were often pictured as decision points within a process workflow diagram. Thus, a rule that said that loans should only be granted to applications that meet the company credit standards might get represented in a flowchart as shown in Figure 10.13.

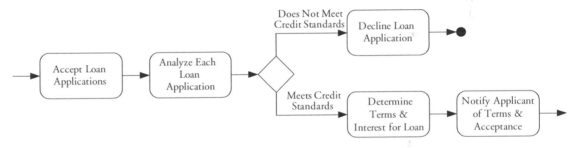

Figure 10.13 A workflow diagram with a business rule that defines a decision diamond.

More complex decisions might also be formalized by means of business or even expert rules. For example, in Figure 10.13, the process analyst might decide to get very explicit about how one determines the terms and interest for a specific loan application. It could easily turn out that one hundred different rules were involved in determining the terms and interest for a specific type of loan. In this case the rules are not shown, explicitly, as a decision box, but are in effect inside the Determine Terms & Interest for Loan activity box. (In many process modeling software tools one can literally click on the Determine Terms & Interest Activity box on a diagram and open a window to the business rules documentation environment.) Clearly the rule represented by the decision diamond was a business rule. Probably the rules used to determine the terms and interest for the loan were also business rules, although some decisions in some processes can become so complex that they are, in fact, knowledge rules. In other words, the rules are not so much defined by explicit policies as by experts who are hired to make the decisions. As process analysts examined ever more complex processes, they found that the capture of business rules was an important part of most business process redesign efforts.

Figure 10-14 suggests some of the relationships we have been discussing.

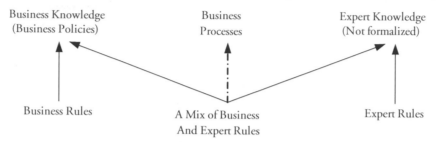

Figure 10.14 Business rules and expert rules.

Business rules are derived from common business knowledge, often formalized as policies, while expert rules are derived from human experts and not formalized. Both are found in business processes analysis efforts.

Just as business rule advocates proposed a top-down approach, most business process architects have urged companies to begin at the enterprise level and define high-level processes—usually called value chains—and then subdivide those to define a hierarchy of business processes. In a similar way, they have advocated that companies align their strategic goals with their value chains and major processes and develop measurement and management systems to support all their processes.

In Chapter 17 we will discuss business process management software (BPMS) products. Most of those products incorporate a business rules engine and we will discuss tools that can automate the use of business rules at that time.

Activities, Job Descriptions and Applications

We need to clarify one final issue: the relationship between activities and the jobs or software applications that implement them. In some simple cases, a single person may be assigned to a single activity—as we assumed the Expense Report Clerk was in our first example. In such a case, an activity description and a job description would just be different perspectives on the same entity. Similarly, we later assumed that a single software application implemented the Expense Report and Payment activity in Figure 10.5. In this latter case, the description of all of the interfaces supported by the Expense Report and Payment activity would describe all the interfaces of the application. These examples are the exceptions rather than the rule.

In most cases, a large process will support many subprocesses divided into many different activities. Some individuals will be responsible for multiple activities. Consider the example of the sales activities outlined in Figure 10.7. Each salesperson would be responsible for all of those activities. Each of those activities would have goals and measures, and each salesperson would be responsible for meeting all of the goals of all of the activities that were included in his or her job description.

Similarly, it might make sense for managers to divide a process into a sequence of activities that describe the order in which things should happen. On the other hand, it might make sense for IT to develop a single application to support every activity in the sequence. Consider a situation where several individuals process common documents that are maintained by a workflow system. The entire process is supported by a single workflow application, and the documents being processed are maintained in a single database. In effect, each person simply edits the document in the database.

We have focused on analyzing processes and activities and defining the order in which they should occur. Once the activity or process descriptions are complete, however, we often reverse the process and lump activities together to define jobs or software applications. Figure 10.10 provides an overview of the process we are describing and illustrates how a redesign team might assign output measures to several activities and how they might be lumped as job descriptions or software applications were designed.

In Figure 10.15 we see that a sales application designed to support the Ergo Chair Sales Subprocess might end up supporting four different activities. Similarly, we see how individuals assigned to the Field Salesperson job might be required to do some or all of the steps defined by three different activities, and be evaluated by output measures associated with the same three activities.

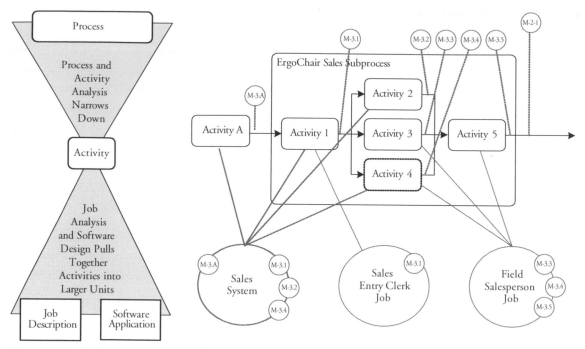

Figure 10.15 Analysis and then synthesis and the assignment of goals or output measures to jobs or systems.

Assume that the manager responsible for monitoring the entire subprocess determines that the subprocess is performing in a suboptimal manner. The subprocess manager's job is to determine what is wrong. He or she will probably begin by checking each of the activities included in the subprocess, as well as the inputs received from Activity A. Once a given activity is determined to be suboptimal—say, Activity 4—the manager still has to determine if it's the sales system that is failing, or the field salespeople who use the system who are performing in a suboptimal manner.

Different organizations track these relationships in different ways. We recommend that process diagrams like the ones described in Chapter 5 be stored in databases managed by software tools and that measures and job descriptions or software systems involved in each activity be stored with the activity in the same database. We'll return to these issues after we have considered the process manager's role in more detail and when we consider the use of software tools to support business processes.

Notes and References

The basic ideas of how to approach the analysis of specific human activity derives from the work of Geary Rummler and others at the International Society for Performance Improvement (ISPI). ISPI grew out of the behavior psychology movement in the 1960s and led to the development of a general theory of how to design effective training and motivational systems, which is, today, generally termed *human performance technology* (HPT) or *human performance improvement* (HPI). For more information, check their Web site: *www.ispi.org.*

Rummler, Geary A., *Serious Performance Consulting: According to Rummler*, Publication of ISPI and ASTD, 2004. This is the best book available on HPT and business processes. Every business process analyst who attempts the analysis of activities that involve human performers should read this book. There is nothing else remotely like it for its clarity and practicality.

Gilbert, Thomas F., *Human Competence: Engineering Worthy Performance*, McGraw-Hill, 1978. Gilbert was one of the people that created human performance technology in the 1970s, and this book provides a thought-provoking introduction to the field. Gilbert is extremely idiosyncratic and can be technical, so you've really got to be interested in human performance issues to get through this.

Gilbert developed the idea of the PIP (potential for improved performance) as a way of measuring the possibility of performance improvement in given situations. In essence, you measure the performance of the best performer(s) and compare it to the performance of average performers. If the gap is very narrow, there isn't much potential for improvement and the variation is likely due to chance. If the gap is great, then you need to find out what accounts for the difference and train or motivate average performers to act like the best performers.

Information on the analysis of sales performance is from a sales performance workshop I gave at ISPI in the seventies.

Curtis, Bill, William E. Hefley, and Sally A. Millor, *The People Capability Maturity Model: Guidelines for Improving the Workforce*, Addison-Wesley, 2002. This is a book that starts with the premises of CMM and then studies how one improves the workforce to move from one level of process maturity to another. Bill Curtis wrote that it was this book that started him thinking of applying CMM to processes other than software processes.

Newell, Allen and Herbert A. Simon. *Human Problem Solving,* Prentice-Hall, 1972. The critical early work on cognitive psychology and artificial intelligence.

Crandall, Beth, Gary Klein and Robert R. Hoffman, *Working Minds: A Practitioner's Guide to Cognitive Task Analysis,* MIT Press, 2006. This book provides a very nice introduction to cognitive mapping and cognitive task analysis.

Lindsay, Peter H. and Donald A. Norman, *Human Information Processing: An Introduction to Psychology,* Academic Press, 1972. This textbook is out of print, but used copies can be obtained from *www.amazon.com* and it provides a really excellent introduction to all the basic cognitive analysis concepts, including mapping.

If you are interested in a more complete guide to acquiring knowledge, and want to get a book that is more advanced than *Working Minds,* I recommend *A Practical Guide to Knowledge Acquisition* by A. Carlisle Scott, Jan E. Clayton and Elizabeth L. Gibson. This book was published by Addison-Wesley in 1991 and represents an excellent synthesis of the techniques used by leading expert systems developers. The same concepts and interviewing techniques described in this book can be just as well applied to the analysis of tasks that knowledge workers face. *Knowledge Acquisition* is no longer in print, but I notice that some used copies are available via *www.amazon.com.*

Davenport, Thomas H., *Thinking for a Living: How to Get Better Performance Results from Knowledge Workers,* Harvard Business School Press, 2005. This is an excellent, high-level look at the problems managers face in dealing with knowledge workers.

Hall, Curt, and Paul Harmon, *The BPTrends 2006 Report on Business Rules Products,* May 2006. In 2006 BPTrends published a report by Curt Hall and Paul Harmon that reviewed business rule technologies and some of the leading business rule products currently in use. This report is free and can be accessed by going to *www.bptrends.com* and selecting BPT Product Reports. I owe many of my ideas on business rules to discussions with Curt Hall.

The OMG has developed a business rules standard that anyone interested in business rules development should study. To access it, visit the OMG Web site and search for: *Business Semantics of Business Rules.*

A good Web site that provides information on the various approaches to business rules is the site of the Business Rule Community, a group that discusses various business rule issues and offers white papers on various topics: *www.brcommunity.com.*

Ross, Ronald G., *Business Rules Concepts: Getting to the Point of Knowledge (2nd Ed.)*, BRCommunity.com, 2005. This is an excellent introduction to the concepts and techniques involved in business rules.

Morgan, Tony, *Business Rules and Information Systems: Aligning IT with Business Goals*, Addison-Wesley, 2002. This is another good introduction to the importance of specific business rules and how they can be used to align business goals with specific processes and activities.

Mitra, Amit and Amar Gupta, *Agile Systems: With Reusable Patterns of Business Knowledge*, ARTECH House, 2005. This is a rather technical book that proposes that organizations develop comprehensive knowledge-based systems to describe complex business processes. This is very much in the spirit of the knowledge-based systems movement of the eighties, and proposes the development of systematic ontologies and inheritance hierarchies that could be used to structure business rule systems. This is a very important book, but only those considering a heavy investment in business rules will want to read it.

Harmon, Paul, and Curt Hall, *Intelligent Software Systems Development: An IS Manager's Guide*, Wiley, 1993. This is an older book, but provides a good technical introduction to the concepts used in expert systems and business rule systems.

Managing and Measuring Business Processes

IN THIS CHAPTER we want to consider how the management of business processes affects the performance of the process. In Chapter 5 we discussed some of the issues that companies face in organizing process management and in Chapter 6 we considered some of the enterprise issues faced by companies trying to organize a corporate performance measurement system. Here our focus is much narrower: we want to consider how a business process redesign team might go about analyzing how a specific business process is managed and what changes they might recommend to improve the specific process.

The work required of a process redesign team varies according to the process maturity of the organization. If the organization is a CMMI Level 4 or 5 organization, it will have an enterprise process management system in place and will already have a performance measurement system defined. In this case, the team will check to see if established process management policies and procedures are being followed. In less mature organizations—and most organizations lie somewhere between CMMI Level 2 and 3—process management will be more informal and the redesign team will have to examine the management of the process carefully to determine if the manager is implementing some basic process management principles. If not, then the process redesign team will have to recommend that more effective process management practices be established and implemented.

In Chapter 4, when we discussed enterprise architecture issues and in Chapter 8 when we discussed how to analyze process problems, we considered two types of management processes. One type operates at a remove from the specific process being analyzed. The scoping effort may identify it and suggest it be included within the scope of the project, but in most cases it will not be included. Thus, the project team may suggest that the management process that generates corporate credit policies change certain policies, but it won't focus on the actual management of the credit policy process. The second type of management process describes what the specific manager in charge of the specific process does to facilitate the day-to-day operation of the process. Figure 11.1 shows the analysis we did of a pizza organization in Chapter 8. Note in this case that the process in scope—the Provide Delivery Service process—has specific management processes associated with its activities. Separately, there are management processes like the removed process that generates company policies and rules.

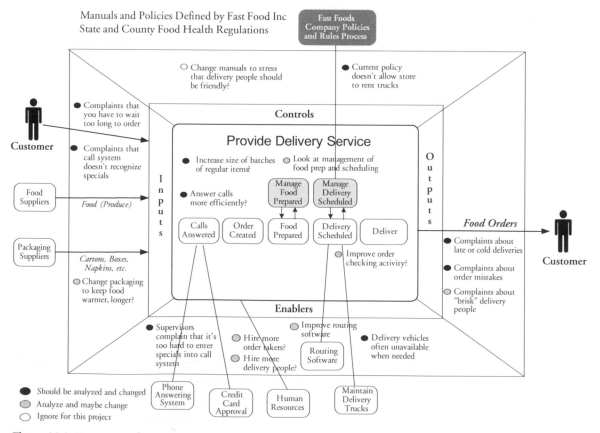

Figure 11.1 Two types of management processes: those at a remove (dark gray) and those associated with the process-in-scope (light gray).

For the purposes of this chapter, we'll ignore the management processes that operate at some remove from the specific process being redesigned and focus only on the activities of the process manager who is responsible for the day-to-day operation of the process we are trying to improve.

Representing Management Processes

In Chapters 8 and 9 we considered what was involved in modeling processes. In most cases, we begin by simply managing the operational processes we are concerned with and assume that each process we identify has a manager. Later, if management seems like something we should focus upon—and it usually is—we can go back and represent management processes. Figure 11.2 shows how we informally represented the management processes involved in the Deliver Pizzas process. In this case we identify the management process that is responsible for the entire Deliver Pizzas process and we represent the management role that is associated with each subprocess within the Deliver Pizzas process. In this case, since we will also be looking at an external process that maintains delivery trucks, we also indicate that we will be looking at the management of the Maintain Delivery Trucks process.

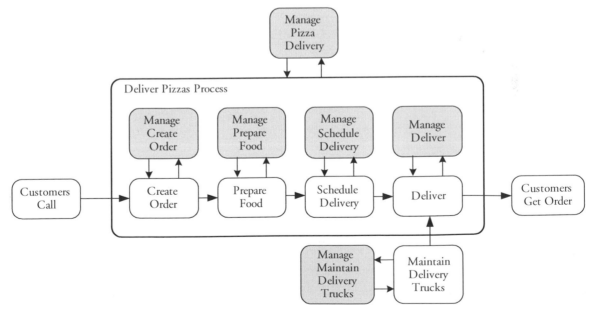

Figure 11.2 A business process diagram that pictures both the regular and the management processes.

In an actual company, some of the processes might be managed by the same person. Thus, for example, there might only be one manager for both scheduling and delivering pizzas and the analysis could be modified to reflect that.

If we create a swimlane diagram, then we usually represent the management of processes and subprocesses on the left vertical axis. In essence, a lane is within the responsibility of a manager. Depending on the level of detail we allow ourselves, we might only show a process or department manager, but in Figure 11.3 we have shown each of the subprocess managers.

By adding to the structure of the swimlane diagram, we can picture the hierarchical relationship between the manager of the food preparation process and the manager of the entire Pizza Delivery process.

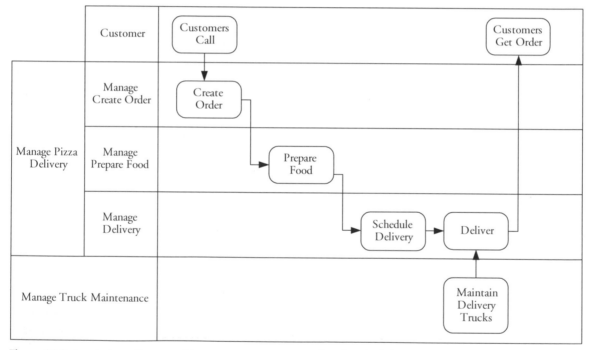

Figure 11.3 A swimlane diagram with management processes listed at the left.

The Process Management Process

Figure 11.4 suggests that the process management process is made up of four major sub-processes: Plan Work, Organize Work, Communicate, and Control Work. Each of these subprocesses, in turn, includes a variety of different activities. Some of the activities, like Establish Plans and Schedules, are quite complex and could easily be classified as processes in their own right. Thus, we stress again that this overview of the process management process is only one possible representation. As we saw in Chapter 5, a number of different frameworks have defined process management processes and

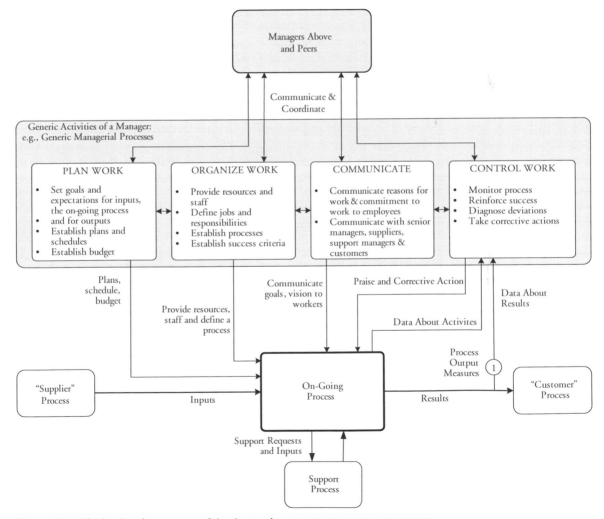

Figure 11.4 The basic subprocesses of the day-to-day process management process.

each has grouped the tasks involved in different ways. It really makes little difference exactly how you conceptualize the process management process at your company, but it is probably best to agree on a single, standard way of talking about the process management process to facilitate effective communication. Companies that have a business process management group usually assign that group the responsibility for training managers in business process management skills. In that case, the BPM group usually standardizes on one generic model of business process management and teaches all managers to use the same terms and to follow the same best practices. Given our preference for Plan, Organize, Communicate, and Control, we will organize the rest of our discussion around those four basic process management subprocesses.

Plan Work

Much has been written on every aspect of management. Every basic introduction to management has sections on setting goals, planning, establishing schedules and establishing a budget. We have nothing to add to the popular or technical literature on any of these topics as they are generally conceived. We can make some specific comments with regard to planning and process redesign.

If you are on a project redesign team and are asked to analyze a process, you will usually begin by figuring out the basic activities or steps that make up the process. Assuming the process has been performed for some time, you can assume that goals, plans, schedules and a budget are in place. As you talk with employees and managers concerned with the operational aspects of the process, you should remain alert for complaints that suggest that employees don't understand the goals of the process or that well-understood plans or schedules are missing. Similarly, you should listen to see that needed resources are provided. If an activity fails to function correctly because it is understaffed or because needed resources are unavailable, you will want to note that, and it will suggest that you will want to talk with the process manager about why he or she thinks those problems have occurred. In an ideal world, when a new manager takes over the responsibility for a process, he or she ought to review all the assumptions and assure that plans, budgets and schedules are adequate for the objectives of the process. If they aren't, they should be altered. Unfortunately, too often a new manager will simply use the scheduling and budget assumptions of a predecessor and this will lead to misalignments as time passes and procedures change.

If the organization you are analyzing takes processes seriously, it may require the process manager to maintain "contracts" with his or her "customers" and "suppliers." We believe this is a very powerful tool, both for planning and for assuring that measurement goals are aligned. Figure 11.5 provides an overview of the possible contracts that any given process manager ought to negotiate and then manage.

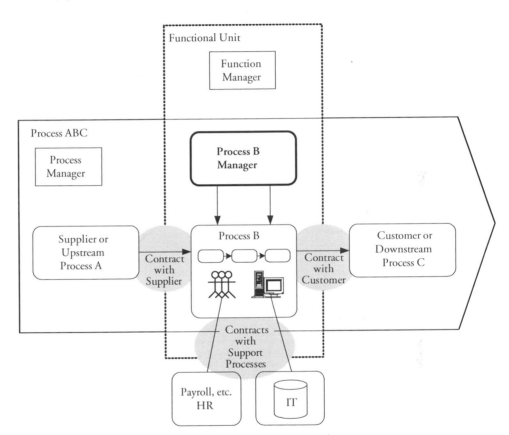

Figure 11.5 Contracts that a process manager ought to negotiate.

Let's begin with the "customer" contract. The process manager ought to sit down with the downstream or customer process or processes and negotiate contracts that specify what his or her process—which we'll term process B—will provide to the customer. This contract, like any good contract, should specify what will be delivered, how it will be delivered, when it will be delivered, and where it will be delivered. It should specify the quality and the quantity of the items to be delivered. It should cover special contingencies, like a situation in which process C suddenly asks for twice the number of items originally scheduled for delivery during the upcoming week. The more specific the contract, the better. Once the contract is drafted, the process B manager needs to get the approval of both his or her functional manager and any higher-level process manager. Obviously, process B's planning, scheduling, staffing and budgeting will all be directly affected by the agreement. The manager of process B can't honestly "sign" a contract to deliver 50 assembled widgets to process C if his or her functional manager will only approve a budget for the assembly of 30 widgets.

When we discussed enterprise measurement systems in Chapter 6 we distinguished between internal and external measures. The customer contract between process B and process C defines process B's external measures. In essence, we are saying that process B will succeed if it provides process C with a set of agreed-upon inputs in the manner specified. That becomes the way we measure the success of process B, of the people working for process B and for the process manager in charge of process B.

If process B and process C were located within a single functional unit, it would usually make the negotiation easer. If process C is in another unit which is still part of a larger functional unit managed by a single manager—say they are both sales processes—that would also make the contract negotiation easier. If process B is located in one major functional unit and process C is located in another, that tends to make the negotiation harder. Similarly, if the two processes are located in different geographical locations or different countries, that can make the negotiation hard. The bottom line, however, is that you can't align processes and you can't assure that process B is delivering real value to the customer without an explicit contract. Your organization might not call it a contract, but everyone has to agree on the desired outputs of process B, or any effort to improve process B is just an exercise in futility.

Once the process manager pins down the outputs of the process, he or she then needs to switch hats and function as the "customer" for other processes. The manager of process B needs to negotiate a contract with process A that will specify that process B will get the inputs it needs to assure it can meet its obligations to process C. If process B can't get an acceptable agreement with process A, then it will need to get senior managers involved or it will need to notify process C that it will be unable to meet the contract that it reached with the manager of process C. In a similar way, the manager of process B will need to negotiate contracts with various support processes to assure process B will have the resources it will need from those processes. It may need help hiring and training new employees, or it may require a new facility or a new software application. It may need new software loaded on the desktop machines of process B employees.

The point is that planning, scheduling and budgeting are all exercises in which a manager determines what can be done within a set of constraints. The constraints are imposed on a process by outputs, inputs and resources. Similarly, alignment with corporate goals are determined by agreed upon inputs and outputs. These needed to be determined before the process manager can generate effective plans, schedules and budgets for the process he or she is trying to manage.

A process analyst examining a process will look to see if contracts exist. If they don't, the analyst will have to generate them, at least informally, simply to determine how well the current process is functioning. Later, when considering recommendations, the analyst would naturally wonder how the process manager could do effective planning and scheduling without a clear understanding of the required output for his or her process, and probably suggest that as a major goal for the redesigned process.

Organize Work

Plans and schedules may assume resources, but then the manager needs to proceed and organize the resources. The steps in the process need to be defined. Jobs and roles need to be defined. Needed equipment and technical resources need to be put in place and coordinated. Once again, in most cases, a new process manager inherits a process that is already functioning. If the manager is sharp, he or she will review all the inherited assumptions. There are two guiding principles that the process manager will want to pursue. First, to be successful the process must meet the output requirements reflected in the contract negotiated with the downstream process. Thus, the first goal of any organizational effort will be to assure the process is organized in a manner that assures that the output requirements can be achieved. Second, once the output requirements are being achieved, the process manager should focus on improving the efficiency of the process itself. If the output requirements can still be met as a result of a process reorganization that reduces the number of employees, or increases the productivity of existing employees, or consumes less resources, that is invariably desirable. This is the time to look for waste and eliminate unnecessary activities. Since a major source of waste is rework, this is also a time to consider how the consistency of the output can be improved.

Put a different way, the first task of the process manager is to design or redesign the process to assure it meets its output obligations. The second task is to work to constantly improve the internal working of the process.

Communicate

So far we've described the process manager's job in rather analytic terms. In fact, of course, process management involves working with people. Some would term this leadership and others might term it teamwork. We simply use the term "communicate" to refer to all of the activities that a process manager must undertake to assure that the process runs smoothly and achieves its objectives.

A quick glance back at Figure 11.4 will suggest some of the types of communication that the process manager has to master. The process manager needs to communicate with the managers of the upstream and downstream processes and with the managers and employees of key support processes. The process manager needs to communicate with his or her functional or unit manager and with any process manager with responsibilities for a value stream that includes process B. Finally, the process manager needs to communicate with the employees of process B. Employees function best if they know why they are doing what they are asked to do. The process manager needs to communicate reasons for the process work and, to the degree possible, communicate commitment to achieving the goals of the process. Once again, there is a large literature on communication and managerial leadership. It's easy to be glib about it, but it's very important and it's usually quite obvious if it's missing or defective when you do an analysis of a process and interview employees and up- or downstream managers.

Consider only one of the many types of communication that's required of a process manager. We have already suggested that the process manager needs to look for opportunities to improve the process and make changes in organization of flow and the tasks performed to assure that the process becomes ever more efficient and effective (or better, faster and cheaper, if you prefer). At the same time that the process manager is looking for opportunities to make changes, he or she should be aware that most people hate to change. Change causes discomfort. It requires learning new things and it results in employees making mistakes as they try to implement new procedures. (The author of this book, for example, does everything he can to avoid upgrading to new software, knowing, as he does, that it will reduce his efficiency and increase his frustration when he tries to figure out a new way of doing things.) The process manager not only needs to identify opportunities for change, he or she needs to be sure the change will really result in a benefit to the organization, and then he or she needs to sell the change to the employees who will be affected by the change.

Control Work

Finally, we come to measurement and the work a process manager must do to assure that goals are met. Obviously, monitoring and control are related to the goals set in the Plan Work process. Similarly, all of the measures used in the process should be linked to the external measures developed during the Plan Work process when the project manager negotiated a contract with the "customers" of the process. In essence, the contract defines process success and, indirectly, it defines the process manager's performance.

The Control process relies on the external measures to define internal process measures. Where the external measures focus on the quality, quantity, and timeliness outputs, the internal measures focus on the cost and the efficiency of the activities, and, in some cases, on the ability of the process to make changes in the internal process to ramp up output or reduce output in appropriate circumstances. At the same time, the smart process manager will develop some leading indicators to make it possible to anticipate output problems.

One way to develop an overview of the kinds of measures that a process manager might consider is to divide the process into subprocesses and activities and consider where one might derive measures. Figure 11.6 uses a simple convention for identifying measures. Here we show a process with four subprocesses and several activities. (We have used a jagged line to reduce the size of the activities in this diagram.) At the top

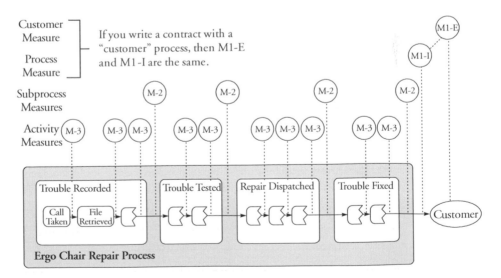

Figure 11.6 Measures for processes, subprocesses and activities.

right, we show the ultimate measure, which is labeled M1-E (Measure 1, External). This is an external measure directly tied to customer performance. The customer could either be a real customer from outside our company, or it could be the downstream process. If we were selling items, it might simply be the number purchased. In the actual situation from which this example is drawn, the company relied on answers to a questionnaire that the company asks a set of customers to complete periodically. Specifically, it refers to the percentage of customers who say they are very satisfied with the repair and the percentage who say that the repair was done in less than four hours.

If you write a contract with a "customer" process, then M1-E and M1-I are exactly the same. If you are dealing with a real customer, you may still have a contract. In most cases, however, if you are dealing with a real customer, there will be lots of customers and you won't have an explicit contract. In that case M1-E will probably be measured indirectly, by tracking sales, by questionnaires, or by some other means. In this case, the organization will need to define its M1-I for itself, and modify its description as it gets feedback from customers. Whether the process manager uses an M1-E or M1-I, that measure or set of measures defines the goal of the process and determines if the process is a success or not. Internal measures that predict the achievement M1 are good. Other internal measures that track cost or process efficiency or flexibility are also useful. In this case, the internal measure is used to determine the overall success of the process. As it happens, the internal measure checks the number of repairs that are done completely and accurately the first time.

A third tier of measures is provided by the four M-2 measures. They check the outputs of the four subprocesses. An example is the second M-2 from the left, which measures the output of the Trouble Tested subprocess. Specifically, this measure checks the percentage of testing errors, the elapsed time in testing, and the time taken per test.

The M-2 measures are checked by both the process manager and by the process managers in charge of subprocess. They measure the success of subprocesses. In effect, well-defined subprocess measures assure that the handoffs between one subprocess and another are up to standard.

The M-3 measures check the success of specific activities. They are monitored by the process managers or supervisors responsible for the specific activities and by the process manager responsible for the subprocess that contains each specific activity.

The worksheet pictured in Figure 11.7 shows how we would record these measures. We haven't listed manager titles or names on the worksheet, but that would probably be done on an actual worksheet.

Process Measures Worksheet			
Process Measures: Ergo Chair Repair Process	M1-I Internal Measure: Quality: First-time accuracy of repairs.	M1-E External Measures: % yes on Q 19 "very satisfactory" % yes on Q 20 "less than 4 hours."	
M-2 Subprocess: Trouble Recorded	Subprocess: Trouble Tested	Subprocess: Repair Dispatched	Subprocess: Trouble Fixed
# or % of inaccurate trouble descriptions % of first-time correct trouble tickets Time per trouble ticket	# or % of testing errors Elapsed time in testing Time per test	# or % of dispatch (address) errors Elapsed time from testing to dispatch # of incorrect dispatches	# or % of "non-fixes" to accurately record problems Elapsed time from dispatch to fix Time per fix
M-3 **Call Taken Activity:** # or % of inaccurate or incomplete trouble descriptions % of trouble tickets returned due to missing/inaccurate information. Time/call Time/ticket **File Retrieved Activity:** # or % of wrong files leading to inaccurate trouble descriptions % of returns due to wrong files. Time per retrieval % of "second" retrievals	*[Incomplete]*		

Figure 11.7 A process measures worksheet is used to record specific measures that will be monitored.

Evaluating the Performance of the Process Manager

We discussed the evaluation of process manager performance briefly in Chapter 6. At this point, suffice it to say that a process manager ought to be held responsible for achieving 1) the output specified, directly or indirectly, with a real customer or with a downstream "customer" process, and 2) process improvements that, over the course of time, render the process more efficient and effective. The first ought to be expected and mandatory. The second should be negotiated between the process manager and his or her boss. In addition, as we have already suggested, the same manager may report to a functional or unit manager and may be responsible for implementing functional goals and policies and for achieving agreed-upon measures required by the functional supervisor.

Figure 11.8 suggests some of the functional and process measures that might be used to evaluate the performance of a manager who is operating as both a functional and a process manager.

Department or function	Typical departmental measures	Typical process measures
Sales department	• Cost of sales • Revenue ($)	• Timely and accurate submission of orders • Timely and accurate entry of new orders • Cost of processing orders
Production department	• Cost of inventory • Cost of labor • Cost of materials • Cost of shipping	• Timely order scheduling • Timely and accurate production of orders • Timely shipment of orders • Cost of unit production and shipping costs
Finance department	• Percent of bad debt • Mean labor budget	• Timely and accurate invoice preparation • Timely and accurate credit checks for new accounts • Cost of processing an invoice
External organizational measures	• Gross revenue • Cost of sales • Growth of customer base • Price of stock	• Percent of on-time delivery • Percent of rejects • Customer satisfaction as measured on survey or index

Figure 11.8 A comparison of some functional and process measures.

Continuous Measurement and Improvement

If an organization establishes process measures that extend from the process to the activity, and if managers continuously check these measures and take actions when there are deviations, then process improvement becomes a part of every manager's job. In effect, measures determine how the activity should be performed. Higher-level measures determine that the outputs of the activities are resulting in the desired task, subprocess, or process outcomes. If any outputs deviate, the appropriate managers should take action.

Figure 11.9 provides an overview of how a departmental group might organize to monitor the results of a given process. In this case, we have used a special variant of our process diagram. On the left side we list all of the managers involved in the hierarchy. Along the top we've listed periods of time and then used rectangles to show who will be involved in review meetings and when they will occur. On the right side we have reproduced a portion of the actual process diagram to show what processes, subprocesses, and activities are being monitored. Most organizations won't include the process detail on the right, and most will have some other way of representing review meetings.

Figure 11.9 lays out a plan that managers can follow to assure that measures are taken and that higher-level processes meet their goals.

Any given activity may fail to produce adequate outputs for many different reasons. Some failures will be the result of a failure in process flow. The work assigned to the activity isn't appropriate or properly understood. But a flawed activity also represents a management failure. Managers are responsible for assuring that the people assigned to the activity understand what they are to do and have the resources to do it. And they are responsible for checking to see that the activity is done correctly, and that corrective feedback is provided if the activity isn't performed correctly.

Any Organization : X Value Chain:

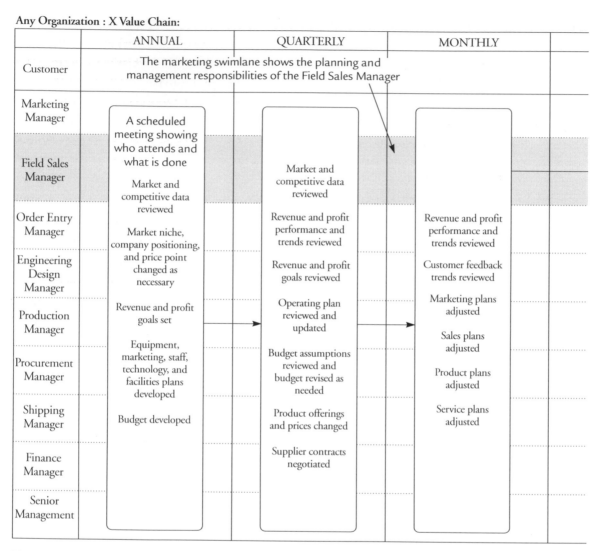

Figure 11.9 A measuring and scheduling worksheet used to schedule meetings to review the success of a process (modified after Rummler).

Any process redesign team that is proposing a major change in the way things are done had better be sure they plan for changes in management. If a specific supervisor is to manage a given activity for new outcomes, the new outcomes need to be clearly specified. Moreover, the changes in the supervisor's job need to be incorporated in the job description of the supervisor's manager, and so on, right up the management hierarchy. If this is done during the redesign of the project, then everyone will know

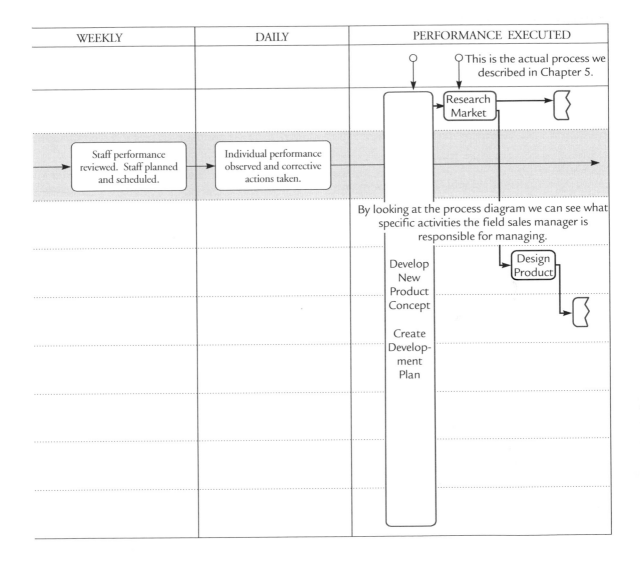

what to monitor, and who is responsible for what outcomes, when the new process is implemented. It may sound like a lot of work, but the alternative is to work hard on revising a process and then watch as it fails during implementation, when employees stick with previous tasks and managers don't spring into action to correct activities to assure that they conform with the goals of the new process.

Management Redesign at Chevron

A nice example of what management alignment can do is illustrated by a redesign effort undertaken by Chevron in 1995. At that time, Chevron was producing one million barrels of oil a day through six different refineries. The company was divided into three major functional units: Refining, Marketing, and Supply and Distribution. The company decided they needed to improve their supply chain system to better integrate their internal processes. According to Peter McCrea, a Chevron VP:

> We recognized that our system for planning and managing the supply chain, from crude acquisition to product distribution, was not working as well as it should. We had been working on this for a long time and were not making much progress. We decided we needed to take a holistic look at the entire supply chain.

The company called in consultants from Rummler-Brache and asked them for help. The consultants, in turn, proceeded through the steps of a process redesign, establishing a redesign team and establishing an overview of the existing process. Beyond that, however, rather than focus on redesigning the sequence of activities that made up the process, the team focused on how the process was currently measured and managed. They scrapped the old corporate operating plan and created a new plan based on linking corporate goals with process measures. Then they assigned managers the responsibility for controlling activities based on these measures. A senior manager was assigned the responsibility for the entire supply chain, and each manager who was responsible for a subprocess became part of his team.

In a report in 1996, Chevron identified savings of some $50 million and attributed a significant portion of that savings to "doing our work a different way, with common plans and measures."

We cite this example to stress two things. A good process redesign, without an accompanying management and measurement plan, often fails to get implemented. If it is implemented, it often fails to get the desired results. A good process redesign, accompanied by a good management and measurement plan, is much more likely to be implemented and successful. And, in some cases, an existing process can be significantly improved, just by implementing a management and measurement plan that assures that the existing process works as it is intended to work.

In an ideal world, one round of process redesign would result in a nearly perfect process and appropriate goals and measures. Thereafter, managers would simply fine-tune the process by studying outputs and taking corrective action whenever necessary. In reality, of course, one round of process redesign improves the process, but leaves some problems that still need to be changed. Moreover, as time passes and employees change, new techniques are introduced, or as customer expectations rise, processes need to be further refined.

In many cases, process improvement is best undertaken by a group of employees working with the manager to refine the process. In the next chapter, we will consider one of the more popular ways of handling more elaborate process improvement efforts.

Notes and References

The analysis of process management is primarily derived from the work of Geary Rummler. The basic concepts were introduced in *Improving Performance*, but have been considerably elaborated in recent lectures and workshops. Ideas about the relationships between day-to-day management and management processes at a distance have been developed in conversations with Roger Burlton.

Other business process theorists have also focused on improving the management of processes:

Champy, James, *Reengineering Management*, HarperBusiness, 1995. As with the original reengineering book, this is more about why you should do it than how to do it.

Hammer, Michael, *Beyond Reengineering: How the Process-Centered Organization Is Changing Our Work and Our Lives*, HarperBusiness, 1997. Similar to the Champy book. Lots of inspiring stories.

In the mid 1970s I worked briefly for Louis A. Allen, a then-popular management consultant. As far as I know, his books are no longer in print, but he introduced me to the idea that managers must plan, organize, lead, and control.

Information on the Chevron process management improvement effort is documented in a white paper: "Strategic Planning Helps Chevron's E&P Optimize Its Assets," which is available from the Pritchett Web site: *www.pritchettnet.com/COmp/PI/CaseStudies/chevroncase.htm*.

Hayler, Rowland and Michael Nichols, *What is Six Sigma Process Management*, McGraw-Hill, 2005. A good book on the role of management in Six Sigma.

12

Process Improvement with Six Sigma

I N THE LAST CHAPTER we saw how managers should be responsible for planning and controlling the business processes they manage. In a sense, planning, organizing, monitoring, and maintaining processes and activities is the everyday job of managers. Redesign projects, which have received most of our attention so far, are the exception, not the rule. At most times, in most situations, companies will want to focus on improving existing processes. In some cases, companies will organize process improvement teams. In other circumstances, the day-to-day process manager can organize a process improvement effort. Continuous process improvement occurs at organizations whose process managers or process teams routinely monitor their own processes and launch their own process improvement projects.

Many companies that aim at continuous process improvement use Six Sigma. In a narrow sense, Six Sigma is a methodology for process change, and is strongly associated with the process improvement methodology we will discuss in this chapter. In a broader sense, Six Sigma is a movement that aims to make all employees aware of the value of process improvement and provides the organizational structure to support a continuous improvement effort.

Six Sigma

At about the same time that Henry Ford created his moving production line and revolutionized auto production, other people were exploring techniques that would let other companies improve their operations. An early practitioner who got a lot of attention was Frederick Taylor, who is usually considered the father of operations research. Taylor published his classic book *Principles of Scientific Management* in 1911. Taylor was obsessed with measuring every step in every process and then experimenting with variations until he found the fastest way to carry out a process. Since Taylor, most large companies have employed engineers who have focused on improving operations. In a similar way, some individuals have specialized in catching defects by inspecting the output of processes. The latter is usually referred to as *quality assurance* or *quality control.*

The quality control movement got a huge boost in the 1980s after an oil embargo prompted U.S. consumers to begin to buy more fuel-efficient Japanese cars. U.S. consumers quickly discovered that Japanese cars were not only more fuel efficient, but were less expensive and better made than their American counterparts. There were fewer defects and problems, and the cars lasted longer.

Table 12.1 provides an overview of the problem that faced U.S. automakers when they began to examine the differences between U.S. and Japanese manufacturing. Clearly the Japanese companies were building cars faster (and thus cheaper) and better than their U.S. rivals.

Table 12.1 U.S. and Japanese auto manufacturing.

	GM Framingham plant	Toyota Takoaka plant
Gross assembly hours (per car)	40.7	18.0
Adjusted assembly hours (per car)	31	16
Assembly defects (per 100 cars)	130	45
Assembly space used (sq. meters per car)	8.1	4.8
Inventory of parts maintained (average)	2 weeks	2 hours

Source: IMVP World Assembly Plant Survey (1986)

Ironically, as U.S. auto companies began to study what Japanese auto companies were doing, they found that the Japanese companies attributed much of their success to an American quality control guru, Edward Deming. (In Japan, the highest prize awarded for industrial excellence is the Deming prize.) Deming had been sent to Japan by the U.S. government in the aftermath of World War II and had worked with Japanese firms to improve their processes.

Deming went beyond U.S. practice and worked with Japanese companies to embed quality control programs into the very fabric of Japanese production lines. U.S. companies traditionally measured the quality of outputs by sampling the products that came off the end of the production line. Deming convinced the Japanese to go beyond that and measure quality at each step of the process. Japanese parts suppliers, for example, learned to coordinate their schedules with manufacturing schedules and to only deliver new parts as they were needed, significantly reducing inventory storage times. This technique, and others, led to improvements that eventually led to a whole new approach to mass production, often called *lean manufacturing.*

In the late 1980s, U.S. companies struggled to become as efficient and effective as the best Japanese producers. Quality control methodologies became very popular in the United States. Over the years, companies have experimented with Statistical Process Control (SPC), Total Quality Management (TQM), and Just-in-Time Manufacturing (JIT). Each of these quality control initiatives contributed to efficiency and better output if the managers of the company were willing to work at it.

Six Sigma is the latest in this series of quality control methodologies to sweep U.S. companies. The Six Sigma approach was created at Motorola in the late 1980s. It was popularized by Mikel Harry, whose work caught the attention of Motorola's CEO, Bob Galvin. Galvin, in turn, spread the Six Sigma approach throughout Motorola, applying it to a wide variety of different processes. Somewhere along the line, Six Sigma became much more than a process control technique and evolved into a systematic approach to process improvement.

In the early 1990s, companies like Allied Signal and Texas Instruments adopted the Six Sigma approach in their organizations. Then in 1995, Jack Welch, the CEO of GE, decided to use Six Sigma at GE. Welch announced that "Six Sigma is the most important initiative GE has ever undertaken.... it is part of the genetic code of our future leadership." More importantly, Welch decreed that, henceforth, 40% of each business leader's bonus was going to be determined by his or her success in implementing Six Sigma. Welch's popularity with the business press and his dynamic style guaranteed that Six Sigma would become one of the hot management techniques of the late 1990s.

Six Sigma originated as a set of statistical techniques that managers could use to measure process performance. Using the techniques, a manager could then make changes in the process to see if it improved the process. Once the process was as efficient as they could get it, managers then used the statistical techniques to maintain the process. As Six Sigma became popular in the late 1990s, it was extended to improve processes far removed from manufacturing. In keeping with the then-current interest in business process reengineering, Six Sigma consultants evolved their methodology to incorporate techniques and definitions from the process reengineering consultants.

Today, for example, most Six Sigma books begin by defining three types of process change efforts: (1) process management, (2) process improvement, and (3) process redesign.

Process management, in the world of Six Sigma, means developing an overview of the company's processes, linking it with corporate strategy, and using it to prioritize process interventions. In other words, what Six Sigma folks would call *process management*, we would call *process architecture*. We prefer to use *process management* more broadly to include how managers' jobs are organized and how managers take responsibility for the processes they oversee, as well as various implementation technologies.

Process improvement, as Six Sigma proponents use it, refers to a set of techniques used to incrementally improve and maintain process quality. We use the term the same way, except that we would include some nonstatistical techniques as well. More importantly, we would make a distinction between *continuous process improvement*, which every manager ought to do as a daily part of his or her job, and *process improvement projects*, which are undertaken to significantly improve the quality of a process in a short period of time.

Six Sigma practitioners use the term *process redesign* to refer to major changes in a process. In other words, they use process redesign the same way we do.

After defining the three types of process change, as we just described them, every Six Sigma book we have ever looked at proceeds to focus almost all of the remaining chapters on process improvement, on how to organize project teams, on how to measure process outcomes, and on the statistical techniques used to analyze outcomes.

None of the Six Sigma books we've seen provide nearly enough information on how to analyze processes. Most simply suggest that the project team should develop a high-level overview of the process (which we'll turn to in a moment) and then suggest the use of "workflow diagrams" if more detail is needed. What this underlines, in our opinion, is that Six Sigma works best with well-understood, currently implemented processes. If extensive analysis of a process is required, we suggest that managers look at books outside the Six Sigma tradition to find useful approaches.

What Six Sigma is very good at is describing how to think about measuring process and activity outcomes, and about how to use statistical techniques to analyze the outcomes and decide on corrective action. We believe that every process manager should study one or two Six Sigma books and use their insights to help define measures for the processes he or she manages. (We've listed several of the best in the Notes and References at the end of this book.) Six Sigma techniques are just as useful when practiced by a manager who is responsible for a process or activity as they are when they are used by a project team that is focused on improving a process or activity. A team approach, however, is often superior in situations where the manager wants to engage and motivate an entire group of employees to improve a process.

In the remainder of this chapter, we will discuss Six Sigma as it is usually presented by Six Sigma consultants—as a methodology that can be used by project teams to improve a process. Before turning to projects, however, we'll take a moment to define the statistical ideas that lie behind the name "Six Sigma."

The Six Sigma Concept

Quality control engineers have always used a number of statistical tools to analyze processes. Six Sigma is a name derived from concepts associated with a standard bell-shaped curve. Almost anything varies if you measure with enough precision. The specification might call for a car door to be 1 meter (100 cm) high. Using a standard meter stick, all of the doors might seem exactly 1 meter high. Using a laser measuring device that is more exact, however, you might find that some doors are 99.70 cm high while others are 100.30 cm high. They average 100.00 cm, but each door varies a little.

Statisticians describe patterns of variations with a bell-shaped or Gaussian curve. (Carl Frederick Gauss was the mathematician who first worked out the mathematics of variation in the early 19th century.) We've pictured a bell-shaped curve in Figure 12.1.

If the items being measured vary in a continuous manner, one finds that variation frequently follows the pattern described by the bell-shaped curve: 68.26% of

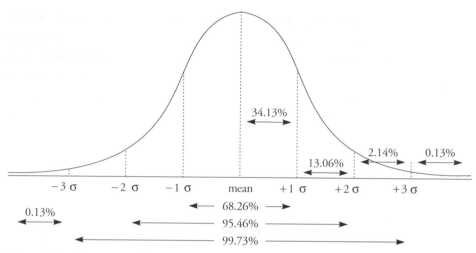

Figure 12.1 The properties of a standard bell-shaped curve.

the variation falls within two standard deviations. In statistics, the Greek letter sigma (σ) is used to denote one standard deviation; 99.73% of all deviations fall within 6 standard deviations.

In Figure 12.1 we show three sigmas to the right of the mean. Imagine that we subdivided the 0.13% of the curve out on the right and inserted three more sigmas. In other words, we would have six sigmas to the right of the mean, and some very small amount beyond that. In fact, we would cover 99.99966% of the deviation and only exclude 3.4 instances in a million.[1] Six Sigma projects rely on formulas and tables to determine sigmas. The only point you should remember is that we want to define what we mean by a defect, and then create a process that is so consistent that only 3.4 defects will occur in the course of one million instances of the process.

---

[1] Technically, there is a difference between a standard normal curve, like the one in Figure 12.1, and a curve used with process analysis. There is a phenomenon called long-run process drift. A curve used in process work generates 3.4 defects per million, and that is defined as the instances that occur beyond six sigmas to the right or the left of the mean. In a normal curve, like the one in Figure 12.1, for reasons we won't consider, one only has to be 4.5 sigmas to the right of the curve to reach the point beyond which the 3.4 defects per million begins.

Returning to our doors and applying our knowledge of standard distributions, you can expect that if the shortest door was 99.70 cm and the tallest door was 100.30 cm, most of the variations in the doors would fall between 99.70 and 100.30. They might not, however, for various reasons. How they vary from a standard distribution would tell a Six Sigma practitioner something about the process. For example, if instead of one curve there were two with two different means, it would suggest that two independent variables were affecting the output. In any case, the chance that a door was more than six standard deviations to the right of the mean, using a process curve, is 3.4 in a million. The goal is to reduce clearly unacceptable output to less than 3.4 failures in a million.

At first, many managers are skeptical of the goal. It seems more appropriate for large manufacturing processes than for more complex processes that are done less frequently. Once one considers a large enough sample, however, Six Sigma isn't always that demanding. How many plane crashes, per million flights, would you accept? How many bank checks per million would you want deducted from the wrong account? How many incorrect surgical operations would you tolerate per week? In all these cases, in a week or a month or a year there are millions of events. In most cases you'd rather not have even 3.4 failures per million. The goal is rigorous, but in many situations it's the minimum that customers should have to expect.

Let's consider another problem. Suppose that the hypothetical restaurant SF Seafood decided to undertake a Six Sigma project and decided to focus on the delivery of meals to diners. The team gathered data by asking customers about how quickly they liked to receive their meals and what they considered an unacceptable wait. The data suggested that half of the customers would prefer their meals in 15 minutes or less. All the customers agreed, however, that meals should arrive within 30 minutes. If a meal was delivered after 30 minutes, all of the customers were unhappy. Using this data, the SF Seafood Six Sigma team prepared the bell-shaped curve shown in Figure 12.2, assuming that they would shoot for an average time of 15 minutes and not tolerate anything over 30 minutes.

In this case Six Sigma refers to the variation on a specific process measure—time from when an order is taken to when it is delivered. The goal the team adopted was to deliver all meals as close to 15 minutes as possible. They were willing to allow some variation around 15 minutes, but wanted to assure that all meals were delivered in less than 30 minutes. In other words, they wanted to achieve Six Sigma and assure that all meals, except 3.4 meals out of a million, would be delivered in 30 minutes or less.

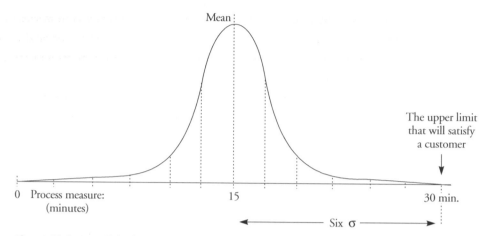

Figure 12.2 A model of a process showing how often dinners are delivered in 15 minutes.

The goal of most Six Sigma projects is to reduce the deviation from the mean. Some projects focus on setting a more rigorous mean. Assume that we decided that we wanted to deliver half of all meals within 10 minutes and all meals within 20 minutes or less. In this case we would set 10 minutes as our target for the mean and 20 minutes at six standard deviations (sigmas) to the right of the mean. The bell-shaped curve would now be even narrower than the one shown in Figure 12.2, and the deviation from the mean would be less. It would require a better controlled, more efficient process to assure that most meals arrive in 10 minutes and no meal ever arrives in more than 20 minutes.

So, Six Sigma refers to improving processes until they are so consistent that they only fail in 3.4 cases out of one million. It also refers to the idea that we establish and measure process goals and a mean and then work to reduce the deviation from the mean. In other words, we work to make the process more consistent, and we use statistical tools to test whether we are succeeding.

The Six Sigma Approach to Process Improvement

In an ideal company, every process would already be mapped and measured by those responsible for managing the process. In reality, of course, most processes aren't mapped or well understood by those who manage them. Moreover, if they are measured, then functional measures are usually the norm. In some companies, managers could read one of the popular Six Sigma books and then implement the ideas by themselves. In most cases, however, it works best if the manager involves the workers in the process of analysis and shares with them the satisfaction of achieving the goals. Six Sigma practitioners always talk in terms of process improvement projects and focus on teams, not on individual managerial efforts.

Many Six Sigma projects begin by helping a management team develop a process architecture. If an architecture already exists, then the Six Sigma practitioner focuses on helping managers identify projects that will benefit most from a process improvement effort.

Process improvement projects based on the Six Sigma methodology are usually short and typically range from 1 to 6 months. In many companies that have adopted the Six Sigma approach, the executive committee chooses two or three processes for improvement every 6 months. Some of the Six Sigma books give the impression that Six Sigma projects tackle value chains or major business processes. They reinforce this impression by discussing processes at small companies or relatively simple business processes. In reality, most Six Sigma projects focus on a subprocess or subsubprocess. Many focus on what we would regard as a single activity.

To clarify this, consider that most Six Sigma projects focus on monitoring two or three measures. If one were to try to monitor an auto production line or the insurance company sales system with two to three measures, one would not get the kind of data that Six Sigma projects need to identify causes and to check that changes are getting the desired results. Put another way, it would take at least a month just to analyze the subprocesses in a large business process like an auto production line or a large insurance sales process.

Measuring an entire value chain or business process with two or three measures is a reasonable thing for a process manager to do. Unfortunately, if the measures suggest that sales are falling or that production is down 5%, they don't usually suggest the cause. In most cases, the process manager will need to examine more specific measures to determine which subprocess or subsubprocess is responsible for the problem. In other words, measures on large processes usually only provide early warning signals that a more detailed study needs to be initiated.

In most cases, Six Sigma projects are not launched to improve large-scale business processes; they are launched to improve subprocesses or activities. Importantly, however, Six Sigma always stresses that measures at any level should be tied back to higher-level processes and eventually to strategic goals.

Six Sigma Teams

Six Sigma projects are usually chosen by a steering committee that oversees all Six Sigma efforts or by the process sponsor or team sponsor. Every project needs a team sponsor or champion. This individual is usually the process sponsor or a member of the steering committee that selected the project in the first place.

The team is headed either by an individual devoted to managing Six Sigma projects or by a manager associated with the project to be improved. In Six Sigma jargon, if the leader is especially knowledgeable in Six Sigma projects, he or she is called a *black belt*. If the leader is a manager who has full-time responsibilities elsewhere and is slightly less qualified, he or she is referred to as a *green belt*. The team is often assigned an internal or external consultant who is a specialist in Six Sigma, and especially skilled in the use of the statistical tools that Six Sigma depends on. This consultant is usually called a *master black belt*. (These designations are usually the result of a combination of experience and passing examinations.)

The team members are chosen because they have expertise in the actual process that is to be improved. If the process is really an activity or small process, the team members are employees who perform the activities or steps involved in the process.

Some Six Sigma practitioners spend a lot of time talking about how good teams are formed and the processes the teams should employ—voting and so forth. We won't go into it here. Suffice it to say that the team leader should know something about team building and team processes, and should apply that knowledge to create an effective team.

The teams meet for 2–3 hours at a time. Initially they meet two to three times a week, but as they shift to data collection, they meet less frequently.

Phases in a Six Sigma Improvement Project

Most Six Sigma projects are organized around a process improvement approach that is referred to as the *DMAIC process*. DMAIC stands for:

- ▶ *Define* customer requirements for the process or service.
- ▶ *Measure* existing performance and compare with customer requirements.
- ▶ *Analyze* existing process.
- ▶ *Improve* the process design and implement it.
- ▶ *Control* the results and maintain the new performance.

Figure 12.3 provides an overview of these key steps or phases and the activities that occur in each step. It also suggests the time required for each step. Some overlap between phases usually occurs.

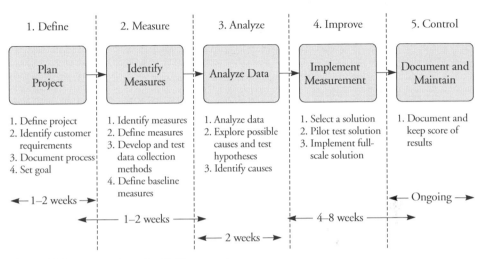

Figure 12.3 An overview of a Six Sigma project.

Obviously the sequence of steps and the times will vary widely, depending on the size and the complexity of the project. In the best case, one will define the goal, create measures, measure, identify some obvious improvements, implement process changes, measure again, and be done. In the worst case, you will identify multiple goals, create measures, measure, identify multiple possible improvements, try some and not get adequate results, try again, decide you need different measures, try again, analyze, try still another process improvement, measure some more, and finally achieve your revised goal. In other words, simple projects run straight through, as shown above. Complex projects recycle through the steps multiple times until they achieve results.

One key to accomplishing Six Sigma projects quickly is having an experienced black belt (full-time project leader) or master black belt (champion). Some elements of each project, like the steps in a process or the customers, are unique to the specific process and must be debated and analyzed by the project team. Other elements, like when to apply what measures and how to set up certain types of measures, can be accomplished very quickly by someone experienced in the Six Sigma process and armed with an appropriate software tool that they know how to use. An experienced consultant can help keep a team moving and get them through other rough spots that would otherwise delay the project for extra weeks.

Not all projects achieve Six Sigma. As most Six Sigma practitioners explain, Six Sigma is a goal. The ultimate idea is to improve the process and to reduce the variation in the process as much as possible. It's the attitude and not a specific target that is most important.

We'll consider each phase of a Six Sigma project in more detail.

Define

In the first phase, a draft charter is usually provided by the project sponsor or team champion. The charter is a clear statement of what the team should accomplish. It should include a brief description of the process to be improved and the business case for improving it. It should also include some milestones and define the roles and responsibilities of the team members. This task is easier if the steering committee has defined a good process architecture and has already defined the scope and goals of the project. If the steering committee hasn't done this, then the Six Sigma team must make some guesses, explore the problem a bit, and then return to the charter and refine it toward the end of the Define phase.

One key to a good charter is a clear understanding of the process to be improved. Like any good contract, the charter should specify who will do what, when. Dates, costs, and a clear statement of the expected results are all important. The team shouldn't allow itself, however, to get pushed into trying to predict the exact changes they will make or exactly how long it will take to reach Six Sigma. Instead, the charter should focus on defining the process to be improved and some initial measures that can be used to judge if the team succeeds.

Six Sigma teams usually put a lot of emphasis on who the customers are and what will satisfy them. The emphasis on the customer that occurs throughout Six Sigma is one of its more attractive features. The customer referred to, of course, is the person or group that receives the product or service produced by the process the team is focusing on. Most groups within organizations produce products for other internal groups. Thus, for example, the customer of Inventory is Manufacturing. The customer of New Product Design is Marketing and Product Engineering, and so forth. Still, it's always good for a project team to begin by focusing on the fact that they produce products or services for some person or group that functions as a customer that they must satisfy. And even when a team focuses on an internal customer, it's always good to define, if only informally, how that customer is linked to some external customer.

The Six Sigma approach to process definition is summed up in the acronym SIPOC, which emphasizes Supplier, Input, Process, Output, and Customer. Figure 12.4 is a rough SIPOC diagram of SF Seafood's Food Service process.[1] SF Seafood only serves dinners, so all data is based on evening dining and not on lunches. The immediate output of the food service process that we are focusing on was a meal on the table. In fact, the team was working on a broader definition of output, customer satisfaction, and a meal and its timely delivery is only one part of that overall output. We'll consider output in more detail in a moment.

Figure 12.4 shows the standard SIPOC approach that most Six Sigma practitioners use. As an overview there's nothing wrong with it, although it usually works a little better when you are describing a concrete process and is a little harder to apply when you are describing a service process. As you recall from our earlier discussion of SF Seafood, the company considers the dining area as one value chain, and the kitchen as another. We are going to focus on satisfying customers who have meals at SF Seafood; hence, in the SIPOC diagram shown we listed four major steps in the food service process. We also listed two other steps that link the waiters to the kitchen and vice versa.

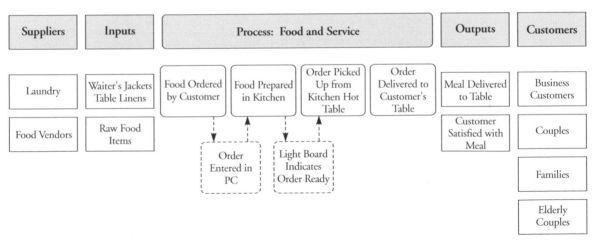

Figure 8.4 SF Seafood's food service process.

In this case we are focusing on both food and service processes. We listed two inputs to the basic process we are focused on—the laundry provides jackets for the waiters and table linens, and the vendors provide the raw food used in the kitchen. We could easily list more suppliers and inputs.

In keeping with Six Sigma policy, we have divided the process—food and service—into three to seven subprocesses or steps. Luckily, there are no complex branches. (If we had considered orders, and included both the delivery of food and drinks, which come from two different processes at SF Seafood, we would have had a harder time developing a neat overview.) As it is, the basic service process doesn't emphasize the food preparation in the kitchen, which is surely going to be a factor in customer satisfaction.

To simplify this case, let's assume that the food preparation process has already been the focus of a different Six Sigma project. The team determined that food was needed quickly and needed to be tasty and hot. They found that they could deliver meals in 9 minutes from the time they received the order on the kitchen PC. Six Sigma work resulted in variations of between 6 and 12 minutes. (Yes, they pre-prepare meals and sometimes use a microwave to heat them.) Thus, we know the characteristics for the Food Prepared in Kitchen activity and can focus on obtaining and delivering the order. It also means that we don't really need to worry about the raw food items delivered to the kitchen, but only about inputs to the food delivery process.

The specific output, in our example, is a meal delivered to the table. That output, however, is part of a broader goal the team is working toward—customers who are satisfied with their meals and meal service. We put most of our effort into identifying customers (or market segments) and arrived at four groups of customers who might have different ideas of what makes a satisfying meal. Customers with kids, our later research showed, prefer food much faster. Couples and elderly customers are willing to wait longer. Business people are in between—although they vary quite a bit—presumably depending on the occasion.

After the team analyzed the process and customers, they turned their attention to the kinds of things about a dinner meal that might satisfy customers. In a sense, this involves asking what kinds of needs customers have. Teams usually list potential requirements on a chart called a CTQ (Critical-To-Quality) tree, like the one shown in Figure 12.5. One starts on the left with the overall output. Then one hypothesizes what might result in the output. If appropriate, one can move on to a third or fourth level, hypothesizing more and more specific or discretely measured requirements.

The initial list prepared by the SF Seafood Dining Six Sigma Team is shown in Figure 12.5. Once the team has arrived at a list like this, it needs to figure out how to determine the role each of these possible requirements actually plays in customer satisfaction.

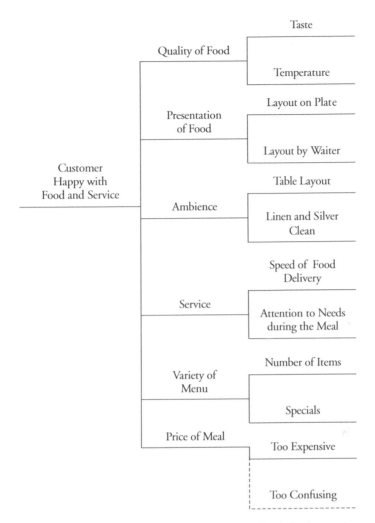

Figure 12.5 A CTQ tree for the SF Seafood meal satisfaction project.

One always needs to test and be prepared to revise. We added the last item (Price of Meal—Too Confusing) to illustrate something the team didn't think of, but which showed up in interviews with elderly couples. It seems that SF Seafood priced all items independently, and some elderly couples were confused about the total cost of the meal they were ordering when they had both a main item and a side order. (SF Seafood decided to change their policy and price specials, which were popular with elderly diners, as single-price meals.) The point, however, is that the team begins with a list and then gathers information to confirm or change the list.

Most Six Sigma books provide detailed discussions of the ways one can gather information from customers. We won't go into them here, but suggest that anyone interested in measuring processes consult one of the Six Sigma books for such details. In brief, most suggest surveys, one-on-one interviews, and focus groups. Other techniques include recording and studying customer complaints, or having team members act as customers and record their impressions. Restaurant Web sites often provide a mechanism that allows customers to evaluate restaurants, and SF Seafood found the local restaurant Web sites a good source of complaints and occasional praise.

Obviously the team will need to gather data about the requirements of all of the different groups or segments of customers. Different types of data-gathering approaches may work better with different groups. For example, SF Seafood found that elderly customers were happy to sit and talk with a maitre d' about what they liked and disliked about their meals. Business people and families, on the other hand, didn't want to sit and talk, although they would take survey forms and some of them would then mail them in.

Based on data gathered, the team usually identifies the most important requirements of customer satisfaction. Six Sigma practitioners put a lot of emphasis on Pareto analysis. Most of us know this mathematical concept as the 80/20 rule. As a generalization, 80 percent of customer satisfaction can be accounted for by 20 percent of the possible requirements. In other words, you can usually narrow the list of requirements that will satisfy customers down to two or three items. They may vary by customer segment but, for each customer segment, it is usually sufficient to track two or three items.

In turns out that for business customers, Taste, Temperature, Speed of Delivery, and Attentiveness during the Meal were considerably more important than the other items on the CTQ requirements tree. On the other hand, for the elderly customers, Taste, Temperature, and Specials were most important.

The team was able to ignore Taste, since that was under the control of the kitchen, but decided to gather data and pass it to the chef, while focusing on improving the dining room service.

The team ends the first phase with a refined charter—a clear idea of the scope of the project, the customers and their most salient requirements, and a set of milestones.

Measure

During the second phase of the project the team develops measures that will let them know how well each key requirement is being satisfied. Most Six Sigma books spend quite a bit of time explaining the concepts underlying statistics and measurement, and provide explanations of formulas that are appropriate for handling the different types of data one might collect. Since different types of data result in different types of curves, it's important that someone understand these things and thus know how to analyze the data and evaluate the results. In most cases this expertise is provided by a master black belt or consultant. Most Six Sigma projects rely on software tools to actually analyze the data. (MiniTab, for example, is a popular statistics analysis tool that is widely used to crunch the data and generate curves.) We are not going to go into measurement theory or discuss statistical formulas. If you need this kind of information, you will want to read a book that covers it in more detail than we can here. Once again, Six Sigma books that do exactly that are listed in the Notes and References at the end of this book.

One Six Sigma author, George Eckes, suggests three measurement principles:

▶ Measure only what is important to the customer.
▶ Only measure process outputs that you can improve.
▶ Don't measure an output for which you have no history of customer dissatisfaction.

Within these constraints, every Six Sigma team must focus on determining how to measure process effectiveness and efficiency. There are basically three things one might measure:

▶ *Inputs.* One can check what was delivered by the supplier to assure that problems do not lie with the inputs to the process. In the case of SF Seafood, there are the linen tablecloths and waiter jackets. We assume that the chef is already checking the quality of the raw food items delivered by suppliers.
▶ *Process measures.* These measures typically include cost, cycle time, value, and labor.
▶ *Outputs or measures of customer satisfaction.* In the SF Seafood case, we might stick with a survey form that we gave to customers when they left the restaurant. There might be some more dramatic form of output measure as well. Consider that some customers are reviewers or evaluators for magazines that assign ratings to

restaurants. In France, upscale every restaurant waits nervously each spring for the new Michelin Red Guide to be published so they can see how many stars they have been awarded. (A restaurant in France that moves from 2 to 3 stars—the highest Michelin gives—typically can double their prices and be assured of a full house every night! Thus, the single Michelin satisfaction rating can more than double a restaurant's annual income.)

In complex manufacturing processes, the best output data is often generated by the receiving group, and the trick is to get it routed back to your group so you can use it. Our dining team, for example, is going to gather data on customers that were dissatisfied with the taste of their food, and then route that information back to the kitchen.

Another way to think about measures is to distinguish between process measures and outcome measures. You can use either, but it's usually best to start with output measures because that's what the customer is most concerned with.

If the process or activity measure is:	Then an outcome you might measure is:
▶ process with a specific goal	▶ strategic goals achieved
▶ quality of work in a specific activity	▶ level of customer satisfaction
▶ time a process takes	▶ on-time delivery
▶ adequacy of staffing	▶ time to answer phone or produce unit
▶ adequate understanding of task	▶ nature and number of defects produced

In all cases, it's ideal to tie the measure to customer satisfaction. This focuses everyone on the basic concept that you aren't doing the work for its own sake, but to provide a product or service that will satisfy and even please a customer. Customers buy products, and they usually have options. If they aren't satisfied, ultimately it makes no difference how the work was done. This is just as true if your customer is another process within your own organization as it is if the customer is someone outside the company. Many IT departments in large companies have learned this in recent years, as companies have outsourced IT functions, applications, or entire IT departments in order to obtain more satisfactory service at a better price. Increasingly, as companies move toward virtual processes and more elaborate outsourcing arrangements, it will become clear to even support groups deep within the company that a process either provides value and satisfies customers, or the customers will end up seeking alternatives.

Some Six Sigma practitioners recommend distinguishing between output measures and service measures. In this sense, "output" refers to features of the product or service you deliver, and "service" refers to more subjective things having to do with how the customer expects to be treated and what kinds of things please the customer. Getting the hamburger, correctly assembled, quickly is an output measure. Getting a smile with the hamburger, or having the waiter remember your name and use it, is a service measure. As a company, if you want to succeed, you have to get output measures right. If you want to be really successful and have loyal customers, you have to get the service measures right as well.

Another way Six Sigma practitioners talk about this is in terms of categories created by Dr. Noriaki Kano, a leading Japanese quality control expert. Dr. Kano developed some measures that can be used to qualify data about customer satisfaction, which we won't go into here, often spoken of as *Kano analysis*. He divided customer requirements into three categories:

▶ *Basic requirements*. This is the minimum the customer expects. If he doesn't get this, he will go away upset.
▶ *Satisfiers*. The additional output or service measures that please the customer. The more of these you get, the happier the customer will be.
▶ *Delighters*. These are things the customer doesn't expect. They are usually things the customer would never put on a survey form because he doesn't even know he should want these things. Having phones available at each restaurant table, for example, might delight some business diners. Having the busboy whisk out an umbrella on a rainy day and accompany customers to their car is another.

If one is unclear, it never hurts to meet with the customer and find out how they judge the products or services they receive from your process. Every department or functional unit has some internal criteria that they measure and seek to meet. In some cases, however, departments end up maximizing goals that aren't important to customers. Imagine a sales organization that places emphasis on closing lots of sales quickly. Ordinarily it seems like a reasonable sales goal, but if manufacturing is struggling to come up to speed on a new product run, lots of sales, quickly, may only make for unhappy customers who don't receive their products in a timely manner. There's no science to choosing the right measure, but the trick is to choose one to three measures that really track quality, efficiency, and customer satisfaction in the most efficient manner. Too many measures waste time. Measures that aren't clearly tied to customer satisfaction risk maximizing some aspect of a process that doesn't really produce results that are important to the customer.

Each measure must be carefully specified so everyone understands exactly how it is going to be determined. Thus, for SF Seafood, one measure will be the time it takes to receive a meal. In this case, we would like to have someone determine the time when the waiter finished taking the order and then later determine when the food is placed on the table. Since SF Seafood uses a computer-based order system, waiters enter each order into a computer that then routes food orders to the kitchen and drink orders to the bar. The orders are placed in a queue on the computer in the kitchen. Waiters can enter a request to expedite an order, and we will need to control for that in our measurements. When the kitchen has an order ready, they enter a code and a light goes on a board that the waiters can see in the dining area. Obviously it would be easy to track when a PC order is placed and when the kitchen enters a code to indicate that the order is waiting on the hot table. The time between the PC entry and the kitchen entry, however, will only tell us how long it takes the kitchen to prepare the meal (i.e., 9, plus or minus 3 minutes). It won't tell us if the waiter went directly from the table to the PC, or went to another table before going to the PC to place the order.

Since the focus of the team's effort is the delivery itself, they decide that they will have to assign an observer to record when orders are taken and delivered. This will need to be someone not otherwise involved in any dining activities to assure that he or she has the time to watch several tables carefully and keep accurate records. Total delivery time is defined as the time between when the waiter takes the order and when he enters it into the computer, plus the time between when the kitchen indicates in their computer that the order is on the hot table and when the order is delivered to the table.

At the same time, the team created a new, simple survey form that they decided to hand out to all diners and request that they complete it and return it by mail. The survey form was on a prepaid postcard.

Without going into the details about how the team classified the various types of measures, or the formulas used to summarize the data, suffice it to say that there are lots of techniques that an experienced practitioner can use to refine the data and provide insights.

The team arrived at a variety of conclusions after looking at the data. One was the conclusion that half the customers preferred getting their meals in 15 minutes and all resented having to wait longer than 30 minutes. This resulted in the bell-shaped curve we presented earlier (Figure 12.2). Since the team was not focusing on the cooking process as such, they needed to factor out the 9 ± 3 minutes of food preparation time. That left 18 to 24 minutes that was controlled by the waiters. (In other words, we subtracted the 6–12 minutes of food preparation time from the 0–30 minutes and arrived at a new curve that reflected the time remaining between food preparation and actual delivery.) The new curve suggested that anything beyond 18 minutes was unacceptable.

If the meal was prepared in 6 minutes, and the waiter took 18 minutes to submit and deliver the order, the customer would get the meal in 24 minutes. If the meal took 12 minutes to prepare and the waiter took 18 minutes to submit and deliver the order, the order would be delivered in 30 minutes. Theoretically, if the waiter knew the meal would be prepared in 6 minutes, he or she could have up to 24 minutes to deliver the meal, but since the waiters never knew how long meal preparation would take, they had to assume that each meal would take 12 minutes. If the kitchen Six Sigma team was able to improve their process so that they could guarantee a narrower variation, then the delivery process could gain more time. But since the goal was to move toward a delivery time of around 15 minutes, this was really irrelevant.

Hence, the new bell curve for the waiters ran from 12 to 30 minutes, with a mean of 21. In other words, a waiter could use up to 18 minutes and always make the 30-minute limit. The goal the team set, however, was to come as close to 9 minutes as possible. The data suggested that it took as long, on average, to place the order as to move it from the hot table to the customer. Thus, a subsidiary goal was to place orders within 9 minutes, coming as close to 4.5 minutes as possible, and to deliver meals from the hot table to the customer within 9 minutes, coming as close to 4.5 minutes as possible.

The team proceeded to gather data on the time it took waiters to place and deliver orders. As the data began to accumulate, they moved to the analysis phase to make sense of it.

Analyze

In many cases the team members have a good idea of the cause of the problems in the process they analyze. They gather data to establish baselines and then want to jump to implementing a solution. In some cases this is reasonable. Waiters, in our example, probably know what takes time and know how they could save some. In more complex cases, however, it isn't so obvious.

Once you have some measurement data, there are lots of ways to analyze what might be causing a problem. Some of them involve defining the process in more detail. Others involve applying statistical tools to the data.

Assuming you have developed a detailed process diagram, you can establish measures for each activity on your diagram. It's also useful to consider how each activity adds value to the entire process. In essence, any given task can be classified into one of three categories:

1. The activity adds value that the customer, whether internal or the ultimate customer, is willing to pay for.
2. The activity is necessary to produce a value-added activity.
3. The activity doesn't add value.

You can always check with the customer to determine which activities add value. You normally wouldn't ask the customer to consider the activities as such, but what they add to the final product or service. This consideration takes us back to the issue of how we choose measures. You could ask, for example, if the customer likes the flowers and the white jackets the busboys wear. If the customer tells you it's a matter of indifference how the busboys dress, you might consider what the purchase and cleaning of the jackets adds to the customer's bill and consider if it might be worth dropping that aspect of the service package.

It's usually easy to identify the activities that add features that customers can identify and value. Those that don't fall in that category are usually placed in category 2. In fact, some activities do need to be done in order that other category 1 activities can be done. Each needs to be challenged, however. Often processes that have been done for a while end up supporting activities that are no longer really required. In all surveys at SF Seafood, customers indicated that napkin rings were of no value to them. Clearly the placing of napkins in rings when setting the table was an activity that could be eliminated. It took time, cost money, and didn't add any value to the customer's dining experience.

Consider a company that installed an email system that allowed salespeople to report their results each day online. For some unknown reason, the company had installed the email system but never eliminated the requirement that the salespeople fill out a Form 2B and submit it on the 30th of each month. In fact, Form 2B only provided information that the sales managers were now already obtaining via the daily emails. Filling out Form 2B was a value-reducing activity. Worse, sales managers continued to log the forms to assure that each salesperson turned them in on time. It's always wise to consider eliminating activities that don't add value. Moreover, if an activity is value reducing, one should check to be sure that no one is measuring that activity.

The analysis of waiter problems at SF Seafood seems straightforward. In fact, those familiar with a small lunchtime restaurant might be surprised that it takes as much time as it does at SF Seafood. It might seem obvious that if the waiter would simply go straight to the PC after taking an order and enter it, it would only consume a minute at the most. Similarly, it might seem if the waiter would go to the hot table as soon as he or she saw a flashing light, delivery of the food couldn't take more than another minute. That would get the total delivery time under 3 minutes. If there were only one waiter per table, they could probably come close to that. Unfortunately, in SF Seafood, each waiter is expected to cover from five to seven tables, depending on the hour. Some waiters are scheduled to begin work when the restaurant opens and there are only a few customers. Then more are added as the numbers grow toward the maximum number between 7:30 to 9:30 in the evening. Equally important, waiters not only take orders, they serve drinks and attend customers who may want help choosing a wine or other drinks, coffee, or desserts. Moreover, as every waiter learns, if you always do only one task at a time, you can never get everything done that needs doing. As long as you are going to get one meal from the kitchen, getting two is better. As long as you are taking an order, taking orders from two tables, one after the other, before placing either order, saves time.

One obvious way to analyze the process is to assign times to each of the tasks a waiter must do and multiply it by the number of tables the waiter is trying to serve. It may be obvious that a waiter should only try to serve four tables rather than five. Or, perhaps, a change that involves the busboys helping the waiters move meals from the hot table to customer tables may save time. If that's a possibility, then we would need to determine exactly what busboys do and what would remain undone if busboys began to do more to help waiters.

This isn't the place to go into such details further. Imagine if we had included the kitchen in our analysis and needed to analyze all of the steps that went into the preparation of a meal, and tried to decide if it would make a difference if the salad chef was more efficient, or if the oven was set 2 degrees higher. Or imagine we were analyzing a production line with hundreds of activities that needed to be coordinated, some of which could be rearranged. The larger and more complex the process, the more problems we need to consider. In some cases, statistical tools become an invaluable way of sorting out the seemingly overwhelming confusion about which activities are really making the most difference in the final outcome.

Six Sigma project managers usually recommend a systematic analysis process. You begin with a comprehensive look for possible causes. Then you examine the possible causes in more detail, gather data as appropriate, and apply statistical tools like regression analysis and scatter diagrams. In the most complex cases, you are forced to design experiments and vary or control one or another aspect of the problem while gathering data. In the end, you usually come back to the 80/20 rule. There may be many causes, but one or two causes (20%) usually account for 80% of the problem. Those are the causes that one initially focuses on in order to make the process more efficient.

Some Six Sigma practitioners talk about problem analysis as a three-stage process:

1. *Open*. Brainstorm to identify as many possible causes as possible.
2. *Narrow*. Use tools or vote to reduce the number of possible causes to a reasonable number.
3. *Close*. Design measures, gather data, and analyze it to determine which causes in fact cause most of the deviation from the mean.

One popular tool used by many Six Sigma teams when they are trying to identify all possible causes is a cause-effect or fishbone diagram. In effect, it's another kind of tree diagram that one examines to whatever depth is appropriate. We've illustrated a cause-effect diagram for the waiting task in Figure 12.6.

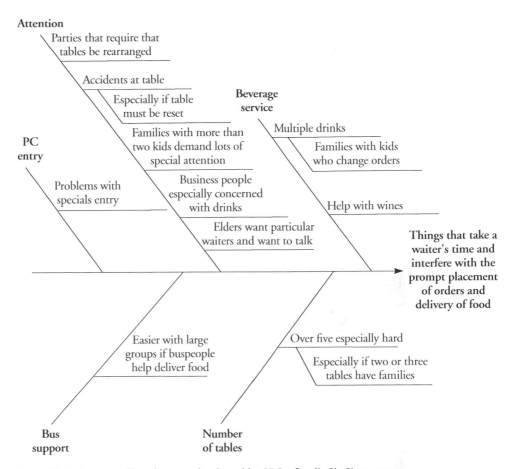

Figure 12.6 A cause-effect diagram developed by SF Seafood's Six Sigma team.

The cause-effect diagram in Figure 12.6 is hardly exhaustive, but it provides an idea of how one identifies a cause, defines it further, and even further if possible. The actual diagram for SF Seafood was much more complex than this. Also, there are some overlapping categories. For example, families with more than two kids are likely to also want to rearrange tables. Moreover, these same tables are the ones that could really benefit from extra help from a bus person.

In the end, the SF Seafood team gathered data on several causes. The team voted on the causes that were really costing the most time. They used a method in which each team member indicated which problem they thought was the worst cause of time delays, the next worst, and the third worst. The results were as follows:

Families with kids	10
Number of tables	8
Tables wanting help with wines	5
Multiple drink tables	3
Lack of busperson help	2
Elders wanting to talk	2
Accidents and spills at table	0
Problems with PC entry	0

One of the issues raised by this analysis was the control and placement of families. This is normally done by the maitre d'. An experiment was developed, and after two weeks it was determined that waiters who didn't have families in their areas definitely provide faster average service. It was also determined that a waiter with six tables that got two groups with more than two kids each was very likely to go over the 18-minute upper limit. As a result, the team decided to change the definition of the process. The new process included a new subprocess—customer seating—and it included the maitre d' placement of customers within the various waiters' areas.

At this point, a Six Sigma team usually gathers lots of data to validate the effect of the different causes identified by the team and to determine their relative salience if possible. We won't consider the various data-gathering techniques or the statistical techniques used by teams to examine the data. In the case of the SF Seafood team, the data confirmed the list that the team generated above.

Improve

As data is gathered and results accumulate, the team begins to think of ways to improve the process. In this case, they are guided by their prioritized list that tells which improvements are likely to result in the largest change.

In the case of SF Seafood, quite a bit of effort was put into determining how the maitre d' could more effectively allocate customers to waiting areas. It was decided, for example, that two groups of families with kids would never be put in the same area. It was also decided that when families with more than two kids were placed in an area, the number of tables the waiter in that area handled would be reduced and the extra table would be reallocated to another waiter. It turned out that an additional waiter was needed for peak weekend periods to keep the number of tables per waiter below five, or four with a multi-kid family.

In addition, it was determined that the restaurant would hire a wine steward and have her available during peak periods. When customers requested help with wines, they were turned over to the steward, who was popular because she ultimately knew a lot more about the restaurant's wines than most of the waiters.

During this period, changes are evaluated and some are put into force. Additional data is gathered to see if the changes are resulting in a more consistent process.

In the case of SF Seafood, changes in customer placement, limits on tables per waiter, and the wine steward resulted in a two-month period in which no diner had to wait longer than 15 minutes for their food. The mean for the order and delivery aspects of the process actually dropped to 8 minutes.

Control

The last phase usually results in a plan to maintain the gains and, sometimes, in new initiatives to improve the process further. Deming, and a wide variety of other experts, has observed that what gets measured gets done.

Large manufacturing companies with production lines constantly sample and evaluate their output. Parts suppliers in sophisticated supply chain systems can only guarantee that their parts are 99.73% defect free because they maintain constant vigilance. This type of quality control costs money and is a necessary part of the process. There are statistical tools that make this kind of control more efficient. Many processes today are monitored by computer systems that derive data from sensors, automatically analyze the data using statistical tests, and report any unacceptable deviations to a human monitor.

In other organizations, once a process has identified and achieved a set of process goals, some of the measures are dropped, since they would otherwise increase the cost of the product. It's important to maintain some measures, however. As we have suggested, measurement and control are a key part of every manager's job and should be done routinely. Process managers should routinely measure customer satisfaction to assure that the process is achieving its goals. Managers responsible for subprocesses need to determine a reasonable compromise between excessive measurement and enough measurement to assure that processes remain efficient and effective. Usually this results in periodic checks, which can become more frequent if problems are detected.

In some cases Six Sigma practitioners recommend that managers develop a response plan, a list of actions tied to specific activities that the manager can take if specific activities within a process begin to deviate significantly from established measures.

The maitre d', who is the process manager for dining service, for example, began to explore ways of using the bus people to save the waiters' time. Overall, however, everyone was happy with the results obtained from the project. The maitre d' discontinued having a person whose job was to time service, but he occasionally asked a waiter to come in 1–2 hours early and time the other waiters just to see that they continued to maintain that 8-minute average. Moreover, once every other month, a week was selected and evaluation postcards were distributed to all diners to continue to monitor their satisfaction. And the maitre d' kept scanning the local restaurant Web sites to see if any complaints showed up there.

Lean

The literature of Lean began with the publication of *The Toyota Production System* (in Japanese) by Taichi Ohno in 1978. (The book wasn't published in English until 1988.) The real book that started U.S. managers talking about Lean, however, was *The Machine That Changed the World,* by James P Womack, Daniel T. Jones and Daniel Roos, published in 1990. In 1997 Womack founded the Lean Enterprise Institute, a nonprofit group that provides training courses and has published a series of books and workbooks to help analysts learn about specific Lean techniques.

Like Six Sigma, Lean began in manufacturing and relies on a variety of statistical and quality control techniques. For awhile, the two movements remained more or less independent. Six Sigma focused on improving the quality and consistency of process outputs and Lean focused on improving the flow of activities and reducing the cost of a process by reducing several forms of waste. More important, the training and consulting companies either focused on Six Sigma or Lean. In the past few years, however, that has changed. Most companies in the Six Sigma market now refer to themselves as Lean Six Sigma companies and offer methodologies that seek to blend the benefits of Lean and Six Sigma.

Interestingly, there has never been a Lean or Six Sigma Association that was in a position to establish a definitive standard for what either Lean or Six Sigma means, or what a green or black belt requires, and each company that provides Lean or Six Sigma training or accreditation follows its own rules.

Most Six Sigma books suggest that Six Sigma practitioners should be interested in three broad areas, the overall management of process change—usually called business process management or BPM—the redesign of processes that require major changes—Redesign—and the improvement of existing processes. In reality, however, most Six Sigma books, until recently, have focused almost entirely on process improvement, just as we have throughout most of this chapter.

There is a specialized area of Six Sigma that focused on new product design, usually referred to as DFSS, Design for Six Sigma, but it is really a special engineering process for designing new products and is only used by a very small and specialized group of Six Sigma practitioners.

Lean, on the other hand, is concerned with both process redesign and improvement, and Lean has both an enterprise ("Flow Kaizen") and a process level ("Process Kaizen") methodology. In essence, Flow Kaizen focuses on improving the flow of the high-level value stream, while Process Kaizen is focused on the elimination of waste. As a further generalization, Flow Kaizen is the concern of senior management while Process Kaizen is the responsibility of the line workers.

Flow Kaizen

The chief tool of the Flow Kaizen practitioner is a high-level diagramming technique called value-stream mapping. Many Lean practitioners skip value stream analysis and jump right to identifying specific sources of waste and removing them. Unfortunately, this often results in local improvements, but rarely results in significant improvements in the overall value stream or in improved products for customers. To really have an impact, you need to begin by streamlining the entire value stream, and only after that, drill down into specific processes to eliminate waste.

Figure 12.7 illustrates a value-stream map. The first thing to notice is that it provides a view of an entire value chain (which Lean practitioners usually refer to as a *product line*). In designing a value-stream map, one begins at the upper right, with the customer (Distribution in Figure 12.7). The customer begins the process with weekly orders. In a similar way, the process ends with the daily delivery of product to the customer. Thus, the value-stream map shows a complete product cycle, from order to delivery.

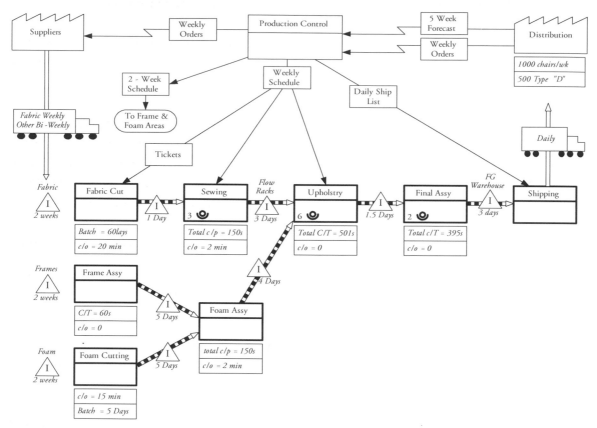

Figure 12.7 A value-stream map (after *Learning to See* by Mike Rother and John Shook).

The second thing to notice is that this is a very high-level view of a process. The entire value chain in Figure 12.7 is broken into eight subprocesses—the bold boxes.

A value-stream map tracks two different types of things. The bold boxes and the wide arrows track the flow of actual product. The thin arrows and boxes track the flow of information (orders, commands, decisions). In addition, there are symbols for customers and suppliers and transportation. The bold clear arrows indicate that the item is "pulled" by the upstream subprocess. In other word, the item is moved on demand. The bold, striped arrow indicates that the item is "pushed." In this case, the subprocess is a batch operation and forwards items to groups, as they are finished. This makes it almost impossible to establish a smooth flow, and Lean practitioners routinely focus on eliminating PUSH processes, replacing them, when possible with Just-In-Time processes. The straight, thin arrow indicates that information is passed between people, while the thin arrow with a kink in it represents an electronic information flow.

The pyramid with a box represents Inventory, and, in most cases, the Map shows what is stored and how long an item is in storage. In some cases, icons are placed within the process boxes to indicate how many operators are involved in a process. Finally, beneath each subprocess box there is a secondary box that contains measurement information. In the map in Figure 12.7 there are, arbitrarily, only two measures per subprocess (and two under the customer box), but there could just as well be more.

Although it isn't shown on the map in Figure 12.7, value-stream maps often place time lines across the bottom that indicate how long product is worked on within each subprocess, and how long product takes to move between subprocesses. Similarly, there are a number of symbols that could be added to indicate where Kanban activities occur. (Kanban activities involve the systematic use of cards to help schedule and manage the flow of products.)

Process Kaizen

Once a Lean team is satisfied that they have the overall value stream running smoothly, they begin to drill down and look at specific processes. In this case they are looking for waste that can be eliminated and this is referred to as Process Kaizen. Lean practitioners begin by defining activities as either value-adding or non-value-adding activities, and try to eliminate as many of the non-value-adding activities as they can. The definition of non-value-adding activities can be tricky, since one needs to distinguish between activities that don't add value but are required to keep the company functioning (e.g., accounting and the tax paying process), and activities that are neither required nor add value. In essence, one examines activities and looks for seven types of waste. The generation of waste suggests a useless, non-value-adding activity. In the Lean world, waste results from seven types of activities: Overproduction, Waiting, Transport, Extra Processing, Inventory, Motion, and Defects.

Overproduction. Overproduction occurs when a process continues to generate outputs after it should have stopped. This occurs because the process does not rely on a Just-In-Time schedule or because it does not get feedback from an upstream process to stop production.

Waiting. Also known as queuing. This refers to periods of inactivity that result when an upstream process does not deliver an adequate supply of a required input on time. Often, as a result, the affected process then proceeds to do non-value-adding work or is engaged in overproduction of some alternative output.

Transport. This refers to the unnecessary movement of materials. Ideally, a work-in-progress should pass from one workstation to another, without being stacked or stored or handled by anyone not directly involved in adding value to the work-in-progress.

Extra Processing. This refers to any extra operations, any rework or any movement of work to storage. It also includes situations in which the customer is asked the same question twice because, although the information was obtained and recorded once, it is unavailable to the second worker.

Inventory. This refers to any excess inventory that is not directly required for current customer orders. It includes both excess raw materials and excess finished goods. Excess inventory might also include marketing materials that are created but never mailed or parts that are stocked but never used.

Motion. This refers to any extra steps taken by employees when they perform their tasks. It refers to employees that have to move to access tools or a telephone and it refers to an employee that has to walk to another area to pick up items that he or she needs to process.

Defects. This refers to any output that is unacceptable to the downstream process or the customer. Similarly it can refer to situations in which incorrect information is entered on forms. All rework is waste.

As you can see, there is quite a bit of overlap between the different categories. The essence of Process Kaizen is to streamline a process so that all work is done in the most efficient manner possible. There isn't much emphasis put on automation in most Lean books, but obviously document-processing workflow systems that scan forms and then move them, instantly, from one workstation to the next fulfill a major Lean goal.

It's easy to see how Six Sigma practitioners can incorporate Lean techniques in their work. Hopefully, however, this book suggests a wide variety of different techniques that Six Sigma practitioners can incorporate and Lean will be adopted by those interested in process improvement right along with new ways of improving process management, new techniques for structuring the performance of jobs, and the use of business rules and BPMS.

TRIZ

Innovation is a hot word at the moment. For the last several years, Six Sigma practitioners have been discussing a systematic approach to innovation called TRIZ. TRIZ (Teoriya Resheniya Izobretate Zadatch) is a Russian acronym for "theory of inventive problem solving." (It's usually pronounced "trees.") It's a methodology that helps people examine problems and develop a number of inventive solutions. A group of Russian researchers, led by Genrich Altshuller, spent several years investigating how people develop breakthrough solutions and refined it into a series of concepts or steps. Just as Six Sigma has recently embraced Lean to extend its scope, many Six Sigma consultants are now incorporating TRIZ elements into their programs to help with the design of new products or new process solutions.

TRIZ can be a bit overwhelming. Altshuller and his co-workers in Russia defined eight evolutionary patterns for guiding strategic decisions, 76 standard solutions for relating engineering elements in a system, 39 problem parameters for characterizing problems, and 40 inventive principles for solving technical contradictions. As with Lean, there are actually two TRIZ methodologies—one for tactical problems and another for strategic problems. The Tactical TRIZ methodology includes the following steps: Define, Model, Abstract, Solve, Implement. Here's how Silverstein, DeCarlo and Slocum define the steps in *INsourcing Innovation*, which is probably the best introduction to TRIZ for Six Sigma practitioners:

> **DEFINE.** The system and problem in question are defined and explored, and the Ideal Final Result (IFR) is formulated based on the contents of the Ideality Equation. A resource model is constructed as a reference for use throughout the DMASI process. Also, the various design challenges are framed in terms of a contradiction. Finally, a financial analysis is conducted to estimate the financial benefits expected from the project.
>
> **MODEL.** The system is modeled using Function Modeling and Substance Filed Modeling. The Function Model enables further understanding of how the elements in the system interact to create contradictions, or to resolve them. In many cases, technical challenges are solved at this stage with some subset of TRIZ's 76 "standard solutions."

ABSTRACT. Using abstract thought, this is when the TRIZ practitioner moves the unsolvable output of the prior two stages into the realm of the solvable. Technical contractions are converted into generic terms per Altshuller's algorithms, then referenced to the contradiction matrix to determine applicable inventive principles. The TRIZ practitioner also uses the Abstract phase to resolve any physical contradictions with the four separation principles.

SOLVE. The generic principles from the Abstract phase are combined with the work done in the Modeling phase to create specific solutions to the specific problem(s) under evaluation. Here, too, is where the powers of abstract thinking are important. Concept selection techniques may also be utilized to determine the ultimate feasibility of various solution pathways.

IMPLEMENT. After creating an implementation plan, the solution selected in the Solve phase is implemented so the problem is eliminated or new revenue is generated. Then the impact of the solution is compared with predicted values identified in the Define phase to confirm the demanded project ROI.

The Strategic TRIZ methodology steps include: Define, Map, Apply, Plot, Implement. In this case, the emphasis is on the evolution of systems and one applies the evolutionary patterns defined by TRIZ to plot how product or processes will likely evolve and to plan accordingly.

When you look at the steps in the methodologies and consider what's involved in each, as described above, you realize that this isn't some informal approach, like brainstorming, where everyone sits around a table trying to come up with new ideas. This is problem solving with a large engineering component and a series of precise models and templates to guide practitioners at each step along the way.

TRIZ isn't something that should be confined to Six Sigma. TRIZ is an approach to systematic innovation. Interestingly, the most innovative work on TRIZ, at the moment, is being published in a series of articles written by Howard Smith for BPTrends. In essence, Smith is reviewing the entire TRIZ literature and developing a systematic approach designed for those involved in process redesign.

Notes and References

[1] The basic flow of the SIPOC diagram is similar to the Project Scoping Diagram we considered in Chapter 8, but it ignores the management of the processes, the controls exerted by policies, rules and other external management processes, and the influence of support or enabling processes like human resources, information technology, and so forth. This just another way of saying that Six Sigma improvement projects focus on narrowly defined processes while redesign projects focus on the broader context, as well as the process.

Taylor, Frederick W., *The Principles of Scientific Management*, Harper's, 1911. For a modern review of the efficiency movement and Taylor, check Daniel Nelson's *Frederick W. Taylor and the Rise of Scientific Management*, University of Wisconsin Press, 1980. Frederick Winslow Taylor advocated the idea that managers had a responsibility to study processes and assure that they were efficient. Taylor emphasized time and motion studies, and motivational incentives to control performance. Workers, who resented being urged to work faster, called the approach "Taylorism."

The automotive data is from an IMVP World Assembly Plan Survey conducted in 1986. I discovered this data in a booklet written by Ken Orr, entitled *Creating the Smart Enterprise: Business Process Reengineering in the Real World*, which was published in 1998 and is available from the Ken Orr Institute. For more information, check *www.kenorrinst.com.*

The International Society of Six Sigma Professionals (*www.isssp.org*) sponsors meetings and training sessions in Six Sigma techniques.

The American Society for Quality (*www.asq.org*) puts on an annual Six Sigma Conference, which is a good place to meet practitioners and learn. The ASQ has a Six Sigma Forum that publishes a newsletter.

For an excellent description of the beginnings of Six Sigma, go to *www.bptrends.com* and search for the article, "The Mists of Six Sigma" by Alan Ramias. Ramias was at Motorola when Six Sigma was born and debunks several myths.

Eckes, George, *The Six Sigma Revolution: How General Electric and Others Turned Process into Profits*, John Wiley, 2001. A good workthrough of all the basics, for managers or practitioners. I'd recommend this be your first book on Six Sigma.

Brassard, Michael, Lynda Finn, Dana Ginn and Diane Ritter, *The Six Sigma Memory Jogger II: A Pocket Guide of Tools for Six Sigma Improvement Teams,* GOAL/QPC, 2002. This is one of several little pocket guides (3" by 5") that summarize everything in a easily accessible form. This is the book I grab when I want to look up a technical term or get a formula. There are several others that are equally useful for more specialized aspects of Six Sigma. Check *www.goalqpc.com.*

Juran Institute, *The Six Sigma Basic Training Kit: Implementing Juran's 6 Step Quality Improvement Process and Six Sigma Tools*, McGraw-Hill, 2001. An expensive but detailed guide to Six Sigma that includes facilitator notes and training modules. For those who want to lead a Six Sigma team.

Harry, Mikel and Don R. Linsenmann, *The Six Sigma Fieldbook: How DuPont Successfully Implemented the Six Sigma Breakthrough Management Strategy,* Currency Doubleday, 2006. This book describes the deployment of Six Sigma at DuPont from 1998 to 2004. It is a great case study in what's involved in making Six Sigma happen at a large company.

Gupta, Praveen, *Six Sigma Business Scorecard: Creating a Comprehensive Corporate Performance Measurement System,* McGraw-Hill, 2004. This book is more specialized, but a good book if you are trying to use both Balanced Scorecard and Six Sigma and trying to figure out how to integrate them.

Webb, Michael J., *Sales and Marketing the Six Sigma Way*. Kaplan Publishing, 2006. This book discusses the application of Six Sigma techniques to sales and marketing problems. It's a great book for anyone who wants to improve sales and marketing processes and it demonstrates how far Six Sigma has come beyond its origins in manufacturing.

Gygi, Craig, Neil DeCarlo and Bruce Williams. *Six Sigma for Dummies*. Wiley, 2005. This is my new favorite as a simple introduction to Six Sigma. It provides a very nice overview of what you need to know.

Sayer, Charlie J. and Bruce Williams. *Lean for Dummies*. Wiley, 2007. A good overview of Lean as it is being used in organizations today.

Ohno, Taiichi, *Toyota Production System: Beyond Large-Scale Production*, Productivity Press, 1988. This is the first book on Lean, published in Japan in 1978. It was translated into English in 1988. This book has the seminal ideas, but is entirely focused on manufacturing problems.

James Womack, Daniel Jones, and Daniel Roos, *The Machine That Changed The World: The Story of Lean Production: How Japan's Secret Weapon in the Global Auto Wars Will Revolutionize Western Industry,* Harper Perennial, 1990. An MIT study of the practices employed at Toyota. This is the book that kicked off the interest in Lean in the U.S. Womack went on to set up the Lean Enterprise Institute, in 1997 (*www.lean.org*). The Lean Enterprise Institute provides training courses and has published a series of books and workbooks to help analysts learn about specific Lean techniques.

Womack, James P. and Daniel T. Jones, *Lean Solutions: How Companies and Customers Can Create Value and Wealth Together,* Free Press, 2005. The latest book by Womack, it contains a lot of good examples of Lean success stories.

Rother, Mike and John Shook, *Learning to See,* The Lean Enterprise Institute, 2003. This is a great introduction to value-stream mapping.

Carreira, Bill and Bill Trudell, *Lean Six Sigma That Works,* AMACOM, 2006. One of several new books that aim to show how Lean and Six Sigma can be combined.

Silverstein, David, Neil DeCarlo, and Michael Slocum, *Innovation Happens Elsewhere: How to transform business as usual into business as exceptional,* Breakthrough Performance Press, 2005. This is a nice introduction to TRIZ by guys who are very much in the Six Sigma tradition.

The most impressive detailed treatment of TRIZ, for those involved in business process redesign, is a series of articles being written by Howard Smith and being published on BPTrends. Go to *www.bptrends.com* and search on P-TRIZ.

chapter

13

The BPTrends Process Redesign Methodology

IN EARLIER CHAPTERS we considered how a company might decide to modify a process or select a specific process for redesign. In this chapter we want to consider how a company might go about redesigning a business process or creating a new process. For our purpose here, we will assume that the process to be redesigned is a reasonably large process and that the company involved wants to do anything it can to make the process more effective. In other words, we will be considering a methodology for a significant business process redesign effort.

This chapter will provide an overview of how analysis, project management, change management, communication and facilitation must all be woven together to achieve results. It will also suggest how a team can be assembled and suggest some of the roles that will be required.

There have been a number of books published describing redesign methodologies. Most focus on major phases, as we do here, and some go into exquisite detail, defining a process with hundreds of tasks or steps. The methodology we describe here is the BPTrends Process Redesign Methodology, which was designed to structure the training of new process change practitioners. We have already introduced the BP-Trends methodology in Part I of this book when we discussed enterprise development. In essence, BPTrends suggests that companies develop a business process architecture and create institutions that will allow the company to prioritize its subsequent process work. We refer to the methodology that puts an enterprise process capability in place

353

as the BPTrends Enterprise Methodology. If this methodology is used, then an enterprise level BPM group will prioritize and scope future business process change efforts. Unfortunately, most companies lack a sophisticated enterprise level process capability, and thus the BPTrends Redesign Process Methodology is designed so that it can either accept information from the enterprise level or generate the information needed for a redesign project from scratch. (See Figure 13.1.)

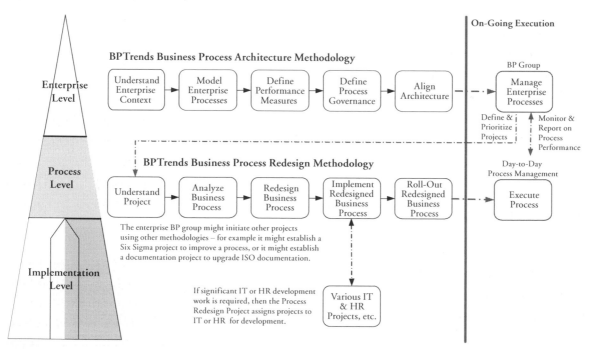

Figure 13.1 The BPTrends Process Redesign Methodology.

The BPTrends Process Redesign Methodology assumes a process redesign project that takes place in five phases. Once the project is complete, it assumes that the process and associated process management system will work together to execute the process on a day-to-day basis, and that one of the things that the process manager will do is to maintain and improve the process on an on-going basis. The methodology also assumes that most implementation phases of most projects will involve other groups, like IT or Human Resources, in the development of components, like training courses and software applications, that will be needed for the new process design.

The BPTrends methodology is designed to provide a framework for a variety of best practices. It assumes that most organizations will already be using specific techniques like SCOR, Balanced Scorecard and Lean Six Sigma. Thus, the BPTrends methodology is designed to provide a project framework into which more specific techniques and practices can be incorporated.

Figure 13.2 takes a somewhat different look at a process redesign project. In this case we picture the five phases in the middle of the diagram, and surround them with some of the broad concerns that anyone contemplating a major process redesign project should consider. Just above the five phases, we suggest that anyone undertaking a process redesign project will need a variety of modeling, analytical and design techniques we focused on in Chapters 8, 9, 10 and 11.

Below the five phases in the center of Figure 13.2, and in addition to analysis and design techniques, we suggest that individuals will need skills in conducting research, interviewing, and group facilitation. In other words, you can't analyze information until after you've acquired it. In most cases, you do this by asking questions of employees and managers who perform the process you are attempting to redesign. In other cases, you must gather and analyze data from reports and historical records that document how the process has behaved in the past.

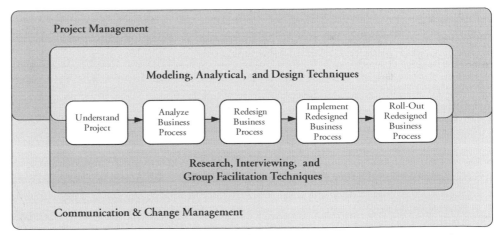

Figure 13.2 An overview of the techniques and skills required to successfully undertake a business process redesign project.

The outer section of Figure 13.2 suggests two more skill sets required for a process redesign project. At the top we list project management. A process redesign project is, first of all, a project. Projects need to be managed and process redesign team leaders need training in project management skills. They need clear goals, a plan, a schedule, a team, milestones and all of the other things that assure that the work gets done in an orderly manner.

At the same time, the project team needs a communication plan. The team manager needs to talk with those working on the project and he or she needs to sell the changes to be made to all the stakeholders who will be affected by the change. Some might prefer to call this *change management*. Whatever it is called, it requires its own set of skills. People resist change and their resistance is only overcome if someone can explain how the change will benefit them. That requires that the person managing the communication understand the needs and interests of each of the processes' stakeholders and manages to communicate with them in terms they understand.

We have already discussed analysis, modeling and design considerations. In this chapter, we will talk more about the management and communication issues. We don't really address interviewing and group facilitation in this book, but we recommend some good books in the Notes and References at the end of this chapter that will provide interested readers with some help in this important area.

We strongly recommend that companies use an experienced facilitator to actually manage a redesign project. The facilitator might come from a redesign group inside your organization, or he or she could be an outside consultant. In either case, the facilitator will probably have his or her own specific approach to business process redesign. What we want to do here, however, is to provide managers and redesign team members with a broad overview of what will happen in almost any large business process redesign effort.

The methodology we describe is best suited for a large-scale effort. Some changes in business processes are routine. They are adjustments made to correct a minor problem or to implement some minor change in the ways things must be done. A change in the price of an item, for example, must be communicated to salespeople, altered in sales catalogs, and changed in software systems. These changes are initiated by the process manager who is responsible for the process or by departmental managers who are responsible for the specific activities that need to be changed. We are not concerned with such routine changes. Instead, we describe an approach that can be used to undertake a major overhaul of a value chain or a major business process.

Major business process redesign projects are usually managed by a steering committee and undertaken by a team that represents all of the functional managers involved in the change. Unlike the less-formal techniques used by managers who need to adjust a process, a major business process redesign effort usually requires a systematic methodology that defines phases and responsibilities and provides the basis for a project plan and schedule. A significant part of the effort will involve keeping senior managers in the loop—communicating with them—to assure their support when it's time to implement the process. This communication process isn't a direct part of business process redesign, but it's vital to assure that the changes get implemented. Assuring that your team has someone knowledgeable to manage the entire project, including all the communication aspects, is another reason we recommend the use of an experienced facilitator.

Why Have a Methodology?

Large projects take time and involve many different people. If they are well planned, they can be conducted efficiently, minimizing the time required of those involved and assuring that results will be obtained in a relatively short time. Outside consulting companies routinely analyze and redesign large business processes in 3–6 months. On the other hand, we know of projects that started off to analyze a process and were still at it 2 years later when the whole project was scrapped. Projects that lose their way usually do so because the people involved don't have a good plan, don't have concrete milestones, and don't have practical criteria that allow them to decide when a task or phase is complete.

What's even worse than a project that gets lost in the swamp of analysis is a project that completes its work and submits a good redesign that never gets implemented. Implementation failures occur because key departments, managers, or employees haven't committed to the project. A good redesign effort requires a lot more than a process redesign. It requires that the company go through a change process that systematically gains the commitments of all relevant stakeholders. At the same time, it requires that the implementation be planned with as much care as the redesign and that managers and employees involved in the process have their job descriptions and incentives changed so that they are judged, and rewarded, when the project meets its goals. If customers or other companies are involved, care must be taken to assure that they are just as committed as your company people are to the new process. Thus, the methodology we describe is not simply a plan for redesigning a process. It's a plan for both a redesign and for securing the support of all the people necessary to assure that the new process will be implemented.

How Does It All Begin?

In the earlier chapters of this book, we described an enterprise alignment cycle. We argued that every organization should establish a process that linked corporate strategy with a business process architecture group. The business process architecture group, in turn, should identify process changes mandated by changes in corporate goals and then generate a prioritized list of projects. Each project should be assigned a sponsor who is responsible for undertaking the project and assuring that the scope of the redesign corresponds with the goals the executive committee and the architecture group set for the project. In this chapter, we won't concern ourselves with the strategic and architectural functions, but assume that, somehow, a senior manager has been assigned goals and the responsibility for improving a business process. Thus, for our purposes here, a project begins with a senior manager who is responsible for undertaking a business process redesign.

What Happens?

Figure 13.1 provides a very high-level overview of the phases in our redesign process methodology. The project begins, in Phase 1, when the responsible manager sets things going. Typically, the manager, who we usually call the project sponsor, retains a project facilitator who will manage the actual process analysis and redesign effort. The facilitator then works with the project sponsor to develop a plan and schedule and to select other individuals to take part in the project.

Ultimately, the planning effort results in a business process redesign team that includes a wide variety of members, including process managers, employees, IT specialists, and others concerned with the process. This team documents the current process, going into only as much detail as seems appropriate.

Once the analysis is complete, the same or a modified team considers various redesign options and arrives at the one they think best. After the redesign is approved, a development plan is created that requires efforts from everyone involved in creating products necessary for the process change.

Finally, after each of the specialized groups has completed its work, the new process is implemented. Assuming all goes well, the new process is used until managers find need to correct it, or until the strategy and BPM group determines that the process should be revised again, in response to still newer threats or opportunities. We'll consider each of these phases in some detail below.

To keep things simple, we are assuming that the process redesign project is confined to a single company or division. Many e-business applications, especially supply-chain-driven redesign projects, involve organizing several companies to work together. The essential process is the same as we will describe, but the establishment of steering committees and design teams can be quite a bit more complex. In some cases, goals and plans may need to be specified in legal contracts before the redesign team can even begin its work. In these cases, a strong BPM group is especially important.

Who Makes It All Happen?

Obviously the names of groups and the job titles will change from one organization to the next. Broadly, however, we assume that the ultimate decisions are made by a group that we'll term the *executive committee*. The executive committee may include a strategy group and a BPM group, or these groups may report to the executive committee. The strategy group provides inputs to the BPM group, which, with the approval of the executive committee, decides what business processes need to be redesigned. However it is organized in any specific company, the executive committee is probably made up of the CEO, the COO, and the heads of major departments and business units. The executive committee is responsible for adopting new corporate strategies and setting corporate goals. Once goals and strategies are adopted, the BPM group is responsible for determining which value chains or business processes should be modified to achieve new strategies or goals, and developing plans to assure it happens. The BPM group may have many of the same members as the executive committee, or it may have more specialists and planners.

A major redesign effort takes time and consumes the efforts of lots of executives and managers. Thus, it is only justified when it is determined that minor changes won't produce the desired result. A major redesign is usually undertaken only if the organization makes a major shift in its strategic orientation, or if a major new technology is to be incorporated that will impact a number of different subprocesses and activities within a major business process.

Once the executive committee decides a process redesign effort is justified, someone must be assigned to oversee the project. If the organization already has a process orientation and process managers, then the person responsible for the project is the process manager, and the project steering team is made up of the team of managers who normally work together to oversee the process. In this case, the project sponsor is either the project manager, or someone directly appointed by the project manager. In companies that do not currently have process managers, a project sponsor must be appointed by the executive committee. Since one of the goals of a serious process redesign effort should be to reorganize the process management system, the person appointed as project sponsor, in this case, is usually the individual who will emerge as the process manager when the redesign is complete. However it's arrived at, the project sponsor is the individual who is ultimately responsible for the redesign project. He or she does not manage the day-to-day work of the redesign team, but is responsible for approving major decisions and working with members of the executive committee to assure broad support for the work of the redesign effort.

At the same time, a *process redesign steering team* should be established. This team usually consists of high-level representatives of all of the departments or functions involved in the process. In some cases, the BPM group serves as a permanent redesign steering team. In other cases, the team is a subcommittee of the executive committee. In any case, you need to create such a team. This team has two key functions. First, it must approve the work of the redesign team and, second, its members need to assure that the managers and employees within each of their respective organizations understand, support, and will implement the redesigned process. The work that goes on with the redesign steering team is just as important as the redesign work itself. The team members must be powerful enough to commit their functional groups and to assure that their managers will be held accountable for a successful implementation effort.

Next, an individual needs to be selected to actually facilitate the process redesign effort. In some cases this individual is a consultant who comes from outside the organization. In other cases he or she comes from a business process group within the company. In either case, it's important that this individual is neutral and doesn't have any stake in, or any commitment to, the functional groups that will be engaged in the redesign effort. The *project facilitator* should be a consultant who understands how to facilitate process redesign. The facilitator does not need to understand how the specific business process works. Instead, he or she should be skilled in working with a design team to assure that they succeed within a reasonably short time. A good facilitator is the key to assuring that the analysis and design occur on schedule and don't get bogged down in an unnecessary analysis effort.

Finally, a *process redesign team* should be established. This group will actually struggle with the details of the process and make the choices about how to redesign the process. The team is usually composed of managers or supervisors from each of the major subprocesses or activities involved in the process. In most cases, technical specialists from human resources and IT should also be included on the project redesign team.

Phase 1: Understanding the Project

Ideally, the goals and overall schedule of any specific process improvement effort should be defined and limited by a charter or plan issued by the BPM group. The plan may have come from the strategy committee or the executive committee. If no project plan exists, the team responsible for the specific business process improvement effort will need to develop a plan. Specifically, they will need to determine the organizational strategy and the goals that the specific process is expected to support, and they will need to define how the specific process relates to other company processes and to company customers and suppliers. In effect, they will need to generate a limited version of the company strategy in order to define and scope their task.

Assume that a BPM group has assigned a priority to the project, created a general plan, and assigned a project sponsor. In that case, the first task of the project sponsor is to identify a steering committee, "hire" a facilitator, and oversee the elaboration of the project plan. In most cases the project facilitator manages the actual day-to-day work of the project. In some cases the facilitator will be an outside consultant, and in other cases it may be an internal facilitator provided by a corporate business process improvement group. In either case, the facilitator will probably begin by interviewing a number of people to assure that he or she understands what everyone expects. In effect, the facilitator begins by checking the completeness of the plan.

Interactions between the project sponsor, the steering team, and the facilitator will also help refine the project plan. The same group should also work together to assemble the process design team—the individuals who will be responsible for actually analyzing the existing process and then developing the new process design.

In most cases, it is the project facilitator who actually writes out a formal planning document and then modifies it after he or she receives inputs from the sponsor and other team members.

Once the project plan and a schedule are completed, they should be reviewed in a joint meeting that includes everyone involved in the project. This is a critical meeting, and the outcome should be an agreement on the scope and goals of effort to be undertaken. If someone's unhappy with the project, this is the time to deal with it. Otherwise, throughout the other meetings and later, during implementation, you are likely to have someone resisting the new process.

Major Activities

Figure 13.3 provides an overview of what's involved in the planning phase. Figure 13.2 uses a process diagram to show who is involved and what happens in what order. Most of the tall activity boxes represent meetings in which members of all the groups get together to review proposals and agree on plans. These meetings and the consensus-building effort that they represent are an important aspect of any major business process improvement project.

Most of the detailed work of this phase is done by the facilitator in conjunction with the steering team.

▶ The executive committee appoints a project sponsor and creates a steering team. They, in turn, appoint a facilitator and a process redesign team. Most of the detailed work is undertaken by the project facilitator, who interviews senior managers and those currently involved with the process. The facilitator creates and presents draft documents for the sponsor and steering team to review and approve.

▶ Refine the scope of the process to be analyzed and redesigned. If the corporate committee created documents describing strategy changes, goals, measures, and a description of how the process should be changed, then one begins with them. (This information can be documented on an *organization diagram* and on an *organization goals and measures worksheet*,[1] or in any other reasonable format.) The

---

[1] In this chapter we will mention several worksheets that can be used to document a process or record decisions about a redesign. We have introduced these worksheets in various other chapters as we discussed analysis and design issues.

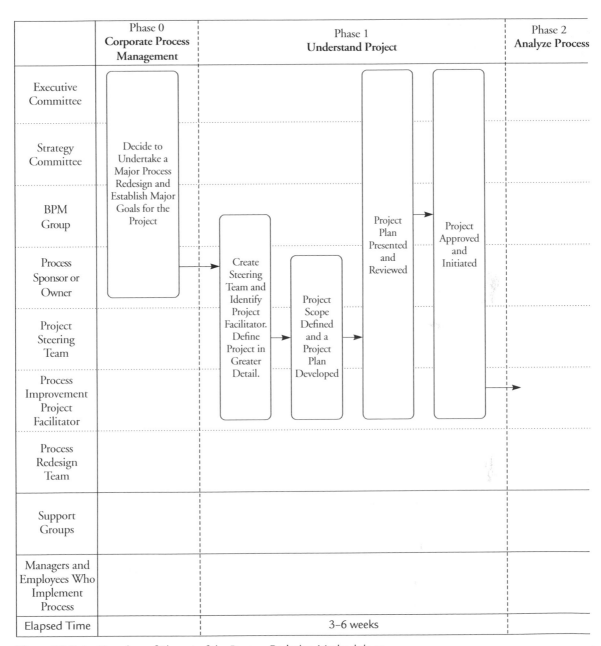

Figure 13.3 An Overview of Phase I of the Process Redesign Methodology.

sponsor, steering team, and facilitator should begin by reviewing everything that has been documented. If no documentation of this sort has been prepared, then the team should create them. Unless the BPM group has already done it, the team should also review or create a *value chain* or *process relationship diagram* to assure that everyone understands how the specific project fits with other corporate processes. If the project is large, the team may want to create a high-level *process diagram*, define the major subprocesses that make up the overall process, and define their relationships. In this case, the team may also subdivide and different groups may focus on different subprocesses, or they may prioritize the analysis and improvement of subprocesses.

▶ Review project goals. The team should review the goals set for the project and explore how they relate to corporate strategy and goals. If the process is large or complex, the team may want to identify which subprocesses lead to which goals or create subgoals for different subprocesses. If a process management system is going to be created or redesigned, then managers from the different functional units should definitely be included on the redesign team.

▶ Once the project is scoped, it needs to be described and a business case for the project needs to be built. We have discussed this in some detail, using the gap model, in Chapter 8. The team will review and document project assumptions, requirements, and constraints. The more familiar the team becomes with the specific process, the more likely it will see alternatives or identify constraints that the corporate committees overlooked. The team should document every assumption and constraint it identifies to clarify its thinking about the nature of the process. Facilities, manufacturing machines, computer hardware, and software systems are often sources of constraints. Changing them, or working around them, can often impose huge costs on a project and render an effective redesign impossible. It's important to find out what constraints might limit redesign as early as possible.

▶ Create a project schedule and budget. As the team learns more about the specific project it is planning, it will either create or refine the schedule and the budget developed by the business BPM group.

▶ Benchmark data describes industry averages for specific types of tasks. Or, in some cases, it describes what competitors have achieved. In most cases it's hard to get good benchmark data, although it's widely available for packaged applications from the vendors and in some industries from associations. If benchmark data is to be used to determine minimal goals for a redesign effort, this fact should be identified in the planning stage and a plan developed to secure it.

▶ Determine who will take part in the actual analysis effort. Identify the members of the process redesign team. In most cases, only some of the members of the team will actually take part in the workshops in which the process is analyzed. The overall team should determine who will take part and arrange for them to be available for the time required. The analysis and design work will take place during meetings, which are often called workshops. It's best to have a neutral, trained facilitator to run the process, and we'll assume one is available throughout the remainder of this discussion.

Outcome

This phase ends with a detailed *project plan* for a specific business process that has been approved by the executive committee, the business BPM group, the process sponsor, and the project steering committee. When everyone agrees on the plan, it's time to begin Phase 2.

Phase 2: Analyze Business Process

The goal of this phase is to analyze and document the workings of an existing process. Some organizations will have already done this analysis. In other cases, the project team will be creating a completely new process, and there will be no existing process to analyze. Still other project teams will decide to skip the analysis of the existing process and focus on creating a new process. Most process redesign teams, however, should develop at least a high-level overview of the existing process simply to provide a starting point for redesign efforts. A few organizations will undertake a detailed analysis of an existing process and then proceed to develop a detailed time and cost model of the current process in order to run simulations to study how specific changes would improve the efficiency of the existing process.

The actual work during this phase is typically accomplished by the facilitator and during meetings between the facilitator and the process redesign team. The team that is to analyze the process meets with the facilitator. Some facilitators prefer to have the team together for several days in a row and to work through the analysis in one push.

Other facilitators prefer to meet for 2–3 hours a day, usually in the morning, every other day for several weeks, until the analysis is complete. There is no correct way to do this. It depends on the company, the facilitator, and the scope and urgency of the project.

The facilitator runs the meetings and helps the team analyze the problem. The facilitator usually draws diagrams and makes lists on whiteboards or large sheets of paper that are put up around the meeting room. The facilitator is usually supported by a scribe (or analyst) who takes notes as the team makes decisions. If a process-modeling software tool is used, it is usually the scribe who uses the tool. The team members don't need to use the tool or worry about it. The main goal of using a software tool is to capture the information and make it easy to print notes and create diagrams to document the process. Between team meetings, the facilitator and the scribe work together to assure that the documentation is accurate and then print documentation so that the team members will have it when they arrive for the next session. A specially designed process-modeling tool makes it possible to document a morning session and then provide printouts of the resulting diagrams in the course of an afternoon. Companies that run intensive efforts, where the team meets every morning, are usually forced to rely on a software tool to assure that the documentation can be prepared promptly between sessions. Software tools are discussed in more detail in Chapters 15 and 16.

Major Activities

Figure 13.4 presents an overview of Phase 2 of the process redesign project.

The activities of this phase are undertaken by the process redesign team, guided by the facilitator.

▶ To assure that things move quickly and smoothly, the facilitator usually reviews the plan and interviews a variety of stakeholders to get up to speed on the process and the problems that call for a redesign. In addition, to assure that the process design team gets off to a fast start, the facilitator will often create a first-draft version of the process. In this case, rather than having the team define the process from scratch, the facilitator begins by proposing an overview of the process and then works with the process redesign team to refine the strawman version. This is a reasonably painless way to introduce *organization* and *process diagrams.* The facilitator puts

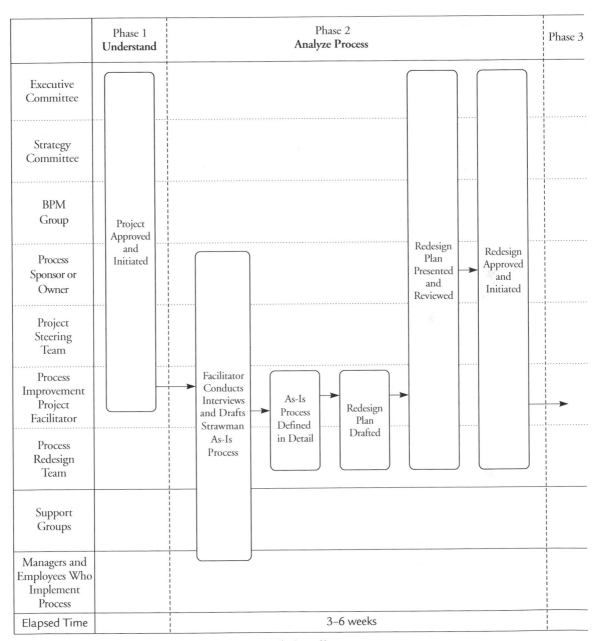

Figure 13.4 An overview of Phase 2 of the process redesign effort.

up diagrams of a process the team is familiar with and talks them through it. The diagrams are easy enough to understand that the team quickly gets into identifying activities or flows that are wrong or missing.

▶ Document the current (As-Is) process. Use *process diagrams* to document an As-Is version of the process. If the process is large, begin with a high-level *As-Is process relationship diagram* that identifies the key subprocesses. Then develop a separate *As-Is process diagram* for each subprocess. Repeat this process until you arrive at an As-Is process diagram that shows activities and describes the process in as much detail as the team feels necessary. The goal isn't analysis for its own sake, but a diagram with enough detail so that the team can easily see what will need to be changed to improve the process and to achieve the project's goals. A good facilitator can help the team focus on creating "just enough" analysis and avoid getting lost in details.

▶ Agree on the names of processes, subprocesses, inputs, outputs, and activities. Different groups often use different terms to refer to the same processes and activities. One important outcome of a process analysis should be an agreement on what processes and outputs should be called. This is especially hard if many different functional groups are involved, and it's very hard if multiple companies are involved.

▶ Identify any "disconnects" or deficiencies in the current As-Is process. Record findings on a *process analysis and improvement worksheet.*

▶ Activities are linked by lines that show where inputs to the activity come from and where outputs go. The lines should be labeled. The flows between activities can be products, documents, information (data), or money. If the inputs or outputs are complex, it is probably worth describing them on a process analysis and improvement worksheet.

▶ Determine necessary characteristics of each activity. As we've said before, we use the term *activity* to describe the smallest unit of process we intend to model. Each activity needs a name, and it should probably also be given a written description to be sure everyone will know just what it entails. An activity can be performed by an individual, automated by a software system, or performed by a combination of a person and a software system. You should note how each activity is performed. In other cases, it may be important to document how decisions are made during an activity. If the flow from an activity branches, it is often useful to include information about how it is determined which path a given output takes. If many different business rules are used to make decisions, it might be worth listing the rules that are applied. If specific goals, subgoals, or quality measures are associated with an activity, they should be defined. All of this information should be noted on an *activity worksheet* or recorded by means of a software tool.

▶ This is another point at which interview and group facilitation skills are required and where a knowledge of change management will pay off. The team will need to interview people, individually or in groups to get information about the As-Is process and its problems. The questions to be asked should be well thought out. Moreover, as team members interview employees, they will also have to answer questions about the changes that might take place. Employees will want to know what the team is trying to accomplish. Employees will usually leave these interviews with an initial bias for or against change, depending on how the project is explained to them. If the team members are skillful in explaining the project in a way that makes sense to the interviewees, and suggest how the work will benefit them, the interviewees are much more likely to support the project in the future.

▶ Develop a process management design. Usually a subset of the entire process design team, made up of managers, meets to document the current management process. As we have suggested, the management process involves organizational, process, and functional aspects. It also involves establishing goals and measures for the process as a whole and for each subprocess and activity. And it involves actually taking measures and evaluating deviations from the expected results. If this has been done in the past, then existing managers should be able to provide specific data on which activities and subprocesses have been performing well or failing in the recent past. Similarly, there should be documentation on corrective actions that have been attempted. If this data doesn't exist, then the As-Is management team should at least document the structure that does exist and develop a document specifying where the management process breaks down. At a minimum, the team should develop a good idea of who is specifically responsible for managing each existing subprocess and activity.

▶ Although we have not emphasized it up to this point, a process redesign effort typically requires changes in both the specific activities that make up the process and the management system that monitors and controls the process in everyday use. In our examination of hundreds of business processes, we have consistently found that there were more problems with the management systems that control the process than with the activities that comprise the process. That is why the team should consider how the management system will support the process before going into the specifics of process redesign. Useless or poorly ordered activities will result in an inefficient process. On the other hand, even a relatively well-designed process that is managed by supervisors who haven't established clear measures or who don't reward behavior that is critical to the success of the process is just as likely to be inefficient. In reality, in any major process redesign effort, we usually find opportunities to improve both the process structure and the management system. We will devote a subsequent chapter to management and measurement problems.

▶ If the team plans to do cost studies, then each activity should be analyzed to determine its cost, the time it takes, the outputs produced per unit of time, and so forth. Time and cost can be documented on an *activity table*, but if you are really going to do cost studies and compare alternatives, then it's much better to use a software product and enter the information into tables associated with the activity on the software product diagrams. This is done on an *activity cost worksheet*.

▶ Refocus on the project goals and challenge old models and assumptions. After the process analysis is complete, it's usually useful to revisit the goals, assumptions, and constraints defined during Phase 1 and to challenge each one. Can it be achieved? Can you do better? Is the assumption or constraint valid? Is there some alternative that will ease or remove the constraint? Revise the goals, assumptions, and constraints as appropriate. This is a good point at which the team might redraw the gap model to summarize what they have learned and what changes they are considering.

▶ Recommend changes in the effort as necessary. If, in analyzing the current version of a process, the team realizes that assumptions are wrong or that opportunities exist that weren't previously recognized, they should communicate their recommendations to the steering team or the executive committee and suggest changes in the scope of the project effort. Do not proceed to a redesign phase with flawed goals or assumptions. That's just a formula for a project that will end in acrimony.

▶ Summarize all the findings in a redesign plan. At the end of the effort, the redesign team should summarize their findings and propose a general approach to the redesign of the process. This redesign plan should take into account all of the assumptions, constraints, and opportunities the team has discovered.

▶ Present and defend the redesign plan before all of the higher-level committees and obtain their approval. Depending on the organization, this may be a public process or it might take place on a one-on-one basis. The key thing, at the end of each phase, is to obtain the approval and commitment of all those who will later have to assure that the new process is actually implemented. As with other employees, the team will need to explain the project in the terms each executive will understand, explaining the benefits of the change for that executive. If an important manager doesn't accept the proposal, it's better to stop and either deal with the objections or come up with a new design. The alternative is to create a plan that will be "dead on arrival," since a key manager won't support implementation.

Outcome

The outcome of this phase is a set of documents and models describing the existing (As-Is) process, a draft plan for the redesign of the existing process, and the support of all key senior managers.

Phase 3: Redesign Business Process

The goal of this phase is to create a design for a new or improved process. In some companies this phase is combined with the previous phase, and the design team moves smoothly from documenting the As-Is process to creating a new or To-Be process. In other cases, this phase is undertaken without having first undertaken Phase 2, or it is undertaken by a slightly different design team.

The actual work during this phase, as with the analysis phase, is normally accomplished during meetings between a facilitator and the process redesign team. The team that is to improve the process meets for 2–3 hours a day, usually in the morning, or for several days at a time, depending on the facilitator and team member schedules. The number of days or meetings will vary greatly depending on the scope of the project and the level of detail being created or redesigned.

Once again the facilitator runs the meetings and helps the team consider alternatives. The facilitator is usually supported by a scribe (or analyst) who takes notes on what the team decides. Between team meetings, the facilitator and the scribe work together to prepare documentation so that the team members will have it when they arrive for the next session. Many software tools include the ability to send results to team members via the Web so they can study them online between meetings.

Major Activities

The major activities in Phase 3 are illustrated in Figure 13.5.

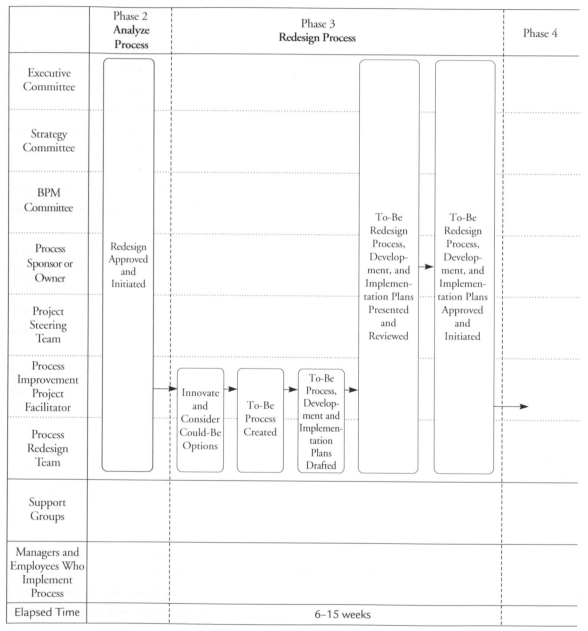

Figure 13.5 An overview of Phase 3 of the process redesign project.

▶ Review As-Is process and improvement goals, and identify specific opportunities to change the As-Is process. Depending on the scope of the design team's mandate and the schedule, the team may focus on very specific types of improvements, or may relax all possible assumptions and speculate about radically different ways of organizing the process.

▶ This is the point at which the redesign team ought to do some brainstorming and consider really innovative options. Generate a list of possible Could-Be processes and consider the benefits of each. If someone is skilled in TRIZ, this is a good point to use this innovation technique to help generate some alternative possibilities. In most cases, the solution will be obvious and the tendency will be to move quickly from the existing process to the obvious To-Be process. That tendency should be resisted, if possible, and some time should be spent considering if a real breakthrough in thinking about how the process is done is possible. A breakthrough isn't likely, but when it occurs it often results in huge savings or sharp increases in productivity, so it's worth considering.

▶ Design the new or improved process. The team's decisions should ultimately result in a new process that is documented on a *To-Be process diagram.* In complex projects, the team may create several alternative *Could-Be process diagrams* and then choose among them. The new design should eliminate disconnects and unneeded activities and streamline the activities, subprocesses, and the overall process whenever possible.

▶ Design a management process to support the new To-Be process diagram. The management process should specify who is responsible for each activity and subprocess. It should also establish measures for activities and subprocesses. This should be indicated on a *role/responsibility worksheet.*

▶ Rationalize reporting relationships. In some cases, changes in a process may suggest a new organizational chart that regroups employees and creates reporting relationships that will allow improved accountability and efficiency. New processes will probably require that employees and reporting relationships be established. In either case, the team should prepare a new organization chart indicating the hierarchy and reporting relationships of employees involved in the new or redesigned process. When appropriate, the process redesign team should review the actual jobs or roles involved in the process, and determine which functional managers will be responsible for which of the new process activities. This information is recorded on one or more *process/responsibility worksheets.*

▶ Cost or simulate new process options. In some cases, design teams will want to compare alternate Could-Be process options to each other or to the current As-Is business process. Or if the process is new, the team may want to simulate it to learn more about it. This can be very valuable, especially if the process is complex. Simulation often reveals problems that no one notices when simply looking at diagrams. To do costing or simulation, however, the team will have to use a software tool and will need the support of someone who has experience in building cost or simulation models. If the team is already using a tool like Proforma's Pro Vision, which is designed to represent To-Be process diagrams and do simulation, it will simply be a matter of entering more specific information about how each of the activities will function. If a spreadsheet is to be used, then the team will want to document the costs and times involved in each activity on an *activity cost worksheet*.

▶ Provide detailed documentation of new activities. If specific activities (i.e., jobs, software systems) are being modified or created, they should be documented on an *activity worksheet*.

▶ When the team arrives at a fully documented To-Be process design, it should arrange to present the proposal to the executive committee, project manager, and steering team. It's important that these groups not only understand the new process but approve it. These are the senior managers who will have to work to assure that the new process is actually implemented. A lukewarm approval from senior management is a recipe for a failed implementation phase.

Outcome

The outcome of this phase is documentation describing the new process and management structure that the design team proposes. This design will probably not be in enough detail to satisfy the requirements of software developers or of job analysts, but it should be sufficient to convey to business managers the exact changes that are being proposed. The redesign plan should be approved by senior managers.

Phase 4: Implement Redesigned Process

The goal of this phase is to acquire the space and resources, create the job descriptions, train employees, set up management systems, and create and test software systems needed to implement the new process.

The work of this phase is handled in a variety of different ways. In some cases, the design team is sophisticated enough to continue to refine the To-Be process diagram into a detailed software requirements document that can guide software developers. In other cases, the design team that created the To-Be process diagram and the activities worksheets will hand their work over to a new team that will develop specific software requirements. Similarly, the original design team may undertake the creation of new job descriptions, salary and incentive structures, and so forth. In most cases, however, they will pass their design on to specialists in the human resources group for detailed specification.

Major Activities

Figure 13.6 provides an overview of the activities in Phase 4.

As Figure 13.6 suggests, Phase 4 involves additional participants in the new process development effort. Although representatives of IT have probably been involved in the earlier phases, at this point they will shift and become active on IT software development teams if new software applications need to be created. Similarly, human resource specialists will probably work with other human performance specialists to redesign jobs and provide needed training if new jobs need to be created or if new skills need to be provided for those already working on the process being redesigned.

The managers on the process redesign team, working with others in their various functional areas, should refine the management systems, managerial job descriptions, and measures required to assure that all managers involved with the new process will understand the changes required and the new criteria by which their performance will be judged.

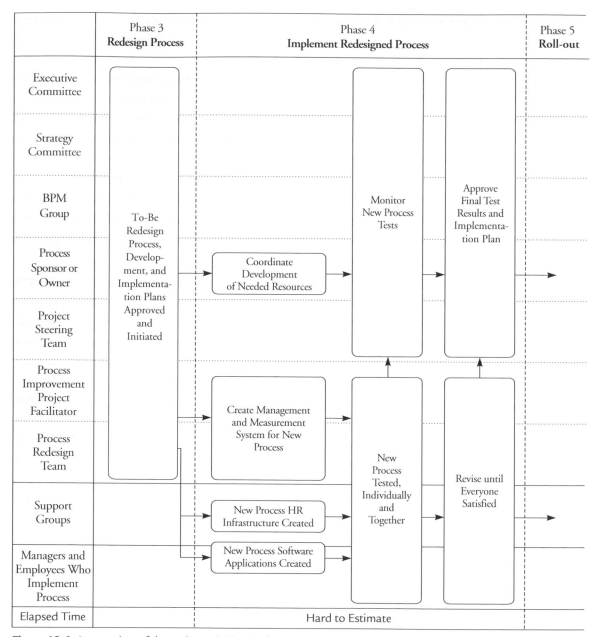

Figure 13.6 An overview of the major activities in Phase 4 of the redesign effort.

Various groups will test their work individually, and then, if it's a large process, it will probably be given some kind of field trial to assure all the pieces work together, before the new process completely replaces the old.

This phase varies in length, depending on the nature of the changes that were selected during the redesign phase. It also varies because different specialized groups may become involved in this phase. Thus, this phase usually begins with the development of a new plan by the steering team, working in conjunction with the various groups that will actually develop the infrastructure needed to implement the new process.

In a typical case, IT people will be engaged to create or acquire new software to implement activities in the new process that are to be automated. In the process they will probably need to refine the To-Be process diagrams to create more detailed *workflow models, use case models,* and any of a variety of other UML software diagrams, depending on the nature of the software application to be developed.

Human resource people will be engaged to create new or modified job descriptions and to negotiate needed changes with unions and existing employees. Training people will develop materials necessary to train employees to perform new tasks. In the course of their work, human performance analysts will probably develop *job diagrams* and prepare *job analysis worksheets.* (See Chapter 6 for a discussion of how human resources might follow up the work of the process redesign team.)

During this same period, the managers involved in the effort should create or refine their management system. If the company is already organized around processes, and the process team is headed by the manager for the process being redesigned, then it will be much easier. In this case, it is a matter of refining how the process management team functions and checking all existing goals and measures to assure that they conform with the changes in the process. If, on the other hand, the company is not organized around processes, this is the point at which they ought to consider doing so. Obviously, a shift in the management of the organization will need to involve the executive committee and cannot be undertaken lightly. A project manager will need to be appointed. Managers currently reporting to department heads will need to be reoriented to become members of the process team and to report to the process manager. Goals, measures, and incentive systems will need to be renegotiated. Some measures and incentives may continue to flow from the department structure, but most should be tied to the overall performance of the process. If a company is really converting to process management, this can easily become a redesign project in its own right.

The alternative: To redesign a process, and then leave subprocess managers responsible to department heads and not to an overall process manager is a recipe for failure. In spite of the redesign, departmental managers will tend to manage to achieve goals chosen for departments and not for the process, and silo thinking will tend to reinsert gaps and disconnects where information and materials are passed between departmental units.

Outcome

This phase ends when the various groups developing infrastructure and materials needed to implement the new process have completed their work and tested their materials.

Phase 5: Roll-out the Redesigned Process

The goal of this phase is to transition to the new process. Many companies have redesigned processes and then failed to actually roll them out. This occurs for a variety of reasons. The foremost reason is that senior managers resist the change. Even managers who recognize that the old process is defective may be unwilling to endure the hassles and problems that changing to the new process will entail. Functional managers may not want to make seemingly minor changes in the way things are done within a department to support the goals of a process that's largely outside the focus of the department. Similarly, employees may resist using the new procedures or the new software systems.

The process sponsor and the steering team should plan for the transition. They should work with senior executives to assure that they have the "push" they will need to get all the relevant managers to try the new process. They should work with middle managers and employees to convince them of the advantages of the new process. In many cases, salaries and incentive systems will need to be changed to assure that managers and employees are rewarded for implementing the new procedures. And they should work with managers responsible for the process, at all levels, to assure that they have management plans in place so that the managers can measure the success of the new process.

Major Activities

Figure 13.7 provides an overview of what takes place in Phase 5.

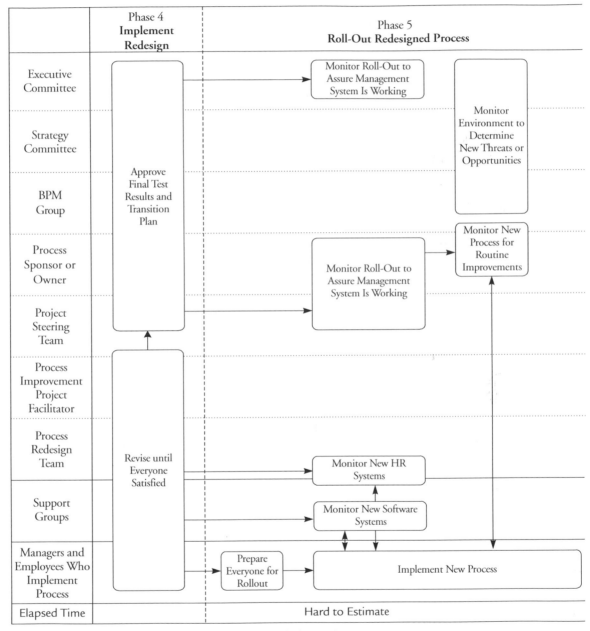

Figure 13.7 Major activities in Phase 5 of a process redesign project.

Few people like change. We all rely on habitual behaviors to make our tasks easier, and change upsets all that. Major changes, in which some employees are laid off and others need to learn to use new software systems, result in even more dissatisfaction. If employees, supervisors, and managers don't see the reason for the change, it's much worse. Thus, a good transition plan calls for meetings that acquaint everyone involved with the nature of the change and the reasons for it.

It also requires managerial pressure to assure there is no backsliding. Senior managers on the project steering team need to communicate to the managers below them their support for the change. The new management system needs to provide ways for senior managers to measure the results of the change, and everyone needs to understand that those measures will be carefully watched to make sure the new process works as designed.

If the change is extensive, then individuals need to be designated so that anyone having problems can get in contact with someone who can deal with the problem. Senior managers should follow up their initial meetings with subsequent meetings to let everyone know that the desired new results are being obtained and that management appreciates everyone's effort.

The activities of this phase vary greatly, according to the nature of the new process, the amount of change required, management support, and the resistance offered by those currently performing the process. In many cases the work of this phase will be subcontracted to a team of change management specialists.

Outcome

The outcome of this phase is a new process. Beyond the transition, managers will need to work to assure that the new process meets its goals and to identify new problems that will require subsequent changes. Maintaining a process is a full-time management job.

Summary

By way of a quick summary, the major phases in a process redesign project include:

▶ Phase 1: Understand Project
▶ Phase 2: Analyze Process
▶ Phase 3: Redesign Process
▶ Phase 4: Implement Redesigned Process
▶ Phase 5: Roll-out Redesigned Process

Figure 13.9 provides a slightly different way of looking at a process redesign project. In this case, we have listed the phases as a series of boxes. Within each box we have listed the key objective and the major steps in each phase. We have also listed the diagrams and the worksheets used in each phase. We have already described the various diagrams in early chapters. We will provide examples of the worksheets in later chapters. We mention them here to lay the groundwork for their use in the case study. In most cases, companies won't use the worksheets, and we provide them only as a way of showing the kind of information that a company needs to gather and the decisions that should be documented.

This overview cannot begin to provide detailed information about what should happen in each phase of a redesign project. Hopefully, however, it provides an introduction, and it should become clearer as we consider a detailed case study in Chapter 16.

Major Steps and Objectives   *Diagrams and Worksheets That May be Used*

Corporate Process Management

    Undertaken by executive committee, strategy committee, process architecture committee, or process sponsor

Determine corporate strategy	Organization goals and measures worksheet
Identify opportunities and threats	Supersystem diagram of organization
Identify corporate processes to be improved	Value chain diagram
Scope projects	
Set general goals for project	

Phase 1: Understand Project

    Undertaken by process sponsor, steering team, and project facilitator

Refine scope of project	Detailed diagram of organization
Establish project schedule and plan	Organization opportunities and threats worksheet
	Project plan and business case

Phase 2: Analyze Process

    Undertaken by project facilitator and process redesign team

Define As-Is process	Detailed diagram of organization
Define As-Is activities	As-Is process diagrams to various levels of detail
Define As-Is management system	As-Is process analysis and improvement worksheet
Identify key disconnects	As-Is specic activity analysis worksheetfi
	As-Is activity cost worksheet

Phase 3: Process Redesign

    Undertaken by project facilitator and process redesign team

Eliminate disconnects and improve process fit	To-Be process diagrams to various levels of detail
Define May-Be processes	To-Be process diagrams with measures
Define To-Be process	To-Be process analysis and improvement worksheet
Define To-Be activities	To-Be specific activity analysis worksheet
Define To-Be management system	To-Be activity cost worksheet
	Process/function role/responsibility worksheet

Phase 4: Implement Redesigned Process

    Managed by project sponsor; undertaken by several specialized teams

Create and test new software needed for new process	To-Be workflow model
Create new job descriptions required	Use case and other software models
Develop training	Job model
	Job analysis worksheets

Phase 5: Roll-out Redesigned Process

    Managed by business managers responsible for the new process

        Manage transition and change

        Manage ongoing process

13.8 An overview of process redesign.

Notes and References

Once again, many of the ideas incorporated in the BPTrends methodology are derived from conversations Roger Burlton and I have had. Other ideas derived from discussions with Geary Rummler.

There are many good books that describe redesign methodologies in more detail. Among some of the best are:

Burlton, Roger T., *Business Process Management: Profiting from Process,* SAMS, 2001. Lots of practical advice.

Jeston, John and Johan Nelis, *Business Process Management: Practical Guidelines to Successful Implementations,* Elsevier, 2006. A new methodology book that provides considerable detail.

Manganelli, Raymond L., and Mark M. Klein, *The Reengineering Handbook: A Step-by-Step Guide to Business Transformation*, American Management Association, 1994. Lots of practical advice and a step-by-step methodology.

Kubeck, Lynn C., *Techniques for Business Process Redesign: Tying It All Together*, Wiley-QED Publication, 1995. Another good book with information on phases and what has to happen when.

Petrozzo, Daniel P., and John C. Stepper, *Successful Reengineering*, Van Nostrand Reinhold, 1994. Another good summary of successful practices.

Grover, Varun, and William J. Kettinger (Eds.), *Business Process Change: Reengineering Concepts, Methods and Technologies*, Idea Group Publishing, 1995. A book of readings. Some of the chapters are excellent and provide information on specific techniques.

There are a number of good books on facilitation. My particular favorite is by Ingrid Bens and is *Facilitation at a Glance!: A Pocket Guide of Tools and Techniques for Effective Meeting Facilitation,* GOLA/QPC, 1999. This small pocket book pulls many techniques together.

chapter

14

The Ergonomic Systems Case Study

THE ERGONOMIC SYSTEMS, INC. CASE STUDY is hypothetical. We did not want to describe problems associated with any specific client. At the same time, we wanted a case that would give us an opportunity to cover the full range of process redesign techniques we have discussed in this section of the book. Thus, we created a case study that blends the characteristics and problems faced by several companies we have worked with in the past several years. (We've never worked with an office furniture company.) With those qualifications, we have tried to make the case study as realistic as possible so that readers will get a good idea of the problems they will face when they seek to implement the concepts and techniques we have described.

We will consider the case study in four parts. First, we will consider how the strategy committee of Ergonomic Systems analyzed their position in the market and arrived at a new position and new goals for the company. Next, we will consider the redesign effort that Ergonomic Systems undertook. To simplify our discussion, we will focus on the redesign of the key Ergonomic Systems Ergo Chair value chain. We will also consider how Ergonomic Systems redesigned their Ergo Chair management system to support the new process design. Finally, we'll comment on the actual transition process and the implementation of the new Ergo Chair process at the company.

Ergonomic Systems, Inc.

Ergonomic Systems, Inc. is a midsize company with sales of approximately $646 million in 2000. It is a subsidiary of a larger company, but it operates independently, and we'll focus only on Ergonomic Systems in this study. The company was initially built around a new design for executive office chairs for high-tech environments. The Ergo Chair is especially designed for executives who spend a significant portion of their time interacting with computers. It's comfortable, has an impressive appearance, and has proved popular with high-tech companies throughout the 1990s. The company has since created a number of other more specialized lines of Ergo Chairs. Recently it has also begun to sell "office environments"—modular units that can be assembled into work areas with features especially useful for workers who are using computers. Indeed, in a major reorganization just after it was acquired in 1999, it changed its name from Ergonomic Chairs to Ergonomic Systems to emphasize its commitment to provide complete office environments and not just chairs.

In addition to chairs and modular office units, the company sells a variety of other high-tech office products, including some desk lamps and several devices to hold and connect computer systems together and power them up or down with a single switch. Throughout the 12-year life of the company, the executive chair line has always been the company's best-known product line. Since 1999, however, the company has begun to reposition itself as an office systems company, stressing its ability to create entire office suites. Meanwhile, larger, more established office furniture companies have introduced lines of executive chairs that have many of the features of the Ergo Chair, and the competition has begun to cut into Ergonomic Systems' growth.

Figure 14.1 provides an organization chart that shows how Ergonomic Systems is organized. It has functional departments, which are subdivided into North American and European groups, and it has vice presidents for each of the company's three major value chains. All VPs and SVPs shown in Figure 14.1 are on the executive committee, along with the CEO. Three of them, the heads of marketing, engineering and design, and finance, are also on the strategy committee, which has its own research staff. Three others, including the VPs for IT, the SVP of Marketing and the VP of Engineering & Design are on a technology subcommittee that is charged with exploring the latest technological options. The business process architecture committee includes the three VPs for product lines and the head of IT.

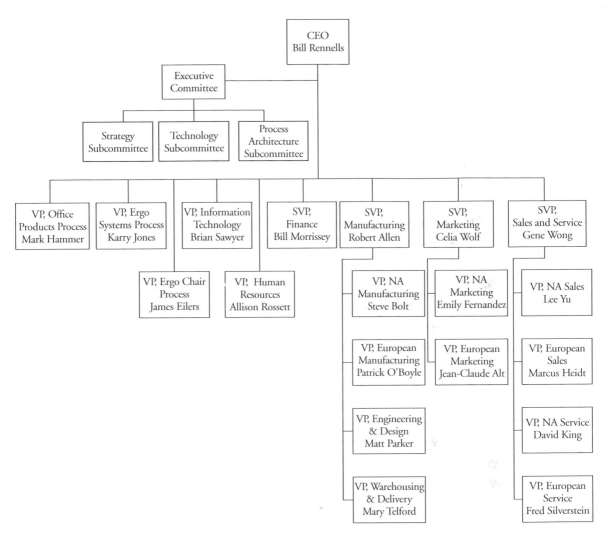

Figure 14.1 High-level organization chart for Ergonomic Systems.

Ergonomic Systems is a process-oriented company and has been since before it was acquired. The company did business process reengineering (BPR) in the mid-1990s and uses a variety of ERP applications they acquired in the late 1990s. It has a matrix organization in which business line managers are responsible for processes, while departmental managers are responsible for activities performed by people in their departments. Ergonomic's business process efforts have recently been revitalized as the company begins to think about how its processes will be changed by the Internet.

Figure 14.2 provides an overview of the company's process architecture. Ergonomic has three value chains, each divided into major business processes. The various support processes, like IT and human resources, aren't shown in the diagram.

Ergonomic Systems manufactures and sells a high-quality line of office chairs and system modules. They are well regarded in the industry and by high-tech companies and have won several awards for their products. An Ergo Chair has been acquired by the San Francisco Museum of Modern Art for its permanent design collection. The company charges a premium price for its products. The company believes that it has about 5% of the market for business and institutional furniture in the United States and slightly less in Europe. The company's sales grew by 5% last year—during a period in which the Business and Institutional Furniture Manufacturers Association (BIFMA) reported that total U.S. sales grew by 4.4%. Ergonomic Systems hopes its office systems products will allow it to continue modest growth. The company's overall strategy, however, is not to become a dominant vendor, but to remain a specialized, high-quality vendor that can maintain a high profit margin. Ergonomic Systems currently has the highest after-tax return on net sales in the industry—12.4%. It has consistently paid its stockholders the highest dividends of any BIFMA member for the past six years.

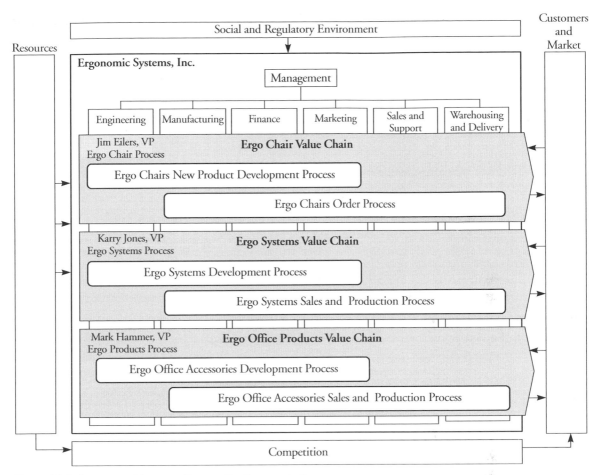

Figure 14.2 Process architecture diagram for Ergonomic Systems.

Figure 14.3 illustrates a worksheet that the executive committee completed at the end of last year, after reviewing Ergonomic Systems' strategy, goals, and performance as part of an annual review.

Organization Goals and Measures Worksheet			
For the Organization as a Whole			
Organization Goals	Measures	Desired Performance	Actual Performance
Ergonomic Systems will sell the best-designed and manufactured office systems for high-tech environments. Our products will consistently command the best prices for high-tech office and industrial settings. We will maintain the highest profit margins in the industry. We will maintain modest growth.	Comparison of sale price of Ergo Chair and two closest competitors After-tax return on net sales Sales growth judged by BIFMA and EuroFMA	Our products will sell for at least 5% more than competitive products. Our after-tax returns on net sales will exceed 10%. Our growth in chairs will be 3% NA and 5% Europe. Our growth in office systems will be 5% NA and 8% Europe.	Results, Fiscal Year 1999: Our products sold for 5.6% more than competitive products. Our profit margins were 12.4%. Our growth in chairs was 4.3% in North America and 4.7% in Europe. Our growth in office systems was 5.2% in North America and 9.3% in Europe.
As Assigned to Specific Value Chains or Processes			
Value Chain	Assigned Goals	Measures	Desired Performance	Actual Performance
Ergo Chair Value	Best-designed chairs Command best price Maintain highest margins Maintain growth goals	Design reviews Sale price comparisons Profit margins Sales growth	Win design competitions, mentions in design press. Chairs will sell for at least 5% more than competitive products. Our profit margins will exceed 80%. Our growth in chairs will be 3% NA and 5% Europe.	New Ergo Conference Chair won gold star in Business Week design awards. Original Ergo Executive Chair added to SF MOMA design collection and given award. Results, Fiscal Year 1999: Our chairs sold for an average of 6.8% more than competitive chairs. Our profit margins were 89%. Our growth in chairs was 4.3% in North America and 4.7% in Europe.
Office System Value				
Office Products Value Chain				

Figure 14.3 Existing Ergonomic Systems goals and measures worksheet.

An E-Business Strategy

When the Internet first burst on the business world in the late 1990s, Ergonomic Systems, Inc. initially decided to ignore it. They had always stressed sales through distributors and targeted ads in high-tech magazines and thought it unlikely that they could sell their expensive chairs online. Within two years, however, they realized they had made a serious mistake. Their leading customers were companies that rapidly adopted new computer technologies and were willing to buy expensive systems online. In fact, they soon began to insist on buying online. In 1999 the Ergonomic strategy committee proposed that Ergonomic Systems make a major effort to transition to an e-business company.

Ergonomic Systems' CEO, Bill Rennells, rejected the initial strategy committee note about e-business and sent a memo to all of the members of the executive and strategy committees. In essence, Rennells said:

Your e-business proposal sounds too much like a popular magazine article that argues that we must all become e-business companies or die. I don't run a company that responds to fads like that. This company is driven by a strategy and by specific goals derived from that strategy. At the moment, our strategy calls for us to sell well-designed, premium-priced office systems to companies whose workers spend a lot of time using computers. We have a well-developed and loyal group of distributors and I'm not sure how using the Internet would play with them. If the Internet or any related technologies can help us achieve our goals more effectively or more efficiently, I'm all for considering how to use them. If we need to have a Web site to sell to our customers, I'm certainly in favor of that. But I don't want to adopt technology for its own sake, or just because other companies are. I'm certainly not interested in changing this company from an office systems vendor into an "e-business company"—whatever that is. We've put a lot of effort into refining our market position and integrating our processes so that they efficiently generate our products. Please reconsider your report carefully, and only resubmit it when you can show how the Internet can help us implement our overall business strategy.

For a while nothing was done because this happened just before talks were initiated that led to Ergonomic Chairs being acquired and repositioned as Ergonomic Systems. Adding new lines kept everyone busy. In 2000, however, even Bill Rennells had become concerned about the Internet. Key distributors had begun to tell Ergonomic Systems that they wanted to buy and obtain information online. This time it was the executive committee that asked the strategy committee to review Internet and Web technologies in the light of what customers were asking for and competitors were doing, and make suggestions about how these new technologies might result in an implementation of the company strategy.

Since the Internet was deemed both a strategic issue and a technological issue, the two subcommittees met together to analyze the potential of the technology and how any use of it might support or change the company's strategy.

The Joint Subcommittee's Review of E-Business

As requested, the joint subcommittee met, assigned research to staff, reviewed the results, and prepared a new report on the opportunities and threats posed by the Internet, Web, and online business activity.

The subcommittee began its report by reviewing the company's existing goals and concluding that none of them would need to be altered in any major way. The goal would still be for Ergonomic Systems to focus on the quality producer and premium-price niche in the office chairs market. The Internet and associated technologies would enable the company to better implement its existing strategy, however, by providing better service to some customers while simultaneously improving the coordination of internal process and developing tighter and more efficient relationships with suppliers. By selling online, the subcommittee suggested that margins and growth could be improved. By modifying the Ergo Chair business process, the subcommittee argued that Ergonomic Systems could save money and thereby increase profit margins. The subcommittee projected that growth could be increased in North America from the current target of 3% to 4%. At the same time, they suggested that sales order cycle time could be reduced by an average of 3 days. All of these assumptions were based on the root assumption that they would be selling 25% of their chairs via the Internet by the end of the year. Online sales of 25% is high for a company switching to the Internet, but several of their key distributors had already indicated that they would switch to Internet orders. In addition, the company decided to reach beyond its distributors and try for direct, or individual, small business sales.

The report noted that everyone was talking about the recent bankruptcies of several dot.com companies, but it also pointed out that Ergonomic has lost two major distributors as a result of Ergonomics' lack of an Internet sales system. It also pointed out that all their leading competitors were continuing to develop their Web sites and stressing online sales, in spite of the dot.com crash. Finally, the report stressed that a survey suggested that the company's image as a company that sold high-tech products to high-tech companies was being undermined by its lack of a Web site.

The strategy committee summarized the opportunities and threats they perceived in Figure 14.4. They realized that some of the opportunities and threats cut across process lines, while others were more specific to the Ergo Chair process that they had been tasked to examine in more detail.

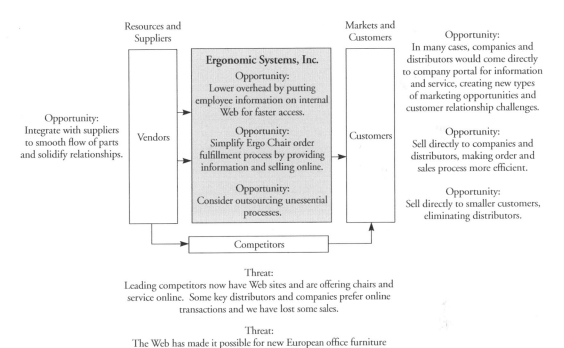

Figure 14.4 Threats and opportunities facing Ergonomic Systems.

The strategy committee also prepared an opportunities and threats worksheet (Figure 14.5) and wrote a report that explained their findings and suggested initiatives in keeping with the company's strategy. In effect, they urged several changes in the company strategy, although not in the company's overall focus.

Organization Opportunities and Threats Worksheet				
Supersystem	Opportunities	Problems/Threats	Action Required	Value Chains or Processes Involved
Customers, Distributors, and Markets	B2C: Improve support to customers that want to use Web and email. B2C: Acquire new customers that will buy online. B2C: Reduce costs of providing support to customers by using email and putting support materials online.	B2C: Losing customers by not providing online access. B2C: Reduce costs of providing support to customers by using email and putting support materials online. B2C: What do we do about shipping single chairs to individuals or small companies? B2C: How much will it cost to produce single chairs on demand?	Major revision of Ergo Chair Value Chain/Order Process to incorporate a Customer Portal or Web site.	Ergo Chair Value Chain/Order Process
Suppliers	B2B: Improve efficiency and smoothness of supply chain system by extending it to all suppliers (reduce inventory). B2B: Improve costs by eliminating existing EDI system. B2B: Make it possible to adjust more quickly to requests for small runs. B2B: Link in key suppliers with supply chain coupled with a more efficient, automatic payment system.	B2B: How do we convert all suppliers to a common set of standards to describe parts?	Major revision of Ergo Chair Value Chain/Order Process/Manufacturing Subprocess to incorporate a Supply Chain System that links Ergonomic Systems to all first and second tier suppliers.	Ergo Chair Value Chain/Order Process

Figure 14.5 Opportunities and threats worksheet for Ergonomic Systems.

Ergonomic Systems Adopts Some New Goals

Two days after Ergonomic Systems' CEO received the report and recommendations of the strategy committee, he scheduled a special meeting of the executive committee. Bill Rennells asked all of the heads of the company's departments who are members of the executive committee, as well as a number of technical specialists, to join him at a nearby resort where they would be isolated from other concerns during the course of their 3-day meeting.

A week later, with everyone gathered at the resort, Mr. Rennells began the meeting by asking Matt Parker, the head of the strategy committee, to summarize their

Organization Opportunities and Threats Worksheet (continued)				
Supersystem	Opportunities	Problems/Threats	Action Required	Value Chains or Processes Involved
Competition		B2C: Leading competitors already offer online sales and have taken key customers. B2B: Leading competitors have already started to link with suppliers and may develop better relationships with our key suppliers. B2B2C: Some of our systems suppliers may begin to sell directly to potential clients, undercutting our prices.	See above.	Ergo Chair Value Chain/Order Process
Resources and Technologies				
Government Regulation and Social Trends				
Organizational Improvements and Operational Efficiencies	B2E: Employee Web site: Provide more information to employees while reducing cost of doing so. B2E: Email: Make it possible for everyone in the company to communicate more efficiently. B2E: Email: Make it possible for management to get information more quickly.	B2E: Email: Company is less secure if company doesn't get involved and set standards and create firewalls for employees already using email.	Develop company-wide email system. Develop a new email-based management information system for Ergo Chair/Order Process. Develop Human Resources Internal Portal or Web site. Create groups in IT to support internal and external portals and company-wide email system.	Ergo Chair Value Chain/Order Process Human Resources Support Process Management Process IT Support Process

recommendations. Following that, given that so many of the recommendations involved the use of information systems, Rennells asked Bryan Sawyer, the VP of IT, to add any comments.

Matt Parker, the head of the strategy committee, began by emphasizing what he considered the main points. There were, he argued, two key things to consider. First, some distributors were buying online, and many more were considering it. Second, the Internet made it possible to increase productivity by improving the flow of communications and data within the company and between the company and its suppliers. He went on to say that several customers, office wholesalers and end users who had previously bought chairs from the company, had inquired about buying online. Second, he pointed out that human resources was now getting more email requests for information about employee pension, health, and benefit plans than phone calls or memos. Next, he pointed out that there was a move afoot by several of the parts vendors who supplied Ergonomic Systems to create an online e-market for ordering parts. He also pointed out that their main competitors, the larger office equipment manufacturers, had introduced Web sites and seemed to be moving to selling online. Finally, he explained that, when marketing and sales costs, discounts, and commissions were added together, it currently cost Ergonomic 22% to sell a $700 chair. By making some assumptions about the cost of doing business over the Internet, he estimated that it would only cost 12% to market and sell a chair online.

At this point the meeting broke up into a heated discussion as different managers challenged Mr. Parker's assumptions. Gene Wong, the head of sales, argued that he was ignoring the fact the most sales were bulk sales and that, in any case, the overhead for maintaining the sales force couldn't be cut the way Parker proposed, since most sales would still come from sales calls and the cost of the sales infrastructure would be almost the same, even if online sales eliminated 20% of the sales force.

Brian Sawyer, the VP of information technology, suggested that if the company was really going to embrace the Internet, it should probably consider pushing direct sales to individuals, something it didn't do at that point. Moreover, he suggested that if they did begin to sell online, they might get more sales overseas and that would create lots of shipping problems that they didn't currently face.

In response to questions about the costs and problems of supporting online sales, Mr. Sawyer explained that they wouldn't be that great. Ergonomic didn't have a very extensive product line, and it wouldn't require a very elaborate application to support online sales. He pointed out that most of Ergonomics' software applications had been created by outside vendors and that they were now offering links to the Internet. In addition, other vendors offered packages that Ergonomic could use to develop a Web presence with a minimum of fuss. He suggested that the company could be ready to sell online within 6 months, if they really decided they wanted to move in that direction. At the same time, he urged the group to consider that they might get a greater return by simplifying their supply chain systems and integrating their existing production system using the Internet.

The VP of marketing, Celia Wolf, argued that Ergonomic was experiencing growing difficulties in expanding their customer base. She argued that the problems resulted partly from their high-end positioning and partly from the fact that the wholesalers they dealt with were increasingly favoring contracts with the larger office equipment companies that could offer them packaged deals across entire lines of office furniture. If they wanted to maintain their current positioning, Ms. Wolf argued, they needed to find a way to significantly increase their market. She suggested that a major move into the European market and sales to individuals who work at home were both priorities. Moreover, she believed that both could be significantly helped by an Internet presence and online sales.

The discussion raged for most of the entire first day. In the late afternoon, Mr. Rennells and the managers created a list of topics to try to resolve and set up groups that would work on each topic during the evening and the following morning. Tomorrow afternoon, after they had heard from the various groups, they would pull everything together, identify action items, and prioritize them.

Without following the twists and turns of the next 24 hours, suffice it to say that by the afternoon of the following day the executive committee had decided to embrace the Internet. They concluded that they wouldn't try to completely change the company overnight, but that they would prepare to support four changes in the way the company did business.

1. They would create a portal that would allow customers and prospects to contact the company via the Web. On the portal they would provide information about the firm, a product catalog, the ability to order either wholesale or retail, and support for products. They decided to initially only support the sale of Ergo Chairs on the Web and only sell chairs online to those who paid in advance or had established credit lines.
2. They would create a new supply chain system with all first-tier Ergo Chair parts suppliers. The supply chain would be linked to the existing production system so that it would automatically generate orders as supplies dropped. The system would also be linked to the company's accounting system so that payments would be transferred to vendors as soon as new parts arrived.
3. They would examine their Ergo Chair value chain to see where they could improve productivity by relying more heavily on the Internet, and they would begin offering

chairs for sale online, via a portal that would also provide marketing information and service support.

4. In addition, they decided to create an internal employee Web site that human resources would manage, to make it easier for employees to obtain information from human resources.

The executive committee decided that the highest priority goal was to develop a portal and begin selling to selected distributors on the Web. Given the key role of the Ergo Chair value chain in achieving this goal, the executive committee decided to set up a task force to review the entire process by which chairs were manufactured, sold, and delivered. In effect, they decided that they were going to redesign the Ergo Chair Order Fulfillment process, and in the process they were going to design and integrate a portal into that process. They also decided they weren't in a position to decide how much change the production process could absorb without thinking about it in a lot more detail. Jim Eilers, the VP of the Ergo Chair process, was designated sponsor of the Ergo Chair redesign effort. He was asked to create a business process redesign task force that would be charged with developing several alternative options and estimating the risk and disruption involved in each and then report back. This task force was to pay special attention to the portal the company would develop to sell chairs online.

Separate task forces would be charged with planning the changes in human resources and in planning the new supply chain system.

To help Eilers with the Ergo Chair value chain redesign effort, Mr. Rennells appointed several members of the executive committee to serve on a steering team to oversee and evaluate the proposed changes.

Phase 1: Understand the Redesign of the Order Process Project

The day after the executive committee concluded its meeting, James Eilers phoned David Sutton. He'd met Dr. Sutton when he'd headed production at Computec, Inc. several years ago. Computec had completely redesigned its Order Fulfillment process with Dr. Sutton's help, and Mr. Eilers remembered how smooth and systematic the effort had been. Eilers wasn't at all sure this effort would be as smooth, since the Internet seemed to impact more aspects of the Ergonomic operations and to raise a lot more questions and controversy about what should actually be done. That, however, in Mr. Eilers' mind, made it even more important that Ergonomic follow a systematic methodology that would give everyone a say and proceed in a manner that everyone could buy into.

Dr. Sutton agreed to facilitate the Ergonomic Systems business redesign process. Dr. Sutton and his associate, Mrs. Lee, arrived at Ergonomic Systems 3 weeks later, and he and Jim Eilers kicked off the redesign planning phase of the project.

The understanding phase took 3 weeks. The steering team had already been appointed and a considerable amount of work on identifying the opportunities and threats had occurred. In this case, the redesign planning effort focused on defining the scope of the project and on preparing a report for the steering committee.

The process sponsor and the facilitator reviewed the value chain diagram provided by the process architecture subcommittee and the opportunities and threats worksheet to assure that they had a clear idea of the scope of the project. At the same time, in conjunction with the process sponsor, the facilitator prepared the detailed organization diagram shown in Figure 14.6 to document how Ergonomic Systems conceptualizes the key relationships between internal functions and its environment.

The steering team was asked to identify individuals who could serve on the process redesign team and assure that they would have the time needed to work on the project. Individuals from each department involved in the process were assigned. Similarly, a mix of managers, supervisors, and workers were assigned to assure that the redesign team had a broad perspective. Individuals from IT and human resources were also assigned.

One of the key decisions that Eilers and Sutton agreed to was that the redesign effort would attempt two things. First, without regard to the Internet-based changes they were mandated to attempt, they would review the current process and look for ways it could be made more efficient. Then, they would see how the mandated Internet changes could improve the process beyond that.

Eilers and Sutton developed a plan that reviewed the goals of the project and established a schedule that would result in a redesigned process in just under 3 months. They presented their plan to the steering committee, received approval, and proceeded to Phase 2.

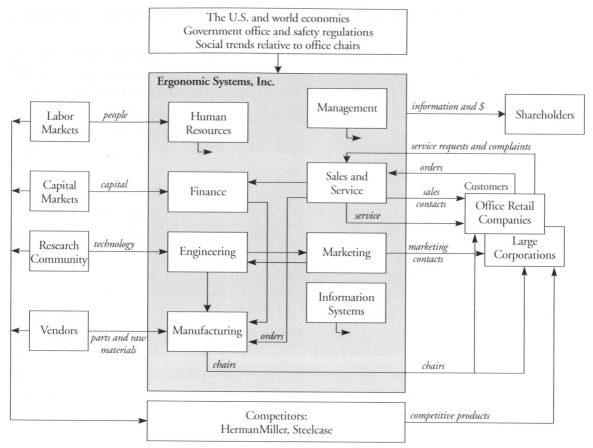

Figure 14.6 Organization diagram for Ergonomic Systems.

Phase 2: Analyzing the Order Fulfillment Process

The week after the steering committee approved the plan for the redesign effort, David Sutton began work on the second phase of the project.

The key to the analysis of the As-Is version of the Ergo Chair Order Fulfillment process was to develop a detailed understanding of how the existing process currently worked. Sutton interviewed each of the process redesign team members to see how they would describe the process and what kinds of problems they would identify. Sutton also talked to a number of managers and supervisors who weren't on the process redesign team to gain a broader understanding of the process and any problems that it might have.

When all the interviews were completed, Sutton and his assistant, Mrs. Lee, worked up a rough overview of the Ergonomic Chairs Order Fulfillment process. Sutton presented this on the first day the process redesign team met to provide everyone with a way of understanding of how they would be documenting the process. He had two versions of the "strawman" process-one printed on 8 1/2 by 11-inch paper for each team member, and another larger version drawn on a whiteboard that covered one wall of the meeting room.

After introductions and a description of the process they would undertake, Sutton began to walk the team through the diagrams. The first diagram was of the entire Order Fulfillment process divided into six subprocesses (see Figure 14.7). The second diagram was a more detailed look at just the Sales and Order Entry subprocess, which they considered in more detail.

Predictably, Sutton was interrupted by members who saw problems with the "strawman" diagram. In some cases, activities had been omitted. In other cases, members wanted decision points made more explicit. Much of the discussion simply involved settling on the level of detail that the first process diagram should include. Once everyone understood that subsequent groups would define each subprocess shown on the high-level process diagram in more detail, things began to move more quickly.

After agreeing on the high-level diagram, the team began to drill down and refine some of the details of how an order would flow through the various order-fulfillment processes. By the end of the first week, the team arrived at a first version of the As-Is diagram. We have shown a portion of that diagram in Figure 14.8. This diagram shows specific activities and identifies the two major software systems used in the Ergo Chair Order Fulfillment process: the Customer Order and Credit System owned by finance and shared with sales, and the Production Management System used by manufacturing.

Ergonomic Systems: Ergo Chairs Order Fullfillment Process

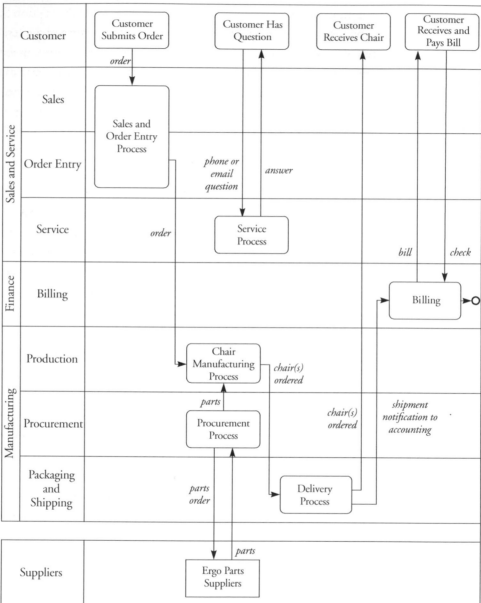

Figure 14.7 An overview of the Ergo Chair Order Fulfillment process.

At this point groups were set up to examine specific subprocesses in more detail. One group from manufacturing wanted to analyze the Production Scheduling process in more detail, while another group, mostly from finance and sales, chose to examine the Credit Check process in more detail. Still another group, made up of managers, focused on describing the measures currently used by managers to evaluate the existing process. Although the process and the management evaluations took place in parallel, we'll ignore discussion of the results of the management subcommittee until a later chapter. We will also ignore the fact that the Order process was slightly different at different locations and that the team designed slightly different processes to describe site variations. In addition, we have also omitted marketing and support activities that would occur beyond the edges of the diagram shown.

Since the next diagram gets quite a bit more complex, we'll shift and only focus on the activities in the Sales and Service Order Entry process and the Finance process as it relates to the Customer orders. (In other words, we'll ignore the Manufacturing process, since it quickly evolves into a supply chain design problem.)

Consider Figure 14.8. It suggests that three departments are directly involved in the Ergo Chain Order process: sales, finance, and manufacturing. Functional groups within each group were identified to make it clear which managers, supervisors, and employees would be responsible for the subprocesses and activities shown on the diagram. Thus, for example, three functions within the manufacturing department were identified: production management system, production, and packaging and shipping. In addition, it was decided that the existing production management software system should be represented as a function since so many different management activities interacted with this system.

A swimlane for customers was placed at the top of the chart. No effort was made to discriminate between customers that were wholesale distributors and those that were the purchasing managers of large companies, although more detailed process descriptions might drill down into that distinction. No individuals were shown on the vertical axis, but two functions were represented by software systems.

Both software systems had been developed in the past and have been in use for several years. One was a financial application that maintained records of customers, undertook credit checks, and prepared invoices. This application had been acquired from an ERP software vendor that specialized in financial packages. The system ran on a mainframe and relied on a database that was an integral part of the application.

Ergonomic Systems, Inc.: Ergo Chair Value Chain: Order Fullfillment Process

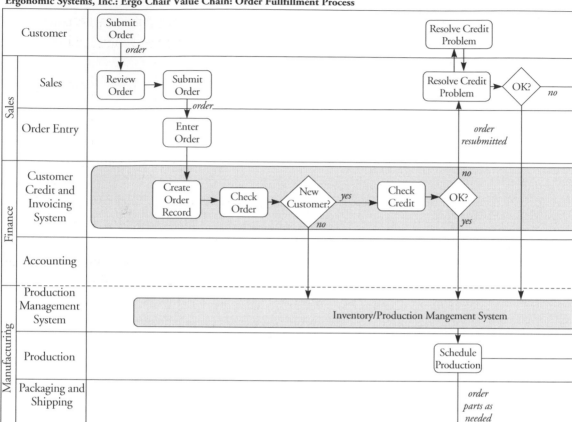

Figure 14.8 As-Is process diagram for the Ergo Chair Order process.

The other application had been developed internally by the Ergonomic Systems IT group. It controlled the inventory and production process. This system ran on a linked set of Unix platforms located at the various manufacturing sites. As each order was entered into the system, a record was created. When the order was approved by finance, the production of the order was scheduled. When the schedule was created, inventory was checked to see if additional parts would be needed for the specific order. If parts were needed, that information would show up on a report. The individual responsible for monitoring inventory would prepare and mail purchase orders to the appropriate parts vendors.

If the customer was new, and especially if the order was large, finance would ask the salespeople to request an advance payment for some or all of the order. Since

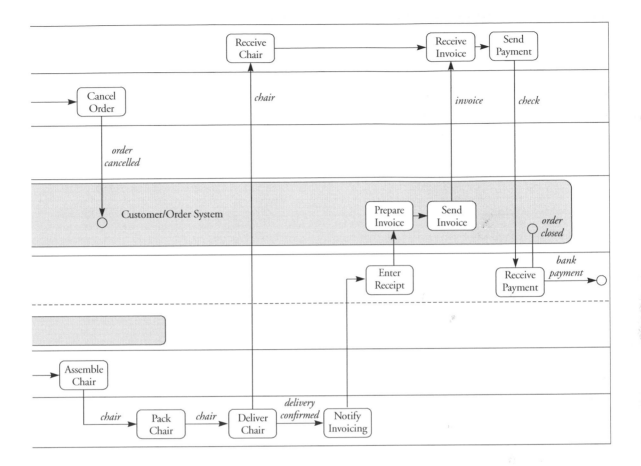

orders tended to be large and Ergonomic Systems had multiple plants and warehouses located close to major metropolitan areas, most shipping was undertaken by trucks owned by Ergonomic Systems. Once orders had been delivered, the shipping group would transmit the customer receipt to finance and they would initiate billing and handle the payment.

Once the basic diagram was complete, the redesign task force considered how it might be improved. Before considering any of the Internet features that the executive committee had mandated, the team discussed disconnects or gaps in the current process.

The group agreed that there were three major problems with the Sales and Order Entry process. Salespeople were sometimes late in submitting new orders, causing delayed delivery. Order entry clerks sometimes misentered orders, causing problems and delays for reentry. And, finally, everyone believed that some of the existing measures were out of line with stated company goals and that managers' measures should be reassessed to assure that they were measuring the right things. The team documented these problems on a process analysis and improvement worksheet (see Figure 14.9).

Process Analysis and Improvement Worksheet

Process or Activity: *Ergo Chair Order Process*   (AS-IS or) TO-BE

Process or Activity Outputs	Desired Performance (Measures)	Actual Performance	Gap (If Any)	Impact of Gap	Cause of Gap	Organization Improvement Action	Activities Which Influences Gap
Salespeople take too long to submit orders.	All orders submitted on day they are signed.	10% submitted 1 day late; 2% submitted more than 2 days late.	12% not submitted on day order obtained.	Order delivery delayed; customer dissatisfaction.	Salespeople too busy. Managers don't stress importance. Delays due to location of salespeople.		
Order details misentered by entry clerks.	All orders entered as submitted by salespeople.	5% misentered.	5% misentered.	Customer dissatisfaction, service calls, delays.	Entry clerk inattention. Nature of transcription process.		
Process measures stress wrong things.	All process measures should be related to value chain and company goals.			Frustration on part of senior managers and employees.	Need to align measures used by managers with corporate goals.		

Figure 14.9 As-Is process analysis and improvement worksheet for Order Entry.

The redesign team suggested that they should not only incorporate a portal into the Order Entry process, but should also equip salespeople with laptop computers and let them enter orders directly. It would eliminate the entry clerk's job and avoid transcription problems. And it was hoped that it would allow salespeople to submit all orders on the day they were received.

The recommendations of the entire order fulfillment team, when complete, were submitted to the steering committee. Once approved, the team was asked to prepare a detailed model of the revised process.

Phase 3: Redesigning the New Order Process

Once the steering committee approved the report and proposal of the process redesign team, they set to work creating a new process map to reflect all of the changes they proposed.

Following the identification of disconnects, the team considered each of the proposed Internet interventions to see if they would eliminate or alleviate the perceived disconnects. In each case, there was quite a bit of discussion about how a specific Internet intervention would change things. The IT representatives were often called upon to discuss what could and could not be done, relative to any specific change. In addition to technical considerations, involving an estimate on the part of IT about their ability to implement the software required for the change, there were concerns about the number and scope of changes being proposed. Everyone agreed that the greater the number of changes, the more difficult it would be to transition the process without significant disruption. Thus, the team decided to divide changes into (1) nice to do and (2) necessary. Only necessary changes would be considered initially. Afterwards, nice-to-do changes would be considered and either included or placed on a list of changes that might be made in the future.

At some point the team also decided they wanted all changes made in 6 months. Thus, if a change could be implemented, in the opinion of IT and the functional managers, within the next 6 months, it was considered a part of this redesign effort. If it would take longer than 6 months, the team decided to place it on a list of things to be considered for a subsequent process improvement effort.

Creating a Portal

The first major change they considered was the creation and incorporation of a Web site or portal. (A portal is really just a set of coordinated Web sites. Thus, rather than having one Web site for prospects that want to learn about company products and another for customers that want to check manuals about specific product features or buy additional chairs, all of the Web sites were clustered behind a single interface that all users arrived at when they entered *www.ergonomicsystemscorp.com* into their browser.)

The team agreed that the Ergonomic Systems portal should support these activities:

▶ General information about Ergonomic Systems
▶ A catalog of all Ergonomic Systems products
▶ A module that would allow prospects to specify Ergo Chair configurations and then buy Ergo Chairs online
▶ A page that would list announcements about part changes and answer frequently asked questions about Ergo Chairs.

Each of these features required considerable discussion, since each had significant process implications. A sketch, developed by the task force, of the basic screens to be included in the initial Ergonomic Systems portal is shown in Figure 14.10.

It was decided, for example, that the general information about the firm would require the creation of a committee with people from the executive committee, marketing, the process managers, legal, and IT. This became a recommendation of the team, since it didn't directly concern the Ergo Chair process.

It was also decided that the catalog of Ergonomic Systems products should include information about all company products, and hence there were recommendations that individuals from the systems group join with the people from the Ergo Chair catalog group to develop this information.

The module that would allow companies and individuals to buy chairs online received a lot of attention. It was decided, for example, that individuals shopping online should pay in advance for chairs they ordered. Since Ergonomics was used to working with established distributors and large companies, it was felt that extending credit to unknown individuals throughout the world was too risky for the systems Ergonomics had in place. Companies and distributors with established credit would be able to buy on credit, but any new individuals or companies would need to provide a credit card or transfer funds before the chair was assembled.

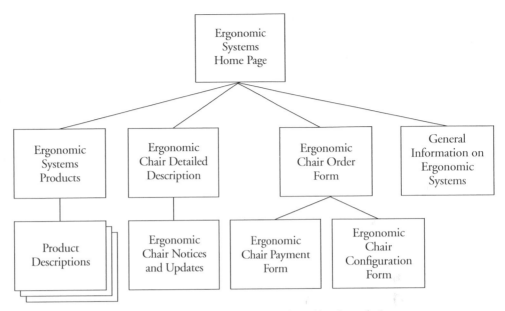

Figure 14.10 A sketch of the Ergonomic portal as envisioned by the redesign team.

They also decided that the purchase module would be designed to allow the customer to configure exactly the Ergo Chair he or she wanted. This, in turn, would require production to revise their procedures so that they could insert single or small orders within their schedule. The production members of the team suggested that they had already been moving in this direction and it could be achieved.

The team decided that they would need to contract with a delivery service to handle individual deliveries, since it would never be cost-effective to use their own trucks to make individual or even small deliveries outside of the major metropolitan areas close to their existing warehouses. They already use UPS to deliver special items, and it was recommended that shipping negotiate with UPS to arrange to handle worldwide delivery of limited runs of Ergo Chairs. At the same time, it was hoped that they would be able to link with production's scheduling system and UPS's tracking system so that online customers could determine when their orders would arrive and track their progress and delivery from the Web site.

It was decided that the Web site should be introduced in an English-only version and that later French and German versions should be developed to support their marketing organizations in those key European countries.

In addition to a discussion of the structure of the portal, the team recommended that an incentive system be developed to compensate salespeople who lost sales to the Web site. In the long run, everyone agreed that if they could convert distributors and large companies to Web site use, the company would save money. In the meantime, however, it was determined that the existing field sales organization should remain in place. That, in turn, meant that salespeople would need transfer payments to assure that they still made reasonable salaries during the transition. The alternative was to have resistance from the field sales staff to use of the Web site by existing customers, and to lose good salespeople who lost income as customers switched to the Web site.

The redesign team also suggested that management consider working out an arrangement with distributors to point their customers to the Ergonomic Web site. In effect, income from sales made through the Ergonomic Web site from transfers from distributor Web sites would be shared with the distributor for 6 months. The team recommended that the systems group consider a similar arrangement with suppliers of items like desk lamps, sold in conjunction with environmental systems. It was thought likely that some of the suppliers used by the systems group would create their own Web sites and that Ergonomic Systems ought to anticipate conflicts and work out a win-win strategy with its suppliers.

Modifying the Sales and the Finance Processes

Since the Web site would allow customers to buy online, everyone agreed that the existing Customer Credit and Invoicing System would need to be extended. In effect, the customer would be creating his or her own order and entering it into the customer database. At the same time, the credit system would need to be extended to allow it to automatically check credit information online. The IT team member explained that all of the major credit card companies already offer the services required. It would only be a matter of generating requests for approval and transmitting them via the Internet to the credit card companies, and then using the responses to confirm the purchase, or trigger an order reversal and an email or letter to the customer indicating that his or her credit card had been rejected. IT believed that the software vendor that had sold them the accounting system in the first place offered modules to do this and that incorporating them wouldn't be too difficult.

The To-Be Process Diagram

Figure 14.11 provides an overview of a portion of the modified or To-Be process that the redesign team arrived at for the Sales and Finance subprocesses. Ergonomic Systems plans on supporting both a manual sales system and an online system. We focus on the changes made to support the online system and only just indicate the manual system that was shown in the As-Is diagram (Figure 14.8). Obviously Figure 14.11 only provides an overview of the changes to be made. The IT group decided to buy a CRM package to manage the online sales and simply described the outputs that the people in the Ergo Chairs processes would need to support. We show two swimlanes for the portal, one for the interface (the Web pages), and one for the software applications that actually do the work once the customer has made an entry on a Web page.

Figure 14.11 incorporates a number of changes in a revised To-Be process. It adds a portal for those who want to use it and incorporates changes in software systems to support that path. It also provides for salespeople to use computers and enter orders directly into the customer system via the Internet.

Notice that accounting no longer needs to make an entry into the order system to generate invoices. The task force working on the Manufacturing process decided to outsource delivery and initiated a contract with UPS. UPS provides automatic electronic notification when chairs are delivered, and that information is now automatically input into the order system. Obviously, customers that pay by credit cards don't get bills. Only established customers are allowed to order with purchase orders, and they are billed after the orders are received. If we had shown a swimlane for the deliver subprocess, we would have included a feedback loop running from the online customer who received chairs via the deliver system's computer to accounting that would have led to a closed order, just as information from the credit card agency provides the accounting group with information about funds transfers.

Obviously Figure 14.11 will need to be defined in still more detail, but we won't go into the additional detail to keep this example limited to a manageable size. Suffice it to say that the redesign team kept at it until they had worked out all the details.

This is more or less the end of our discussion of the process redesign effort, and at this point the facilitator and the redesign team might prepare a report for the steering committee. Similarly, it might draft a plan to show what kinds of development effort

Ergonomic Systems, Inc.: Ergo Chair Value Chain: Order Fulfillment Process: Sales and Finance Subprocesses

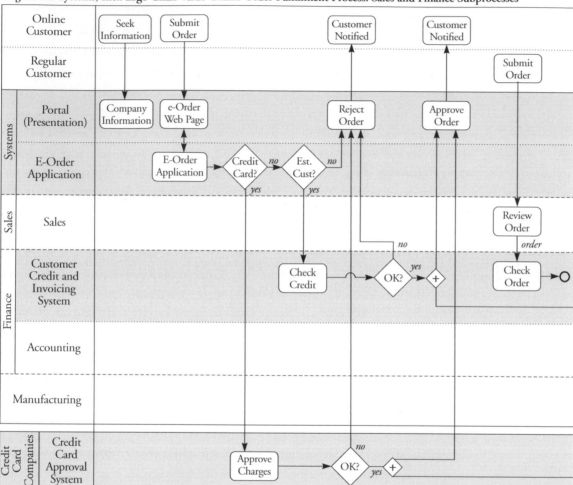

Figure 14.11 To-Be process diagram of Ergonomic Systems' revised Order Entry process.

would be required before the changes could be implemented. Before that, however, we need to return to the issue of management redesign, which we set aside at the beginning of Phase 2.

Refining the Management System

At the same time that the various teams were discussing processes and designing the new portal interface and the supply chain that now links manufacturing to its parts

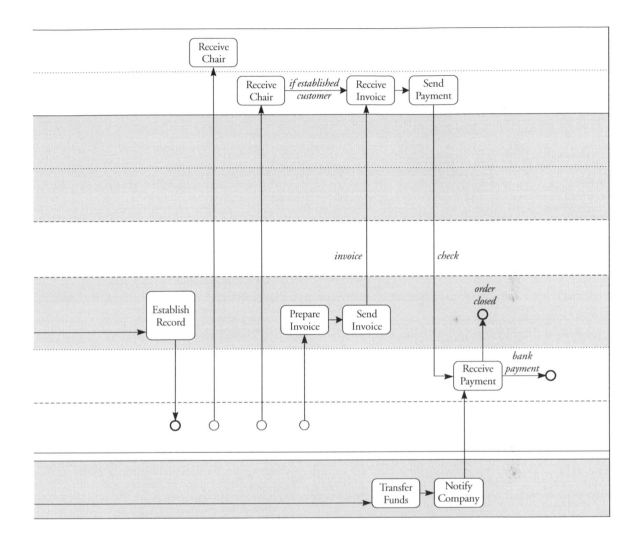

suppliers, a group of managers was formalizing the new management system. Like most companies, Ergonomics had always spoken of aligning its corporate goals to process and departmental goals. Similarly, as at most other companies, the alignment had always been an informal process. As part of the overall Ergo Chair process redesign, management made a commitment to create a more formal management system.

Figure 14.12 looks only at the Sales, Systems, and Finance functions as they relate to the new Ergo Chair Order process. To keep this diagram simple, we've collapsed several of the activities to make it easy to see what managers are involved in this process.

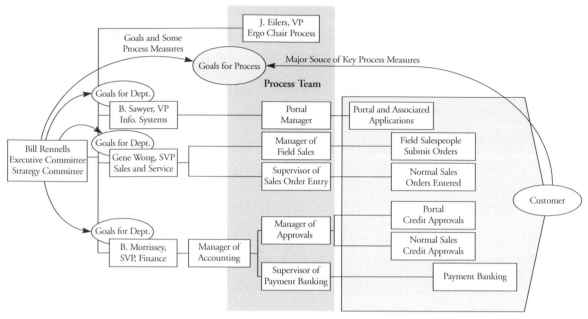

Figure 14.12 The flow of goals and measures.

In the simplified view shown in Figure 14.12, we see that the source of all goals for Ergonomic Systems is the executive committee and the CEO. Bill Rennells delegates two types of goals. Some goals are established for department heads and relate to the performance of the functions themselves. Things like profitability per salesperson, cost per sale, and sales reports might be delegated directly. Similarly, accounting standards and the ability to pass standard audits would be delegated to the SVP of finance. Data security requirements would be delegated to IT.

When it comes to the Ergo Chair Order process, however, goals for the whole process ought to be established by the executive committee working with the process manager, Jim Eilers. Those goals, in turn, should be turned into broad process measures that Eilers is responsible for monitoring and controlling.

Eilers then delegates subgoals for the process to function managers who are responsible for specific subprocesses or activities within the process.

Recall that Ergonomics already has an organization goals and measures worksheet (see Figure 14.3). The goals and measures listed on that worksheet for the Ergo Chair value chain include the following:

Goals	Measures	Desired Performance
1. Best-designed chairs	Design reviews	Win design competitions and mentions in design press
2. Command best price	Sale price comparisons	Chairs will sell for at least 5% more than competitive products
3. Maintain highest margins	After-tax returns on net sales	After-tax return on net sales exceeds 10%
4. Maintain growth goals	Sales growth	Growth in chairs will be 3% NA, 5% Europe

When Sutton and the managers on the Ergonomics redesign team sat down to discuss goal alignment, they sorted out the corporate goals as follows:

1. This goal was for the new product development process. It didn't apply to Ergo, except as the Ergo marketing communications people worked to bring the chair line to the attention of editors and juries.
2. This goal was used to set the prices, after comparing Ergo's price with other chairs.
3. This goal directly applied to the Order Fulfillment process and required that the process be as efficient as possible. The process was currently efficient, but changes to incorporate a portal should increase the efficiency of the process, not decrease it. Thus, proposed changes would be carefully evaluated to see if they helped maintain efficiency.
4. This goal applied to the Ergo sales manager and his team and was delegated directly to the respective sales groups.

As a part of their planning for the conversion to the use of a portal, the executive committee established a corporate strategy that entailed providing information about and accepting orders for Ergo Chairs via an Internet portal. The executive committee also set goals. The process was to be redesigned and the portal was to be up and running in 8 months. In the following 12 months, 20% of the orders for Ergo Chairs were to be taken via the portal. It was hoped that online orders were to reduce the cost of sales by 3%. Customers were to indicate their satisfaction with the availability and ease of use of the portal on surveys.

As the team approached these ideas, they formalized two additional goals:

5. Assure that customers are happy with Ergo chairs.
6. Assure that customers who use the portal are happy with the experience.

Both of these goals were going to be measured by surveys that Ergonomics planned to undertake periodically.

In order to clarify their thinking about these goals, the management team developed Critical-to-Quality trees for each goal. (CTQ trees, Sutton explained, are a popular Six Sigma tool that can be used on any goal-setting project.)

The team decided that customers were pleased when they got the chairs they ordered quickly and exactly as ordered, and with a correct bill (see Figure 14.13).

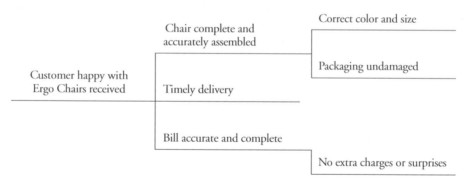

Figure 14.13 A CTQ tree for the Ergo Chairs Order Fulfillment process.

Some of these goals reinforced the concerns the team had already uncovered as regards occasional misentry of order information. The team was satisfied that its billing system generated accurate and complete bills, provided it got an accurate order. The rest of the items were passed to the group that was working on the manufacturing process.

The team then proceeded to focus on a CTQ tree for the Sales and Order Entry process, since that would be the process affected by the new portal. In this case, they came up with the CTQ tree shown in Figure 14.14.

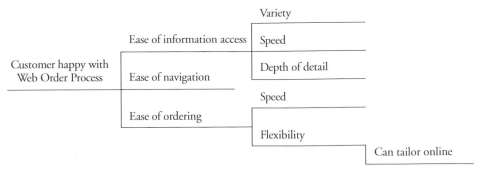

Figure 14.14 A CTQ tree for the Ergo Chairs Sales and Order Entry process.

The team realized that most of these would depend on the work of the software developers who created the portal. For the purposes of measurement, however, the team considered their goals, and then created some measures that they figured would allow the process manager to know if the portal succeeded.

They created a survey form that asked questions about the various items on the CTQ tree and suggested that someone be assigned to email copies of the survey to all of their customers for the first 2 months after their site was launched to determine if they were meeting these goals.

Eilers had to sit down with the various senior managers involved in the redesign and allocate subgoals and agree with the managers on measures. All the managers, for example, committed to providing the people needed to get the redesign done on schedule. The IT group was given the responsibility for creating a high-quality site. They agreed to work with Eilers to interview leading customers to determine what they wanted on the portal. Eilers would turn the customers' requests into a survey that would be used, in the future, to measure customer satisfaction with the site. The survey would not only ask questions about the overall content and ease of use of the site, but it would also ask about the speed of approvals, responses to online inquiries, time to delivery, and so forth.

Most of the redesigned site depended on software automation, and thus IT took a particularly heavy responsibility for the effectiveness and efficiency of the new process. At the same time, however, the SVPs of sales and service and finance agreed to performance measures for the processes that were performed by employees reporting to their departments. In each case, the SVPs, in turn, delegated specific measures to subordinates, and ultimately measures were established for each activity and for the employees who performed the activity.

In the future, when Eilers or any of the SVPs responsible for portions of the Order Fulfillment process undertake a process improvement effort, they will already have the goals and measures needed to judge how well they are doing. They may decide to use a program like Six Sigma to try to refine the process and narrow the variation in performance, but they won't need to start from scratch. In fact, given the use of off-the-shelf software for much of the IT aspects of this effort, a Six Sigma would more likely be applied to the manufacturing assembly process, which includes more manual effort and is more susceptible to the kinds of techniques that a Six Sigma effort would employ.

Figure 14.15 shows how the measures that the management team developed were ultimately assigned to specific subprocesses within the Order Fulfillment process.

This same exercise was repeated and specific goals were associated with each activity in each of the subprocesses.

Most organizations develop role/responsibility worksheets to show how each manager's goals will be aligned with the process goal. In Figure 14.16, we have reproduced a worksheet that the process sponsor, Eilers, and the North American sales manager, Lee Yu, prepared for a meeting of the task force. This worksheet was refined by the managers, and then other versions of the worksheet were employed by each manager to establish goals for their subordinates. Ultimately, each employee's job description was checked against the activity manager/supervisor's goals and measures to assure that employees understood how their work related to activity outcomes and thus, ultimately, to the achievement of process goals. In the end, there was a set of 24 role/responsibility worksheets defining every manager's and employee's goals for the Chair Order Fulfillment process.

Ergonomic Systems: Ergo Chairs Order Fullfillment Process

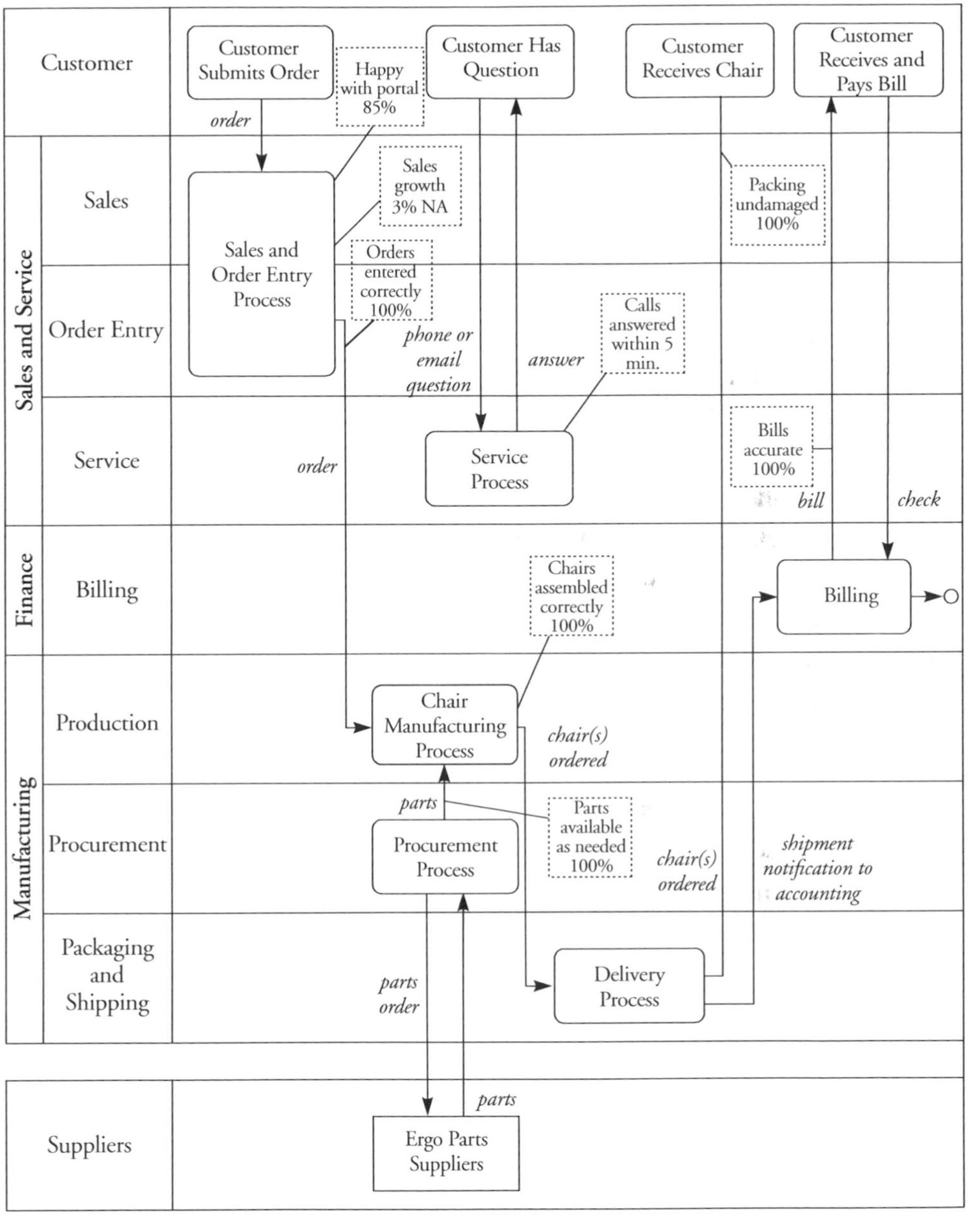

Figure 14.15 Measures established for each subprocess within the Order Fulfillment process.

Process/Function Role/Responsibility Worksheet							
Function: *Sales and Service*			Process: *Ergo Chair Order Process*				
Process	Subprocesses	Activity, Job, System Responsibilities, and Goals					
		Role: *Field Sales Manager—NA*		Role: *Order Entry Supervisor*		Role: *Sales Support Manager*	
		Activity or Step	Goals	Activity or Step	Goals	Activity or Step	Goals
Sales and Order Entry	Sales and Order Entry	Sales	3% Growth in NA	Order entry	Entered on day received. Entered 100% correctly.		
Service Process						Service calls answered.	Calls answered within 3 minutes.
						Service call follow-up.	Any promised materials mailed within 24 hours. Other material mailed within 3 business days.

Figure 14.16 Process/function role/responsibility worksheet.

Phase 4: Implement Redesigned Business Process

Once the steering committee had approved the revised Ergo Chair value chain design and plan, the process supervisor appointed his assistant to coordinate the implementation phase effort.

A major part of the effort involved the information technology (IT) department, which was going to have to develop the new company Web portal and revise the existing finance and manufacturing systems. IT had had representatives on the redesign team, and they believed that they could extend the redesign documents developed during Phase 3 to provide the requirements document that IT needed before they could begin their work. The IT members drafted the requirements document, and then the entire redesign team met again to review the requirements and sign off on them.

For many organizations the requirements definition phase is fraught with danger. In Ergo's case, however, since it had already produced process diagrams, it was much easier for the Ergo business and IT people to agree on the requirements document. Most organizations spend a significant amount of time and money defining requirements. Organizations that have already defined their processes will usually spend much less and will produce a better quality system.

Teams of senior managers from various departmental groups were assigned the responsibility for meeting with credit card companies, parts vendors, and UPS to work out contracts for the new relationships that Ergonomic Systems proposed to enter into with them.

Human resources was assigned the task of modifying or developing new job descriptions where jobs had changed and developing new compensation and incentive plans to accomplish some of the specific changes required by the new design.

The group whose efforts would take the most time was IT, which figured it would need a full 6 months to create and test the new software. Thus, everyone else was assigned tasks within that overall framework, and the rollout was scheduled to begin 7 months hence.

Phase 5: Roll-out the New Order Process

Some organizations revise processes and then, when they try to implement them, find it impossible. The new process is introduced, but within weeks or months everyone is back to the old way of doing things. The revision effort has seemingly disappeared without any effect. When this happens, organizations tend to play the blame game: the supervisors didn't support it, or the workers simply sabotaged the effort.

We have not experienced significant difficulty in implementing redesigned processes. We attribute our success to four factors.

First, we don't undertake a project unless we have a steering team and a process sponsor. We explain to those individuals, up front, that their job is to make the change happen. If they can't commit to the changes, we want to know early. If they sign off on the phase reviews, then we expect them to apply the pressure required to get their folks to implement the resulting process redesign.

Second, we don't undertake a problem without a clear statement of the scope of the project. If a company has a good process architecture and can pinpoint the process or subprocess to be changed, that's good. In most cases they don't, and we need to spend some time defining what will and won't be included. First, you need to agree on the activities that are to be included. Then, you need to decide if you are only going to work on the flow, or if you can also change management systems and jobs. Similarly, is the redesign team able to designate the use of automation and other technologies? You need to be clear on any limits on the nature of the redesign. All these issues will get resolved if you work through the phases we recommend and have the meetings we suggest to assure that all the issues are aired with everyone who is a stakeholder. If you reach a point in the process where you can't get agreement on scope, or if management or employee jobs get excluded, then you really want to examine if the project should proceed. Nobody likes to drop a project, but it's better to drop one and shift to something else than proceed when you don't have agreement. If you go past Phase 2 and don't have agreement, you can be pretty sure that implementation is going to be rocky, and there are going to be problems and recriminations in the end.

Third, we don't believe that process redesign should be undertaken separate from management system development. A sure recipe for disaster is to introduce a new process while managers are still being judged by older criteria or are using older measures to judge employee success. The whole system has to be integrated. A major redesign should always be accompanied with a goals and measures alignment effort. When the new process is rolled out, usually on a trial basis and then fully implemented, managers are measured on criteria developed to assure that the new process works as it should. Measures are taken more often during the initial months, and managers are provided feedback. Assuming that senior managers are committed, it is quickly obvious which junior managers are meeting their goals and which aren't, and corrective action is taken.

Fourth, we don't believe that process redesign should be undertaken separate from the people who must implement it. The redesign team ought to have employees (and people from other companies when a multicompany process is being designed) on the design team who represent all major groups whose work will be changed. When jobs are being changed or eliminated, plans must be established to handle the changes in a fair manner. Employees should understand the goals and measures and how they relate to company success, and should sign off on them just as the managers do.

We aren't suggesting that meeting all four of these criteria is always easy. We do insist, however, that they are as much a part of the process as any new software or any new process model. Ultimately, people do the work. And ultimately managers are responsible for seeing that the work gets done. Process redesign requires the active help and consent of these individuals, or it won't get done. A good bit of any redesign effort involves selling the new process to everyone involved and getting their commitment.

Ergonomic Systems did all these things. They had the full support of senior managers and prepared a management measurement plan that provided specific measures and linked 40% of managerial bonuses to meeting the new goals. They obtained the commitment of employees. Some salespeople were laid off, but not many, since the portal was only going to generate about 20% of the company's sales in the first few years. The salespeople realized that a portal was inevitable and liked the way Ergonomic Systems approached it gradually. They liked the fact that Ergonomics provided them with laptops and provided training to make them more skillful and efficient. Some clerical jobs were eliminated, but most of the clerks were assigned to other jobs within the company. Everyone hoped that the new portal would not only make the company more efficient, but that it would lead to growth and the creation of new job opportunities.

The software was ready on time, and the new process was implemented 8 months from the day the redesign started, just as management requested. There were some problems in the first few months, but by the end of 12 months everything was running smoothly and the new goals were being met. They actually achieved a slightly larger conversion to portal use and a 4% reduction in overall process costs. Management was happy with the results and began to think of what other lines they could sell online.

Notes and References

This is a hypothetical case, not a specific company we have helped.

IMPLEMENTATION LEVEL CONCERNS

I N THIS THIRD PART we consider some of the issues that today's companies face when they seek to implement process changes. There are a number of topics we could address, from training design to software development. Because space is limited, we are going to focus our discussion of implementation level concerns on three of the topics that are most important to today's business process managers.

We'll begin in Chapter 15 with a look at process modeling software. Any company that is serious about doing enterprise work needs a process modeling tool that can capture information about processes and store it in a repository. By using the same tool and storing information from multiple projects into a single repository, a company begins to create an asset that it can enhance as it does more process work.

In Chapter 16 we will look at Business Process Modeling Suites. BPMS software products not only let companies capture process diagrams, but go well beyond that and automate the day-to-day execution of those processes. BPMS is an exciting new approach to the management of processes that will revolutionize how we think of processes and IT by the end of this decade.

Chapter 17 will focus on Enterprise Resource Planning (ERP) and related applications and consider how companies can use ERP applications to support process automation efforts. We will then go beyond today's ERP applications and consider how ERP and BPMS are likely to merger in the next decade to provide companies with much more powerful and flexible process management environments.

Chapter 18 provides a recapitulation of the main points we have made and some final recommendations.

15

Software Tools for Business Process Analysis and Design

T HIS CHAPTER BRIEFLY DESCRIBES the range of business process modeling tools. We illustrate how modeling tools can be used by showing how a software modeling tool might be used in the development of the Ergonomics case study we considered in Chapter 14.

Why Use Business Process Software?

We have already suggested that a wide variety of different groups are engaged in different aspects of business process change. Those involved in process automation, for example, already use software development to aid them in their work. They use modeling tools to define and document requirements. They use UML, MDA, or CASE tools to generate code. Similarly, those involved in workflow automation development use workflow tools to model applications and then rely on those same tools to implement the results. Increasingly, companies are exploring the use of BPMS software to automate the runtime management of large business processes.

Business analysts and professional business process practitioners usually rely on software tools especially developed to support business process modeling and redesign. We refer to these tools as *professional business process modeling tools.*

Business managers engaged in business process analysis and redesign, on the other hand, are less likely to use software tools. Surveys suggest that a large number of managers prefer written descriptions. Many use simple graphical or illustration tools, like the introductory version of Microsoft's Visio, to quickly create flow diagrams. There's nothing wrong with either written descriptions or simple graphics when one is doing informal analysis. When one wants to do something that can be saved, accessed by others, and reused, however, a software tool is needed that can store the models and the associated data in a database. A database designed to store information about business processes is usually termed a *business process repository*.

Many business process teams rely on a *recorder* to capture group discussions in a business modeling tool. During analysis and redesign, a facilitator usually works with a business process project team to capture the existing or As-Is process and then to create a To-Be diagram. These sessions usually take place on two or three mornings during each week of the project. The facilitator usually stands in front of the group and makes notes on a whiteboard. Thus, each day the newly modeled process needs to be documented and changes need to be incorporated in earlier models. A tool makes it easy to record the results of a morning session and to print out neat versions of the organization and process diagrams for the participants. Some facilitators work with an associate who sits at the back of the room and records the session in a business process modeling tool. Others simply use the tool themselves to record the results in the afternoon following the morning session. Since modeling tools can save versions, it's easy to record different proposals so the group can document alternative versions of a solution.

Integrating paper documentation that shows processes and subprocesses, goals and measures, and the cost and capacity assumptions made about activities can be quite complex, but a tool makes it easy to keep all the information in a single file, providing a huge increase in the efficiency and productivity of the documentation process.

Some process modeling tools make it possible to simulate processes, so teams can study alternatives or check to see how the process would perform under different flows or constraints. Some managers use tools to track results of measures, and in these cases the tool becomes a management aid.

Finally, if a company is serious about developing a process architecture and expects to keep track of ongoing changes in processes and subprocesses, they need a tool to manage and maintain all of their process descriptions. Ideally, the company should agree on modeling standards so that the outputs of business process redesign teams can be smoothly integrated into the overall model maintained by the process architecture committee.

The Variety of Business Process Tools

There are dozens of different software tools that can be used for business process change projects. Figure 15.1 shows how BPTrends defines the business process software market. The overlapping circles suggest that many products combine features from different technologies. In many cases, the software vendors began by offering one type of tool—say a business rule tool—and then, as the market evolved, have begun to reposition themselves as something else—a BPMS vendor, for example. BPTrends uses the overview in Figure 15.1 to define software product markets and has produced a series of popular, free reports that describe the different niche markets and the specific products available in each niche.

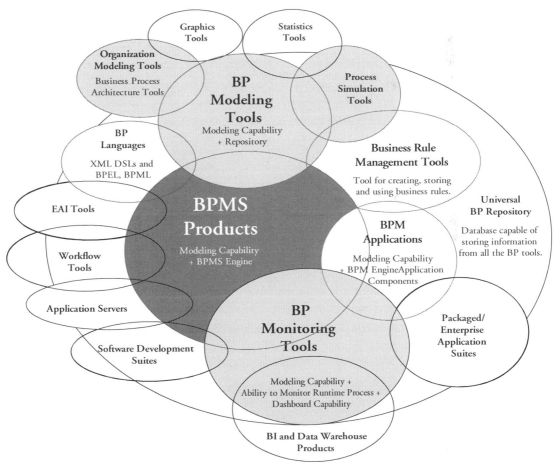

Figure 15.1 The business process software market as defined by the BPTrends Web site.

Table 15.1 provides definitions for some of the different types of tools shown in Figure 15.1 and suggests who might benefit most by using them. We have provided generic names although, in fact, the various tools go by a wide variety of different names.

Table 15.1 An overview of some of the software products that can aid in business process change.

Software products	Users		
	Executives, business and line managers engaged in informal business process improvement	Executives, business and line managers, BP team leaders, and employees engaged in business process redesign or improvement projects	Software analysts and developers engaged in developing applications to improve business processes
Organization Modeling Tools. Software tools that aid in the analysis of corporate strategy, competitors, customer needs, and threats and opportunities for process improvement. Tools that maintain enterprise process architectures.		Professional BP modeling tools	
BP Modeling Tools. Software tools that aid business teams in the analysis, modeling, and redesign of business processes. Includes methodologies, modeling tools, activity documentation, simulation, and costing tools.	Graphic and illustration tools	Professional BP modeling tools	Professional BP modeling tools
Business Rule Tools. Software tools that aid business teams in defining business rules for processes. May support the evaluation of rules for decision making.		Business Rule Tools	Business Rule Tools
BP Monitoring Tools. Software tools that aid in creating management measurement systems for business managers responsible for managing or implementing new business processes. Includes tools that monitor ongoing business processes.		Process monitoring and measurement tools	

Table 15.1 (continued)

Software products	Users		
	Executives, business and line managers engaged in informal business process improvement	Executives, business and line managers, BP team leaders, and employees engaged in business process redesign or improvement projects	Software analysts and developers engaged in developing applications to improve business processes
Statistics Tools and BP Modeling Tools. Software tools that aid in process improvement projects.		TQM tools, Six Sigma tools, professional BP tools with statistical utilities	
Packaged ERP Applications. Software applications that actually automate business processes. Includes ERP, CRM, and other packaged applications organized to support process automation. Tools that are tailored to help tailor ERP and other packaged applications.			Packaged applications from ERP and CRM vendors, tools from ERP and CRM vendors, professional BP modeling tools with extensions to support ERP development
Software Modeling Tools. Software tools that allow software developers to model processes and create software applications.			UML modeling tools, MDA tools, CASE tools
BP Modeling Tools with Support for Frameworks. Software tools that support the development of specific types of applications (e.g., tools that support the use of the SCOR supply chain framework and methodology).		Professional BP tools with extensions to support SCOR or other frameworks or methodologies.	
BPMS Products. Software tools that allow analysts to model processes and that then automate the execution of the process at runtime. May also include rules, and monitoring capabilities. Combines features of older workflow and Enterprise Application Integration products.	BPMS products can support executive dashboards to let senior managers monitor processes as they execute	BPMS products make it relatively easier for manager to make changes in processes being managed. Some tools support changes while the process is being executed (Dynamic updates.)	BPMS products are initially developed by business analysts & software developers and are maintained by them. Allow software developers to integrate software applications into business processes.

Some of the tools described in Table 15.1 are narrowly focused. Others fulfill more than one function. Thus, for example, there are business process modeling tools that are simply designed for that purpose. There are also UML, MDA, or CASE tools that include business process utilities so business managers can develop process diagrams that can then be converted to UML diagrams for software development. There are workflow tools that combine business process modeling and the actual execution of a workflow application.

There are well over 100 business process software tools on the market at the moment. In part, that reflects the variety of ways that companies are approaching business process change. It also reflects the immaturity of the market. We predict that in the course of the coming decade a few business process modeling tools will emerge as the most popular, and most of the other vendors will disappear. At the moment, however, since companies cannot know for certain which vendors will prosper and which will fall by the wayside, they would be wise to approach standardizing on any one tool with considerable caution.

A Professional BP Modeling Tool

In the remainder of this chapter, we'll only focus on the more sophisticated business process modeling tools.

Figure 15.2 provides an overview of the key features we expect from a professional business process tool. It provides interfaces in which users can create organization and process diagrams. Unlike the simpler tools that only create diagrams, professional tools store the model elements in a database, usually called a *repository*, so that any information gained can be reused. Similarly, whenever a user creates a modeling element on a diagram, the user can click on the modeling element and enter information about the element. Thus, if we create an organization diagram and name six departments, we can later create a process diagram and have those six department names automatically inserted as the names of the swimlanes. Similarly, if we create a process called Sell Widgets, and then define a number of activities that occur within the Sell Widgets process, we can click on the Sell Widgets process in any diagram it occurs in and get to the diagram that shows the activities within Sell Widgets.

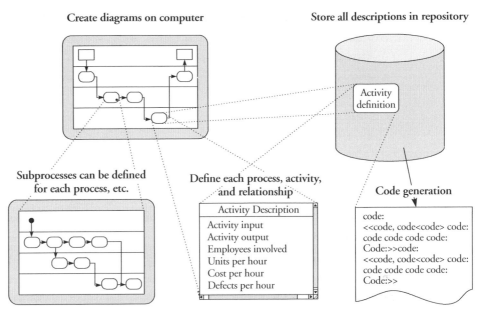

Figure 15.2 Key features of a professional business process modeling tool.

The heart of every professional business process modeling tool is a database, or BP repository, in which all elements of a business process and all of the relationships between those elements are maintained. Graphic tools that only support diagrams are equivalent to pages of paper that have a process diagram on them. Each page or diagram is a thing in itself. Creating one diagram doesn't help you create the next. A professional business process modeling tool, on the other hand, stores each element in the BP repository. Thus, as you create one diagram, you are storing information about processes and relationships that you can use on subsequent diagrams. As you proceed, you rely less and less on drawing new elements and more and more on telling the database what previously entered elements you want to place on your diagram.

Most business process tools support some kind of code generation, if for no other reason than to allow users to pass information about a process to other process tools. Increasingly, business process tools will support an XML business process language. Most also support UML or some software language so that software developers can begin where business managers leave off. Code generation isn't a feature that business process redesign teams need, but it can certainly make it easier when a business process team wants to hand off a redesigned process to a software development team.

There are a number of other features that we don't show in Figure 15.2. For example, if the tool is going to be used for Six Sigma projects, it's nice to have statistical utilities or a clean interface to a popular statistical package. If the tool is going to be used with a methodology like the Supply Chain Council's SCOR methodology, the tool should probably offer frameworks for templates for SCOR models.

Similarly, many of the more powerful business process tools offer simulation. Simulation means that you can enter information about how activities will process throughput and then introduce inputs into a process and see how they are handled. You might specify, for example, that a given activity, Activity C, with one employee can tune 12 widgets an hour. If you find that the typical throughput is 20 widgets, you are either going to have to add an employee to that activity, or the simulation system is going to show widgets piling up and waiting to be processed by Activity C. The analysis of simple systems rarely demands simulation, but complex processes, with multiple paths and loops for exception handling and product tailoring, usually benefit from simulation. Most supply chain developers can benefit from tools that support simulation. Similarly, creating customer-oriented e-business systems usually benefits from simulation. It's one thing to track four or five requests through a process, and it's another thing to go online and have hundreds of requests come in more or less simultaneously. If your processes are going to respond to varying levels of customer demand and require the support of a wide variety of subsystems, depending on the nature of the customer request, then you should be doing simulation during process design.

As important as simulation can be, teams must be aware of the time and effort required to enter all the data required for a major simulation. The world's leading auto manufacturers use simulation all the time to refine their manufacturing processes, but to do it, they employ teams of simulation experts with strong mathematical and statistical backgrounds. On the other hand, if you use a tool that supports simulation and only want to check how a specific subprocess will work under some specific set of circumstances, it need not be too tedious. We generally urge clients to consider simulation. But we also suggest that they make sure that the cost of any simulation effort will justify the time and cost of formalizing a model and providing sufficient detail for effective simulation. In fact, we usually recommend they use a consultant who specializes in simulation. If it's worth simulating, it's usually worth hiring someone who can quickly set up an effective simulation.

Modeling the Ergonomics Case

Now let's consider how using a professional business process modeling tool would have helped us as we analyzed and designed a new order fulfillment process for Ergonomic Systems, Inc. In this example, we'll assume that the facilitator is working with the Ergonomics process redesign team. The facilitator is aided by an assistant who sits at the back of the room and constantly creates models in the business process modeling tool.

We could have used any of a dozen tools to illustrate how the Ergonomics' example could have been implemented. In 1996 BPTrends published a free report in which it reviewed fourteen professional business process modeling analysis tools.

In this chapter we will use Proforma Software's ProVision Workbench to illustrate how a process modeling tool could be used to model Ergonomics processes. We will also show screen shots of another popular BP modeling tool, MEGA International's MEGA 2005, to illustrate how other business process modeling products can provide similar capabilities.

One of the reasons that we chose ProVision is because the tool uses a notation very similar to the notation we have used in this book, which is a cross between the Rummler-Brache notation and UML activity diagrams. In fact, ProVision supports several different notations, and you can change the notation that appears on the screen by simply pulling down a menu and selecting another notation. We chose ProVision's version of the Rummler-Brache notation so that you would have no trouble understanding their diagrams.[1]

An Organization Diagram

Let's assume that when the Ergonomics business process redesign team started, they created an organization diagram, showing how Ergonomics related to the environment outside of Ergonomics. Then they refined the diagram to show the major departmental units or functions that occur within the company.

In Figure 14.2 we pictured an organization diagram for Ergonomic Systems. Figure 15.3 shows how that same diagram would be pictured in ProVision.

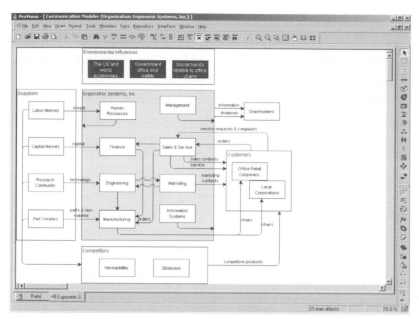

Figure 15.3 ProVision screen in which an analyst has created an organization diagram of Ergonomic Systems.

If you compare this diagram to the one shown in Chapter 14, you will see only minor differences [1]. ProVision provides pop-up windows with symbols like the rectangles shown on the screen in Figure 15.3. A developer simply clicks and drags to place one on the diagram. Then, the analyst types a name for the function. This seems simple, but in fact, once you have placed the Manufacturing box and labeled it, you have also created an entity in the database, called Manufacturing, which knows what other entities it is related to as you link that rectangle to others with arrows.

Process Diagrams

Let's assume that our business process team now turns to defining the existing order fulfillment process. In this case, our analyst would open a new window for a process diagram. ProVision would prompt the analyst to see if he or she wanted to use the departments defined in the organization diagram to create swimlanes on the process diagram. Assuming the analyst clicked YES, a process diagram with labeled swimlanes would appear. The analyst might want to rearrange the order of the swimlanes by dragging some up or others down, but the basic structure of the process diagram would be in place.

Assuming the business process team went through the same process they did in defining the As-Is order fulfillment process in Chapter 16, our analyst would end up with a similar process diagram. Figure 15.4 shows the diagram created in ProVision for the Ergonomic Systems As-Is process. In this case we reproduce the diagram that ProVision would print on demand. On the screen, we would only see a portion of the entire diagram. By printing it, however, we create a diagram that is as wide as needed.

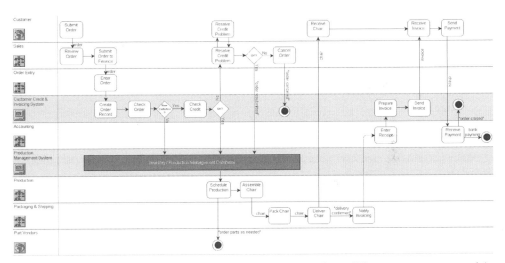

Figure 15.4 As-Is process diagram of the Ergonomics Order Fulfillment process created in ProVision.

You can compare Figure 14.11 to 15.3 to see the slight differences. ProVision uses a symbols to label swimlanes, for example. The globe indicates that the function described in that swimlane is outside the organization being analyzed. Thus, both the customer at the top and parts vendors at the bottom are tagged with globes. A small PC icon is used to mark systems functions, and an organization hierarchy icon is used to mark swimlanes that describe departmental functions. Otherwise, the two diagrams are remarkably similar.

Just as we created departments on the organization diagram, we create processes and decision points on the ProVision process diagram by selecting elements from a pop-up window and dragging them to a location. Similarly, as we give names to the processes, we create database entries. In this case, the database not only knows of the existence of a process, and relationships between that process and others, but knows which department is responsible for the process.

In Figure 15.5 we reproduce the To-Be diagram that was created in ProVision. In this case, the analyst started by creating the As-Is diagram. Later, as the team began to change the process, the analyst saved the As-Is diagram and then took a copy of that diagram and modified it as the team modified the process in their meetings. Once again, we have reproduced the printed version of the To-Be diagram to make it easier to see the entire To-Be process diagram. You can compare this with the To-Be diagram in Figure 14.11 in the last chapter.

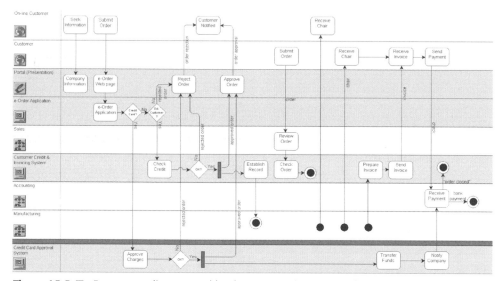

Figure 15.5 To-Be process diagrammed by the Ergonomics process design team in ProVision.

Once again, Figures 15.5 and 14.11 are very similar. We didn't develop any diagrams that showed the details of what happened inside the boxes shown in Figure 14.11. If we had and we wanted to represent them in ProVision, we would click on one of the boxes in Figure 15.5 and indicate we wanted to do a detailed diagram. At that point, ProVision would create a new diagram, and we could create a subprocess diagram. ProVision would then mark the box on Figure 15.5 with an indicator to show that a more detailed description was available if we double-clicked on that box.

Figure 15.6 shows how MEGA 2005 would represent a process. In this case, the diagrams are using BPMN notation and the swimlanes are vertical rather than horizontal.

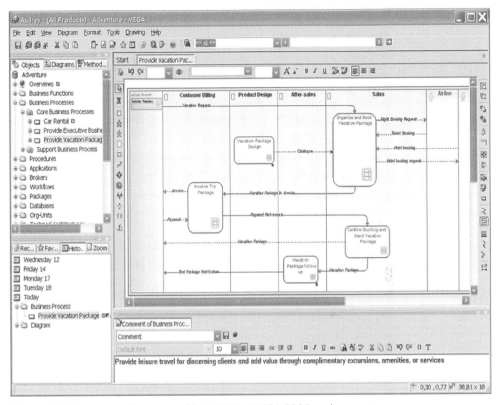

Figure 15.6 A process diagrammed in MEGA's MEGA 2005 environment.

As with ProVision, MEGA 2005 creates a BP repository entry every time a user creates an object for the model.

Other Diagrams

In the text, we have used a variety of worksheets to capture more specific information. In ProVision, one simply clicks on a given box, opens a window, and enters more detailed information on forms associated with each diagramming element. Figure 15.7 shows a window opened for an activity and information that we've entered.

Figure 14.15 in the last chapter illustrated how measures could be associated with each subprocess in the Order Fulfillment process. It would be easy to associate those measures with subprocesses in ProVision simply by opening each subprocess box and inserting the measurement information. It would also be possible to print out lists of the measures assigned to each department or functional group.

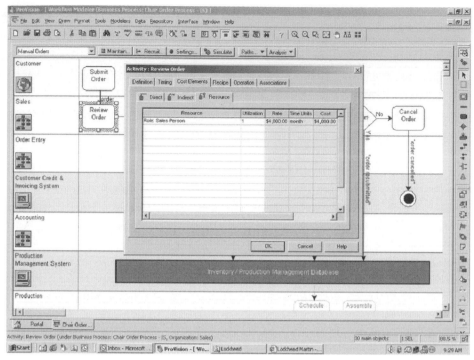

Figure 15.7 ProVision screen showing a process diagram and a window opened in which a developer can record information about a specific process.

In addition, ProVision supports almost any matrix an analyst can think of, all driven by information accumulated in the repository. Thus, for example, when we have entered as much as we want, we could ask for a matrix that showed us which departments were responsible for which activities, and ProVision would offer us a matrix.

Process Simulation

Another important feature that ProVision supports is process simulation. The Ergonomic Systems team in the last chapter could never have simulated their redesigned process without using a software tool.

To illustrate simulation, we started with the As-Is diagram of the Ergonomics sales process. The As-Is diagram had already been created, and we didn't need to change the diagram in order to run the simulation. We did have to open each activity box that would be involved in the simulation and provide information about what would occur in that activity and how long it would, on average, require. For each activity shown in Figure 15.8, we entered data and assumptions. Thus, for example, we assumed that there were only two salespeople available for the Review Order activity and that they were also responsible for calling customers about credit problems. Ask yourself if you thought of this as a problem when you looked at this diagram in the previous chapter.

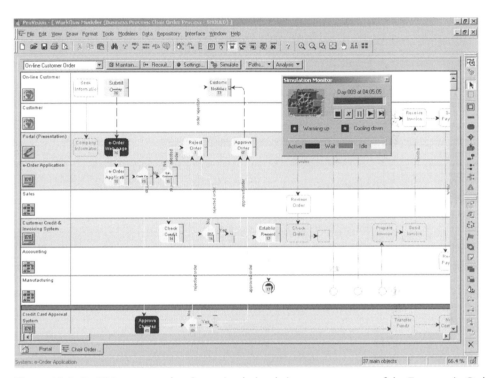

Figure 15.8 ProVision screen showing a simulation being run on a part of the Ergonomic Order Fulfillment As-Is process.

In Figure 15.8 the Review Order activity is black, indicating that it is active. Making only modest assumptions about the number of orders coming in and the number that need to be checked for credit problems, and how long each activity takes, our process quickly grinds to a halt. Basically, when one salesperson is checking a credit problem, the other salesperson, alone, can't keep up with the orders. We would need more salespeople, or we would need someone else assigned to handle credit problems if we wanted this process to run smoothly.

Figure 15.9 illustrates the matrix we created in ProVision that shows the data collected from the simulation. We highlighted the column labeled Postponed Time. Postponed time is the amount of time the activity spent waiting for resources (in this case, salespeople) to become available. So, out of the 80-hour simulation duration (we ran the simulation for ten 8-hour days), the first two sales activities were waiting for available salespeople for a total of 24 and 28 hours.

	Activity	Occurs	Idle time	Work time	Delay time	Pending input time	Stall time	Postponed time	Congested time
1	Chair Order Process - IS(Manual Orders)	1.00	401.20	96.00	73.33	0.00	0.00	57.13	0.00
2									
3	Sales		124.66	66.50	60.50	0.00	0.00	55.63	0.00
4	Cancel Order	2.00	53.20	0.50	0.00	0.00	0.00	1.48	0.00
5	Resolve Credit Problem	7.00	28.59	7.00	21.00	0.00	0.00	1.62	0.00
6	Review Order	79.00	5.42	39.50	39.50	0.00	0.00	24.55	0.00
7	Submit Order to Finance	78.00	37.45	19.50	0.00	0.00	0.00	27.99	0.00
8									
9	Customer Credit & Invoicing System		235.35	3.83	0.00	0.00	0.00	0.00	0.00
10	Check Credit	38.00	78.49	1.27	0.00	0.00	0.00	0.00	0.00
11	Check Order	77.00	78.44	1.28	0.00	0.00	0.00	0.00	0.00
12	Create Order Record	77.00	78.42	1.28	0.00	0.00	0.00	0.00	0.00
13									
14	Order Entry		41.19	25.67	12.83	0.00	0.00	1.50	0.00
15	Enter Order	77.00	41.19	25.67	12.83	0.00	0.00	1.50	0.00

Figure 15.9 ProVision screen showing grid with information on the wait time for each activity in the simulation.

This quick and trivial illustration points to the value of simulation. Increasingly companies will want to run simulations on processes they are redesigning and then maintain the simulations so they can use them in the future to test any proposed changes in the existing processes. Mature process companies will maintain simulations and routinely use them for process improvement projects.

Using Tools to Maintain Architectures

So far we have spoken of using a modeling tool to help in analyzing and redesigning a process. In Chapter 3 we spoke of business process architectures and the need to maintain an overview of all the processes supported by a company. This task would be nearly impossible without the use of software tools. In effect, a tool like ProVision or MEGA can store one business process after another, keeping track of the individual processes, and holding them ready for simulations to check possible changes. At the same time, it can examine multiple processes to identify where common activities occur in more than one process. The amount of detail involved in this effort could overwhelm a business process architecture committee if it didn't have a way of automating the task.

The Use of Business Process Software Tools

The Ergonomic process redesign team would probably not have finished much faster using a business process modeling tool. If the team only met every other day for half a day, the analyst would be able to create the needed diagram by hand or in a simple diagramming tool. The tool would probably have made the facilitator's job easier and might have resulted in nicer diagrams, but it would not have changed the overall time required for the redesign. Without the tools, however, the team could not have run a simulation, and that might have changed the ultimate design assumptions.

On the other hand, once the Order Fulfillment process had been redesigned in ProVision, all of the information about the process would be stored in a single software file. Future changes in the process would be easy to effect. A manager could quickly record any improvements made in the process. More importantly, a tool would allow the team to undertake simulations to answer a variety of questions. How many additional employees would need to be assigned to assembly if we were to double the number of orders each month or each week? Would bills still arrive at customer sites at the same time, and so forth?

When the Ergonomic redesign team was done, the managers responsible for the process could each place a copy of the process on their computers so that they could answer questions of that kind for themselves. A copy could also be provided to the Ergonomics business process architecture group so they would have an up-to-date, detailed description of the Order Fulfillment Process and could run their own simulations in the future when other changes were proposed.

While we don't recommend any specific business process redesign tool, we would never undertake the facilitation of a major process redesign effort without using a business process modeling tool, and we wouldn't recommend anyone else do so either. Different facilitators or analysts with different goals will prefer some tools over others. This is a matter of pragmatics and individual taste. Overall, however, any company that seeks to incorporate process into their culture should regard a process modeling tool as a tool that every manager should use, just as they use spreadsheet software or word processing programs.

In the late 1970s, we worked on a project that introduced spreadsheets in one of the largest banks. At the time, we used mainframes and the interfaces weren't very good. We developed a system that would support 12 individuals, the heads of the bank's 12 divisions, who had to prepare quarterly projections. The project met a surprising amount of resistance. Each of the 12 senior vice presidents had a person who reported to them whose primary function was to prepare spreadsheets. Those individuals worked on large pads of paper and used adding machines to crunch numbers. It would take hours to work out a spreadsheet describing a set of assumptions for a division for the next quarter. You can imagine the assistant taking the results to the SVP, who would look at it, consider the results, and then suggest that they change two assumptions. "Assume we have a 6% turnover instead of 5% and let's assume we get 25 new loans at each branch rather than 24." At this point the faithful assistant would trudge back to his or her desk and start the process over again. Don't think about the huge amount of time used by this manual process, however. Focus instead on how often the SVP would change his or her assumptions. Everyone is always under pressure, and no one has time to go through laborious cycles like this for weeks on end. The SVP would make some changes, check the results, suggest a few more changes, and then go with one of the spreadsheets. There was no time to explore lots of alternatives.

The availability of software spreadsheet programs with relatively friendly interfaces that run on personal computers has changed all that. Today, an SVP can sit at his or her desk and make one change after another. In the course of an hour or two, an SVP can examine the impact of hundreds of different assumptions. It's hard to imagine that SVPs don't understand their financial operations a lot better today than they did in the 1970s. Moreover, it's safe to assume that an SVP can make changes much quicker when things change. You can imagine an SVP checking loan sales data each day and making changes in assumptions and revising estimates that same day.

What spreadsheets have done for the way business managers think about their cash flow, process modeling tools and BPMS products will do for the way business managers understand and manage business processes. This change is just beginning, but it will gain momentum throughout the decade. A manager with a process description on a software tool not only understands what is happening, he or she can make changes and run simulations to see how things can be changed or improved. In the near future, managers will need to modify business processes much more frequently than they do today to keep up with environmental and technological changes. Business process modeling tools will make that possible.

Notes and References

[1] The ProVision diagrams were developed for the first edition of *Business Process Change*, before BPMN had been completed. Each of the leading business process modeling vendors now supports BPMN. Thus, if these diagrams had been generated today, the minor differences between this older (Rummler-Brache notation) and BPMN would disappear. Thus, initial events would be circles and not black dots and terminal events, for example would be bold circles and not "targets." Similarly all the branching gates would be represented as diamonds.

To obtain information on most of the leading BP modeling vendors, go to *www.bptrends.com* and click on BPT Product Reports and then look at the 2006 Process Modeling report. Process Modeling tools keep changing. BPTrends will update the modeling reports annually to reflect the evolution of these products.

For more information on Proforma or ProVision Workbench, and to download a trial version of their business process modeling tool, check *www.proformacorp.com*.

For information or to download a trial version of MEGA International's MEGA 2005 product, go to *www.mega.com*.

16

Business Process Management Suites

BUSINESS PROCESS MANAGEMENT SUITES (BPMS) are software products that evolved in the past few years. In essence, they combine features previously found in (1) workflow and document management tools, in (2) enterprise application integration (EAI) tools, and in (3) business process modeling tools and well as (4) new technologies derived from the Internet.

In the 1970s and 1980s, IT groups created software applications at the request of departmental or functional units. Thus, the accounting department has accounting applications and an accounting database. Similarly manufacturing and sales each had their own applications each with its own database. In the 1990s, in conjunction with the emphasis on business process reengineering, companies began to struggle to integrate departmental activities into processes that crossed departmental boundaries. This immediately put pressure on IT to find ways to make it easy for departmental applications and databases to work together and exchange information. The three different types of software tools mentioned above evolved to help facilitate this change.

Workflow tools were created to make it easy to manage processes in which employees processed documents. In essence, an incoming document was scanned and placed in a database. Then a digital copy of the document was sent to an employee's computer when the employee needed to interact with the document. At a minimum, workflow systems speeded processing by eliminating the time otherwise required to physically move documents from one employee's workstation to the next. Instead, as soon as one employee finished working on a document and selected SEND, the database system would place a copy of the edited document in the queue of the computer terminal of the next employee who needed to work on the document.

At the same time, other software developers focused on building software systems that would manage a diverse set of software applications. Rather than try to redesign an application originally designed to work only for one department to work with other applications, a whole set of applications were interfaced with a single *enterprise application integration* (EAI) tool that would move information from one departmental application to another, as needed. EAI tools made it possible to operate a number of applications as if they were integrated.

Stepping back from the specific EAI tools, we can see that IT tried to solve the problem created by diverse software applications by creating a new application that managed other applications. Similarly, workflow systems sought to integrate employee efforts by providing each employee with a computer and then using a workflow application to manage the movement of work from one computer to another.

The limit on both early workflow and EAI solutions was the lack of a common infrastructure. It was expensive to wire diverse things together using the infrastructure technologies available in the early 1990s. All that began to change in the late 1990s when companies discovered the Internet. The Internet was created by the government and used a set of common, open standards. Equally important, the Internet was designed to operate over ordinary telephone lines. As the Internet evolved rapidly in the late 1990s, a number of technical standards like SOAP and XML were created that made it even easier to interface older software systems and applications with the Internet. That process continues today and most companies are now moving to the Service Oriented Architecture (SOA), the latest set of open Internet standards that make it even easier to integrate applications.

By 2002 a number of different authors and vendors were talking about creating a new type of software that would combine the features of the Internet, workflow software EAI and process modeling to create a product capable of managing the execution of business processes. In essence, the workflow elements would manage the human activities within the process and the EAI elements would manage the software applications and databases used during the execution of the process. Everything would be integrated via the Internet and the open protocols created for the Internet. This vision has been variously termed BPM (business process management) or BPMS (business process management suites, or software). We have discouraged the use of BPM and opted for BPMS, since BPM was already in use and is widely used to describe all kinds of business process work, including much that won't be incorporated in the new software applications.

A BPMS product is a software tool that one can use to develop one or more BPMS applications. A BPMS application is an application that is managed and executed by a BPMS tool. Thus, a BPMS application describes a business process and incorporates a BPMS engine that will execute the business process in real time. Imagine a BPMS application to manage insurance claims processing. The claims processing process is described and can be examined by either the business managers or by IT developers. When an actual claim arrives, the application manages the processing of the claim. In fact, the BPMS application is a template of the process, just like any workflow diagram. When the application is asked to manage a specific instance, it creates a copy of the template and then maintains the data related to the specific claim in a file in a database. Unlike the template that shows decision points and multiple branches, a real instance reflects specific decisions and only follows a single path.

If the interfaces are good and the business managers can read a basic process flow diagram, the business manager is in a unique position to make or request changes in the business process. The key here is that the actual software applications and databases and the data being processed by employees are all maintained independently of the BPMS application. By simply changing the diagram or the business rules in the BPMS application, the business manager can immediately change the way the application functions. In the best case, the business manager can make specific changes. In any case, the business manager can communicate with IT by describing a process change without being concerned about the underlying implementation details. A BPMS application assures that, from then on, the business managers and IT developers will communicate by talking about specific processes.

BPMS represents an evolutionary development with major roots in business process modeling, CASE, workflow, rule-based systems, EAI, and packaged applications. Today, vendors who would formerly have positioned their products in one of these categories have repositioned their products and now refer to them as BPMS products.

Gartner estimated the revenue from BPMS sales would reach between $520 and $543 million in 2003, and estimates that the BPMS market will be generating more than $1 billion by 2009. Forester, of course, had projected a much higher estimate. Keep in mind that most of these sales are sales that would have been recorded as workflow or EAI sales two years earlier. Nevertheless, many companies are interested in business process and are buying BPMS products to explore the possibilities.

The Importance of Process Diagrams and a BPMS Engine

In essence, a BPMS product is a software package that allows a business manager or business analyst to describe process and, later, as needed, to modify the process. From a software architectural perspective, one could describe BPMS as a new layer of software that sits above other software applications and uses business process specifications to determine when to call those other software applications.

The BPMS product must includes a process-diagramming interface for the business analyst to use to define the process to be managed and a BPMS engine that generates instances of applications when they are needed and terminates them when they are completed. There's quite a bit more to it, but let's start with a simplistic overview. In Figure 16.1 we picture the two core BPMS elements. One is a graphical modeling environment that allows the developer to create a description of the business process. (In the case of the example in Figure 16.1, the process consists of five activities, labeled A through E.) The other main element is a BPMS engine that follows the script implicit in the process description and manages the creation of instances as specific cases are processed. In effect, a business analyst describes what is to be done, and the engine then "reads" the description, whenever the process is executed, invoking each implementation component in order.

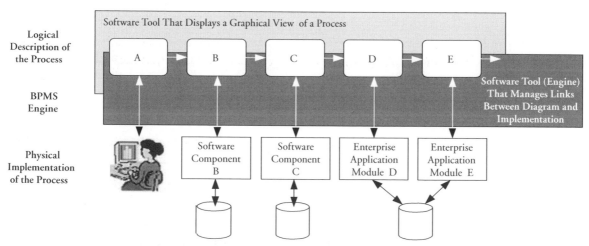

Figure 16.1 The two core elements of a BPMS product.

Notice that the BPMS system in Figure 16.1 is managing both employees and software applications. In other words, BPMS can combine the ability to manage human tasks (usually called workflow) and software systems (usually called EAI). Obviously the BPMS system interacts with employees by means of a computer interface, sending requests for information or decisions to employee terminals, waiting for a response, and using the responses to continue executing the process.

Let's be sure we understand the primary value proposition of those who advocate the use of BPMS systems. BPMS systems should make it possible for managers or business analysts to change how processes work without having to ask IT to reprogram. Some claim any business manager would be able to do this, but that's unlikely, except in the case where the business manager feels really comfortable with software systems and process diagrams. (Recall that most business managers today do NOT define processes with diagrams. Instead they use text outlines.)

Figure 16.2 illustrates a process modeling interface offered by one of the BPMS vendors. This particular interface is based on the BPMN notation we have discussed in this book.

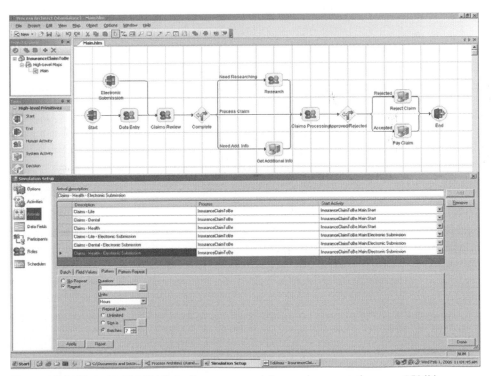

Figure 16.2 Global 360 BPM Suite features a modeling environment that uses BPMN.

Figure 16.3 suggests how a business analyst might have used the process design tool in a BPMS package to change a process diagram and thereby automatically change the way the process is executed at runtime. We assume that the same underlying implementation components are still in place and that they function as they did in Figure 16.1. Now, however, the order in which they are invoked has changed. Whenever the process is executed, the BPMS engine will read the new diagram and execute the steps in the new order. Moreover, the changes have been accomplished without the intervention of IT developers.

We have pictured the changes in the flow of the process as a change in the arrangement of the activities in the diagram. Some tools allow the user to literally change the way the arrows connect to boxes to effect this redesign. Other tools rely on business rules that state how decisions are made and what activities follow certain decisions. In those cases, the manager or business analyst can achieve the changes by simply editing the business rule statements. In this case, the BPMS engine is executing business rules rather than simply following a workflow description.

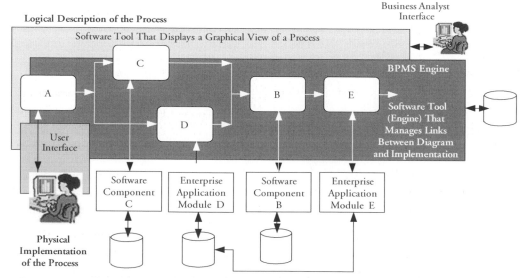

Figure 16.3 A BPMS product has been used to reorganize how the process is implemented.

The ability of a BPMS product to re-establish links to underlying software components without the intervention of an IT programmer requires a rather flexible BPMS engine. We will discuss the implications of this flexibility a bit later. Meantime, we want to underline what the BPMS package did NOT do. The BPMS product, as we have defined it, did not create any new components. It simply allowed the business analyst to rearrange the order in which existing components were used. Some BPMS advocates have suggested that BPMS products will "automatically" generate the code needed to provide new implementation functionality. We don't believe that will be a key part of most BPMS products. On the other hand, some products will allow developers to create code in the tool and, thus, to capture business rules that will structure or supplement the functionality of existing software applications.

Before that, however, let's consider the elements required by a comprehensive BPMS that we have not yet discussed.

What Features Might a BPM Suite Include?

Figure 16.4 provides an overview of one possible architecture for a BPMS product. The BPMS product here would be a rather comprehensive tool or suite.

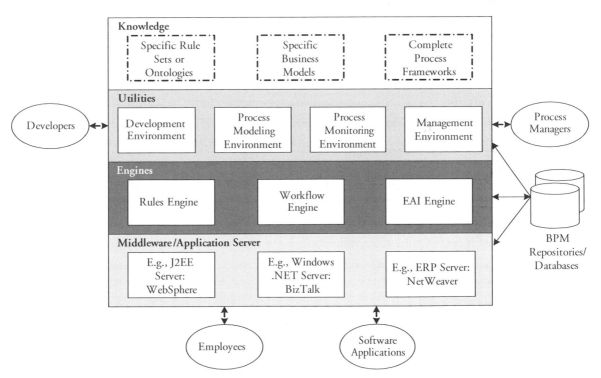

Figure 16.4 An Architectural Overview of a Business Process Management Suite.

To simplify our discussion, we have divided the BPMS package into four layers. The bottom layer is labeled Middleware/Application Server. Any BPMS product needs to be able to manage the access of other software applications. A few BPMS products handle these functions, but most rely on existing middleware and application server products to provide this support. The most popular platforms are IBM's Java server, WebSphere, and Microsoft's Windows .NET BizTalk server. The leading packaged application vendors offer their own servers to facilitate access to their ERP and CRM applications. Thus, SAP offers NetWeaver that manages the access to many of the SAP modules that companies use.

The heart of a BPMS product consists of the engine that manages the runtime execution of the business process instances. Most BPMS products offer two or three engines. One engine manages the execution of the workflow aspects of a process. At a minimum the engine locates the appropriate employee's terminal and routes information to and from the employee. Most workflow engines do a lot more. Many, for example, will generate "task lists" for the employee, defining exactly what the employee is expected to do. Others will monitor groups of employees and determine which employee is available or has the skills required for a specific type of task.

A second BPMS engine (the EAI engine) usually manages the calling and coordination of the software applications required for the execution of a process. These engines turn other software applications on and off, move data to and from databases, and manage all the associated activities.

A third engine is typically used to manage the maintenance and execution of business rules. When a decision point is reached, the rule engine will determine which business rules apply and then examine them to determine the appropriate decision.

Most BPMS products have a history in workflow, document management, business rules management, or EAI. Typically the vendor has a strong engine for the execution of the kinds of activities they have historically specialized in, and is working to extend or acquire the other engines. Thus, today, if you want to manage processes that are primarily people-based, you will want to talk with a BPMS vendor that has a historic strength in workflow. On the other hand, if you want to develop an application that will be primarily software-based, you will probably fare better if you work with a vendor with a strong EAI background. As the market evolves and mergers continue to occur, BPMS products are gradually acquiring strong engines for all different types of applications. Equally important, they are gradually rewriting their software so that it is well integrated and so that users can deal with simple interfaces that allow them access to all of the different engines and capabilities of the BPMS product.

The third layer includes utilities that are required for the development of a BPMS application. The business analyst needs a development interface that he or she can use to describe the process to be managed. The business manager needs an interface that will make it easy to modify the application as the process changes. Both need a modeling environment that provides a graphic overview of the process that will be executed when the application is used. Similarly, both need an environment that will make it possible to capture data as the process is being executed so that the business manager can determine how the process is performing. In addition, many tools provide a spreadsheet-like interface so that everyone can see and edit the business rules that are used in the process. In the worst case, the BPMS product has been assembled from many different, earlier products and there are a variety of incompatible interfaces that the manager and developer must master. In the best case, the vendor has created common interfaces that let the analyst or manager move easily and smoothly between the various elements that must be coordinated, managed or changed.

Most early BPMS tools limited themselves to the three layers we have just described. Recently, however, a number of BPMS tools have begun to include knowledge elements that make it easier to create specific types of business process applications. Consider that you might want to create a BPMS application to manage the day-to-day execution of a bank process. In that case, a BPMS tool that came with sets of business rules typically used for major bank processes, or with workflow diagrams that describe typical bank processes, would save you time as you sought to create your bank application. Similarly, a BPMS package that provided the Supply Chain Council's SCOR framework of process and performance measures would make it a lot easier to quickly create a supply chain management system. Predictably, as BPMS products become more mature, some BPMS vendors will specialize in specific industries and include sophisticated packages of knowledge elements with their products.

BPMS and BAM

Business activity monitoring (BAM) is a term that's been around for several years. It refers to any of several different approaches to gathering information about processes and providing that data, in some form, to managers. Most analysts assume that, ultimately, any BPMS solution will be combined with a BAM solution to assure that managers can monitor the process and the BPMS system to assure that they are both performing as they should.

Most BPMS products being sold today provide a limited type of monitoring. They record events, as they occur, summarize that information and provide the data on a manager's interface. This kind of monitoring is appropriate for supervisors who have immediate responsibility for the specific process. Assume we were using a BPMS application to manage a call center, assigning incoming calls to operators according to their availability. In this case, the BPMS system would let the supervisor know how many calls each of the various employees handled in a given time period. This kind of event monitoring is pictured in Figure 16.5 in the lower gray box.

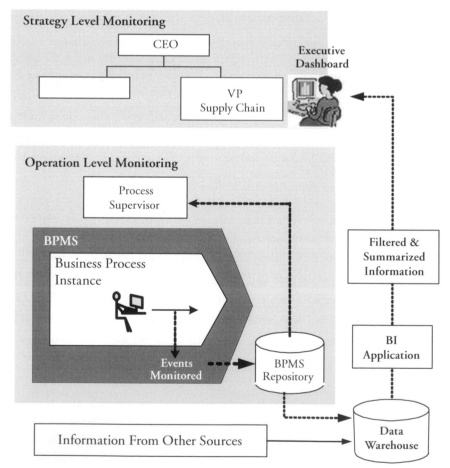

Figure 16.5 A BPMS tool can either provide information to the process supervisor or it can combine and filter the information for a senior management dashboard.

More sophisticated monitoring requires quite a bit more technology. To create an executive dashboard that would provide useful information to a vice president responsible for a large business process, for example, we would need to combine data from specific processes with information from many other sources. We might also want sales data, data about recent customer surveys, or data from suppliers. All this data would need to be accumulated in one place—in a data warehouse, for example—and then it would need to be analyzed and filtered so that only summary data was provided to the senior manager. The analysis and filtering operations usually rely on data mining systems and on *business intelligence* (BI) techniques. Only a few BPMS products provide the additional technologies to support data warehouse, BI and executive dashboards.

Figure 16.6 illustrates a dashboard developed for an executive using IBM's BPMS product. This dashboard relies on a wide variety of data sources and is filtered by a business intelligence application.

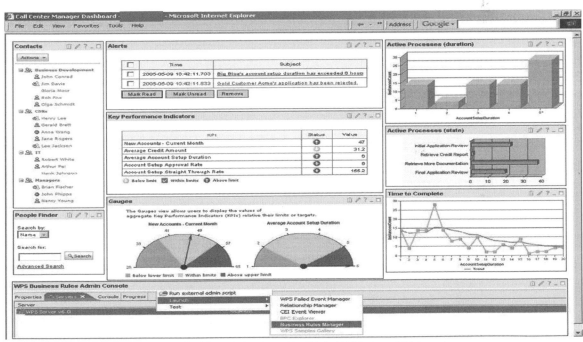

Figure 16.6 A senior management dashboard developed in IBM's WebSphere BPM product.

At the beginning of 2007, a growing number of traditional data warehouse and BI vendors were beginning to explore the BPMS market. As BPMS products become more mature it is likely that they will incorporate data warehouse and BI elements to provide more sophisticated BAM capabilities.

The BPMS Technology Continuum

Stepping back from the idea of a BPMS product, let's consider the elements that go into a BPMS solution, more broadly. In essence, we have turned the diagram in Figure 16.3 and pictured it as a continuum that runs from a software language at one extreme to a complete application at the other. (See Figure 16.7) This continuum suggest a range of products that BPMS vendors could offer.

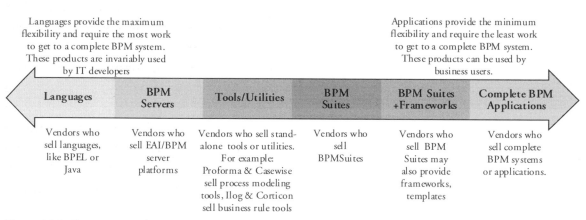

Figure 16.7 The BPMS Product Continuum

Imagine you wanted to create a BPMS application to manage your corporate supply chain. If you have a team of very skilled software developers, they might propose developing the whole application, from scratch, in a software programming language like Java or C. To simplify things somewhat, they might want to use a programming language especially designed to represent business processes and manage the execution of business processes. The Business Process Execution Language (BPEL) is an example of such a language. To save time, the design team might decide to use an Application Server like IBM's WebSphere or Micrcsoft's .NET BizTalk Server. In both cases, the vendors have built utilities into the tool that provide support for BPEL.

To save even more time, the development group might decide to buy a process modeling software package from a vendor that specializes in process modeling. Using a tool like Proforma's ProVision or MEGA's Modeling Suite, one can quickly create process diagrams of unlimited complexity and generate BPEL from the diagram.

If the team really wanted to save time, they might decide to buy a complete BPMS suite, like IBM's WebSphere BPM suite, or Global 360's Enterprise BPM Suite. To save even more time, if a BPMS supply chain application were already available, the development team could just skip development altogether and buy the complete application.

There are lots of packaged applications for sale. The difference between a conventional ERP application and a BPMS-enabled application is that the BPMS application incorporates the elements found in a BPMS product. With a BPMS application, the user can examine the actual flow diagram that guides the process, check the business rules used to make decisions, and change them, as needed. In other words, a BPMS application is designed so that users can examine the underlying process models and can modify the decision rules used in the application.

The problem, of course, is that even a generic BPMS supply chain application might not do what your company wanted done. If you bought the application, you would have to tailor it, and it might turn out to cost as much to tailor the application as it would to develop it from scratch using a BPMS tool. If your supply chain was really large and complex and you needed to integrate with lots of applications developed at your company over the last two decades, you might find that even a BPMS suite lacked the needed utilities and your design team might decide to program their own BPMS package.

In other words, depending on your needs, you might want to buy a product that lies anywhere along the BPMS product continuum. Most companies will probably fall near the middle and find that a BPMS product will serve their needs. But others will want to use basic elements, like BPEL programming language or modeling tools and others will want and hope for BPMS products tailored for their industry, or for complete applications that will serve their needs. Predictably, vendors are readying products that will supply any of these needs.

BPEL

The Business Process Execution Language (BPEL) is the short name for BPEL4WS (for Workflow Systems). BPEL4WS was originally announced in August of 2003 by

BEA, IBM, and Microsoft. Soon after the initial announcement, which described what BPEL4WS should be able to do but fell short of specifics, the draft specification was submitted to OASIS, a standards organization, for completion. The originators were joined by many others and the completion of BPEL was given to the OASIS committee, which has now nearly completed the specification. Unfortunately, even the first version of BPEL is really only an EAI language—it doesn't incorporate the elements needed to describe and support workflow processes that include employees. Thus, BPEL will continue in committee and, eventually, a second or third version of BPEL will emerge that supports most of the core functions we associate with BPMS. In the meantime, vendors may claim to support BPEL but, in fact, they must supplement BPEL code with their own proprietary code to actually accomplish anything interesting, and thus BPEL doesn't buy the user very much. Later, after more sophisticated versions become available, BPEL may be a viable programming option and it will probably make it easier to move applications from one BPEL-compliant product to another, but that time probably won't arrive for several years.

BPMS and SOA

A BPMS product could use any of a variety of different infrastructure techniques to link to software applications. Historically, each of the EAI tools created their own engines to effect the access and linkages. In the last 3–4 years, however, the rapid rise of open Internet standards has focused most developers on a new approach that is usually termed the service oriented architecture, or just SOA.

SOA depends on the Internet and a collection of Internet protocols, including XML, SOAP, UDDI, and WSDL. It depends on organizing software applications as software components that can be called via the Web. A manager considering how his or her company can outsource business processes while still maintaining control over the outsourced processes doesn't need to know any of the details. He or she simply needs to know that SOA is a cost-effective way to organize and integrate distributed software assets.

BPMS does not require SOA, but SOA certainly requires BPMS. Services don't make any sense without the context that business processes provide. Conversely, the runtime automation of business process assumes an underlying layer of services, middleware and, ultimately, software components, and SOA currently provides the most cost-effective way to organize that infrastructure. Even human-focused BPMS systems designed to automate the work of teams of employees still assume the existence of the middleware and software needed to send information to employee desktop PCs and to store the results in appropriate databases.

The Business Process Management Initiative (BPMI.org), a group launched in 2002 whose stated purpose was to encourage the use of business process management systems, certainly recognized this and assumed, from their earliest meetings, that they were creating an XML-based language that would sit on top of a stack of SOA protocols. Similarly, the Object Management Group (OMG) has had this comprehensive vision for several years, and has worked slowly but surely to create a set of standards that would support the integration of components, middleware, services, and process descriptions. Ultimately, this common vision led to the merger of the two organizations and it guides their efforts, today.

Figure 16.8 provides an overview of one possible way of representing the layers that make up a service oriented architecture. Broadly, there are four layers, a software and data layer, a layer of components/interfaces, a layer of business services and their

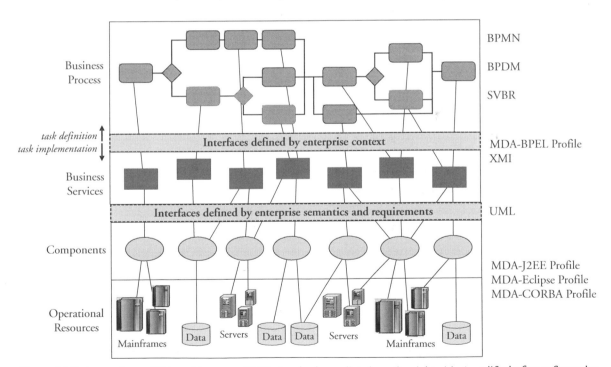

Figure 16.8 Layers in an SOA architecture. OMG standards are listed on the right side (modified after a figure by Mike Rosen).

interfaces, and, on top, a business process. In essence, specific processes are associated with services. The services, in turn, access components, and they, in turn, provide access to software applications or data.

The hope is that, eventually, business people will be able to focus on the business process layer and make changes there, using BPMS tools that will more-or-less automatically rearrange activities on underlying layers. The reality today, however, is that most companies are working to create systems that integrate all these layers and that both BPMS developers and SOA developers need to worry about all aspects of the architecture. Thus, most BPMS efforts involve teams of business and IT people working together.

We have highlighted some of the BPMI and OMG standards on the right side. Some, like BPMN and UML, are involved with notation. Others are involved in defining interfaces, in defining the semantics of rules, and in defining how software design models will generate J2EE or CORBA code. From the OMG's perspective, all of the various models and standards are held together by their model driven architecture (MDA) but, viewed more broadly, MDA is simply a technology that supports the development of BPMS/SOA systems. The ultimate integration of the next generation of BPMS products will depend on the completion and acceptance of the many BPM and XML standards that are today being developed by various standards organizations.

Choosing a BPMS Product

We are not going to recommend a specific BPMS product. Instead, we simply want to point out some things about the current state of the BPMS market, circa early 2007. We suggested earlier that the idea of BPMS originated around 2002. The first BPMS products appeared in 2003. Today there are some 150 vendors who suggest that they are selling BPMS products. Most are small and new. We have also suggested that most BPMS vendors came from another technological area. Thus, for example, some analysts divide BPMS products into four groups:

▶ Integration-Centric BPMS products – tools that have strong roots in EAI
▶ People-Centric BPMS products – tools that have strong roots in workflow
▶ Decision-Centric BPMS products – tools that have strong roots in rules processing
▶ Document-Centric BPMS products – tools that have strong roots in document processing

▶ Monitoring-Centric products – tools that have strong roots in performance monitoring, BI and analysis

Figure 16.9 provides another way to think of the different capabilities of a BPMS product. In this case, we picture a "radar diagram" that we have used to evaluate BPMS products. We begin by creating one branch for each feature set that is important to us. Along each branch we indicate the criteria we use to determine if the product lacks the feature, has some of the desired capability, or implements the feature in the best possible way. We make notes about the uses a particular company wants to make of the BPMS product, to help users think about what's most important to that particular company. Then we map each product we are considering unto the radar diagram. Using dotted and dashed lines, and shading, it is easy to map and compare several applications.

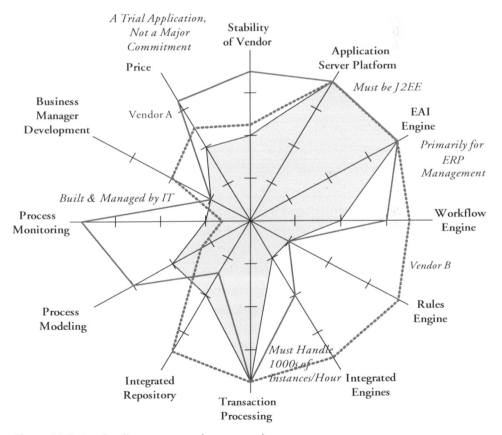

Figure 16.9 A radar diagram comparing two products.

The shaded area on Figure 16.9 suggests what some particular company decided it absolutely needed in any BPMS product it considered. The two lines show how two specific BPMS products were evaluated. In this case, neither provided the minimal functionality that the company felt it required. We provided this example not to provide a definitive way of evaluating BPMS products, but to suggest how to approach the problem, and to underline the fact that the acquisition of any real product, at this point in time, will involve a series of compromises.

The BPMS Market

Now let's step back a bit further and consider the BPMS market more broadly. To help with that, let's take a detour and review Geoffrey Moore's generic analysis of new technology markets. Geoffrey Moore is a high-tech marketing guru who has been involved in numerous technology launches and who wrote a very popular book, *Crossing the Chasm*, which describes the lifecycle of new technologies and the problems they face gaining widespread acceptance.

New technologies, according to Moore, are initially adopted by Innovators, companies that are focused on new technologies and are willing to work hard to make a new technology work in order to gain an early advantage. Innovators have their own teams of sophisticated technologies and are willing to work with academics and vendors to create highly tailored solutions.

Once the Innovators prove that a new technology can be made to work, Early Adopters follow. Early Adopters are not focused on new technologies, as such, but on new business approaches that can give them a competitive advantage. They are less technologically sophisticated than Innovators, but still willing to work hard to make a new technology perform, if they see a clear business advantage. (See Figure 16.10.)

The market for a new technology doesn't really get hot until the Early Majority are convinced to adopt the technology. The Early Majority represent some 35% of the market. They won't adopt new technology until they consider it well-proven. In fact, they aren't interested in technology at all, and don't have a lot of sophisticated technologists who are willing to struggle with the technology. They wait for case studies to show that the technology really gets the benefits that are claimed. And they insist on products that make it easy for less sophisticated developers to deploy the technology quickly, without significant difficulties.

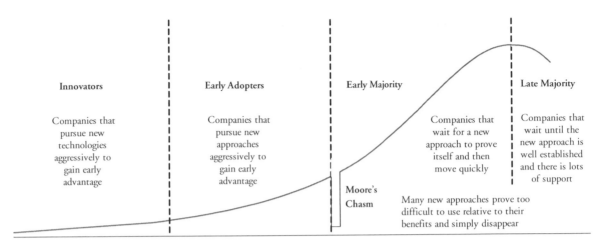

Figure 16.10 Moore's Technology Adoption Life Cycle Curve.

Moore's Chasm falls between Early Adopters and the Early Majority. Lots of technological innovations that are tried by Early Adopters fail to gain sufficient acceptance to pass the criteria of the Early Majority. The new technology gets lots of publicity, for awhile. Conferences are launched to provide information about the technology and it's described in glowing articles in all the high-tech magazines and business publications that are always touting the next new thing. Ultimately, however, the technology fails to produce enough concrete proof of usability and benefits to convince the Early Majority to make an investment.

The Late Majority, like the Laggards who lie even further to the right, are reluctant to spend money or take chances on new approaches. They wait till their competitors among the Early Majority have started gaining benefits from the technology, and then follow suit, reluctantly.

When you go to conferences and hear vendors talking about the technological features of their product and why it's better technology than whatever came before, you are in an Innovator's market. When the market begins to transition to Early Adopters, you begin to hear more business cases and get information on specific benefits. This is also the time when vendors begin to worry about wider acceptance, and become concerned with standards, user interfaces, and assuring their products can work with legacy applications. If the technology is really successful and crosses the chasm, the technology shows tend to drop away, and the vendors begin to show up at traditional business shows and promote their products as a cost-effective way to solve a class of business problems. The majority don't care about technology. They just want to solve business problems quickly and effectively and to stay ahead or at least even with their competitors.

When a new technology is first introduced, lots of relatively small vendors rush to offer products. As long as the market is small, ironically, the number of vendors is large. No one vendor makes very much money, but they are full of hopes, each believing that their technological approach is superior. As the market grows and customers become a little more sophisticated, they begin to demand more comprehensive products and features like support for evolving standards. It is not uncommon for products to go through three to four generations in the course of 2–3 years. The cost of constantly developing new versions of one's product, coupled with the need for more aggressive advertising, forces the smaller vendors to search for capital to continue to remain competitive.

Sometime during the Early Adopter phase of the market, the major vendors begin to incorporate the technology into their more comprehensive offerings, and promote the technology. In effect, the large vendors guarantee that the new technology is safe. As the competition heats up, most of the small vendors disappear. Some are acquired by large vendors. Many decide to specialize in industry- or niche-specific markets. Others simply fail to earn enough money to survive. The key thing, however, is that Majority companies only buy from established vendors who they are reasonably confident can provide the rather extensive support they will require and who they are sure will still be in business 5 or 10 years from now. Thus, if a new technology succeeds in crossing Moore's chasm, the leading vendors will be companies like IBM, Microsoft, and SAP. One or two of the new startups may have been successful enough to have grown into a 100-million-dollar company and still be viable in the Majority market, but most won't make it.

Obviously, we've discussed Moore's analysis framework in order to apply it to the BPMS market. BPMS is somewhere in Early Adopter phase. There are still lots of small vendors competing and the rhetoric is still pretty technical. The large vendors like IBM, Microsoft, and SAP are active, but still have rather immature offerings, and have yet to really commit their considerable marketing resources. Standards work is underway, but the needed standards aren't available yet. There have been some acquisitions and a couple of dropouts, but the market is still focused on technology, on creating early applications that can establish real benefits for the BPMS approach, and on figuring out how to create integrated, easy-to-use packages that a Majority company might want to purchase.

One of the complexities of the BPMS market lies in the comprehensive nature of the BPMS vision. It's conceivable, if BPMS can deliver on its promise, that worldwide processes, like global supply chains, will be managed by BPMS tools that will not only facilitate rapid changes in the processes, but organize the companies' ERP applications more effectively than in the past, while also providing senior managers with comprehensive, real-time monitoring. The scope of this vision suggests just how complex the products are going to have to be if they are really to scale to handle these kinds of processes. At the same time, it suggests that lots of established vendors—process modeling vendors, workflow vendors, EAI vendors, ERP and CRM vendors, Rule, BI and data warehouse vendors—will all need to figure out how to play together in this arena if successful products are to be brought to market. Indeed, it is possible that the real market will be an industry-specific market, rather than a generic process market, since it may prove to be easier to integrate all the elements for an industry than to arrive at a generic, universal BPMS solution.

We expect that it will be at least 3–5 years before BPMS products are ready to cross the chasm and be widely used by the early majority. That won't take place until major vendors like IBM, BEA, Oracle, SAP and HP put their weight behind BPMS and offer and promote sophisticated products. Meantime, everyone is experimenting to determine how BPMS can be most effectively used. And, given the different capabilities of different groups of products, it will be awhile before anyone understands what mature BPMS products will be capable of doing.

We believe that BPMS products will play a major role in the development of the corporate use of business processes. Before a company is ready to automate its processes, however, it first needs to understand them and be confident that the process works well. Most companies are only modeling their processes and don't have good process measurement systems or good process management systems in place. Most large companies will want to explore the use of BPMS, but most would be well-advised to focus on getting their processes modeled and organized before they begin to try to develop automated business process management systems.

Process Modeling Tools vs. BPMS Suites

You might imagine that, since a BPMS product includes a business process modeling environment, BPMS products would replace process modeling tools. It might happen in a decade, but its not likely to happen much sooner. At the moment, the two groups of products are used for different purposes. The process modeling tools were developed to help business people analyze and redesign processes. The leading process modeling tools have been around for over a decade and are much more mature than newer BPMS products. The best of them have simple modeling notations with lots of supporting utilities that make it much easier for business people to capture information about their processes. Moreover, lots of companies use their process modeling tools as an interface for their business process repository, and have stored multiple processes in the repository. Leading companies have used the tools to create business process architectures and rely on the tools to keep track of complex relationships between different processes, measures and resources that support the processes. Many have recorded detailed cost and performance data for specific activities and use simulation to test possible process changes.

BPMS products are much less mature. Most have process modeling environments, left over from when the tools were EAI or workflow tools. These modeling environments are suitable for IT developers and some business analysts, but aren't nearly as friendly as they will need to be if business managers are to use them. BPMS products are designed to support the runtime execution of large business processes. As such, they are much more complex than stand-alone process modeling tools, and much more expensive. As BPMS tools mature they will undoubtedly get better modeling environments and add support for repositories and process architecture work. Eventually, as managers become familiar with BPMS they may feel comfortable enough to do their initial analysis and redesign in these tools. For the moment, however, most companies should focus on redesigning and improving processes, not on automating them. BPMS automation is only in the early adopter phase. Thus, business managers use business process modeling tools for architecture and for process redesign and improvement. BPMS tools are primarily used by software developers and by business analysts working on BPMS application development.

Creating a BPMS Application

There is, to date, no widely accepted methodology for BPMS application development, although some vendors offer their own suggested procedures. In part, this is because BPMS is new and few companies have developed enough BPMS applications to have a good understanding about what works best. In addition, as we have suggested, there are in fact a number of rather different products all going under the BPMS label. Thus, the approach one might follow to develop a human-centric BPMS application (workflow) is different than the approach one might follow to create an integration-centric BPMS application (EAI) or a decision-centric BPMS application (rules-based). Some companies model and redesign their processes in conventional business process modeling tools and then move the application over to a BPMS environment for runtime execution, while others develop directly in the BPMS tool. There's little consistency and no one has enough experience.

Stepping back from specifics, we can offer one very important piece of advice. Don't start a BPMS project until you are sure that process you intend to manage with the BPMS application is already running as you want it to run once it's a BPMS application. In other words, do not try to combine a process redesign project and a BPMS application development project. Both types of projects are demanding and require different skill sets and combining them is a recipe for a failure. Do redesign or improvement using the techniques we described in Part II of this book. Once you have processes you are happy with, consider setting the process up in a BPMS environment for day-to-day management and execution.

Getting a BPMS application up and running is an IT implementation project. The problems we have heard about are classic software-development problems and have little to do with process work, as such. Companies have had trouble getting the infrastructure right. Companies have developed applications in one tool and then realized that the application wouldn't scale to support the number of transactions they wanted to run on a daily basis, and so forth. As we have suggested, companies are still learning about BPMS, so don't attempt to automate an application that you can't afford to have fail. Get some experience with BPMS before you attempt anything too challenging.

With all these qualifications, imagine a world in which your major business processes were defined with process modeling and you could literally watch as instances flowed through the different activities that made up your application. You could notice bottlenecks as they began to occur, and you could change business rules and watch how they changed the activities that were taking place. BPMS offers a world in which processes are more central and better managed than ever before. It offers a world in which managers can observe the work being done and change the process, as needed, in something close to real time. They are a solution for lots of the demands that today's managers face. Leading companies are investing in BPMS because they see its potential and want to use it to gain a competitive advantage over their rivals. In a decade, we expect that BPMS applications will be as widely used as ERP applications are today. The trick, in the meantime, is planning your transition to this technology.

Notes and References

BPTrends has developed a report that describes the popular elements in BPMS products and describes most of the leading products to facilitate an initiation evaluation of the available products. The report is free and updated yearly and provides a good way for those new to BPMS to develop a better understanding of the many different products being offered at this time. To access the report, go to *www.bptrends.com* and choose the BPMS Report.

There is ambiguity about the phrase *business process management*. Executives tend to use it in a generic sense to refer to managing processes. People in the workflow and XML business process language area often use *BPM* and *Business Process Management* as synonyms for BPMS to refer to systems that automate business processes. Also keep in mind that some people will use Workflow or Enterprise Application Integration (EAI) as synonyms for BPMS.

Smith, Howard, and Peter Fingar, *Business Process Management: The Third Wave*, Meghan-Kiffer Press, 2003. This book kicked off the current interest in BPMS tools and applications. It's a bit over the top, but it presents the case for BPMS with lots of enthusiasm.

Khan, Rashid N., *Business Process Management: A Practical Guide*, Meghan-Kiffer Press, 2005. Of the books published that have sought to explain BPMS products, this is the one I think offers the most practical and straightforward presentation.

White, Stephen, "Using BPMN to Model a BPEL Process," BPTrends, March 2005. This paper on BPTrends walks through the way BPMN notation can be used to generate BPEL, the language underlying some BPMS products.

Owen, Martin, "BPMN and Business Process Management," BPTrends, March 2004. This paper on BPTrends discusses the use of BPMN for BPMS development.

Rosen, Michael, "BPM and SOA: Where Does One End and the Other Begin?" BPTrends, January 2006. Mike Rosen has written a series of articles on BPTrends describing the relationship between BPM and SOA. This is the article where he introduced the diagram used in Figure 16.8, but all of the articles are worth reading.

There are no books that really describe a methodology for BPMS development. Derek Miers has published two papers on BPTrends that suggest what such a methodology might look like.

Miers, Derek, "Keys to BPM Success," BPTrends, January 2006.

Miers, Derek, "Getting Past the First BPMS Project," BPTrends, March 2006.

Chappell, David, *Understanding BPM Servers*, *www.bptrends.com*, January 2005. This is a nice summary of how Microsoft is approaching BPMS with its BizTalk Server.

The International Conference on Business Process Management is a yearly event at which researchers gather to explore the inner workings of BPMS technologies. BPM 2007 will be in Australia and the web address is: *http://bpm07.fit.qut.edu.au/* Each year the conference publishes its proceedings via Springer under the general title: Business Process management. If you are interested in technical issues involved with BPMS, these technical papers can be useful.

zur Muehlen, Michael, *Workflow-based Process Controlling: Foundation, Design, and Application of Workflow-driven Process Information Systems*, Logos Verlag Berlin, 2004. A technical book on the theory of BPMS with a special emphasis on process control.

The Web address of the Workflow Management Coalition is *www.wfmc.org*. The WfMC was founded in 1993. It's a consortium of major workflow users and workflow vendors. WfMC meets frequently to discuss key workflow issues and has developed a number of workflow standards.

Moore, Geoffrey A., *Crossing the Chasm*, HarperBusiness, 1991.

A search on BPMS on *www.bptrends.com* will generate a large selection of articles. This field is changing very rapidly and new articles are being published each month.

17

ERP-Driven Redesign

I N   T H E   1 9 9 0 S , many companies installed off-the-shelf applications from a variety of companies, including SAP, Peoplesoft, Baan, J.D. Edwards, and Oracle. Initially, these vendors stressed that they sold applications that performed certain common tasks that companies faced, like those in accounting, inventory, and human resources. Later, in response to the widespread interest in business process improvement, these same companies began to reposition themselves. They developed templates or blueprints that showed how groups of their modules could be linked together to create business processes. In line with this transition, people began to refer to these groups of applications as enterprise resource planning (ERP) applications, and recently some have added customer relationship management (CRM) applications and manufacturing applications. In essence, the vendors introduced a layer of EAI or workflow that allowed companies to specify or modify the flow of control from one ERP module to another.

One leading advocate of this approach is Thomas Davenport, one of the consultants who had kicked off the business process reengineering movement in the early 1990s. In 2000, Davenport wrote *Mission Critical: Realizing the Promise of Enterprise Systems*. He argued that a packaged application approach allowed companies to integrate and improve their software systems. He was careful to qualify his argument and say that the use of software only worked within a broader business process architecture, but when implemented in such a context, Davenport believes that packaged applications can help a company to rapidly integrate diverse processes.

In the last few years J.D. Edwards was acquired by PeopleSoft, which was, in turn, acquired by Oracle. Meanwhile, Microsoft has entered the market and is developing packaged software for smaller companies In 2004, all of the ERP vendors combined made around 50 billion dollars. Obviously, the ERP market is much larger than the early BPMS market. At the same time, however, most companies are unhappy with the installation problems and the maintenance costs of their ERP software. One of the major drivers of BPMS development has been the hope that BPMS will make it easier to manage ERP. Thus, although BPMS is just beginning to gain momentum, it seems likely that, in a few years, ERP and BPMS vendors will find themselves merging or competing to offer companies more flexible business process solutions.

Processes, Packages and Best Practices

Vendors like SAP, Peoplesoft, and Oracle often refer to their applications as "best processes." They argue that they developed their modules after studying what worked best at several companies and that the modules represent very efficient ways of handling the processes and activities they support. In fact, of course, these modules represent "average processes." In many cases, they are an advance on the applications that companies had before, but once a company decides to use SAP, Microsoft, or Oracle modules in their human resources department, then their HR processes will be the same as those of their competitors who are using the same modules from these same vendors.

Compared to the business process improvement approach we advocated throughout this book, the use of ERP applications occurs in reverse order. In effect, you begin with a solution—a new inventory application from SAP—and proceed to modify your existing inventory process to accommodate the inputs and outputs of the new inventory application. It is still possible to begin by analyzing the existing process, substituting the new SAP module or set of modules during the design phase, and then making the adjustments necessary to use the modules effectively. But the heart of this kind of ERP redesign effort is to accommodate the way your company works to the ERP application and not the other way around.

We think ERP applications represent a reasonable approach to improving a wide variety of business processes. If the processes are easy to automate and add little value to your overall business, then there's no reason why you shouldn't simply rely on efficient, average solutions, and focus your energies instead on core processes that do add significant value. Let's face it, managing payroll deductions or handling an office inventory database are enabling processes that need to be done, but they rarely add anything to the bottom line.

The problem comes when companies try to use ERP applications for tasks that are not routine and decide to tailor the ERP applications to better fit with the way their company does business. The various ERP applications are, essentially, database applications; they manage database operations. Each of the ERP vendors has its own favorite database, and it's very hard to modify the internal workings of ERP applications once they are installed. If your company acquires a payroll application and then decides to tailor it, you will find that the value of buying an off-the-shelf application diminishes rapidly. Moreover, the maintenance costs will rise in the future. When new versions of the ERP application are released, they won't work at your organization until the new ERP modules are modified to match the previous modifications you made. If you find yourself considering ERP applications, and simultaneously planning to make lots of modifications in the ERP applications you buy, you are probably making a mistake. If the process is really a routine process and adds little value, it's probably better to change your workflow and use the application in its standard version. If you really can't live with the vanilla version of the ERP application, then you ought to ask yourself if you really want to buy an ERP application in the first place. (We'll return to this problem later in this chapter.)

There are vendors that sell applications or that develop applications that offer more flexibility than the standard ERP applications and in the long run don't cost as much if you want a highly tailored application or know you will want to change the application frequently. On the other hand, of course, these applications will probably not integrate with other modules as well as the standard ERP modules do, and that will add to the cost of the more specialized applications.

The ERP vendors have recently experienced problems as companies have begun to rely more on the Internet. Most ERP applications were designed to be self-contained systems, tightly linked with and relying on a proprietary database management system. The ERP systems were not prepared to support distributed data management. Most aren't especially good at working with other ERP applications, and they were totally unprepared when companies began to want to integrate applications into Web portals or into supply chains that communicated over the Internet. In the past few years, most of the ERP vendors have redesigned their systems and have begun to release new ERP applications designed to communicate via the Internet. In most cases, however, this adds another layer of complexity to the problems of integrating applications into e-business systems.

A Closer Look at SAP

Let's take a closer look at SAP, the dominant ERP vendor. SAP provides overviews, which it calls *business maps*, of processes that it offers in a number of industry-specific areas. Specifically, it offers business maps, or what we would call *process architectures*, in each of these areas:

Discrete industries
- Aerospace and defense
- Automotive
- Engineering and construction
- High tech

Process industries
- Chemicals
- Mill products
- Mining
- Oil and gas
- Pharmaceuticals

Financial services
- Banking
- Insurance

Consumer industries
- Consumer products
- Retail

Service industries
- Media
- Service providers
- Telecommunications
- Utilities

Public service
- Healthcare
- Higher education and research
- Public sector

Figure 17.1 illustrates one of SAP's business maps. In this case we have illustrated SAP's telecommunications business architecture. On the left side SAP lists the functional areas or, in some cases, large-scale business processes. On the right, in each row, are the processes included in the general category listed on the left.

SAP Telecommunications Business Architecture					
Enterprise Management	Strategic Enterprise Management	Business Analytics	Business Intelligence and Decision Support	Accounting	Workforce Planning and Alignment
Customer Relationship Management	Marketing and Campaign Management	Sales Management	Dealer Management	Customer and Retention Management	Customer Care
Sales and Order Management—Standard Products	Product Selling	Contract Management		Order Management	Service Activation
Sales and Order Management—Customer Solutions	Sales Cycle Management	Site Survey and Solution Design	Contract Management	Project Management	Order Management and Fulfillment	Provisioning
Service Assurance	Service Agreements	Customer Trouble Reporting	Customer Trouble Management	Trouble Resolution
Customer Financials Management	Credit Management	Prebilling	Convergent Invoicing	eBPP	Receivables and Collections Management	Dispute Management
Supply Chain Management	Supply Network Design	Demand and Supply Planning	eProcurement	Production Planning and Execution	Supply Chain Coordination	Warehouse Management
Network Lifecycle Management	Demand Planning	Requirements Planning	Investment Management	Network Design and Build	Operation and Maintenance
Value-Added Services	Content and Intellectual Properties Management	Advertising Management	Mobile Business and Wireless ASP	eLearning
Business Support	Human Resources Operations Sourcing and Deployment	Travel Management	Financial Supply Chain Management	Treasury/Corporate Finance Management	Real Estate

Figure 17.1 SAP telecommunications business architecture.

Thus, one functional area is Service Assurance, and there are four SAP processes under that function heading: Service Agreements, Customer Trouble Reporting, Customer Trouble Management, and Trouble Resolution. Figure 17.2 shows the specific SAP components or application modules that are used to implement (automate) each process.

Notice that although the various components have different names, they often have the same component number. This suggests that the components are, in fact, subcomponents or modules of larger SAP applications, or that they rely on the same database for stored information. As we suggested earlier, SAP has reengineered its software applications to move them from a client-server architecture to a component architecture, and the original design often shows through.

SAP Telecommunications Business Architecture				
Service Assurance	Service Agreements	Customer Trouble Reporting	Customer Trouble Management	Trouble Resolution
SAP Components Available	- Service Contracts (C17) - Service Level Agreements (C17) - Service Event Management (C17)	- Capture of Customer Trouble Ticket (C17) - Diagnostic Engine to Aid Resolution (C6, C17) - Call Management with Front-end Close Support (C17) - Site Visit Scheduling (C17, C5) - Internet Trouble Self-Service (C17)	- Work Request Management (C17, C5) - Workflow-Based Execution and Exception Management (C5, C17) - Correlation of Customer Troubles to Network Troubles (Future) - Trouble Ticket Reporting	- Sophisticated Diagnosis Engine (C17) - Field/Mobile Service (C17) - Work Dispatching/Scheduling (Future) - Material/Spare Part Management (C6, C8) - Capture of Resolution Data for Future Diagnosis (C17)

Figure 17.2 SAP components used to implement the four processes under Service Assurance.

We illustrated SAP's telecommunications business architecture so you can compare it with the eTOM business framework developed by the TeleManagement Forum, which is pictured in Chapter 3 as Figure 3.5. The eTOM architecture was developed by a task force of telecommunications managers and uses terms that are probably more familiar to those in the telecommunications industry. The SAP architecture was also developed by a telecom industry group organized by SAP. The resulting framework uses more generic process names since it relies on existing SAP modules whenever possible. In addition, keep in mind that the eTOM architecture was designed to describe a set of processes that might or might not be automated at any given telecom company. The SAP architecture, on the other hand, only lists software components that SAP sells or plans to sell, or that an SAP-associated vendor sells. Each software component may be entirely automated or it may provide user interfaces, so that employees can use interface screens to monitor or control the processing undertaken by the component.

Figure 17.3 illustrates a different SAP business architecture—in this case, the architecture for insurance. Notice how similar the lists of functional areas or large-scale processes are. Also notice that functional areas near the top and bottom of the diagram describe processes that are very similar to those listed on the telecommunications business architecture in Figure 17.1. Once again, the insurance architecture was developed by industry representatives in conjunction with SAP, and, as before, it relied on standard SAP modules whenever possible.

SAP Insurance Business Architecture				
Enterprise Management	Strategic Enterprise Management	Business Analytics	Business Intelligence and Decision Support	Accounting
Customer Relationship Management	Customer Engagement	Business Transaction	Contract Fulfillment	Customer Service
Sales	Sales Planning	Account and Contract Management / Acquisition and Sales Management	Commission Management	Collections and Disbursements
Claims	Claim Notification	Proactive Claims Management	Claim Handling and Adjustment	Claims Accounting
Policy and Product Management	Market Research	Product Definition and Administration	Policy Management	In-Force Business Administration
Reinsurance	Reinsurance Underwriting	Reinsurance Claim Handling / Reinsurance Accounting	Retrocession	Statistics and Reporting
Asset Management	Asset Allocation	Portfolio Management	Portfolio Accounting	Portfolio Controlling
Business Support	Human Resource Operations Sourcing and Deployment	Procurement	Treasury	Fixed Asset Management

Figure 17.3 SAP business architecture for insurance companies.

If a company decides to work with SAP, the SAP representative provides the company with a detailed description of the SAP business architecture and the processes making up each component and asks the company managers to choose which they want to use. Once a company has chosen the modules or processes they want to acquire, they can tailor them by changing names to match the terminology already in use at the company or by changing the actual processes themselves to conform more closely to practices at the specific company. It's especially difficult to link SAP components to other components that you use at your company, or to mix modules from more than one ERP vendor.

Tailoring also takes quite a bit of time. More importantly, once an SAP process is tailored, it's harder for the company to use new SAP updates. Before the company can install the updates, the company must first tailor the updates to match the existing SAP modules you have already tailored. The cost of tailoring SAP applications rapidly eats into the cost savings that one hopes to get when one buys off-the-shelf software, and raises maintenance costs. A company gets the best buy when it acquires

SAP modules and uses them without tailoring, or creates add-on modules that don't change the basic SAP modules.

SAP is in the business of selling processes or components that are very similar. They have created some unique modules for each industry, but, overall, they still rely on the initial modules they introduced in the 1980s, which include core accounting, inventory, and human resource functions. There's nothing wrong with using standard modules, but any business manager should realize that many competitors are also using SAP modules. Thus, using an SAP process doesn't give a company a competitive edge, but simply provides the company with a clean, modern implementation of a software process.

So far we've looked at the business architecture view of SAP processes. Once you have settled on a specific component, you can obtain a more specific process diagram. SAP uses diagrams from the ARIS product of IDS Scheer. Both SAP and IDS Scheer are headquartered in Germany. (The founder of IDS Scheer, August-Wilhelm Scheer, is a software engineering theorist who has written several books on business process modeling and software development. He is currently on the advisory board of SAP.) The IDS Scheer annual conferences, Process World 200x, are major events in Europe and North America each year and provides a good overview of the ERP-driven approach to business process improvement. Other process modeling vendors, like Popkin, MEGA, and CASEwise, also have relationships with SAP.

Figure 17.4 provides a process diagram of a process used by a car retailer. The diagram begins at the top of the page and flows down.

The rectangles with rounded corners represent activities. The six-sided boxes represent events or decision outcomes that occur during the process. The small circles represent decision points or describe the logic of a flow. Thus, the circle with ^ represents AND. If two events are joined by an AND, then both must occur before the next process can occur. (The circle with XOR inside represents *exclusive OR*, which means that one or the other must occur, but not both.) The person or department responsible for the processes appears at the right in an oval. On the left, in thin rectangles, are documents that are accessed, modified, or stored in a database.

SAP is widely used, and thus there are lots of programmers who understand and use ARIS process diagrams like the one shown in Figure 17.4. In addition, ARIS supports a number of other diagrams, including one that has swimlanes and is more like the diagrams we have been using in this book. The diagram in Figure 17.4, however, is the standard ARIS process diagram.

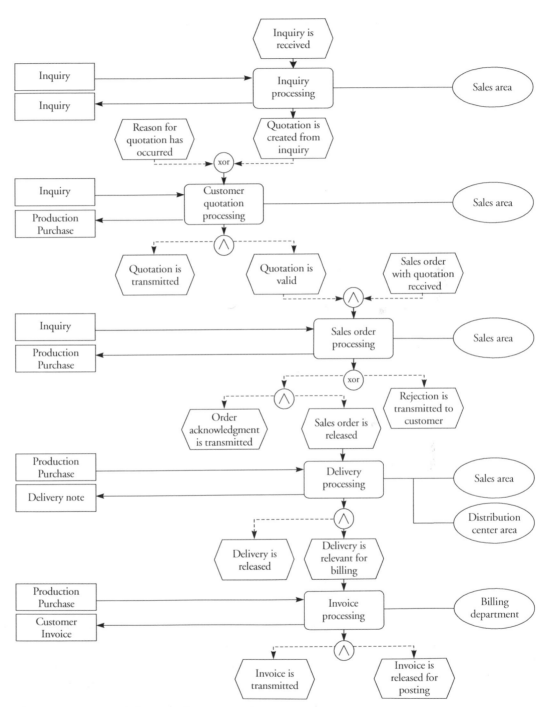

Figure 17.4 SAP/ARIS diagram of a new car sales process.

Figure 17.5 presents the same information that is shown in Figure 17.4 using the process diagram notation we have used in this book.

Auto Sales Process

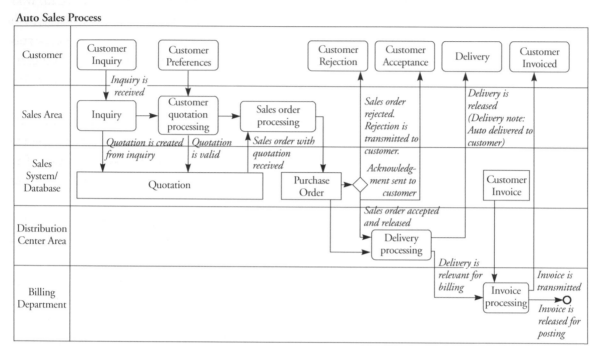

Figure 17.5 A retail car sales process in our notation.

As you can see in Figure 17.5, there is a clearer distinction between events that a customer performs, documents that are inside the sales system, and events that define the flow of information in the process. By simply scanning along a swim lane, one can quickly see all the places the retail dealer interacts with the customer. Similarly, using other swimlanes, one is provided with a better idea of who is responsible for which activities. Note that all the activities pictured in Figure 17.5 are mixed employee/IT activities. In other words, in each case an employee must enter information into the sales database from a personal computer.

We have omitted most of the logic flow notation. In some cases we show two arrows arriving at a box. Our notation does not tell us if both inputs are required, if either one is sufficient to start the process, or if both are required before the process starts. These are issues that software developers must resolve before they can develop software, but they are issues that managers often ignore when they are defining business processes.

The process notation used in the SAP reference model by ARIS is designed to tell its users more about the control flow between processes. On the other hand, it doesn't emphasize the relationship between process and the customer, or make it as clear who is responsible for what activities. As a strong generalization, the diagrams we use are better for managers who want to analyze and design business processes. The diagrams used with the ARIS methodology are better suited for software developers who must implement a system that relies heavily on the management of documents that reside in SAP systems.

Figure 17.6 illustrates another type of SAP diagram. In this case, an e-business process that relies on the Internet to pass information between three parties—customers, an insurance company, and companies that repair cars—is illustrated. The processes or activities are shown in six-sided boxes. The flow is indicated by the fact that some boxes abut others.

SAP calls the diagrams shown in Figure 17.6 C-business maps, which stands for collaborative business maps. In essence, this is a special kind of ARIS diagram to illustrate simple e-business interactions.

What we like best about Figure 17.6 are the business benefits and value potentials that SAP includes on the right and left sides of the basic diagram. In essence, SAP lists reasons why specific activities will save or make companies money. When they have specific data, they indicate it as a value potential, and usually add footnotes to indicate the source of the data. Thus, in the example in Figure 17.6, we see that SAP predicts that approving auto repairs online will result in cost savings, and suggest that Diebold Deutschland found that it saved them 40% of the cost of the activity.

All of the business architectures and C-business maps are available on SAP's Web site: *www.sap.com*. SAP offers collaborative business maps in CRM, supply chain management, product lifecycle management, e-procurement, marketplaces, financials, and human resources. The kind of benefits SAP lists are most reliable when a company implements a standard process. There isn't much data available on the more industry-specific processes, which only emphasizes that the ERP-driven approach is usually best employed when a company wants to automate processes where the logic is relatively simple and where the processes don't add much strategic value.

SAP Insurance C-Business Map: Loss Notification and Automated Claims Handling

This C-Business Map is designed for the insurance industry. It shows how three parties—a customer, an insurance company and a service provider—use the Internet to exchange information about an insurance claim. The map shows h the benefits of collaboration. Efficient and pro-active claims management reduces claim expenses and enhances customer se rvice. These benefits save time and money.

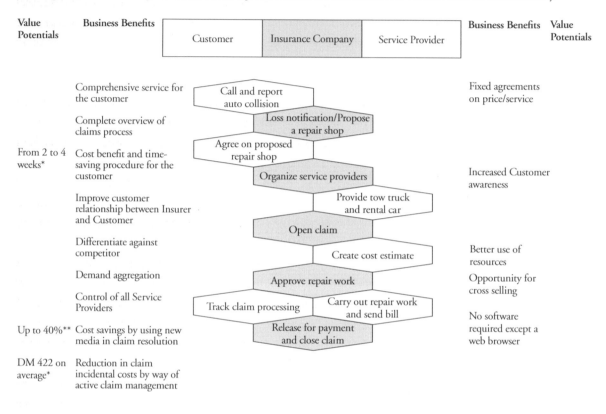

Source: *German insurance company; **Diebold Deutschland GmbH

Figure 17.6 SAP C-Business map of an Internet-based auto claims process.

Implementing an ERP-Driven Design

In a review of ERP implementation efforts, the Gartner Group argued that the most important thing is the training of end users. This follows directly from the nature of the business process redesign efforts that are driven by ERP applications.

In essence, you begin with an architecture and choose components to use. Then you turn to specific process sequences and choose specific activities to implement.

As a result, you have selected a whole set of processes and activities that you intend to install at your company with a minimum of changes. Some activities will be fully automated, but most of the activities you select will require that employees learn to use interface screens on PCs to enter or retrieve information from the SAP databases that form the core of any SAP system. That may sound simple but, in fact, depending on what your employees are doing now, you will need to teach employees an entirely new process.

Consider an auto dealer that used a less sophisticated system. The salespeople talked with customers and eventually filled out a form, which they then used when they phoned to see if a car with the desired characteristics was available. At some point, assuming the car was available, the salesperson would negotiate a price and then take a brief break to get the manager's approval of the deal being struck. The order in which the salesperson performed those tasks, and the verbal exchange with the customer while all the details were being attended to, was probably quite specific to individual salespeople. Once the SAP system is installed, our salesperson is going to have to learn to carry on his conversation while entering information into a computer. The SAP system assumes that the manager approves online, and that the supplier determines the availability of the car online, and so forth. It's probably going to take quite a bit of training before the salesperson feels comfortable with the new process. And the auto example is relatively simple, since it largely follows the sales process already used in auto retail showrooms. Other processes that rely on the use of databases can rearrange the steps in an established process in a much more confusing manner.

SAP is not the only ERP vendor that offers architecture and business process diagrams. Oracle and Microsoft both have something similar. Figure 17.7 illustrates a process map developed by Siebel and IBM to show how Siebel's CRM software could be organized with IBM's BPMS WebSphere software.

Most companies begin with an analysis of their As-Is process. Then they "overlay" the ERP modules they intend to install, eliminating the subprocesses and activities that the new ERP applications will replace. What one obtains is a new diagram with lots of disconnects. The interfaces to the ERP applications are PC interface screens (links to database documents). The trick is to create a new To-Be diagram that ties each of the existing activities that remain to ERP modules that have been inserted. Once you have done that, you need to review which employees will be doing what tasks and revise job descriptions accordingly. And then you must provide the training necessary to assure that people can do their new jobs.

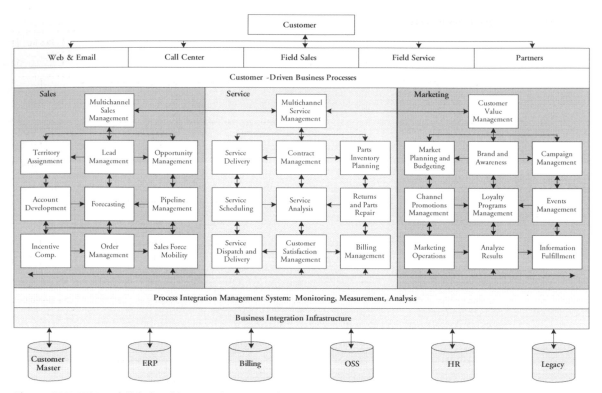

Figure 17.7 IBM and Siebel architecture for CRM (after a report from IBM and Siebel).

One technical problem involves the "translation" of diagrams. We recommend the use of the type of process diagrams we have introduced in this book. These diagrams make it easier for managers to see how processes work and who is responsible for what activities. Thus, to "overlay" a set of SAP activities, you need to do a translation of the SAP diagram, along the lines illustrated in Figure 17.5. This probably isn't something the redesign team should attempt, but something that the facilitator or someone in the IT department should be able to do for the team.

Figure 17.8 illustrates a sales order system that relies on two different ERP modules. The ERP Sales Quotation application is essentially an application that checks an inventory database to determine if ordered items are in stock. The ERP Sales and Distribution application is an application that creates a printed bill of lading. The Sales Order System is an automated system that could be on a company portal, or it could simply be an application that is accessible online to retailers who sell your company's products.

E-Commerce Sales Quotation Process

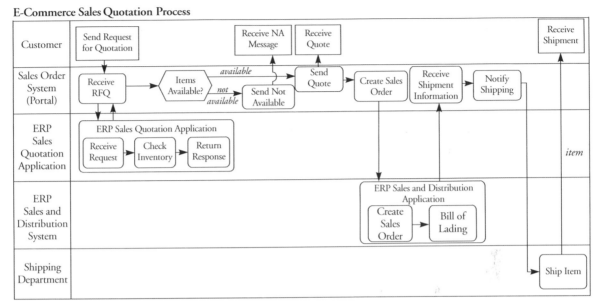

Figure 17.8 A process that interfaces with two ERP applications.

In this example, we've shown some of the activities that occur inside each ERP application. In most cases we would simply have a single process box to indicate each ERP application. The people working on the process really don't need to know exactly what goes on inside the ERP applications. What they need to know is what inputs they need to make, what outputs are made, and who has to process the inputs and outputs. In this example, since the customer is interacting with an automated system, the inputs to the ERP applications are made by the sales order system, which is itself a software system. If this system replaces a process that involved employees, then appropriate changes would be required. The output of this process is a request to shipping (a bill of lading) to send an item to a customer. Shipping needs to know to accept such an order and how to handle it. Assuming employees are working in shipping, we would probably want to do another process diagram to define just what happens in the Ship Item subprocess.

The main point here, however, is that you can create swimlanes for ERP applications and indicate how the ERP applications interface with existing process flows. Preparing for a transition to the use of ERP applications means understanding exactly how the ERP applications will interact with your existing processes, and then training your people to handle the ERP inputs and outputs when the system is implemented.

Before we discussed ERP-driven redesign, we considered workflow. In essence, ERP systems are also workflow systems. Instead of designing a unique workflow system with a workflow tool, one simply chooses ERP components or processes to assemble into a system. Underneath, however, the ERP vendor provides a workflow engine that passes control from one component or process to the next. An IT manager can use the ERP management system to exclude specific documents from a particular process or to quickly modify the order in which processes are used. By combining precoded processes with workflow, companies gain considerable control over basic processes.

Microsoft recently announced that it would be entering the ERP market. Microsoft argued that existing ERP vendors had not provided for small and midsize businesses, and it hopes that it can use XML and the Internet to create a new generation of ERP applications.

Case Study: Nestlé USA Installs SAP

A good example of a company that used ERP packages to reorganize their business processes is provided by the U.S. subsidiary of Nestlé SA, a Swiss food conglomerate. Nestlé USA was created in the late 1980s and early 1990s via acquisitions. In 2002 it included seven divisions which collectively sold such popular brands as Alpo, Baby Ruth, Carnation Instant Breakfast, Coffee-Mate, Nescafe, Nestlé Toll House, Power-Bar, Stouffer's Lean Cuisine, SweeTarts, and Taster's Choice. In 2002, the company employed some 16,000 employees and earned about $8 billion in revenues.

In the mid-1990s the various companies that make up Nestlé SA were all operating as independent units. In 1997 a team studying the various company systems concluded that, collectively, the companies were paying 29 different prices for vanilla—which they all purchased from the same vendor. The study wasn't easy, since each company had a different number or name for vanilla and purchased it via completely different processes. Just isolating vanilla and then determining a common unit price required a considerable effort.

In 1997, Nestlé USA decided that it would standardize all of the major software systems in all of its divisions. A key stakeholder team was set up to manage the entire process. By March 1998, the team had its plan. It decided it would standardize on five SAP modules—purchasing, financials, sales and distribution, accounts payable, and accounts receivable. In addition, the stakeholder team decided to implement Manugistics' supply chain module. The team considered SAP's supply chaining module, Advance Planner and Optimizer (APO), but it was brand-new in 1997, and they decided to go with the better-known Manugistics module that was specifically designed to work with SAP modules.

Before even beginning to implement SAP modules, people from the divisions were gathered and spent 18 months examining data names and agreeing on a common set of names. Vanilla, for example, would henceforth be code 1234 in every division.

Somewhere along the line, the project to install SAP modules also became a Y2K program. By moving to standard software that was guaranteed to be free of bugs associated with date problems that might occur when applications started dealing with dates subsequent to December 31, 1999, the companies would avoid any Y2K problems. Unfortunately, this placed a deadline on the entire implementation effort—it had to be done before January 1, 2000.

As the various SAP applications began to roll out to the divisions, the stakeholder team managing the entire effort began to get lots of unpleasant feedback. Jeri Dunn, the VP and CIO of Nestlé USA, explained that, in hindsight, they had completely underestimated the problems involved in changing division cultures or modifying established business processes. By the beginning of 1999, the rollout was in serious trouble. The workers didn't understand the new SAP modules, and they didn't understand how the outputs they were now getting would help them do their jobs or manage the processes they were responsible for.

It was at a major meeting in early 1999 that Dunn was given responsibility for the project. Among the other conclusions reached by this executive committee meeting was that the Y2K deadline would be ignored. Henceforth, they would figure out the implementation requirements for each SAP module and then let that specification guide their schedule. They decided that it was relatively easy to install SAP modules, but that it was very hard to change business processes and to win the acceptance of the people responsible for assuring those processes operated correctly. They also decided that much more care needed to be taken to determine just how the SAP modules would interact with the processes and applications that would remain in place.

At the same time that Dunn took over, a new director of process change was hired, and a process manager (VP) for the supply chain was promoted to help Dunn on the remainder of the project. In most cases, the team now began to focus on modeling processes and defining process requirements and then creating a plan to install the SAP modules. Several installations were delayed for months or years to accommodate groups that were not prepared for the process changes required. As we go to press, the Nestlé transition is coming to an end. The company spent approximately $200 million on the transition. Dunn claims that the project has already paid for itself. The new planning processes, for example, make it possible to project Nestlé USA-wide demand more accurately and to save significant inventory and redistribution costs. The VP for Nestlé USA's supply chain, Dick Ramage, estimates that supply chain improvements have accounted for a major portion of the $325 million that Nestlé has already saved as a result of the SAP installation.

Dunn says she's happy with the SAP applications and very happy that all of the companies are now using the same basic processes. Still, in an article on the transition in *CIO Magazine* in May 2002, Dunn claimed that if she had it to do over again, she'd "focus first on changing business processes and achieving universal buy-in, and then and only then on installing the software."

Nestlé USA's use of ERP applications and their problems are typical of most large companies that have elected to rely on ERP applications to drive major changes. The company embraces the ERP applications in hopes that they can organize and standardize their software applications and databases across departments and divisions. Most large companies have started on this path and found that it takes much longer and is more painful than they had hoped. Few have completed their ERP transitions. The problem lies in the fact that the ERP applications aren't a solution. They are a tool to use in changing business processes. This isn't something that IT can do by itself. The transition must be conceptualized as a business process transition and guided by business managers. The ERP applications must be installed as part of the overall business process redesign effort, not as an independent activity. Used in an appropriate manner, ERP applications offer a powerful tool to aid in business process redesign.

Using BPMS to Improve ERP Installations

Most large companies have installed packaged ERP and CRM applications in the course of the last decade. Some have installed the same vendor's ERP applications throughout the company while others have installed a mix of packaged and best-of-breed applications. Figure 17.9 provides a very abstract way of looking at an ERP installation. Imagine a company that has a process with three activities. To automate the activities, or at least to support the employees performing the activities, while simultaneously gathering data that can be provided to managers, the company decides to install an ERP system. To keep things simple, the company buys all its ERP modules from a single company and thereby assures that the modules will all talk to each other and will store their data in a common database, making it much easier to generate reports. The vendor has three modules that support the three activities. Luckily, Activity 1 is so similar to the assumptions made by the corresponding ERP application that no tailoring is required. Unfortunately, both Activity 2 and Activity 3 include steps and flows that are performed differently than the two ERP modules normally handle them. Thus, IT agrees to tailor the two ERP modules. We represent this with the little boxes inside the modules, which we hope suggests some tailoring.

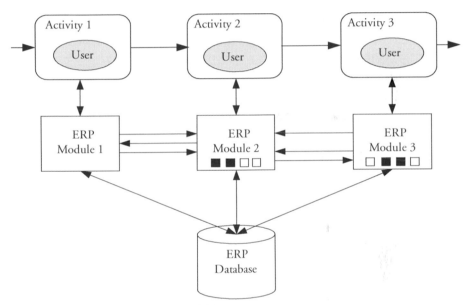

Figure 17.9 ERP modules support activities.

When the ERP application is finally rolled out—for it took quite some time to tailor the ERP modules—everyone was happy. Later, however, when the ERP vendor moved from Version 2.0 to Version 3.0, modules 2 and 3 had to be tailored all over again. In a short time the company realized that it was going to have to keep paying and changing its ERP applications as each new version of the ERP software is released.

Unfortunately, the problem we have described is only the tip of the ERP iceberg. If the company involved is a large international company, it probably rolled-out ERP to its different branches and subsidiaries over the course of several years. Moreover, to keep everyone happy, IT keep tailoring ERP applications to support the local practices of groups in each of the branches and subsidiaries. Let's imagine that ERP module 2 records sales data and that ERP module 3 prepares a statement for the customer. The European division uses both ERP modules 2 and 3, tailored for their way of doing business. The Indian subsidiary and the Japanese subsidiaries also use ERP modules 2 and 3, but each tailored in a slightly different manner. In other words, when the ERP vendor moves from Version 2 to Version 3, the company is actually going to have to buy several copies of module 2 and several copies of module 3 and then tailor them to replace all of the different versions of those modules it is using throughout the world.

Multiply this by a dozen different business processes and you have anywhere from dozens to hundreds of different ERP applications running in a large international organization. The costs of this approach can be staggering. Figure 17.10 suggests the ERP multiversion problem that most large companies face.

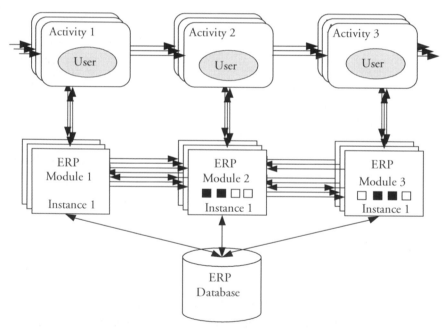

Figure 17.10 Multiple instances of ERP supporting a variety of similar, but slightly different sales activities.

A quick glance at Figure 17.10 suggests that three different units all do a rather similar activity—recording sales data in the case of Activity 2—and that huge savings could be achieved if all divisions and subsidiaries agreed to perform the same activity in the same way. Then the company could tailor one module to support the common activity and not have to support multiple versions of ERP module 2.

Several companies have launched efforts to significantly reduce the number of different ERP applications they have to support. To do this, they are turning from IT to the business units and creating enterprise-wide process managers. Thus, Company X now has a worldwide sales manager and a worldwide procurement manager, and so on. Each process manager is charged with creating a standardized process that will subsequently be supported by a single instance of ERP. Other benefits of enterprise standardization rapidly emerge, as training is also standardized, reporting becomes more consistent, and it becomes easier to move sales people from one business unit to another, but let's stay focused on ERP.

Figure 17.11 shows a matrix that was developed by one company that is trying to get control of its ERP applications. In this case we have placed the traditional organization chart on its side and have the CEO at the left rather than at the top. As you can see, the company has created a global process board and identified one sponsor for each major process area. In fact, to get to the organizational structure shown in Figure 17.11 the company had to create a business process architecture and define its major business process area. Having done that and assigned process sponsors, the sponsors then convened meetings that brought together managers from throughout the world. We've highlighted the sales process on Figure 17.11. The Sales process sponsor held meetings with the sales managers from all the company's departments and divisions. Together they worked out a common sales process that each unit could follow.

Once the company's worldwide sales process manager pulls together people from all the business units, he or she will hear all the reasons why sales are different in Europe than in the U.S. or Japan. There is always some truth in these claims, but if one's goal is a companywide process, and it's backed by senior management, it can usually be achieved, especially at the high-level. Once the process is standardized it is possible to configure single instances of ERP to support the new standard processes.

We've been impressed by the number of CEOs who are determined to make this happen and by the results they are generating. In some cases the companies have had ERP for years and are simply tired of the costs and problems associating with supporting multiple different versions of their ERP software. In other cases companies are just

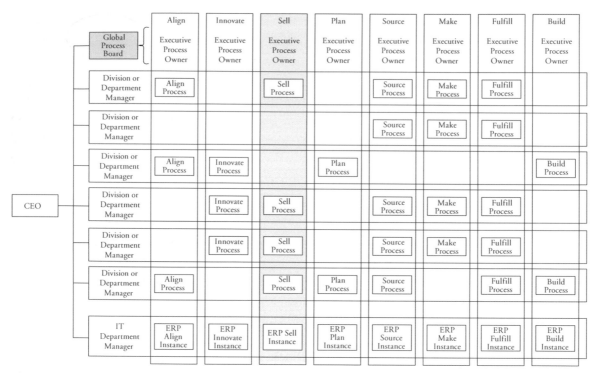

Figure 17. 11 A company that has created process sponsors in order to standardize processes.

installing ERP, have learned from others, and are waiting to install ERP modules until they have arrived at standard processes. They are determined that they are only going to install a single instance. In either case, the road to improving the ERP installation lies through enterprise process redesign and standardization. Figure 17.12 illustrates the goal of Company X.

As we began to meet with CEOs and CIOs and hear these stories, we began to worry that they are simply creating process silos that will be just as troublesome in a few years as the departmental and business unit silos they currently struggled with. Consider Company X. In Europe it sells large manufacturing equipment. In Japan it sells small commodity items. Surely the two types of sales are different. Remember how we discussed Porter in Chapter 2 and concluded that competitive advantage only accrued to companies that were able to integrate all the processes in a single value chain in the best possible way. Surely if one wanted to create a well-integrated value chain for large manufacturing equipment and another for the sale of the small

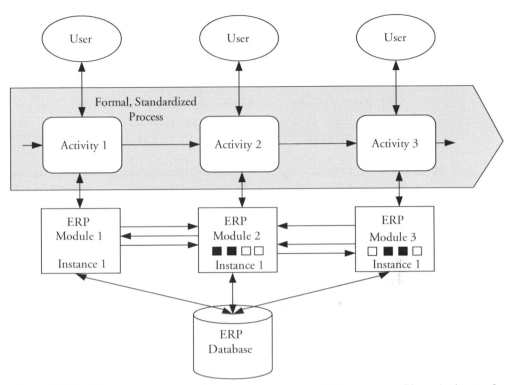

Figure 17.12 All business units are using the same process, which is supported by a single set of ERP modules.

commodity items, one would modify the sales process in different ways to integrate with and to support the different marketing and manufacturing processes.

ERP and BPMS

Without knowing it, Company X is preparing to move to BPMS. They now have the enterprise level process managers and teams and they are now struggling with how to keep their simplified ERP structure while simultaneously allowing different divisions to tailor their processes to better integrate with the overall goals of their specific value chains. Someone from one of the BPMS vendors is going to find his or her way to this company and explain to them that BPMS can provide the best of both worlds. They can use a BPMS product to separate the dependencies between the ERP modules and to provide tailoring, within the BPMS package, without having to tailor the ERP modules. At that point they will have a single instance of ERP and the ability to tailor specific processes.

Figure 17.13 illustrates where Company X may end up in a few years after it has installed a BPMS package to manage its sales process. In this case the standard process has been defined in a BPMS product. Rather than tailoring the ERP modules, all the tailoring that needs to be done is done within the BPMS tool. We've represented these as activity boxes 1 and 2 on Figure 17.13. (Put more technically, one creates business rules within the BPMS environment that analyze and prepare data to be submitted to the ERP modules. As an added benefit, the ERP modules can be managed by the BPMS tool rather than compiled together. Thus, now the BPMS product manages the ERP and allows the user to make changes rather easily, avoiding the problems companies with large compiled sets of ERP modules now struggle with.) Company X may very well find that they can use the BPMS system to tailor their basic sales processes to support multiple value chains while simultaneously maintaining a single instance of ERP.

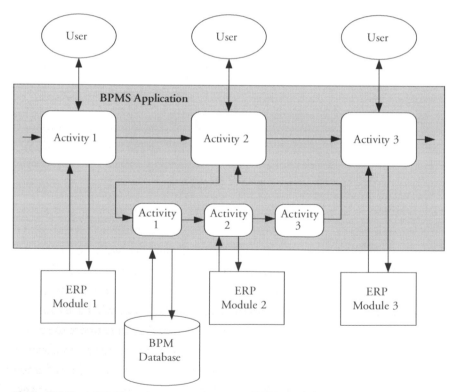

Figure 17.13 A BPMS product managing a set of ERP modules.

In a completely rational world, we might advise Company X to skip the phase they are in and move to a BPMS effort. In reality, however, BPMS is still a new technology and the Company X people are a bit too conservative to jump on a new technology. They are, however, very much aware of how much the multiple versions of ERP modules are costing them, and they have the motivation to try to eliminate that problem. And they have figured out that they will need to control processes, at the enterprise level, to achieve the single instance of ERP. Thus, Company X has moved into enterprise process work in a very serious way and is, in essence, preparing itself for more process work in the future.

We have been impressed with what we've seen. Many BPM gurus in the 1990s urged companies to focus on enterprise process work and to assign enterprise level process managers. In reality, most companies focused on specific process redesign efforts. Today, a surprising number of large companies have definitely moved beyond one-off process redesign efforts and are focused on process management and corporate-wide process standardization. It's a major step forward and will undoubtedly lead to even more interesting things in the future.

The scenario we have just suggested illustrates the problem that ERP vendors face. One of the most popular uses of BPMS software to date is to create process management systems that can manage ERP applications. By keeping the ERP applications generic and doing any special tailoring in the BPMS application, the company reduces its costs and increases its control and its ability to change rapidly. The company also gains the ability to mix applications from different ERP vendors, since the BPMS product can potentially manage whatever database the company wants to use and keep it independent of any particular ERP module.

This movement constitutes a clear threat to the dominance of the leading ERP vendors, and, if it proceeds, will significantly reduce the importance of ERP software at leading companies. ERP vendors have responded by seeking to generate their own BPMS solutions and offering them as alternatives to other BPMS products. Thus, SAP is developing NetWeaver, Oracle is working on its own BPM Suite and Microsoft is developing its BizTalk server. Broadly speaking, each of these products is primarily an application integration tool. The ERP vendors will have trouble matching what the BPMS vendors can do because they are trying to support their existing installed base while simultaneously innovating, and that's hard for any software vendor. While the leading BPMS vendors support business processes with lots of employee activities, the ERP vendors have traditionally focused on automated processes and will have to come up to speed with expanded workflow capabilities to match the capabilities of the best BPMS vendors. Similarly, the ERP vendors have traditionally designed their products for IT developers, as the ARIS diagram we showed earlier suggests. The ERP vendors will also have to rethink their entire positioning if they hope to create products with interfaces that are friendly enough to allow managers to modify processes.

ERP vs. BPMS Applications

Keep in mind that BPMS products rely on BPMS engines (e.g., a workflow engine, a rules engine, an EAI engine) that can interpret code at runtime. Most ERP products are designed to be compiled. That means that once the code is ready to run it is nearly impossible to change. Thus, for most ERP vendors to support the kind of flexibility that BPMS vendors offer, they would have to rewrite their software, shifting from one software architecture to another—and that will be both expensive and very disruptive for their current customers.

Let's consider a CRM vendor that has made the transition. Chordiant Software was founded in 1997 to create and sell software for customer resource management (CRM). Unlike most ERP software, Chordant's software was written in a modern language, Java, and was architected to support Internet delivery and easy integration with other Java component-based systems. Thus, unlike most other enterprise application vendors, that will have to retrofit their products to support the BPM paradigm, Chordiant was designed from the beginning to support a BPM approach. The product components are used by processes which, in turn, are defined and managed by a BPM engine. This means that a user can alter any element of any module running in the Chordiant environment. Figure 17.14 illustrates the Chordiant CRM Suite.

The heart of the Chordiant CRM Suite is Process Design Tool, in which any process can be examined and modified. The Chordiant BPM engine controls the execution of the processes and the invocation of components.

In addition, the Chordiant BPM suite has three tailored interfaces that provide employees with access to data and to the various processes clustered with each interface. Thus, when a call center employee contacts a customer, a portion of the interface shows all the data on the customer. Chordiant is designed to allow the business analyst to easily link in non-Chordiant databases and legacy applications into a larger process. In fact, the Chordiant system can automatically combine data from multiple database

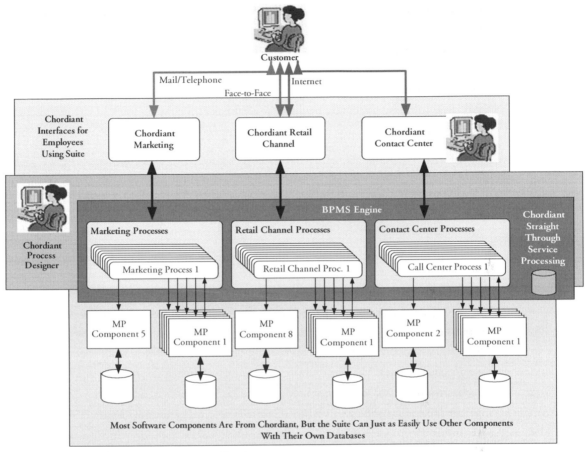

Figure 17.14 Chordiant's CRM/BPMS application.

sources and present a consolidated overview of relevant data. Another part of the same screen shows the employee what processes are available. Typical processes that the employee might invoke include Change of Address, Lost Credit Card, Change of Credit Card Limit, and Closing an Account. Once the employee selects a process, the interface presents the employee with a Work List, and guides the employee through the steps involved in the process. Thus, Chordiant provides a nice example of a BPM suite that is tailored to support employee activities rather than the activation of entirely automated components.

As you can see in Figure 17.14, the Chordiant BPM suite comes with three sets of pre-defined processes. One set of processes is designed to help marketing managers plan and manage marketing campaigns. Using one of these processes, for example, a marketing manager is guided through the steps required to plan a campaign in which customers are offered incentives to upgrade. This campaign can subsequently be implemented by either Retail Channel processes, as when a customer goes to a company Web site to shop, or via Call Center processes that are triggered when a customer calls the company. Since the business analyst has control over each of the processes in each of Chordiant's major process groups, the analyst can tailor the marketing campaign process, and subsequently tailor exactly how the resulting marketing campaign is implemented by specific Call Center processes.

Let's take a closer look at how Chordiant supports BPM development. The screen shot that follows as Figure 17.15 is derived from an Automobile Insurance Claims Management system that Chordiant developed for delivery on IBM platforms. The place to start, with any BPM product, is to consider how Chordiant supports processes. Chordiant has a development tool, the Business Process Designer, shown in 17.15. Since Chordiant comes with an extensive set of customer facing processes, one can use the Process Designer to examine any existing Chordiant process. The business analyst can examine the flow and modify it, if desired. Obviously some activities depend on others and the analyst is constrained from reordering or eliminating certain activities with dependencies, but is otherwise free to alter the diagrams to specify how specific processes will be executed.

Each of the individual process boxes shown in Figure 17.15 can be opened and the properties of each activity can be examined or changed. As a generalization, most Chordiant processes are manual processes that require employees to make decisions. Thus, most processes are associated with worklists that structure the tasks the employee should perform.

Another way that business analysts can tailor processes is by modifying the business rules used to guide decisions. Chordiant incorporates a business rule engine that the analyst accesses via a "spreadsheet," that makes it easy to see which rules are being used to make decisions. The business analyst can quickly modify rules to change outcomes. Suppose, for example, that your company wanted to modify a specific process to increase the credit requirements for a specific type of transaction. It would simply be a matter of changing the appropriate rules that were used to determine credit worthiness for clients and you would automatically change the credit criteria used in a given activity.

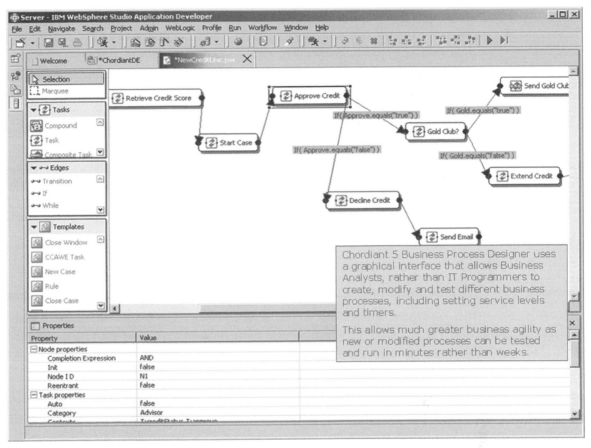

Figure 17.15 Chordiant's Business Process Designer screen.

Once the manager and the business analyst are satisfied that the processes supported by Chordiant are tailored for their needs, they have an application and are ready to use the software to manage actual processes as they are executed.

Chordiant is designed to support Internet-based deployment. Thus, individual marketing managers, call center operators, or customers interact with Chordiant processes via a browser interface. In other words, a specific employee simply signs on, from his or her computer, and accesses the browser screen needed to undertake his or her work.

Chordiant uses a single interface screen to manage all customer-facing processes. The screen is divided so that a given employee can view data on the right side of the screen and available processes on the left side of the same screen. The underlying

Chordiant system executes the processes as defined by the business analyst. When the system is first set up, it is linked to various company and external databases and appropriate legacy applications so that any data needed to execute a process is available to the employee. Thus, for example, if the employee is working in the call center and a customer calls to report an accident, the employee is quickly provided all company data on the customer on the right side of the screen, in an integrated view.

Many readers probably think of Chordiant's customer-facing applications as applications similar to applications from other enterprise software vendors. This is not a fair comparison, and it is the BPM engine that makes all the difference. Packages from other vendors may provide graphics to describe the processes that their modules implement, and they may allow limited changes in the way modules or rules are used in actual processing. In fact, however, without a BPM engine, the process models are simply a kind of documentation. The modules themselves, and the rules they contain, are already coded and locked in compiled software modules.

Chordiant applications, on the other hand, are being managed and executed by the BPM engine. The process is actually being assembled dynamically, as users make inputs during the course of the process. Thus, depending on a user response, different rules will be called and the process that is generated will change. The BPM engine not only allows managers to modify processes as needed, it assures that the processes themselves change in real time.

From all we've said, you might conclude that we don't think most ERP vendors will be able to transition and generate the kind of highly flexible BPMS applications that company will be demanding in the next decade. In fact, we think it will be hard and we don't expect the small ERP vendors to manage it. The large ERP vendors—SAP, Oracle, and Microsoft—have enough resources and technical sophistication that they ought to be able to do it. Indeed, they are already making a major effort, and we expect them to intensive their effort in the years ahead. Thus, although it is easy to think of ERP and BPMS as separate technologies, in fact they will merge in the years ahead. The BPMS vendors will add application-specific knowledge to their products and the ERP vendors will add BPMS engines to their suites. We expect some interesting mergers as the ERP and BPMS vendors struggle to figure out how to create the best applications for their customers.

Notes and References

Davenport, Thomas H., *Mission Critical: Realizing the Promise of Enterprise Systems*, Harvard Business School Press, 2000. Having helped launch the BPR movement, Davenport noticed that by the late 1990s many companies were implementing process change with packaged applications from ERP vendors. He wrote this book to report on his investigations of the whole trend. When Davenport wrote this, he was the director of the Institute for Strategic Change at Andersen Consulting. Davenport is now director of the Business Process Institute at Babson College. For more information, check *www.babson.edu.*

The software and business process theorist that has dominated the ERP space is August-Wilhelm Scheer, who is the head of the Institut für Wirtschaftsinformatik at the University of Saarlandes in Germany. Scheer started by developing techniques for modeling software systems and founded a company, IDS Scheer GmbH, to promote his approach and to sell a software tool, ARIS. Today, IDS Scheer is a major business process modeling and consulting company. The ARIS approach is used by SAP, the largest packaged software (ERP) vendor, which is also headquartered in Germany. Some of Scheer's books include the following:

Scheer, A.-W., *ARIS—Business Process Modeling* (3rd ed.), Springer, 2000. This book focuses on process modeling, especially as it is done with ARIS in SAP R/3. A book for IT developers, not business managers.

Scheer, A.-W., *ARIS—Business Process Frameworks* (3rd ed.), Springer, 1999. This book focuses on the ARIS approach to process redesign using SAP R/3 products and the ARIS software tool. It talks about aligning strategy and processes, but is a book for IT developers and not business managers.

Scheer, A.-W., *Business Process Engineering: Reference Models for Industrial Enterprises* (2nd ed.), Springer, 1994. The book lays out Scheer's basic approach to process reengineering. A book for IT developers, not business managers.

All of Scheer's book are very technical and written for software architects, not business managers. For information on IDS Scheer, check *www.ids-scheer.com.*

The main source of information on SAP and the diagrams used in this chapter was the SAP Web site: *www.sap.com.*

Curran, Thomas, and Gerhard Keller, with Andrew Ladd, *SAP R/3 Business Blueprint: Understanding the Business Process Reference Model*, Prentice Hall, 1998. A good introduction to the use of SAP modules to model business processes. Lots of detailed ARIS examples. A book for IT developers, not business managers.

Conference Board Study, ERP Post Implementation Issues and Best Practices, December 2000.

Worthen, Ben, "Nestle's ERP Odyssey," *CIO Magazine*. May 14, 2002, pp. 62–70.

Special Report from IBM and Siebel Systems, *Reinventing the Integrated Customer-Driven Enterprise,* IBM, 2002. (Siebel has since been acquired by Oracle.)

Woods, Dan and Jeffrey Word, *SAP NetWeaver for Dummies*, Wiley, 2004. A good introduction to NetWeaver, SAP's evolving BPMS entry.

Forndron, Frank, Thilo Liebermann, Marcus Thurner and Peter Widmayer, *mySAP ERP Roadmap: Business Processes, Capabilities, and Complete Upgrade Strategy,* SAP Press, 2006. This book describes how SAP is modifying its ERP modules (converting them to mySAP modules) that will be able to run with NetWeaver.

IDS Scheer's ARIS software tool is reviewed on the BPTrends Web site, *www.bptrends.com.*

SAP has created a special Web site within their SAP Community Network for business process experts (BPx) that is designed to help business analysts learn about the latest developments in BPM. Visit *www.sdn.sap.com/irj/sdn/bpx* for more information.

18

Conclusions

THIS BOOK WAS WRITTEN to provide managers and Six Sigma and BPM practitioners with an introduction to the concepts and techniques needed for business process change and to provide them an overview of some of the options they will have when they undertake business process change. In keeping with this goal, we have considered a wide variety of different business process topics. Complete books have been written on several of the topics we treat in a single chapter. We have provided references to books and Web sites in the Notes and References that were placed at the end of each chapter to help interested readers pursue various topics in more detail. Our goal here was not to make readers into masters of tactical details, but to give them the basics they need to think strategically about how they should approach business process change in their organizations.

In this final chapter we want to briefly reiterate the major themes we have emphasized in this book.

First, there is the idea that organizations are systems. Things are related in complex ways, and we only understand organizations when we understand them as wholes. We believe that every manager should be able to draw an organization diagram of his or her organization at the drop of a hat. That would demonstrate at least a high-level acquaintance with how various functions relate to each other and to suppliers and customers.

Second, we believe that the best way to understand how things get done and how any specific activity is related to others is to think in terms of processes. Process diagrams provide a good basis for demonstrating that one understands how things flow through an organization, from supplies and new technologies to products and services that are delivered to customers. In an ideal world, we'd like every manager to be able to access a process model of the process he or she is managing by going to the company's business process Web site. We believe that a basic acquaintance with process diagramming techniques is just as important for today's manager as familiarity with spreadsheets and organization charts.

In the 1990s it was sufficient to understand processes. Today, leading companies are moving beyond specific processes and trying to integrate all of the company's process work into enterprise tools that make it possible for senior managers to monitor and control the organization with process technologies. Today this is being facilitated by business process modeling tools and repositories, and by exciting new approaches like business process frameworks. By the beginning of the next decade, leading companies will be using BPMS applications to manage large-scale business processes on a day-by-day basis. At the same time, companies are focusing on realigning their Key Performance Indicators on processes and establishing process management system. Thus, today, a manager not only needs to understand specific processes, but he or she needs to understand how all of the processes in the company combine into a business process architecture. Figure 18.1 reproduces the BPTrends process pyramid and highlights some of the different types of concerns and alignments that today's manager should understand.

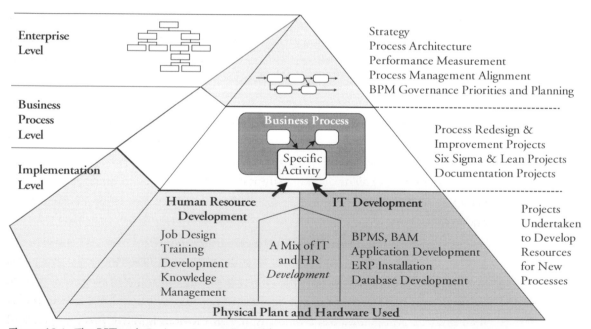

Figure 18.1   The BPTrends Business Process Pyramid.

At the same time, managers need to understand how the different processes are aligned to strategy and value chains and to a variety of enterprise resources. Figure 18.2 shows how processes can be the key to understanding and organizing what is done in a company. A business process architecture provides everyone with an overview of how all the activities in the organization relate to one another and contribute to satisfying customers. A well-understood process shows how each activity relates to every other and where departments must interface in order for the process to be effective and efficient.

The same process diagram provides the basis for defining measures and aligning those measures with organization strategies and goals, departmental goals, and process and activity measures. This, in turn, defines the responsibilities of individual managers and supervisors. Each manager should know exactly what processes or activities he or she must plan and organize and just which measures to check in order to monitor and control the assigned processes and activities.

Drilling down in the diagram, well-defined activities provide the framework on which a whole variety of organizational efforts can be hung. Each activity should generate data on inputs and outputs, on time and cost. Activities are the basis for cost-based accounting systems. They are also the key to analyzing jobs and developing job descriptions and training programs.

Activities also provide a framework for organizing knowledge management efforts, feedback systems, and decision support systems. And they also form the basic unit for the database systems and for defining requirements if the activity is to be automated.

As enterprises become more mature in their understanding and use of processes, they learn to constantly adjust their processes and to align the activities within a process in response to changes in their external environment. As each strategy change results in a process change, it also results in changes in the management and measurement systems and in all of the other support systems that are tied to the processes and activities. Thus, the process architecture becomes the heart of enterprise alignment and organizational adaptation.

We are constantly asked how to get started. You start from wherever you are. You need to make a major management commitment to do enterprise-level process work. If your management isn't ready to make such a commitment, you will need to work on processes and build up some credibility while looking for a sponsor in your senior management group. The SEI's maturity model provides a pretty good overview of

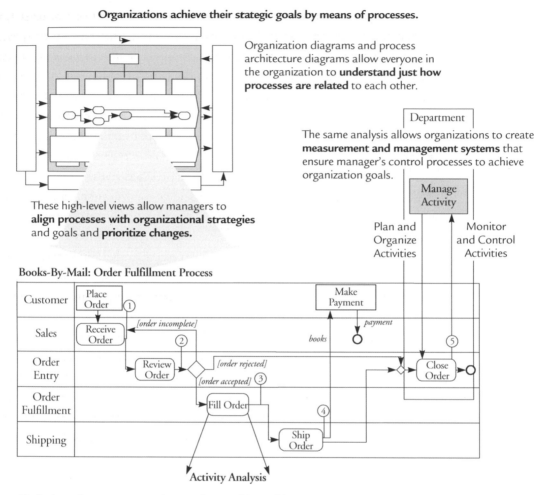

Organizations achieve their stategic goals by means of processes.

Organization diagrams and process architecture diagrams allow everyone in the organization to **understand just how processes are related** to each other.

The same analysis allows organizations to create **measurement and management systems** that ensure manager's control processes to achieve organization goals.

These high-level views allow managers to **align processes with organizational strategies** and goals and **prioritize changes.**

Activity Analysis

Basic data: Inputs, outputs, time, and cost of the activity.

Job analysis: Employees involved in activity. Job descriptions and performance support system. Training available to support employees engaged in this activity.

Communications: Feedback that should flow from this activity to other activities or to senior management.

Knowledge management and decision support: Business rules used to make decisions required for this activity. Other knowledge required by those performing this activity.

Automation and IT systems support: Data required to perform this activity. Requirements for automating this activity. Software applications and components that automate this activity.

Figure 18.2 Process is the key to understanding an organization.

how most companies evolve. (See Figure 18.3.) Companies begin at level 1, without processes. They move to level 2 as they develop some processes—usually within departments or divisions. They move to level 3 when they start to work on organizing all their processes together into an architecture. They move to level 4 when they develop the process measurement and management systems necessary to truly control their processes. Increasingly, this will be the point at which leading companies will seek to install BPMS applications. Installing them if your organization is at a lower level is probably a waste of time. Finally, companies move to level 5 and use Six Sigma or something very similar to constantly optimize their processes.

Moving up the CMM scale requires a major commitment on the part of an organization's executives. It isn't something that can be spearheaded by a departmental manager or a business process committee. It requires the active support of the CEO and the entire executive committee. Moreover, it isn't something that can be done in a single push or in the course of a quarter or even a year. Business process management and improvement must become part of an organization's culture. Process improvement must become something that every manager spends time on each day. It must become one of the keys to understanding how the entire organization functions.

If business process improvement is to be ingrained in the organization, then improvement itself must become a systematic process. Every organization needs a BPM group to support senior management just as they need a finance committee to be available to provide financial information. The process architecture committee should be constantly working to align and realign corporate processes to corporate strategies and goals. As goals and strategies shift, process changes must be reprioritized and new process redesign or improvement projects must be undertaken. Just as senior executives receive daily or weekly reports on financial results, they should receive daily or weekly reports on how the various processes are achieving their assigned measures and what efforts are being undertaken to improve processes that fail to meet their goals. This kind of reporting assumes a matrix management structure, where there are managers with specific responsibilities for seeing the processes perform as wholes.

At the same time, most organizations benefit from a Six Sigma program that makes all employees aware of the need for constant process improvement. A well-organized and integrated Six Sigma program is a major step toward creating a process-centric culture.

At the tactical level, process redesign and improvement have changed and will change more in the near future. In the early 1990s, when most managers first learned

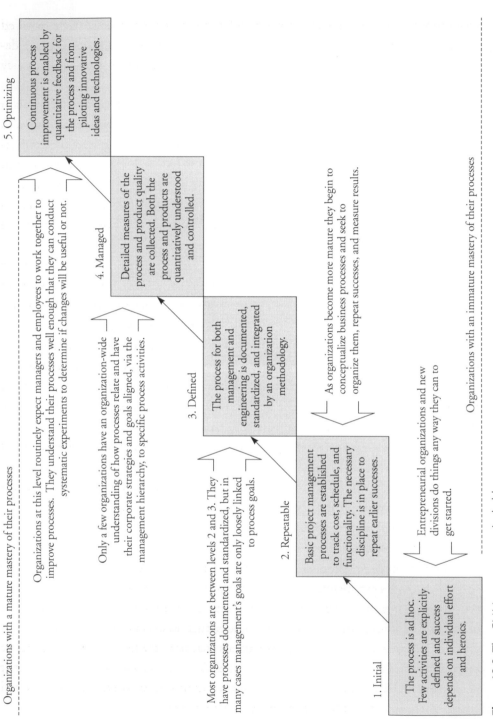

Organizations with a mature mastery of their processes

5. Optimizing

Continuous process improvement is enabled by quantitative feedback for the process and from piloting innovative ideas and technologies.

Organizations at this level routinely expect managers and employees to work together to improve processes. They understand their processes well enough that they can conduct systematic experiments to determine if changes will be useful or not.

4. Managed

Detailed measures of the process and product quality are collected. Both the process and products are quantitatively understood and controlled.

Only a few organizations have an organization-wide understanding of how processes relate and have their corporate strategies and goals aligned, via the management hierarchy, to specific process activities.

3. Defined

The process for both management and engineering is documented, standardized, and integrated by an organization methodology.

As organizations become more mature they begin to conceptualize business processes and seek to organize them, repeat successes, and measure results.

2. Repeatable

Basic project management processes are established to track cost, schedule, and functionality. The necessary discipline is in place to repeat earlier successes.

Most organizations are between levels 2 and 3. They have processes documented and standardized, but in many cases management's goals are only loosely linked to process goals.

Entrepreneurial organizations and new divisions do things any way they can to get started.

1. Initial

The process is ad hoc. Few activities are explicitly defined and success depends on individual effort and heroics.

Organizations with an immature mastery of their processes

Figure 18.3 The CMM process maturity ladder.

about process redesign, the organization and improvement of processes were regarded as tasks that should be handled by business managers. In effect, a redesign team determined what needed to be done. They only called the IT organization in when they decided they needed to automate some specific activities.

Today, the use of IT and automation has progressed well beyond that early view of business process redesign. Increasingly, companies and information systems are so integrated that every process redesign is also a systems redesign. Today every IT organization is heavily involved in business process redesign. The Internet, email, and the Web have made it possible for IT organizations to achieve things today that they could only dream of in the early 1990s. Information systems are making it possible to integrate suppliers and partners—and in many cases, customers—in networks that are all made possible by software systems.

More important than technologies, however, is IT's new commitment to working with business managers to improve processes. In essence, the business process becomes the new basis for communication. IT will increasingly focus on offering solutions that improve specific processes, while keeping in mind how specific processes relate to other processes. As BPMS techniques evolve, we will see IT architects and business managers working to automate major business processes as BPMS applications that will facilitate rapid change and provide real-time monitoring capabilities for senior executives. The successful development of large scale BPMS applications will bring IT and business managers together as never before.

To commit to managing an organization in a process-oriented manner requires that you commit to an ongoing process of change and realignment, and, increasingly to business process management systems. The world keeps changing, and organizations must learn to keep changing as well. We have pictured this commitment as a cycle that never ends and is embedded within the core of the organization. We term it the *enterprise alignment cycle*. (See Figure 18.4.)

The process organization is constantly monitoring its external environment for changes. Changes can be initiated by competitors, by changes in customer taste, or by new technologies that allow the organization to create new products. When relevant changes occur, the organization begins a process that results in new processes with new characteristics, and new management systems that use new measures to assure those processes deliver the required outputs. Organizations can only respond in this manner if all the managers in the organization understand processes. We hope this book will have done a bit to make the reader just such a manager.

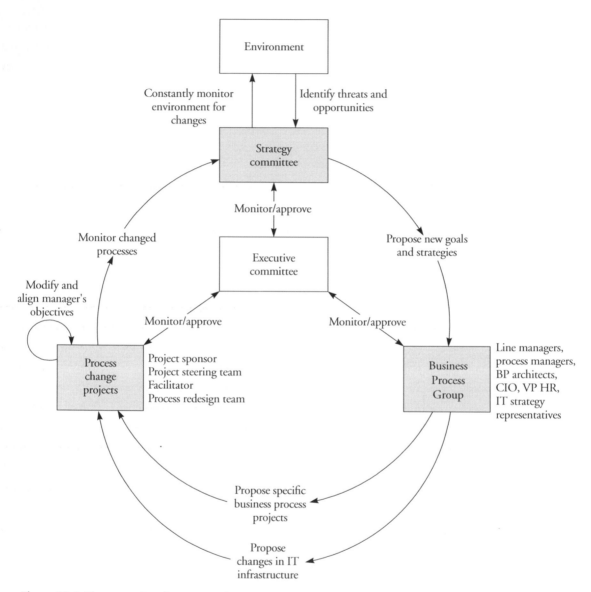

Figure 18.4 The enterprise alignment cycle.

I

Business Process Modeling Notation BPMN CORE NOTATION

There are many process notations that have been used over the years to represent more complex process flows. The one that has the most support today is the Business Process Modeling Notation (BPMN), which was developed by representatives of the leading business process modeling vendors under the auspices of BPMI, the business process interest group of the OMG, an international standards organization. BPMN comes in two versions, a core notation set, which can be used by business people, and an extended notation set, which provides the details to represent processes for automation. In BPTrends classes we only use the core BPMN symbol set. This core set is identical with the OMG UML Activity Diagram notation and nearly identical with the Rummler-Brache notation, and is thus as close to a universal notation as exists today.

We have added some of the BPMN extended notation that we often use in business diagrams.

The core BPMN symbols are as follows:

An Activity. A generic term for work that a company performs. Activities take time. Activities can be composed of activities. Complex activities include Processes and subprocesses. In extended BPMN notation a symbol within the Activity box indicates that the process has subprocesses that have been modeled.

An Event. An event is something that happens during the course of a business process. An event is a point in time. Events include triggers that start processes, messages that arrive that disrupt processes and the final production of products, services or data that result in the end or termination of a process or subprocess. In extended notation symbols can be placed within the circle to specify things about the nature of the even.

A Gateway. A gateway is used to show the divergence or convergence of a sequence flow. This might indicate forking or merging activities, or it might indicate a decision that determines which of two or more subsequent flows is to be followed. In extended notation symbols are placed within the diamond to specify things about the gateway. They might indicate, for example that all preceding activities need to be done before the next activity occurs.

A Sequence Flow. An arrow is used to show the order that activities will be performed in a process. A sequence arrow does not imply that a physical output, information, or people move from one activity to the next, though they may. It simply suggests that a subsequent activities is performed next in the normal course of accomplishing the process. Labels can be associated with the Flow arrows to indicate when decision paths are being followed or when things or information is flowing along the arrow.

A Message Flow. An dashed arrow is used to show that messages (information) flows between two organizations or individuals.

A Data Object. Data objects are artifacts that do not have a direct effect on the sequence flow or the message flow of processes. They provide information that activities require to produce what they produce.

An Association. Used to associate text or other annotations to activities or arrows on a diagram.

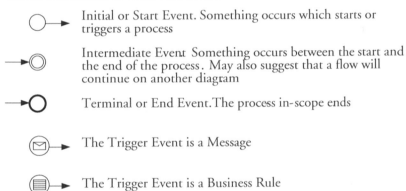

A Pool with Swimlanes. A pool provides a context for a set of activities. Departments or Roles or Participants are described in the boxes on the left. Activites and flows are indicated in the rectangles on the left. The top swimlane is normally reserved for the customer of the process.

Two pools are used to indicate the organizations or individuals within separate organizations are coordinating their work on a common process.

In extended BPMN notation, some of the elements in the core notation are "extended" to provide more information. Examples:

A Few Extensions of the Event circle:

Initial or Start Event. Something occurs which starts or triggers a process

Intermediate Event Something occurs between the start and the end of the process. May also suggest that a flow will continue on another diagram

Terminal or End Event. The process in-scope ends

The Trigger Event is a Message

The Trigger Event is a Business Rule

A Few Extensions of the Gateway Diamond

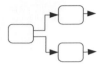

Parallel Processing—The flow divides and the same information goes to both subsequent activities. No decision required

Condition 1

Condition 2

DECISION – Only one path is followed by a given flow – either Condition 1 applies OR Condition 2 applies

MERGE (OR-Join) The flow continues when one of the possible inputs arrives

MERGE (AND-Join) Process only proceeds when inputs from both streams are joined together

Some Other Notations That We Occasionally Use

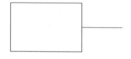

System/Thing. A rectangle with square corners thats linked to a process suggests that the process interacts with something that isn't a process – e.g., a thing or a database system

The Activity Is Modeled In More Detail. A square with an X inside an activity box indicates that there is another diagram that shows what occurs inside this activity.

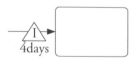

Inventory Is Maintained. A triangle with an I inside and a time period indicated below means that inventory is being maintained. In this case the activity immediately following the triangle has 4 days of inventory that it is maintaining. Thus any new flow goes into inventory and is then used 4 days later.

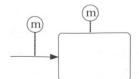

Measurement Taken. A circle with "m" and a number inside a circle, attached to a flow arrow or an activity suggests that we will monitor results at that point.

II

Business Process Standards

Most people in most companies don't care about standards. They simply do their jobs without thinking about the fact that their work is greatly simplified by the many common agreements about how things are to be done. It doesn't make any difference whether we drive on the right or the left side of the road, but it's a huge convenience that everyone within a particular geographical area agrees to do one or the other. Similarly we all benefit by having a limited number of screw formats, so that two sets of screwdrivers will work in almost all cases.

We have discussed Geoffrey Moore's technology adoption lifecycle model in other chapters. The model is pictured in Figure A-II.1. In essence, Innovators take new technology just out of the universities and labs and try to use it to make breakthroughs that will give them significant competitive advantage. They are willing to invest significant resources to figure out how to make the technology work for them. Early Adopters take technologies that are a little further along and try to develop applications before their competitors do and thus gain advantage. Like Innovators, Early Adopters have strong technology groups. Early Majority companies wait until after a technology has proven itself, and then they adopt the new technology. But Early Majority companies don't expect to have to develop new technology or struggle with immature tools. More important, for our purposes here, they expect standards to be in place. In other words, standards development, at least in technological domains, is an activity that is carried on by vendors and sophisticated users during the Early Adopter phase of the technology lifecycle. It isn't something that most companies are interested in working on—they expect it to be completed by the time the technology is ready for widespread use. In some cases, technologies that fall into the Chasm and disappear are those that fail to develop workable standards during their early years.

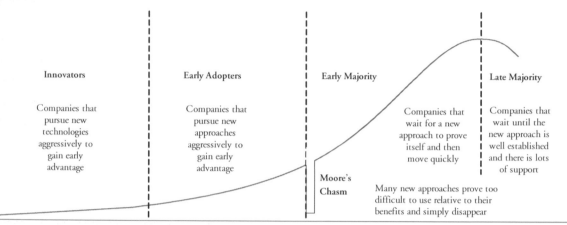

Figure A-II.1 Geoffrey Moore's Technology Adoption Lifecycle (after Geoffrey A. Moore, *Crossing the Chasm*, Harper-Business, 1991).

The other thing to understand before discussing standards is the difference between a *de facto* standard and a *de jure* standard. *De jure* (in law) standards are established by standards groups or industry consortia. *De facto* (in practice) standards are defined by communities without any formal agreement. Windows is the Microsoft operating system that over 90% of PC users depend upon. It is the *de facto* standard for operating systems, and any vendor that wants to sell software for PCs would be well advised to support it. In complex and rapidly evolving environments, *de facto* standards are often more important than *de jure* standards, which usually take longer to develop. Put somewhat differently, if leading vendors can't agree on a common standard, they let the market decide, and the vendor that achieves the *de jure* standard wins.

With these considerations in mind, we want to spend a few minutes considering the standards in the business process world today. To organize the discussion a bit more, we'll divide standards into three broad sets, according to who uses them. *Enterprise Level* standards are used by business managers to assist in analyzing and organizing enterprise initiatives. *Business Process* standards are used by business managers and business process practitioners when they undertake business process change projects. This area is the most difficult to organize because the individuals who undertake business projects vary so much. In some cases business managers and employees undertake business improvement projects. In other cases business analysts and other IT-oriented individuals undertake process automation projects. *Implementation* standards are specific to technologies used by those charged with developing solutions to process problems. Most of the standards in this area are IT standards that structure how software is developed or how software tools interface with each other.

We can hardly consider all of the business process standards that exist or are being developed today, but we want to provide a high-level overview. Obviously we have structured the discussion and assigned standards to categories that reflect my experience. Others would surely arrange some of these standards differently, and several of the standards that we consider in one category could just as well be placed in another category. But we need to simplify a bit to provide an overview.

Enterprise Level Business Process Standards

Enterprise Level Business Process standards are used by executives and senior business managers to help organize their overall understanding, evaluation, and management of a business's performance. In addition, some organizations have BPM groups that report to executive committees and they use enterprise level standards as tools to do manager evaluations and to prioritize process interventions.

Probably the most widely used business process standard, at the enterprise level, is Kaplan and Norton's Balanced Scorecard approach to managerial evaluation. This is a de facto standard and predictably takes many forms. The various spin-offs of Kaplan and Norton's approach have enough in common, however, that most companies can immediately answer "yes" or "no" if asked if they are using a Balanced Scorecard approach.

The most impressive business process standard at the enterprise level is the Supply Chain Council's SCOR framework and methodology. SCOR was developed by supply chain managers as a tool they could use to build and evaluate multicompany supply chain processes. It is being rapidly generalized to serve as a standard for defining, benchmarking and evaluating the entire value chain. In its expanded version, it is either called SCOR+ or SCOR/DCOR/CCOR (for supply chain, design chain, customer chain operation reference models). We predict that SCOR+ will grow in importance as more senior executives embrace a process-centric approach in the years ahead. VRM is an alternative approach, which is very similar to SCOR+. eTOM is another framework that is tailored for the telcom industry. (We fully expect to see other industry-specific frameworks in the near future.)

The Europeans have a quality standard for organizations, EFQM, that is attracting a lot of attention on the part of companies that are doing process architecture work in Europe, although it has not reached the U.S. yet.

Another standard that is sometimes used at the enterprise level is the Software Engineering Institute's (SEI) Capability Maturity Model Integrated (CMMI). Most companies use CMM to evaluate the performance of their IT processes, in which case CMM would be a process level standard. A few organizations, however, use it to evaluate all their business processes to determine how the entire organization is evolving and in those cases it can function as an enterprise level tool.

The U.S. government's various agencies rely on the Federal Enterprise Architecture Framework (FEAF). FEAF is potentially an enterprise tool, and is used that way by a few agencies. Most use it as an approach to IT architecture, in which case we would classify it as an IT implementation standard, like Zachman.

We've summarized some of the business process standards we're considering in Figure A-II.2.

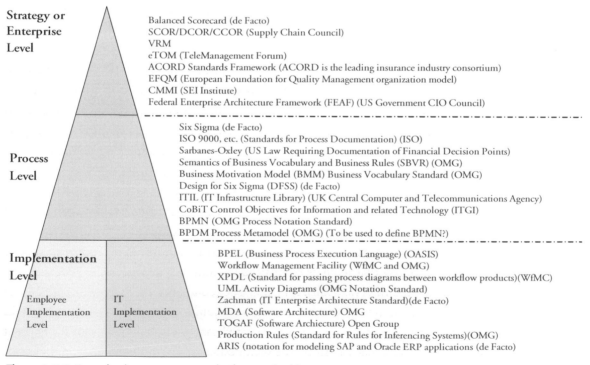

Figure A-II.2 Some business process standards organized by users.

Process Level Business Process Standards

The process level is all about business process redesign and improvement projects. The standards on this level help managers, employees, business analysts, and human performance analysts change how specific processes work.

By far the most important standard at the process level is Six Sigma, another *de facto* standard that is defined differently by different companies and standards groups. Most of the variations on Six Sigma, however, bear enough of a family resemblance to be easily identified. Six Sigma provides a generic process improvement methodology (DMAIC) and a large collection of tools that process improvement teams can use to improve processes. Most Six Sigma books suggest that Six Sigma practitioners consider BPM (management), process redesign (Design for Six Sigma or DFSS) and process improvement (DMAIC). In reality, most Six Sigma practitioners are focused on DMAIC. Lean represents a separate methodology that focuses on eliminating waste from process flows and is now usually considered one of the tools that Six Sigma teams ought to employ—so, perhaps, we ought to call this standard "Six Sigma/Lean." In any case, most leading companies have trained a large number of their employees in Six Sigma and regularly undertake a large number of improvement projects guided by the overall Six Sigma/Lean approach.

Almost as widespread as Six Sigma is the ISO 9000 standard. (This standard has many variations on 9000, but most people can recognize it by this designation.) In essence, ISO 9000 is the International Standards Organization's specification for defining business processes. Many leading European firms and governments require companies to define their processes using ISO 9000. Unfortunately, this standard has become a "checklist" item and most companies create their ISO 9000 documentation rapidly and then shelve it. There are efforts under way to make ISO 9000 more meaningful for modern business process work, but, at the moment, ISO documentation has little impact on how processes actually work at companies.

In the U.S., most companies have worked to generate documentation for Sarbanes Oxley, a U.S. law that requires companies to show they can track the processes that generate key financial decisions. Like ISO 9000, Sarbanes Oxley represents an opportunity for a firm to make a significant leap forward in understanding its processes. In reality, Sarbanes Oxley has been implemented too quickly and will most likely result in more shelfware that will sit on the shelf beside the ISO 9000 documentation.

The OMG has recently put its imprimatur on a rules standard (and an associated Business Motivation Model) originally developed by the Business Rules Community that defines standards for defining corporate vocabulary and policies and business rules. Financial companies are very active in this area, and this standard will help those companies organize their ontology and their business rule efforts.

There are several business frameworks in industry or domain-specific areas that are useful in helping a process team design or evaluate existing business processes. A good example is ITIL (a standard for IT support processes) and CoBiT (a standard for IT management processes). Both are of growing interest to companies that want to standardize their IT processes throughout the company.

For years, business process modelers have used a wide variety of workflow notations, including, for example, IDEF0 and Rummler-Brache. Most of the popular process modeling tools support these two notations and provide variations of their own. Today, however, there is no *de facto* standard that most business people rely upon. When you consider that we know of several companies that now document their business processes with flow diagrams and have classes that teach employees to read the diagrams that describe the tasks they are to perform, you realize that a standard business process notation would be useful.

The best candidate, at the moment, is the BPMI/OMG's Business Process Management Notation (BPMN). The good news is that the notation was developed by a team from the leading process modeling vendors, and, in its core version, provides the basic notation business people need. The bad news is that it is also designed to generate a business process execution language (BPEL) and that, to do that, it has lots of notation that business people clearly don't need or understand. In addition, now that BPMN is controlled by the OMG there will be an effort to merge BPMN with UML Activity Diagrams. In fact, in their simple forms, BPMN and UML Activity Diagrams are hardly distinguishable from Rummler-Brache diagrams and either could be used by business people. Both, however, are usually described in their more elaborate forms and quickly become overwhelming for business people. So, there are some standards for business modeling, but it isn't yet clear if one of them will become the *de facto* standard in this area.

Business Process Standards for Implementation

Once a business team has redesigned a process, there are various groups that can become involved in preparing for implementation. HR teams may be asked to develop new job descriptions, hire new people or retrain existing employees. IT groups may be asked to develop software. Corporate property management groups may be asked to relocate plants, buy new trucks, or build new distribution centers, etc.

Most of the business process standards in the implementation area, at the moment, are IT standards. They are either designed to help IT professionals gather business requirements and design or tailor software applications, or they are designed to assure that companies can store process information in a common data format or pass models from one software tool to another.

BPEL, the OASIS process execution language, has gotten the most attention. BPEL is closely associated with BPM Suites, but, broadly speaking, only a few BPMS applications have actually been developed using BPEL, and none of them have been developed entirely in BPEL. The current version of the language is simply too limited to support sophisticated BPMS development and any vendor that uses BPEL supplements it with other code. This will change as the BPEL standard evolves, but at the moment BPEL is still a work in progress.

Closely related to BPEL are standards like XPDL and the Workflow Management Coalition's Workflow Management Facility. These standards were developed to support workflow systems and will need, eventually, to be merged with BPEL or some similar language and expanded to support the BPMS applications we will start to see in the next few years.

The OMG's UML is clearly established as the notation system for those engaged in software development. MDA and TOGAF are both candidates for structuring the SOA-oriented applications that BPMS tools are going to generate. And the OMG's Production Rule specification will eventually standardize the way business rules are stored in inference-based systems that are increasingly being used in financial companies to manage their business rule systems.

Zachman's Enterprise Architecture is the *de facto* standard for enterprise architects focused on cataloging the IT assets of the company, but causes no end of confusion when people confuse it with a business process architecture standard and try to use it as a business management tool.

Finally, ARIS, IDS Scheer's notation and tool, is the *de facto* notation for diagramming ERP applications. It is used by SAP for their diagrams and has been adopted by Oracle and Microsoft. In its ERP form, it's a notation that only software developers understand, and underlines the need for a different notation for business managers. It is, however, widely used by IT developers working on ERP-based process implementations. Just don't plan on showing an ARIS diagram of your new ERP application to your CEO.

The Future of Standards

We've only considered a few of the many standards being used by business process managers and developers. The variety is impressive. The key to developing standards is to understand what group will use them and what activities will be facilitated by the existence of a standard approach. When IT tries to get business people to use one of their software-oriented standards, it usually leads to an unsuccessful project. Similarly, when business people provide process models to IT, developed in one of their preferred notations, it usually means that the requirements are insufficiently specified. These problems will only become more complex as companies try to figure out how to use BPMS tools and create BPMS applications.

We are most hopeful about the SCOR+, VRM, ACORD's Standards Framework and eTOM frameworks and the idea that high-level value chain frameworks will make it possible for companies to create enterprise process architectures that will, in turn, make it easier for senior managers to understand processes, monitor performance, and prioritize their process improvement initiatives.

At the same time, we think the OMG's MDA architecture has the potential to define how different standards can interface effectively with each other while each preserving the characteristics that make them valuable for their particular user groups.

As we indicated at the beginning, most business process people aren't interested in standards. As time goes by, however, everyone will benefit if companies agree to use some common conventions. Hopefully the leading companies and vendors working on standards today will find ways to develop common conventions within a flexible architectural system that will make it possible for all of the different groups engaged in business process work to accomplish their work in the manner they find most effective, while still communicating with each other.

Index

About the Author

Paul Harmon is a Co-Founder, Executive Editor and Senior Market Analyst at Business Process Trends—*www.bptrends.com*—the most trusted and accessed source of information and analysis on trends, directions and best practices in business process management.

He is also a Co-Founder, Chief Methodologist and Principal Consultant of BPTrends Associates, a professional services company providing executive education, training and consulting services for organizations interested in understanding and implementing business process management.

His business process work dates back to the late 60s when he worked with Geary Rummler managing the overall development and delivery of performance improvement programs. He has worked on major process change programs at Bank of America, Wells Fargo, Prudential and Citibank, to name a few.

Paul is authored or co-authored over twelve books and is the co-author and editor of the BPTrends Product Reports, the most widely read reports available on BPM software products. He is an acknowledged BPM thought leader and noted consultant, educator, author and market analyst concerned with applying new technologies and methodologies to real-world business problems. He is a widely respected keynote speaker and has developed and delivered executive seminars, workshops, briefings and keynote addresses on all aspects of BPM to conferences and major organizations throughout the world.

Edwards Brothers Malloy
Ann Arbor MI. USA
November 12, 2013